"Written as a contribution to an
volume deserves a readership ac ....u...i.s, ior
example, will find Tyler Wittman's brilliant account of Aquinas's Trinitarian
theology to be necessary reading. May this volume's Trinitarian reflections
have a healing and unitive effect, not only among the evangelicals involved
in the debate, but also across ecclesiastical lines so that we 'may all be one'!"

—Matthew Levering,
James N. and Mary D. Perry Jr. Chair of Theology, Mundelein Seminary,
and coeditor of *The Oxford Handbook of the Trinity*

"This new collection of Trinitarian studies is theologically sensitive, biblically
attuned, and historically concerned. Everyone interested in the future of Trinitarian theology within evangelical Protestantism will find this book a good
and encouraging guide."

—Lewis Ayres,
Durham University and Australian Catholic University

"In recent years, the waters of evangelical Trinitarian theology have been
roiled and muddied by unfortunate debates about the subordination of the
Son. The very fine essays collected in this volume make genuine progress in
exegetical, biblical, as well as historical and systematic theology, and they will
do much to help bring an end to this debate."

—Thomas H. McCall, Professor of Biblical and Systematic Theology,
Trinity Evangelical Divinity School and Professorial Fellow in
Exegetical and Analytic Theology, University of St Andrews

"Orthodoxy matters. Who is the God we are confessing, worshiping, and
living for in faith and obedience? Who is the God whom we long to share
eternal communion with on the new heaven and the new earth? What theological cultures are we receiving? It is incumbent upon the church to retrieve
an orthodox confession and pass that down to the next generation. *Trinity
without Hierarchy* addresses the different academic, dogmatic, historic, and
practical camera angles of a contemporary debate regarding whether there is
hierarchal distinction between the persons of the Godhead. The impact of this
teaching has already left a heavy fingerprint on the church. As a laywoman, I
see who pays the price when academics try to apply an unorthodox view of
the Trinity to gender relations. What will the continuing intergenerational
impact be if we do not call for renewal of the orthodox faith?"

—Aimee Byrd,
author of *Why Can't We Be Friends?* and *No Little Women*,
cohost of "Mortification of Spin"

"First, open theism; now, eternal functional subordination of the Son. Evangelical theology has shown itself to be soft at the very point on which the gospel depends: the doctrine of the triune God. This collection of essays rightly reminds us that the primary purpose of Trinitarian theology is to enable the right reading of Scripture and to preserve the integrity of the gospel message, not to serve as a template for human social relations. The authors of *Trinity without Hierarchy* carefully examine key New Testament texts, as well as the work of past and present theologians. The result is a compelling and comprehensive case that evangelicals are most biblical when they adhere to the catholic and orthodox tradition."

—Kevin J. Vanhoozer,
Research Professor of Systematic Theology,
Trinity Evangelical Divinity School

TRINITY
WITHOUT
HIERARCHY

Reclaiming Nicene Orthodoxy in Evangelical Theology

MICHAEL F. BIRD &
SCOTT HARROWER

EDITORS

Kregel
Academic

Trinity without Hierarchy: Reclaiming Nicene Orthodoxy in Evangelical Theology
© 2019 by Michael F. Bird and Scott Harrower

Published by Kregel Academic, an imprint of Kregel Publications, 2450 Oak Industrial Dr. NE, Grand Rapids, MI 49505-6020

The Greek font GraecaU is available from www.linguistsoftware.com/lgku.htm, +1-425-775-1130.

ISBN 978–0–8254–4462–3

Printed in the United States of America

19 20 21 22 23 / 5 4 3 2 1

Graham Cole,
in thankful appreciation,
for his leadership and service
to Christ the King.

Contents

PREFACE

Theologians of a Lesser Son

MICHAEL F. BIRD

I entered the debate about the eternal functional subordination of the Son to the Father with two articles coauthored with my former colleague Robert Shillaker. There we argued *contra* Kevin Giles that an economic submission of the Son to the Father did inform relationships within the immanent Trinity; and we concurrently argued *contra* Bruce Ware and Wayne Grudem that this had very limited relevance to issues of gender roles, and that furthermore we should probably drop the language of subordination since it was flirting with Arianism.[1] As far as I could tell, Ware and Grudem were clearly not Arians; they did not deny the eternality of the Son, they affirmed that the Son was of the same substance as the Father, and they believed in their own minds that they were orthodox Trinitarians. That said, their language of "subordination" certainly bothered me, but I erstwhile assumed that such scholars were using the term not in its actual sense, but as more of a clunky yet effective way of correlating the economic Trinity with the immanent Trinity and safeguarding the personal distinctions within the Godhead. I imagined that their preference for "subordination" was akin to how Karl Barth used the term "modes of being" (*seinsweise*), not because he was a modalist, but because he wanted to avoid the philosophical baggage attached to the words for "person" used in both the

---

1. Michael F. Bird and Robert Shillaker, "Subordination in the Trinity and Gender Roles: A Response to Recent Discussion," *TrinJ* 29 (2008): 267–83; idem, "The Son Really, Really Is the Son: A Response to Kevin Giles," *TrinJ* 30 (2009): 257–68.

fourth- and twentieth-century discussions.[2] For myself, I much preferred Wolfhart Pannenberg's notion that Jesus's divine sonship implies his obedient self-
distinction from the Father, but it is a horizontal rather than a vertical obedience, principally about *taxis* ("order") rather than *archē* ("authority").[3]

However, after reading and rereading several volumes by complementarians, where the language of subordination and hierarchy are championed, I
am now convinced that Grudem, Ware, and others were arguing for something analogical to a semi-Arian subordinationism.[4] The Trinitarian relations
being advocated by such scholars are not identical to Arius, since proponents
identify the Son as coeternal with the Father and sharing the same substance
as the Father. In addition, I think it is fair to say neither are Eternal Functional
Subordination (EFS) advocates pure semi-Arians, because they do not think
Jesus is merely like the Father nor do they consider the Son to be the Father's
creature. Those caveats aside, they resemble a species of semi-Arianism, called
"homoianism,"[5] by virtue of three things: (1) an overreliance on the economic
Trinity in Scripture for formulating immanent Trinitarian relationships, (2)
leading to a robust subordinationism characterized by a hierarchy within the
Godhead, (3) consequently identifying the Son as possessing a lesser glory
and majesty than the Father.[6]

Problems abound with this subordinationist and/or quasi-homoian
complementarianism view of the Trinity, not least in how advocates describe
the theological lay of the land and map their own position within it. For a start,
one wonders if it wise to divide perspectives into so-called "feminist" views
of the Trinity in contradistinction to so-called "complementarian" views of
the Trinity.[7] I submit that this classification tells us more about the classifiers
than it does about the *status quaestionis* in contemporary Trinitarian discussions. A historical taxonomy would normally refer to "orthodox," that is to
say Nicene-Constantinopolitan formulations, over and against "heterodox"
positions, such as Arianism, Sabellianism, and Tri-theism. Going further,
within orthodox Trinitarianism, one could opt to distinguish "Classical" from
"Social" configurations of the Trinity.[8] On close inspection, then, the descrip-

2. Karl Barth, *Church Dogmatics*, trans. G. T. Thomson (Edinburgh: T & T Clark, 1969), 1/1: 406–31.

3. Wolfhart Pannenberg, *Systematic Theology*, 3 vols., trans. G. W. Bromiley (Edinburgh: T & T Clark,
   1991 [1988]), 1:308–17.

4. See Wayne A. Grudem, *Systematic Theology: An Introduction to Biblical Doctrine* (Grand Rapids:
   Zondervan, 1994), esp. 250–51; Bruce A. Ware, *Father, Son, and Holy Spirit: Relationships, Roles, and
   Relevance* (Wheaton, IL: Crossway, 2005); Bruce A. Ware and John Starke, eds., *One God in Three
   Persons: Unity of Essence, Distinctions of Persons, Implications for Life* (Wheaton, IL: Crossway, 2015).

5. For a good introduction to homoianism, see R. P. C. Hanson, *The Search for the Christian Doctrine of
   God: The Arian Controversy 318–381* (Edinburgh: T & T Clark, 1988), 348–86.

6. A similar observation is made by Tom McCall, *Which Trinity? Whose Monotheism? Philosophical and
   Systematic Theologians on the Metaphysics of Trinitarian Theology* (Grand Rapids: Eerdmans, 2010), 186.

7. Wayne A. Grudem, *Evangelical Feminism and Biblical Truth* (Wheaton, IL: Crossway, 2012).

8. As done in Jason S. Sexton, ed., *Two Views on the Doctrine of the Trinity* (Grand Rapids:
   Zondervan, 2014).

tion of "feminist" and "complementarian" views of the Trinity do not represent historical categorizations or even correspond to contemporary schools of Trinitarian thought. Thus, to insist on views of gender roles as the single criterion for classifying Trinitarian formulations is a strange move. It is also a categorization that is, to be frank, utterly bizarre in that it subordinates Trinitarian doctrine to a very narrow band of anthropology (i.e., gender roles); it even turns out to be a meaningless categorization when it is realized that complementarian and egalitarian advocates both can affirm a non-subordinationist Trinitarian theology.

The problem, as I see it, is that a quasi-homoianism was drafted into the complementarian narrative by a small cohort of theologians in order to buttress their claims about gender roles and to define what distinguishes them as complementarians. In which case, something like homoianism is being utilized as scaffolding for complementarianism with the result that a defense of complementarianism involves a defense of a quasi-homoianism. Now it is quite clear that not all complementarians will allow their views of gender roles in the church to be tethered to this quasi-homoianism since many complementarians will regard such a formulation as extrinsic to their accounts of gender roles and will simultaneously wish to affirm an orthodox and Nicene Trinitarianism in which there is no subordination. Indeed, this book proves that very point since it comprises of several essays written by a mixture of egalitarian and complementarian scholars who are all singularly united in their articulation of a non-subordinationist and non-hierarchical account of intra-Trinitarian relationships. This is fatal to the quasi-homoianistic brand of complementarism because it demonstrates that a Nicene and orthodox Trinitarian theology ultimately transcends and even unites those with different convictions about gender roles, marriage, and family. Clearly, then, one does not have to hold to a homoian and hierarchical view of the Trinity in order to be complementarian.

The central thesis of this book is that the evangelical consensus, in keeping with its catholic and orthodox heritage, affirms that the Trinity consists of one God who is three distinct and equal persons, and the distinctions do not entail subordination or hierarchy. As such, this volume tries to do two things. First, it constitutes a robust restatement of Trinitarian orthodoxy with special attention paid to a non-subordinationist and non-hierarchical account of the relationships within the Godhead. Second, it attempts to wrestle the doctrine of the Trinity away from the trenches of American evangelical debates about gender and authority.[9]

---

9. In this sense, the volume issues a challenge to the complementarian wing of the evangelical church to reconsider whether one sibling in their family has gone a bridge too far in trying to anchor gender roles in a particular articulation of the Trinity that potentially risks mutating into homoianism. See a similar plea by Millard J. Erickson, *Who's Tampering with the Trinity? An Assessment of the Subordinationist Debate* (Grand Rapids: Kregel, 2009), 259.

With those goals in mind, it is my hope that the following presentation of Nicene trinitarianism is as clear and persuasive as Wayne Grudem's description of the deity of Christ, and our critique of quasi-homoianism is as effective and forceful as Bruce Ware's refutation of Open Theism.[10] Hopefully, one day, we can all be united together and recite the wonderful words of the Athanasian Creed, which says of the church's faith:

> Nothing in this Trinity is before or after,
>> nothing is greater or smaller;
>> in their entirety the three persons
> are co-eternal and co-equal with each other

And

> For the person of the Father is a distinct person,
>> the person of the Son is another,
>> and that of the Holy Spirit still another.
>> But the divinity of the Father, Son, and Holy Spirit is one,
> their glory equal, their majesty co-eternal.

The editors would like to thank the editorial team at Kregel for their massive efforts in bringing this book to completion, Mr. John Schoer for doing the indices, and the authors for their contribution and collaboration in this project.

---

10. See Wayne A. Grudem, *Systematic Theology: An Introduction to Biblical Doctrine* (Grand Rapids: Zondervan, 1994), 543–63; Bruce A. Ware, *God's Lesser Glory: The Diminished God of Open Theism* (Wheaton, IL: Crossway, 2000); idem, *Their God Is Too Small: Open Theism and the Undermining of Confidence in God* (Wheaton, IL: Crossway, 2003).

Introduction

MICHAEL F. BIRD

The objective of this volume is to provide a non-hierarchical and pro-Nicene account of intra-Trinitarian relations. This will be achieved by exemplifying instances of Trinitarian interpretation of the New Testament, appropriating insights from historical theology, and offering reflections by systematic theologians on the subject of the Trinity. Our contributors are diverse in terms of age, gender, denomination, views of ministry, and geographical distribution. However, they are all united in their concern that evangelical accounts of the Trinity remain fiercely committed to a catholic and orthodox theology of the Godhead. Evangelical theologians, who claim to be biblical and orthodox, are not at liberty to dispense with eternal generation, nor to substitute roles of authority for Nicene terms for articulating the relationships between the divine persons. Thus, the contributors of this volume engage in a robust defense of Trinitarian hermeneutics and Nicene orthodoxy.

The essays that follow are broken down into three sections: biblical perspectives on the Trinity, insights from historical theology, and perspectives in systematic theology.

Biblical Perspectives on the Trinity

Although the word "Trinity" is not found in the New Testament, nonetheless, Trinitarian doctrine is the result of the church's exegesis of Scripture and its philosophical reflections on the language of Scripture. The aim of theology proper has been to develop a framework and grammar to describe Scripture's coherence and to rule out erroneous configurations of the Godhead.

The Gospel of John was vital in the church's christological controversies by providing the textual terrain and grammar upon which the controversies were largely fought. This gospel, more than any other, also shaped the church's Trinitarian discourse and how it articulated both the Son's agency and unity with the Father. Thus John's Gospel cannot be ignored in any study of immanent and economic Trinitarian relationships. To this end, Adesola Akala examines how the Gospel of John, which mostly portrays the Son's submission to the Father, also effectively expresses the Son's equality with the Father. She argues that John's Gospel ingeniously unveils Jesus, who is divinely equal with God, as the *Son sent by the Father* into the world to fulfill a salvific mission. Then, using John 5 as a case study, she surveys how pro-Nicene theologians have understood the theme of subordination in the Gospel of John without negating the Son's equality with the Father. Her conclusion is that the Son's eternal divinity and equality with God is uncompromised by his mission into the world for the salvation of humanity.

In regards to 1 Corinthians 11:3–11, with the language of headship for God over Christ and man over woman, Madison Pierce offers a direct counterpoint to complementarian readings of this passage which stress God's economic authority over the incarnate Christ, which is projected into eternal immanent relations between Father and Son, and then made the template for male-female relations in terms of authority and submission. First, Pierce proposes that the God-Christ relationship expressed in 1 Corinthians 11:3 is at best analogically representative of eternal subordination, but is not the sum of immanent Trinitarian relations. Second, she highlights the importance of *taxis* ("order") over *archē* ("authority") for understanding the Father-Son relations and how the persons are distinguished by their number and sequence within the Trinitarian *taxis* and not by any rank discerned in their economic operations. Third, Pierce presents lexicographical evidence that *kephalē* in 1 Corinthians 11:3 has the meaning of "first" and "prominent." The result is that God is prominent over Christ in a manner that reflects the dynamics of pro-Nicene *taxis* language use, that is, unity of purpose at the same time as economic differentiation. Paul's intention, Pierce claims, is not to establish relations of authority for the Corinthian church but to set forth the right worship for men and women given their distinctiveness. Consequently it would be misleading and inadequate to ground gender relationships between men and women within a reading of Corinthians 11:3 that postulates hierarchy between God and Christ. Finally, applying the concept of *redoublement* (French for "repeating") to the topic, Pierce contends that God is the Father only insofar as he has a Son and vice versa for the Son. This entails that the primary matrix for understanding their relationship is not authority and subordination; rather, it is unity and mutuality. She concludes rather that we do best to remember that according to Paul the Trinity is characterized by *taxis* rather than *tiers*.

In the epistle to the Hebrews, another christologically rich document, Amy Peeler examines how the Father-Son relationship depicted there informs Nicene orthodoxy. According to Peeler, Hebrews discloses that while God the Father and God the Son are both distinct persons, nonetheless, both persons are equally and gloriously sovereign and they act out of the one divine will to rescue humanity. The author uses paternal and filial language to communicate the uniquely intimate relation between two distinct persons of the Godhead. In contrast, supporters of subordination commit a category mistake by equating the Father's primacy in relation to the Son with the Father's authority over the Son. Yet the author of Hebrews argues that there never was a time when the Father's authority was distinct from the Son's, since Father and Son are mutually dependent upon the other, and upon the Spirit. The language of sending and being sent does not pertain to the Son's submission, but more properly expresses differentiated roles to achieve the one divine will which is human salvation. Peeler concludes that in a theological reading of Hebrews there was and is mutual authority but no submission. That is because authority was given by the Father to the exalted Son as a reiteration of the equal glory, will, and power that the Son shares eternally with the Father.

Ian Paul has the gargantuan task of exploring how the book of Revelation describes the relationship between Jesus and God the Father. He begins with examination of the opening greeting of the book as well as the worship of God and the Lamb in Revelation 4–5. His conclusion is that while Jesus and the Father are distinguished, nonetheless, Jesus shares in the being, actions, and worship of the one God. In addition, the book of Revelation is far from binitarian, since it has a germinal Trinitarianism in that the Spirit is the agent who activates life in the present and in the age to come, and so participates in and effects the salvific work of God the Father and Jesus Christ. In the end, Revelation explicitly attributes the roles and functions of God to Jesus, God and Jesus are regarded as equal persons in the Godhead, and John the Seer presents the Spirit as acting for both God and Jesus. Paul's final comment is quite apt: "Nicene belief in God as Trinity is the only doctrinal and theological framework which can make sense of the narrative shape and diverse imagery of the book of Revelation in its depiction of the threefold identity of God."

Insights from Historical Theology

Trinitarian orthodoxy developed, we might say, like a slow-cooked BBQ. It took time for theologians, especially in the patristic period, to develop a lexicon and grammar for explaining what Scripture affirmed about the Father, the Son, and the Spirit (e.g., they are all divine, all persons, and all equal), developing a language that could not be used in double-speak for affirming mutually exclusive ideas (e.g., *homoousios*), and identifying which configurations of the Trinity were unbiblical or incoherent (e.g., modalism, tri-theism, and subordinationism). As such, any discussion of the Trinity will inevitably involve analysis of patristic, medieval, reformation, and modern Trinitarian discussion. The

Trinity is a doctrine, not a text, so it requires us to investigate how theologians of the past have developed and defended Trinitarian orthodoxy.

Peter Leithart demonstrates from Athanasius how any account of hierarchy within the Trinity is notoriously problematic. The Father can never be said to act independently of himself, even hypothetically, because unless the Father eternally begets the Son, he would not be the Father. This is the heart of Athanasius's axiom: No Son, no Father. Hence, the Father never *chooses* to act through the Son and Spirit, he is constituted as Father because he works in cooperation with the Son and the Spirit. Leithart then proceeds to demonstrate from Athanasius's exegesis of 1 Corinthians 1:24 how the mutual dependence on the divine persons is basic to Athanasius's account of Trinitarian theology. Here Athanasius judges that the Son is not an expression of God's wisdom and power, but is its very contents. The Father has no wisdom or power that is not identical to the Son. By implication, the Father is neither wise nor powerful without the Son. Thus, God is his power because the Father has proper power of his own that *is* the Son begotten by the Spirit. God is identical to his wisdom because the Father has eternally begotten a Son through the Spirit, a Son who *is* his word and wisdom. Athanasius's account of the Trinity rests on mutuality not hierarchy.

Amy Brown Hughes's chapter focuses on Gregory of Nyssa's specific contribution to a mode of Trinitarian discourse that came to characterize the thought of the Nicene Cappadocians such as Gregory of Nazianzus and Basil of Caesarea. She points out that Gregory played a crucial role in the establishment of theological language and concepts that locate divine unity at the level of being, while preserving the distinction of the Trinity from all other being, and avoiding hierarchies within the Godhead. During the volatile period of Trinitarian deliberation that was the late fourth century, the overarching question for Gregory was how to conceive of God as one undivided essence as well as three distinct persons. According to Brown Hughes, Gregory's theological method allows for a speaking of God that both resists hierarchical notions of God that lead to the subordination of the Son and the Holy Spirit, and provides the church with a meaningful way to speak about God.

Tyler Wittman brings medieval scholasticism into the discussion with a study of Thomas Aquinas's account of God's inner life which attaches material significance to the divine names through the distinction between theology and economy. By focusing especially on the principles of Aquinas's inquiry, Wittman demonstrates how it frames what we can and cannot say about God's inner life through privileging the essential intelligibility of the personal names of the Father, Son, and Holy Spirit. The relevance of Aquinas's apophatic yet contemplative approach is seen through the example of how he navigates the language of "authority" in Trinitarian discourse. Then, moving on to early modern theologians, especially in the Reformed tradition, Wittman shows that this same commitment to characterizing the inner-Trinitarian relations in minimalist terms is complemented by the traditional distinction between theology and economy. The latter distinction in particular helps theologians such as Francis Turretin, Amandus Polanus, and John Owen situate the differentiation of authority between the Father and Son within God's economic condescension. Though the language of "authority" has figured into Trinitarian theology for a long time, it has always done so differently than it does in contemporary debates. The conclusion Wittman reaches probes the contrasts between traditional and revisionist accounts of "authority," and he suggests that the older approach for expressing and speaking about the Trinity remains the most promising avenue.

T. Robert Baylor examines the relevance of the *pactum salutis* to the eternal functional subordination debate. Drawing on the writings of John Owen, Baylor contends that early Reformed accounts of the covenant of redemption between the Father and the Son to redeem the elect were intended precisely to undermine any notion that subordination is an eternal personal property of the Son. For Owen, the whole of God's redeeming work is grounded in a voluntary agreement between the Father and the Son. The Son's subordination to the Father was eternally willed as part of that agreement, but it was not naturally inherent to his relation to the Father as the Son. This is because the Son's subordination to the Father is not to be grounded in the Son's relation of origin. Instead, the subordination of Christ in the economy of grace refers us to a dependence that the Son has upon the Father in virtue of a new relationship established within the *pactum salutis*. According to Owen, it is the covenant, and not the processions, which form the sole foundation of the Son's dependence upon the Father. What is more, covenants can only be made on a voluntary basis, so that the Son was absolutely free in making this covenant. As a result, Owen ultimately grounds the Father's authority over the Son in the Son's own freedom and will. Owen seemed to be of the mind that, if the eternal Son was naturally subordinate to the Father, then his obedience in the economy would have been necessary rather than the free act of grace that it is. For Owen, then, the love and grace of the Son's mission is apparent not simply in the fact that he was humbled by the Father, but that, in his absolute freedom, the Son humbled himself and willed to take on flesh for our sakes.

Jeff Fisher looks at perspectives among Protestant scholastics on the Trinity and the intra-personal relationships therein. Fisher covers several notable Protestant theologians—Peter Martyr Vermigli (1499–1562), Girolamo Zanchi (1516–1590), Theodore Beza (1519–1605), Zacharias Ursinus (1534–1583), Francis Gomarus (1563–1641), William Ames (1576–1633), and, Francis Turretin (1623–1687)—all of whom consistently maintained the eternality and equality of the Father-Son relationship within the Trinity. Fisher explains how these theologians endeavoured to qualify and clarify almost every instance where the charge of the Son's subordination to the Father might possibly arise. They married together the eternal generation of the Son with the Son's divine aseity. In the fusion, they maintained that the Son was *homoousion* with the Father, and therefore, in the eternal generation of the Son as a person, the divine essence was "communicated" to the Son. Accordingly, the Son was not in any sense inferior to the Father; indeed, the Son was operation- ally subordinate to the Father only in his role as the incarnate mediator. The Protestant scheme, then, was not eternal functional subordination, but rather something better described as *preincarnate functional obedient subjection*, since these theologians would reject any sense that the Son's subordination corresponded with his eternal divinity or even his personhood. In a distinc- tively Protestant way, they supposed that the preincarnate submission of the Son to the Father was exclusively because of the triune plan that he would assume the office of the mediator and not because of his personal relationship as Son to Father. Fisher shows how the Protestant scholastics insisted that the order of subsisting as first, second, and third persons within the Godhead did not refer to a chronology of origins or to a hierarchy of authority. There is, then, no historical support among the Protestant scholastics for the view that the Son is relationally subordinate to the Father eternally.

Jules Martínez-Olivieri examines the christological method of the propo- nents of eternal functional subordination and finds it wanting. All christo- logical formulations imply something about the Father-Son relationship and Martínez-Olivieri contends that a faithful Christology should be based upon the depiction of God's hypostatic activity in the economy of redemp- tion, concurring with the creedal confessions of Nicaea and Chalcedon. However, advocates of "eternal functional subordination" (EFS) fail to uphold this because they are attempting to trace hierarchical human gendered rela- tions from a hierarchical conceived view of the Trinity. The divine persons are not differentiated by relations of origin—generation and procession—as normally claimed by tradition, but by active roles and expressions of author- ity and submission. Martínez-Olivieri regards this as a "conjecture" and "innovation," which makes the Son's place in the Trinity contingent upon his role within creation and thus impugns divine aseity and freedom. Further confusion appears over the Son's two wills, human and divine, which for EFS proponents anchor claims that the Son's divine will was for incarnation not equality with the Father. Yet a divine will that is not identical to the Father's will implies a separate centre of consciousness indicative of tritheism. In the end, Martínez-Olivieri regards EFS as following a liberal tradition in theol- ogy that has attempted to conceive of the Trinity as a means to justify certain models of social organization.

Among modern theologians worthy of consideration, John McClean mines Wolfhart Pannenberg for perspectives that can contribute to the debate about intra-Trinitarian relationships. According to McClean, Pannenberg's doctrine of God makes much of the submission of the Son to the Father in the historical life of Jesus. This self-distinction of the Son from the Father turns out to be, because of the resurrection, also the movement of unity of the son with the Father. Thus Pannenberg's view, shaped by his eschatologi- cal metaphysic, is that God's triune life takes up the economic movements in such a way that it is not marked by submission and authority but by intimate dynamic love between the persons of the Trinity. Pannenberg posits the Father's monarchy while simultaneously claiming that the Son is the locus of the monarchy of the Father, rendering the Father as dependent upon the Son. Of course, McClean does find some aspects of Pannenberg's Trinitarianism to be problematic, not least of all Pannenberg's attempt to transpose all the economic relations of the Father and the Son into an account of eternal mutually dependent relations. McClean finds the classical approach preferable whereby the economic submission of the Son is understood in a twofold way: first, the proper submission of the incarnate Son to the Father as temporary; and second, human submission is the fitting analogical expression of the *ad intra* Father-Son relation which we signify by the phrase "eternal generation."

Perspectives in Systematic Theology

The role of systematic theology is to resource biblical and historical theology in order to provide a contemporary restatement of the Christian faith. That restatement often engages in competition with other contemporary restatements of the faith. Accordingly, our systematic contributors deploy the tools of their craft to contend that some complementarian expressions of the Trinity are running the gauntlet of not Arianism but a semi-Arianism.

Stephen Holmes contends that within Anglophone evangelical theology and church life there has been much debate over the idea of eternal functional subordination or "eternal relationships of authority and submission" (ERAS). To ask whether EFS/ERAS are adequately Trinitarian, he says, we must first define "Trinitarian." Following Michel Barnes, Holmes argues that the only possible definition is historical. To be Trinitarian is to hold to the doctrine developed in the fourth-century debates. Insisting on a strong distinction between the divine life *in se* and the economic acts of God rules out any appeal to, for instance, the *pactum salutis* in an attempt to defend EFS/ERAS. A consideration of the Father-Son relationship suggests two possible defences of such positions, one relying on finding an eternal analogue to the economic ordering of the divine acts, and the other pressing Father-Son language to suggest that the relationship of eternal generation might entail something like EFS/ERAS. An examination of what must be said concerning the simple divine essence, however, excludes both these possibilities. According to Holmes, therefore, EFS/ERAS, or any similar doctrines, are incompatible with classical Trinitarianism.

Graham Cole provides an essay that very much summarizes the theme of the volume where he exhibits his concerns about any claims pertaining to the eternal subordination or submissiveness of the Son. He identifies the current debate as largely an internal one among social Trinitarians as to whether the Trinity is egalitarian or hierarchal and so authorizes relationships of that nature. His objection to hierarchal formulations of Trinitarian relations is that it creates "tiers" of authority within the Trinity which resonate with species of Arian theology. He, too, sees current expressions of subordination-ism as rehearsals of the semi-Arianism of the Blasphemy of Sirmium. While Arian and semi-Arian expressions of subordination need to be differentiated, Cole—following John Murray—sees the danger of collapsing the economic Trinitarian actions into the immanent Trinitarian ontology, simply because operations and essence are related but are not strictly the same thing. What is more, using any view of the Trinity to presage views of gender and ministry is likely to prove problematic in the end.

James Gordon offers a critical engagement with Philip R. Gons and Andrew David Naselli concerning the equality and distinction of persons within the Godhead. Gons and Naselli contend that their position on EFS is no more problematic than eternal generation or eternal procession. Further, they argue that their position fits within traditional orthodox Christianity. Gordon demonstrates that Gons and Naselli's claims are either unfounded or unorthodox. Moreover, they do not meet their initial hopes for their work, which was to overcome McCall and Yandell's well-known arguments against EFS. Firstly, Gordon shows that Gons and Naselli's view of divine and personal properties entails four distinct divine beings: God, the Father, the Son, and the Spirit. Secondly, Gordon demonstrates that Gons and Naselli drive a wedge between the divine essence and the persons in such a way that the result diverges from the mainstream Christian doctrine of God. This, together with other claims about unique personal properties for the Father and the Son, undermines Gons and Naselli's claim that their doctrine of God fits within historic Christian orthodoxy. Gordon then moves to a descriptive section on how prominent theologians including Aquinas and Anselm dealt with the issues at hand. Gordon advances the classical position (classical for both Catholics and Protestants) that the divine essence consists of nothing more than the simple divine essence, which is equal to the relations and attri-butes of the divine persons who are Father, Son, and Holy Spirit. Hence, what distinguishes the persons is their opposed relations to one another rather than any "additional" personal properties. Within this account of God, the Son's fitness for incarnation—as opposed to the Father and the Spirit—is not based on a unique property of subordination to the Father. Indeed, to posit a personal property distinction between the Father and the Son would under-mine not only the unity of God, but also the value of what is *divinely* revealed and accomplished by the Son in salvation.

Scott Harrower critiques Bruce Ware's Trinitarian hermeneutics and theology as exemplified in Ware's volume *Father, Son, and Holy Spirit: Rela-tionships, Roles, and Relevance*. Harrower contends that Ware's appeal to "Rahner's Rule"—where the "economic" Trinity is the "immanent" Trinity—is a misstep because Rahner's rule is capable of strict or loose readings. What is more, the "strict" applications create some serious problems especially if one introduces Jesus's relationship to the Spirit, meaning that Ware must utilize Rahner's Rule very selectively. On top of that, Harrower asserts that

Ware's work is full of inconsistencies at the level of its use of Scripture and its postulation of relationships between the members of the Godhead. According to Harrower, Ware's strict employment of Rahner's Rule is not exegetically warranted and as such does not provide a secure basis for the doctrine of God.

Finally, Scott Harrower offers a second contribution, something of an epilogue to the volume, talking about the value of creating a theological culture that endures. He uses Isaac Newton, William Whiston, and Samuel Clarke as his examples of how seventeenth- and eighteenth-century Anglican academics gradually slid toward semi-Arianism, then into Arianism and even into full-on deism and unitarianism. He warns: "The point to note here is that sub-Nicene tendencies in one generation may well lead to committed sub-trinitarian and non-Trinitarian believers in the next." Thus, it is vital that we do not allow the theological cultures of our churches, colleges, and seminaries to get wishy-washy, nonchalant, confused, or loose with Trinitarian doctrine. The best way to avoid sliding into Arianism is to call out people who start building semi-Arian slides.

Summary

The debate about the Trinity within North American evangelicalism has certainly ratcheted up in the last eighteen months.[1] It has become increasingly clear to many that a hierarchical account of the Trinity with a semi-subordinationist Christology is neither biblical nor orthodox.[2] In this book, we add our own voices to the discussion as to what it means to be truly Trinitarian, to make Nicaea normative for doctrine and practice, and to be overwhelmingly orthodox and catholic by conviction when it comes to speaking about God. It is the conclusion of the editors, and by implication of the contributors too, that whom evangelicals believe in—or should believe—is a Trinity without hierarchy of authority or gradations of glory and majesty. The apostolic and evangelical faith is to confess one God and three equal persons, distinguished by relationships of origin, not by degrees of authority and glory.

---

1. See Kevin Giles, *The Rise and Fall of the Complementarian Doctrine of the Trinity* (Eugene, OR: Cascade, 2017) and Logos Mobile, TH361, "Perspectives on the Trinity: Eternal Generation and Subordination in Tension," Faithlife Corporation, 2017.
2. See Fred Sanders and Scott Swain, eds., *Retrieving Eternal Generation* (Grand Rapids: Zondervan, 2017).

CHAPTER 1

Sonship, Sending, and Subordination in the Gospel of John

ADESOLA AKALA

T he key to understanding the Johannine Jesus is the gospel's pronounced portrayal of the Son *sent by the Father* into the world to proclaim and bestow eternal life. John 20:31 clearly defines the gospel's purpose: "These have been written so that you may believe that Jesus is the Christ, the Son of God; and that believing you may have life in His name."[1] In the Fourth Gospel, therefore, Christ is uniquely presented as the divine Son sent into the world by the Father. Those who believe in the Son's message will obtain eternal life, and as God's children, partake in the divine relationship (1:12).

Jesus in John's Gospel is the Father's emissary; accordingly, his obedience to the salvific mission is inevitably emphasized. The following narrative analysis shows how the Son's submission to the Father in the mission is strategically unveiled within a Johannine "theology of sending."[2] In the Prologue (1:1–18), the Son is introduced emphatically as divinely equal with God the Father. Interspersed within the ensuing narrative are "conflict passages" where the

---

1. Scripture references are from the *New American Standard Bible: 1995 Update* (LaHabra, CA: The Lockman Foundation, 1995).
2. The phrase "theology of sending" is attributed to Rudolf Schnackenburg. See Rudolf Schnackenburg, *Jesus in the Gospels: A Biblical Christology* (Louisville: Westminster John Knox, 1995), 248.

Son emphasizes his divine equality with the Father. In these pericopes, the Son simultaneously explains his obedience and devotion to the Father using the subordination language expected of emissaries. As the Son's mission draws to an end, in the Farewell Discourse and Prayer (13–17), he commissions his disciples to continue the salvific mission, following his example of submission to the Father. Throughout the Johannine narrative, the Son's submission to the Father is unveiled entirely within the framework of his life-giving message and mission in the world.

The Prologue (1:1–18)

In the Gospel of John, the Prologue is the *terminus a quo* of the Son's mission from the Father. Introduced as the divine *Logos* who is coeternal and coequal with God (1:1–5), the Son's eternality and divinity is established at the onset of the narrative. It may be argued that by underscoring the Son's equality with the Father before introducing his sonship, the Prologue is emphasizing divinity and equality with God over the Gospel's ensuing portrayal of the sent Son.[3] The Prologue also foreshadows the opposition to the divine mission (1:10–11), which would lead to the Son's affirmations of divine commission and pronouncements of obedience to the Father. At the end of the Prologue, the eternal *Logos* is unveiled as God's incarnate Son, who is in the world to reflect the Father's glory, grace, and truth to humanity (1:14–18). This responsibility of the Son as the Father's representative in the world is the context within which the subordination texts emerge in the conflict passages.

The Conflict Passages

Rejection by the Jewish religious elite is the catalyst that drives the Johannine portrayal of Jesus as Son sent from the Father. In the gospel, Jesus's actions such as breaking the Sabbath laws lead to controversies and confrontations. These conflicts force Jesus to defend himself by proclaiming both divine equality and unity with the Father on the one hand, and on the other, obedience and submission to the Father's will. The Son's assertions follow a pattern—the Father has sent the Son into the world and the Son is obeying by speaking the Father's words and accomplishing his works. Most of the subordination texts appear within this repeated explanation.

The first conflict occurs in chapter 5, where Jesus heals a lame man and is accused of breaking the Jewish Sabbath laws. Responding to this accusation, Jesus replies that he and the Father are at work together (5:17), implying that all the Son's words and works on earth are equal to and synchronous with the Father's. Since Jesus equates his actions with the Father's, the religious leaders interpret his statement as a claim of equality with God (5:17–18). In a lengthy monologue, Jesus reveals how he and the Father work together, affirming both

---

3.   Adesola Akala, *The Son-Father Relationship and Christological Symbolism in the Gospel of John* (London: T & T Clark, 2015), 219.

his equality with, and subordination to the Father: the Son can do nothing apart from the Father (5:19, 30); he carries out the same actions as the Father (5:19–20, 30); he accomplishes the Father's works to prove that the Father sent him (5:36); both the Father and Son raise the dead and grant eternal life (5:21); the Son's voice will raise the dead because he shares the Father's life (5:25–26); the Father authorizes the Son to execute eternal judgment (5:22, 27–30); both the Father and Son share equal honor (5:23); acceptance of the Son's message is equivalent to belief in the Father who sent him (5:24). These statements show how Jesus's submission to the Father in the work of salvation is rooted in his unity and equality with God.

In chapter 6, Jesus miraculously multiplies five barley loaves and two fish to feed five thousand people (6:1–13). The next day, the crowd challenges Jesus to produce more bread, to which he responds that *he* is the true Bread of Life. During this exchange, Jesus gives further insight into the Father-Son relationship and the divine mission: He is the one on whom the Father has set his seal (6:28); his hearers are to believe in him whom the Father has sent (6:28); the Father gives true bread from heaven which provides life for the world (6:32–33); all whom the Father has given to the Son will come to him (6:37); the Son has come from heaven to fulfill the will of the Father who sent him (6:38); the Father's will is that none given to the Son will be lost, but raised in the eschaton (6:39); the Father's will is that those who believe in the Son will have eternal life (6:40); only those drawn by the Father will come to the Son (6:44); those who hear the Father and learn from him are drawn to the Son (6:45); only the Son has seen the Father (6:46); the Father has sent the Son, the Son lives because of the Father and whoever feeds on the Son will live also (6:57). In chapter 6, the Son's submission is based on his representation as the Bread of Life sent by the Father from heaven to give humanity eternal life.[4]

Further controversy ensues in chapter 7, where the source and authority of Jesus's teaching is questioned (7:14–15). Jesus insists that his teaching originates from the Father who sent him (7:16), that those who desire to do God's will recognize the source of his teaching (7:17), and that he seeks the Father's glory (7:18). To validate the divine authenticity of his teaching in this chapter, Christ refers to his sending from the Father five times (7:16, 18, 28, 29, 33).[5]

Jesus's claim in chapter 10, that he is the Good Shepherd who lays down his life for the sheep, causes division among his audience (10:1–21). When pressed to admit whether or not he is the Christ, Jesus points to the works he has accomplished in his Father's name (10:22–26). Again in his defence, the Son stresses his relationship with and agency from the Father: The Father and Son know each other (10:15); the Father loves the Son because

---

4. The word "life" (*zōē*) occurs eleven times in the Bread of Life Discourse (6:22–71); "eternal life" (*zōē aiōnios*) occurs five times.

5. Cf. 7:16, 18, 28, 29, 33.

he lays down his life for the sheep (10:17); the Son has received this charge from the Father (10:18); the Son's works are performed in the Father's name (10:25); no one will be able to take from the Father those he has given to the Son (10:29); the Son and Father are one (10:30); the Son reveals the Father's works (10:31, 37); the Father has consecrated and sent the Son into the world (10:36); the Father and Son indwell each other (10:38). In this chapter, Jesus emphasizes the extent of his obedience to the Father, namely, his impending crucifixion. Simultaneously, Jesus also affirms his unity and divine equality with the Father.

Chapter 12 narrates the prophetic rejection of the Son (12:37–43) and the Son's appeal for people to believe in him. Speaking of his relationship with the Father, Jesus states: whoever believes in and sees the Son also believes in and sees the Father who sent him (12:44–45); the Son speaks on the authority of the Father, who has sent and commanded what he should say (10:49); the Father's commandment is eternal life (10:50). In this conflict passage, the Son attempts to overturn the people's rejection of his agency by pointing to his obedience to the Father.

The Farewell Discourse

In the Farewell Discourse (chs. 13–16), Jesus meets with his disciples before the crucifixion, and prepares them for his departure by reaffirming his relationship with the Father: The Father is glorified in the Son (13:31–32; 14:13; 15:8); no one comes to the Father except through the Son, thus, knowing and seeing the Son is equivalent to knowing and seeing the Father (14:6–7, 9); the Father and Son indwell each other (14:10–11, 12, 20; 16:32); the Son acts on the Father's authority, and the Father works through the Son (14:10–11); the Son is returning to the Father (14:12; 16:10, 17, 28); the Son will ask the Father to send the Holy Spirit in the Son's name (14:16–17, 26; 15:26); the Father loves those who love the Son (14:23; 16:27); the Son speaks the Father's words (14:24; 15:15); the Son is returning to the Father, therefore the Father is greater than the Son (14:28);[6] the Son loves the Father and is obedient to him (14:31); the Son is the vine and the Father is the vinedresser (15:1); the Father loves the Son (15:9); the Father answers prayers made in the Son's name (15:16; 16:23, 26); all that the Father has, belongs to the Son (16:15).

The subordination texts in the Farewell Discourse reiterate aspects of the Son's mission in the world as the Father's representative. The disciples also learn about how they are to continue the mission following the example of the Son's obedience to the Father.

---

6. The Father's priority in this notable subordination verse can be attributed to his act of sending the Son, who at this point is about to return to the Father after having completed the mission in which he was sent: "I go to the Father, for the Father is greater than I."

The Farewell Prayer

The final cluster of subordination texts in the Gospel of John occurs in the *terminus a quem* of the Father-Son relationship—the Farewell Prayer. This prayer expresses the Son's obedience to the Father in the divine plan of salvation and refers to his sending by the Father six times (17:3, 8, 18, 21, 23, 25). Jesus mentions what the Father gave him to accomplish the mission: authority to grant eternal life (17:2); work to accomplish (17:4); believers (17:6–7, 12, 24); words to speak (17:8); glory (17:22, 24). In the prayer, the Son reiterates that he has glorified the Father (17:4); manifested the Father's name (17:6, 26); given the Father's words (17:8, 14) and the Father's glory (17:22). Contingent to this portrayal of submission, however, is the Son's oneness with the Father (17: 11, 21, 23), which is demonstrated in their sharing all things (17:10), including eternal glory (17:5). In this prayer, "Jesus portrays himself as an example to his disciples in his earthly life and ministry . . . a model Son, a paradigm of sonship for believers whom he calls to come into relationship with the Father as children of God."[7] The Son is expressing his devotion and obedience to the Father in the salvific mission—the disciples are to continue the mission in the same manner.

Sending Theology in the Gospel of John

From the above narrative analysis, the sending of the Son by the Father is evidently a distinguishing Johannine theological theme. The Father is characterized by his sending the Son into the world and the Son incessantly identifies himself in relation to the Father who sent him.[8] Virtually every time the Father is mentioned in the Johannine narrative, some aspect of the Son's emissary role is also narrated.[9] In the Gospel of John, therefore, the word "send" occurs thirty-seven times in context of the Father-Son relationship,[10] compared to only fourteen occurrences in the Synoptic Gospels combined. Most of the subordination texts in the Gospel of John are embedded in passages where the Son defends or explains his earthly mission. In these conflict passages, the word "send" occurs twenty-seven times—more than 70 percent of the total occurrences in the Gospel of John.[11]

---

7.   Akala, *Son-Father Relationship*, 219.

8.   The Father's unique title in John's Gospel is *ὁ pempas [patēr] me* ("one who sent me" or "the Father who sent me"). Cf. 1:45; 4:19, 44; 6:14; 7:40; 9:17.

9.   Paul N. Anderson, "The Having-Sent-Me Father: Aspects of Agency, Encounter, and Irony in the Johannine Father-Son Relationship,'" *Semeia* 85 (1999): 37.

10. References to the Father sending (Gk. *apostellō* or *pempō*) the Son in the Gospel of John are as follows: 3:17, 34; 4:34; 5:24, 30, 36, 38; 6:29, 38, 39, 44, 57; 7:16, [18], 28, 29, 33; 8:16, 18, 26, 42; 9:4; 10:36; 12:44, 45, 49; 13:20; 14:24; 15:21; 16:5; 17:3, 8, 18, 21, 23, 25; 20:21.

11. In the Conflict Passages, Farewell Discourse, and Prayer, "send" (Gk. *apostellō* or *pempō*) occurs twenty-seven times. Cf. *apostellō*: 5:33, 36, 38; 6:29, 57; 7:29; 10:36; 17:3, 8, 18, 21, 23, 25; *pempō*: 5:23, 24, 30, 37; 6:38, 39, 44; 7:16, 18, 28, 33; 12:44, 45, 49.

Jesus's sonship and submission cannot be understood outside of the plan of salvation for humanity. The Son's subordination to the Father is that of an emissary sent into the world to act and speak words that will lead people to eternal life. For the message of eternal life to be received and believed, the Son must convince his hearers that he has been sent by God and that he is acting and speaking in obedience to a heavenly directive. At the same time, the Son asserts his coequal and coeternal status with the Father, and affirms that his works and words are synchronous with God's. The Johannine portrayal of Jesus's sonship is deeply entwined with his role as emissary from the Father, and thus accounts for the Gospel's language of subordination.

Pro-Nicene Theology and the Gospel of John

The subordination language in the Gospel of John was at the center of the Arian heresy that erupted in the first quarter of the fourth century. Arianism viewed the Son as inferior to the Father, a distinct being who was created as a derivative copy having only some of the Father's attributes.[12] On May 20, 325 C.E., more than two hundred church delegates from the Roman Empire convened in Nicaea to discuss the contentious Arian heresy, which essentially denied the Son's eternality and equality with God the Father. The orthodoxy that corrected the Arian heresy was articulated in the Nicene Creed, which expressed in Johannine language a declaration of eternality and equality in the Father-Son relationship: *We believe in one God, the Father almighty, maker of heaven and earth, of all things visible and invisible; and in one Lord, Jesus Christ, the Son of God, begotten from the Father, only-begotten, that is, from the substance of the Father, God from God, light from light, true God from true God, begotten not made, of one substance with the Father, through whom all things came into being, things in heaven and things on earth.* These christological principles in the Nicene Creed were revised and expanded in the ecumenical councils of 381, 431, and 451.[13]

The councils used the Gospel of John as a primary document for the support of pro-Nicene Christology.[14] By the time the Arian heresy emerged, the Gospel of John had recovered from the "Johannophobia" of the first and second centuries.[15] Irenaeus of Lyons in his *Against Heresies* had made

---

12. Lewis Ayres, *Nicaea and Its Legacy: An Approach to Fourth Century Theology* (Oxford: Oxford University Press, 2004), 15–16.
13. Constantinople (381), Ephesus (431), and Chalcedon (451).
14. Kyle Keefer, *The Branches of the Gospel of John: The Reception of the Fourth Gospel in the Early Church*, Library of New Testament Studies 332 (London: T & T Clark, 2006), 1. See also Harold W. Attridge, "Johannine Christianity," in *The Cambridge History of Christianity. Volume 1: Origins to Constantine*, eds. Margaret M. Mitchell and Frances M. Young (New York: Cambridge University Press, 2006), 125.
15. "From the end of the second century on, there is virtual agreement in the Church as to the authority, canonicity and authorship of the Gospel of John." Carson, *Gospel according to John*, 28. For discussion of the reticence of early church theologians' usage of John, or lack thereof, see Charles E. Hill, *The Johannine Corpus in the Early Church* (New York: Oxford University Press, 2004); Keefer, *The*

extensive use of the Gospel of John to refute gnostic Christianity,[16] making the gospel a powerful theological tool for the refutation of heresy and establishment of orthodoxy. The Gospel of John thus provided the language for articulating the christological debates of the third century and beyond.[17] T. E. Pollard sums up the role of the gospel in pro-Nicene orthodoxy: "From the very beginning of the controversy it was St John's Gospel, the pre-eminent New Testament witness to the divine Father-Son relationship, which provided Arius' opponents with their most powerful arguments."[18]

John's Prologue provided a theological basis for the Son's eternality and equality with the Father; it also shaped the doctrine and language of *homoousios* ("one substance with the Father"),[19] which was enshrined in the Nicene Creed. The Johannine narrative introduces Christ in the grandeur of divine glory and subsequently unveils him as Son in the humility of his mission to humanity. Due to this distinct dualism, the Gospel of John became an equivocal text that lent itself to both sides of the debate regarding the Son's equality with, and subordination to the Father. Pro-Nicene theologians not only vigorously attacked the way Arians used John's Gospel to deny the Son's eternality and equality with the Father; they simultaneously used the subordination texts in the Gospel in defence of orthodoxy. In sum, Johannine theology framed pro-Nicene theology. The following analysis of John 5 demonstrates how pro-Nicene theologians interpreted subordination texts to affirm the eternal and equal divinity of the Son with the Father in context of his life-giving mission in the world.

Sonship, Sending, and Subordination in John 5

In John 5, Jesus heals a lame man on the Sabbath thereby instigating the ire of the Jewish religious leaders, who accuse Jesus of breaking the Sabbath laws (5:16). In Jesus's defense, which happens to be his longest, uninterrupted

---

Branches of the Gospel of John; J. N. Sanders, *The Fourth Gospel in the Early Church* (Cambridge: Cambridge University Press, 1943).

16.   Irenaeus vindicated John's Gospel as the *regula veritatis*, and used it to establish the main standard by which theological orthodoxy is to be measured. Sanders, *Fourth Gospel*, 72, 86–87.

17.   Francis Moloney, *The Gospel of John*, Sacra Pagina 4 (Collegeville, MN: Liturgical Press, 1998), 21.

18.   Pollard also notes that Arian documents provide little evidence of the usage of John's Gospel. T. E. Pollard, *Johannine Christology and the Early Church* (Cambridge: Cambridge University Press, 1970), 146. The importance of Johannine language in defining the Father-Son relationship and articulated in fourth-century pro-Nicene theology is affirmed by Ayres. See Ayres, *Nicaea and Its Legacy*, 15.

19.   A standard connotation of the term *homoousios* was membership in a class, a generic similarity between things that were, in some sense, coordinate. However, the term became problematic because it also conveyed biological or material analogies, such as the generation of a human son by a human father. Ayres, *Nicaea and Its Legacy*, 94–95. According to Andrew Louth, *homoousios* became the hallmark of later ecumenical debates and councils. Andrew Louth, "The Fourth-Century Alexandrians: Athanasius and Didymus," in *Cambridge History of Early Christian Literature*, eds. Frances Young, Lewis Ayres, and Andrew Louth (Cambridge: Cambridge University Press, 2004), 278.

speech to opponents in the gospel (5:19–47),[20] he offers insight into his relationship with the Father as divine Son and representative. The passage, therefore, contains key subordination verses.

Jesus's defense in 5:17 is a declaration of equality with God,[21] "My Father is working until now, and I Myself am working." The implications in this statement are so clear that the religious leaders plot to kill Jesus, on the grounds of breaking the Sabbath law, and more importantly, on the grounds of blasphemy (5:18; cf. 10:33).[22] The basis of the blasphemy charge is Jesus's claim that he is equal with God, the divine Law-giver; their works are the same.[23] Jesus is claiming "the fundamental powers of God."[24] The Gospel has made it clear from the start that Jesus is God precisely as the Father is God (1:1, 18), therefore, to hear it implicitly from Jesus's own lips, and explicitly from his opponents, is a confirmation of the fact.[25] The declaration of divine equality in 5:17 is important for interpreting the subordination texts in the ensuing passage (5:19–47). [26] Underlying the Son's professions of obedience and submission to the Father in the divine mission is their shared equality and unity. As Jesus claims equal rank with the Father, he also declares that his works are in obedience and on the Father's delegated authority,[27] thus, signaling the two-dimensional nature of the divine relationship as it unfolds in the narrative.

In his *Discourse against the Arians*, Athanasius approaches 5:17 by first castigating the Arian heretics for interpreting the verse to mean that the Father "made the Son for the making of things created."[28] The Son, argues Athanasius, is not a mere instrument for the Father's use nor was he taught to be creator; rather, Christ does the Father's work by virtue of his "being the Image and Wisdom of the Father."[29] Commenting on 5:17–18, Augustine also attacks the Arians: "Behold, the Jews understand what the Arians do not understand. The Arians, in fact, say that the Son is not equal with the Father,

---

20. Michaels, *John*, 306–307.
21. *Contra* Keener, who argues that Jesus is not claiming equal rank with the Father. Keener, *John*, 1:647–48. Other scholars argue contrary to Keener. See Michaels, *John*, 304; Urban C. von Wahlde, *The Gospel and Letters of John*, 3 vols. (Grand Rapids: Eerdmans, 2010), 2:225.
22. For an explanation of the Jewish notion of blasphemy in this passage see Keener, *John: A Commentary*, 2 vols. (Peabody, MA: Hendrickson, 2003), 1:647. See also Ramsey J. Michaels, *The Gospel of John* (Grand Rapids: Eerdmans, 2010), 305.
23. *TDNT*, 3:352.
24. von Wahlde, *John*, 1:405.
25. Michaels, *John*, 305.
26. Andreas J. Köstenberger, *John* (Grand Rapids: Baker, 2004), 184.
27. According to Keener, "Neither the lowly obedience nor the implication of deity should be overlooked." Keener, *John*, 1:648. See also Leon Morris, *The Gospel according to John*, The New International Commentary of the New Testament (Grand Rapids: Eerdrmans, 1971), 278.
28. *NPNF²* 4:363–64.
29. *NPNF²* 4:363–64.

and hence it is that the heresy was driven from the Church."[30] In other words, although the Jews did not agree with Jesus's claim, they recognized that Jesus believed that he was equal with the Father. Explaining the Son's equality in John 5, Augustine states, "He did not make Himself equal, but the Father begat Him equal. . . . He usurped not equality with God, but was in that equality in which He was begotten."[31] Christ's equality with the Father is, therefore, as eternal as his generation from the Father. The term "equal" (*isos*) in 5:18 expresses the notion of equal nature and will—the essential and perfect equality that the Nicene term *homousios* was designed to defend.[32]

Next, Jesus explains that because of his oneness with the Father, he is not blaspheming: "the Son can do nothing of Himself, unless it is something He sees the Father doing; for whatever the Father does, these things the Son also does in like manner" (5:19). The Son's essential equality and unity with the Father is evident in the fact that the Son does nothing on his own (cf. 5:30; 7:17, 28; 8:28; 12:49; 14:10). The Son and Father are jointly and equally active in the mission to the world; their oneness is demonstrated in synchronous action. The phrase "can do nothing of Himself" (5:19; cf. 5:30) was used by the Arians to portray the Son as incapable of any action, and therefore inferior to the Father.[33] Patristic pro-Nicene theologians did not view 5:19 as a suggestion of the Son's inability or inferiority; their interpretations defended the Son's divinity and equality with the Father.

For Athanasius, Jesus in 5:19 was expressing how the Father manifests his works through the Son on earth. Athanasius comments, "Where the Father is, there is the Son, and where the light, there the radiance; and as what the Father worketh, He worketh through the Son."[34] In his commentary, Cyril of Alexandria explains how it is naturally impossible for the Son not to desire to do the Father's works, in other words, the Son is saying, "by the laws of uncreated nature, I ascend to the same will and action as God the Father."[35] Cyril concludes that the word "cannot" in 5:19 shows "the stability of the Son's substance and his inability to change into something other than what he is."[36] Hence, the Son is intrinsically equal with the Father in every action. Hilary of Poitiers, in *De Trinitate IIV* comments, "He told them that, because the power and the nature of God dwelt consciously within Him, it was impossible for Him to do anything. . . . His liberty of action coincides in its range

---

30.   *NPNF*[1] 7:116.

31.   *NPNF*[1] 7:187, 188.

32.   *TDNT*, 3:353.

33.   According to Ayres, probably because of its use by the Homoians in the 360s, John 5:19 was the subject of extended discussion by Christian theologians. Lewis Ayres, *Augustine and the Trinity* (Cambridge: Cambridge University Press, 2010), 233.

34.   *NPNF*[2] 4:370–71.

35.   *ACT, John* 1:143.

36.   *ACT, John* 1:146.

with His knowledge of the powers of the nature of God the Father."[37] In other words, "cannot" denotes not the Son's inequality with the Father, but rather, his inseparable power with the Father, which is inherent in him by birth and by sharing the Father's nature.[38] Gregory Nazianzen's *Fourth Theological Oration* asserts the unity of the Father and Son: "It is impossible and inconceivable that the Son should do anything that the Father doeth not."[39] Gregory Nyssa explains that the Son is "equally provident" with the Father because they exhibit a "communion of nature" and purpose to do the same things.[40] In his commentary on this verse, Augustine addresses the Arian heresy that the Son "is surely less, not equal" because in 5:19, Jesus is trying to show that he is not equal with God in order to offset the anger of the Jewish leaders.[41] For Augustine, the word "cannot" in 5:19 means "the works of the Father and of the Son are inseparable."[42] The pro-Nicene theologians viewed John 5:19, not as a negative assertion of incapability and inferiority, but rather, as insight into the Son's co-divinity with the Father, which is expressed in unity of thought and equality of action.

An intriguing aspect of the Son-Father relationship in John 5 is the Son's act of "seeing" what the Father is "doing" (5:19–29).[43] The pro-Nicene Church Fathers did not view this claim by the Son as one of subordinate imitation. Hilary argues that when in 5:19 the Son declares that he does the same things he sees the Father doing, their actions are equal.[44] Cyril of Alexandria points out that based on the actions of seeing and doing in the Father-Son relationship, Arians view the Father as the sole originator of the Son's works. Cyril regards this Arian argument as ultimate ignorance, for "how could he [the Father] ever originate anything alone by his own power, since he has the Son as his operative power for everything . . . who is with him eternally and who reveals his will and activity in every matter?"[45] Thus, for Cyril, the Father and Son work in unison and simultaneously, in a way incongruent of imitation. Augustine states clearly that the actions of the Son do not imitate the Father; rather, their works are simultaneous, for "it is by the Son that the Father does"; therefore, Augustine concludes, "let the heretic be convinced: The Son is equal to the Father."[46] In his book, *Augustine and the Trinity*, Lewis Ayres

---

37. *NPNF*² 9:336.
38. *NPNF*² 9:177, 178.
39. *NPNF*² 9:630.
40. *NPNF*² 5:144.
41. *NPNF*¹ 7:190–91.
42. *NPNF*¹ 7:218.
43. Due to its emphasis on divine revelation, verbs of seeing occur more in the Johannine Gospel than the Synoptics. The three verbs of seeing, *horaō, theaomai,* and *phaneroō,* occur altogether more than forty-five times in the Gospel of John.
44. *NPNF*² 9:178.
45. *Ancient Christian Texts (ACT), John,* 1:147.
46. *NPNF*¹ 7:194.

examines how Augustine and other pro-Nicene theologians understood the Son's action of "seeing" the Father without being "thought to act subsequently to the Father or as one subordinate in power."[47] Ayres notes that in 5:19, these patristic theologians mostly viewed the Son's seeing as a consequence of his generation from the Father and his sharing divine essence or nature.[48] Both Greek and Latin pro-Nicene Fathers all view the Son's seeing as an intrinsic part of what it means for him to possess divine nature and power.[49]

In 5:20, Jesus declares that the Father will show Him "greater works"; these greater works are explained in the next verse, "just as the Father raises the dead and gives them life, even so the Son also gives life to whom He wishes" (5:21). "Greater works," therefore, refers to the main purpose of the Son's mission on earth—the bestowal of eternal life to humanity through resurrection from spiritual death. Rather than view 5:21 as a subordination text, Cyril of Alexandria teaches that since God is the one who has the power to resurrect from the dead, Jesus is establishing his equality with the Father.[50] Hilary explains that because they share the same nature, the Father and Son have equal power to raise the dead.[51] Likewise, Augustine argues that the Son's power is not different from the Father's, like that of a servant or an angel; rather, "the Father and the Son have one substance, so also one will."[52] For Augustine, therefore, "the power of the Father and of the Son is the same, and also the will is the same."[53] John 5:21–22 portrays the Son and Father willing and working together to grant spiritual life.

The bestowal of eternal life by the Father and Son is directly connected to the notion of judgment. In the Gospel of John, judgment is the refusal to believe in the Son sent by the Father. For this reason, the Son inevitably assumes the position of Judge, which is why he declares in 5:22, "the Father has given all judgment to the Son" (cf. 5:27). This verse further establishes the Son's deity, for in the Old Testament, God is Judge;[54] hence, both the Son and Father are equally honored (5:23). Judgment was taking place as Jesus was teaching—those responding to the voice of the Son of God were rising to eternal life (5:25). Within this context of life-giving mission, Jesus states, "just as the Father has life in Himself, even so He gave to the Son also to have life in Himself" (5:26).[55] How did the pro-Nicene Fathers interpret this verse?

---

47.   See chapter entitled "Showing and Seeing," in Ayres, *Augustine and the Trinity*, 230–50, esp. 233–34.
48.   Ayres, *Augustine and the Trinity*, 236.
49.   Ayres, *Augustine and the Trinity*, 237, 240.
50.   *ACT, John*, 1:189.
51.   *NPNF*[2] 9:125–26.
52.   *NPNF*[1] 7:141.
53.   *NPNF*[1] 7:123.
54.   Cf. Gen. 18:25; Pss. 50: 4, 6; 58:11; 75:7; 96:13; 98:9; Isa. 2:4; 33:22; 66:16; Dan. 7:9–10.
55.   This statement should be understood against the Old Testament background of God as the source of life (Gen. 2:7; Deut. 30:20; Job 10:12; 33:4; Pss. 27:1; 36:9). Morris, *John*, 283.

In *Four Discourses against the Arians*, Athanasius explains that like the Father, the Son has always had life; the "Son's Godhead is the Father's Godhead, and thus the Father in the Son exercises His Providence over all things."[56] Cyril of Alexandria comments that Jesus is speaking in human terms, "mixing the message fitted for human nature with God-befitting authority and majesty."[57] Based on this explanation, Cyril rephrases Jesus's words: "Though I am now like you and I appear as a human being, promise to raise the dead and threaten to bring judgment. The Father has given me the power to give life. The Father has given me the authority to judge."[58] For Cyril, therefore, Jesus is explaining the source of the life he bestows to humanity in terms his opponents understand, namely, as a divine Son sent by the Father, and as an emissary equipped and authorized to fulfil the life-giving mission. The Son's life, Cyril asserts, originates together with the Father's life, by reason of their shared divine nature.[59] In *On the Councils*, Hilary fiercely defends the Son's equality with the Father, stating that anyone who views 5:26 as a denial of Jesus's divine essence should be anathema.[60] The life spoken of in 5:26, explains Hilary, signifies the substance and the life of *both* the Father and Son, for the Son's origin is a "perfect birth of the undivided nature."[61] In the following words, Hilary eloquently refutes any notion of the Son's subordination in 5:26:

> There is no diversity in the likeness of the essence that is born and that begets, that is, of the life which is possessed and which has been given. For though God begat Him of Himself, in likeness to His own nature, He in whom is the unbegotten likeness did not relinquish the property of His natural substance. For He only has what He gave; and as possessing life He gave life to be possessed. And thus what is born of essence, as life of life, is essentially like itself, and the essence of Him who is begotten and of Him who begets admits no diversity or unlikeness.[62]

Finally, Augustine argues that 5:26 refers to the Son's generation from the Father.[63] In *Homilies on John Tractate XLVII*, the theologian states that there is no lessening of the Son because he "is said to receive of the Father what He possesses essentially in Himself."[64] Furthermore, Augustine explains, the Father does not add gifts to the Son as though the Son were imperfect; rather, the Son's gifts are part of his begetting, for the Father "gave Him equality with

---

56.   *NPNF²* 4:414.
57.   *ACT, John*, 1:156.
58.   *ACT, John*, 1:156.
59.   *ACT, John*, 1:156.
60.   *NPNF²* 9:8.
61.   *NPNF²*
62.   *NPNF²*
63.   For more on the Son's eternal generation, see Kevin Giles, *Eternal Generation of the Son: Maintaining Orthodoxy in Trinitarian Theology* (Downers Grove, IL: InterVarsity, 2012).
64.   *NPNF¹* 7:265.

Himself, and yet begat Him not in a state of inequality."[65] Pro-Nicene exegesis viewed the Father's act of "giving life to the Son" through the lens of the Son's eternal generation from the Father—a divine state of contemporaneous existence in which the Son exerts power equal with the Father's, in order to impart eternal life to humanity. The Son's eternal generation does not equate with eternal subordination.

The Patristic commentaries on verses in John 5 examined above are by no means exhaustive; nevertheless, they demonstrate how pro-Nicene exegesis refuted implications of the Son's subordination, even within his role as the Father's emissary. Pro-Nicene theologians refuted Arian claims of the Son's subordination by painstakingly stressing the Son's equality with the Father—they interpreted the subordination language in the Gospel of John in light of the Son's incarnate, human state, and his mission of redemption and salvation.

Conclusion

The Johannine theology of sending ties Jesus's divine sonship to his agency from the Father, making the gospel's subordination language inevitable. The subordination conundrum in John's Gospel, therefore, stems from the theological tension originating from the narrative portrayal of the Father who *sends* his *equally divine* Son into the world as his unique emissary.[66] In the narrative, in every instance where the Son uses subordination language, his essential equality and oneness with the Father is clearly affirmed. As highlighted by patristic pro-Nicene theologians, the Johannine Jesus is eternally equal with the Father; his divinity supersedes his delegated role as the Father's emissary.

The Gospel's unique presentation of Jesus is a clear invitation to enter into divine relationship with the Son and his Father. To this effect, the sending Father works together with and through the sent Son in the life-giving mission to humanity. Through the Johannine portrayal of Jesus, believers have a clear picture of how to relate to the Father within the divine relationship. The devotion and obedience demonstrated in the earthly mission is an example to Jesus's followers, who have been commissioned by him just as he was commissioned by the Father (17:18; 20:21). Believers in Christ are to relate to God as subordinate and obedient children who continue the Son's life-giving mission in the world.[67]

---

65. *NPNF*[1]
66. Akala, *Son-Father Relationship*, 218.
67. Akala, *Son-Father Relationship*, 219.

Bibliography

Akala, Adesola. *The Son-Father Relationship and Christological Symbolism in the Gospel of John*. London: T & T Clark, 2015.

Anderson, Paul N. "The Having-Sent-Me Father: Aspects of Agency, Encounter, and Irony in the Johannine Father-Son Relationship." *Semeia* 85 (1999): 33–57.

Attridge, Harold W. "Johannine Christianity." In *The Cambridge History of Christianity. Volume 1: Origins to Constantine*. Edited by Margaret M. Mitchell and Frances M. Young, 125–43. New York: Cambridge University Press, 2006.

Ayres, Lewis. *Augustine and the Trinity*. Cambridge: Cambridge University Press, 2010.

_____. *Nicaea and Its Legacy: An Approach to Fourth-Century Theology*. Oxford: Oxford University Press, 2004.

Carson, D. A. *The Gospel according to John*. The Pillar New Testament Commentary. Grand Rapids: Eerdmans, 1991.

Elowsky, Joel C., ed. *Cyril of Alexandria: Commentary on John*. 2 vols. Ancient Christian Texts. Translated by David R. Maxwell. Downers Grove, IL: InterVarsity, 2013.

_____. *John 1–10*. Vol. IVa. Ancient Christian Commentary on Scripture. 2 vols. Downers Grove, IL: InterVarsity, 2006.

Giles, Kevin. *Eternal Generation of the Son: Maintaining Orthodoxy in Trinitarian Theology*. Downers Grove, IL: InterVarsity, 2012.

Hill, Charles E. *The Johannine Corpus in the Early Church*. Oxford: Oxford University Press, 2004.

Keefer, Kyle. *The Branches of the Gospel of John: The Reception of the Fourth Gospel in the Early Church*. Library of New Testament Studies 332. London: T & T Clark, 2006.

Keener, Craig S. *The Gospel of John: A Commentary*. 2 vols. Peabody, MA: Hendrickson, 2003.

Kittel, Gerhard, and Gerhard Friedrich, eds. *Theological Dictionary of the New Testament*. Translated by Geoffrey W. Bromiley. 10 vols. Grand Rapids: Eerdmanns, 1964–1976.

Köstenberger, Andreas J. *John*. Baker Exegetical Commentary on the New Testament. Grand Rapids: Baker, 2004.

Louth, Andrew. "The Fourth-Century Alexandrians: Athanasius and Didymus." In *The Cambridge History of Early Christian Literature*. Edited by Frances Young, Lewis Ayres, and Andrew Louth, 275–83. Cambridge: Cambridge University Press, 2004.

Michaels, J. Ramsey. *The Gospel of John*. Grand Rapids: Eerdmans, 2010.

Moloney, Francis. *The Gospel of John*. Sacra Pagina 4. Collegeville, MN: Liturgical Press, 1998.

Morris, Leon. *The Gospel according to John*. The New International Commentary of the New Testament. Grand Rapids: Eerdrmans, 1971.

Pollard, T. E. *Johannine Christology and the Early Church*. Cambridge: Cambridge University Press, 1970.

Sanders, J. N. *The Fourth Gospel in the Early Church*. Cambridge: Cambridge University Press, 1943.

Schaff, Philip, ed. *The Nicene and Post-Nicene Fathers*. Series 1 &2. 1886–1889. 14 vols. Repr. Grand Rapids: Eerdmans, 1956.

Schnackenburg, Rudolf. *Jesus in the Gospels: A Biblical Christology*. Louisville: Westminster John Knox, 1995.

Von Wahlde, Urban C. *The Gospel and Letters of John*. 3 vols. Grand Rapids: Eerdmans, 2010.

CHAPTER 2

Trinity without *Taxis*?

A Reconsideration of 1 Corinthians 11

MADISON N. PIERCE

When one thinks of "submission" and/or "subjection" in the New Testament, Paul typically comes to mind. This is especially true of his *Haustafeln* (household codes), which outline submissive relational dynamics between slaves and masters, children and parents, and wives and husbands (Eph. 5:21–6:9; Col. 3:18–4:1). Elsewhere Paul presents another relationship with language similar to submission: God is the "head" of Christ (1 Cor. 11:3). This along with other so-called Pauline "subordination" texts portrays the Son in submission to the Father. But when? Does Paul envision Christ in submission to God *eternally*? If so, how does that accord with the theology of early Christianity?[1]

I contend that pro-Nicene theology and the doctrine of the Son's eternal subordination are incompatible.[2] According to pro-Nicene theology, the

---

1. Many thanks are due to Benjamin G. White and Joseph R. Dodson who read an earlier draft of this essay and to Richard Davis and Benjamin E. Reynolds who allowed me to discuss the material at various stages and provided some much-needed encouragement.

2. "[Pro-Nicene] theology is not sufficiently defined by reference to Nicaea alone, but only by reference also to a number of the key principles within which Nicaea was interpreted as teaching a faith in three co-ordinate divine realities who constitute one nature, power, will and substance" (Lewis Ayres, *Augustine and the Trinity* [Cambridge: Cambridge University Press, 2014], 43; see also Lewis Ayres, *Nicaea and Its Legacy: An Approach to Fourth-Century Trinitarian Theology* [Oxford: Oxford University Press, 2004], 236–40).

Father and Son (and Spirit) are of one divine will and one essence, and their operations are inseparable. Further, the Trinity evinces difference without hierarchy—a concept these early theologians called *taxis* or "order." These tenets stand among many components of pro-Nicene theology that cannot be reconciled with an "eternal relation of authority and submission" (ERAS) or "eternal functional subordination" (EFS). This essay will argue that *taxis* offers a helpful framework for understanding the description of the Father-Son relationship in 1 Corinthians 11:3. Namely, "God is the head of Christ" because he is first in order. The primary concern for Paul is the distinction between man and woman, and the analogy to this divine relationship offers a model for equity *and* distinction. To establish this, I will first outline previous readings of 1 Corinthians 11:3, primarily that of Kyle Claunch. This will lead into an introduction to *taxis* in Trinitarian theology. Since "head" is frequently interpreted in terms of authority, I will discuss some alternative proposals for the meaning of *kephalē*, which will lead into a final reading of 1 Corinthians 11 that focuses on other helpful categories for understanding Paul's theology proper.

Previous Readings of 1 Corinthians 11

In Paul's first correspondence with the Corinthians, he moves from a discussion about guarding one another's conscience—doing that which is *beneficial*, not just *permissible* (10:23–11:1)—to a discussion of proper attire in worship (11:4–16). But as Paul makes the transition, he says:

> Be imitators of me, as I am of Christ. Now I commend you because you remember me in everything and maintain the traditions even as I delivered them to you. Now I want you to understand that the head of every man is Christ [*pantos andros hē kephalē ho Christos estin*], the head of a wife is her husband [*kephalē de gynaikos ho anēr*], and the head of Christ is God [*kephalē de tou Christou ho theos*]. (1 Cor. 11:1–3)[3]

Most readings of this passage focus primarily on the function of the "head" metaphor for male-female relationships, but do not adequately address how that interpretation affects the Father-Son relationship.[4] For example, Ciampa and Rosner say that "[i]n this context the word [*kephalē*] almost certainly refers to one with authority over the other," which suggests a cohesive under-

---

3. Scripture quotations are from the ESV unless otherwise noted. I will opt to translate *ho anēr* and *hē gynē* as "man" and "woman" (respectively), but I think this is a point of tension in the text. *If* hierarchy is in view, then the marital relationship seems to be the primary referent; however, if created order, then a more general reference to the sexes seems more appropriate. The language used in major translations (NIV, NASB, KJV, NRSV, NLT; contra ESV, NRSV) and commentaries (e.g., Ciampa and Rosner, Fee, Thiselton) tends toward the latter.

4. I will opt in many instances to speak in terms of "Father" and "Son" rather than "God" and "Christ," since the antecedent of "God" is sometimes challenging to ascertain in discussions about the deity of Jesus.

standing of "head" in this verse. But later they argue the uses of the term are not identical: "although the language used for each relationship is the same, the precise nature of the relationship is determined 'according to the occasion.'"[5] But what is the "nature of the relationship" represented by *kephalē* when Paul speaks of God and Christ? Ciampa and Rosner leave this question unanswered.

Along similar lines, Joseph Fitzmyer summarizes what he sees as the "clear sense" of the verse as follows:

> As God is preeminent over Christ, so Christ is preeminent over every man, and man is preeminent over woman. . . . The whole verse is but another way of affirming what Paul has already asserted in 3:23, "You belong to Christ, and Christ to God." This principle so enunciated shows that Paul is indeed propounding a hierarchy.[6]

What Fitzmyer does not clarify is the scope of the hierarchy between the Father and Son. Is he implying the eternal submission of Christ?

Richard Hays does take into account the implications of the Father-Son relationship, even allowing it to alter his conclusions regarding the text somewhat. For example, he claims that for the Corinthian women "[t]he head covering—whatever it may have been—symbolized their femininity and simultaneously their inferior status as women."[7] Here and elsewhere he affirms "patriarchal" elements of the text, but later he offers an "approach" to the "problem" of hierarchy in the text:

> If . . . we now read 11:3 through the lens of a theological tradition that affirms Christ's full participation in the Godhead, then we must ask ourselves how this affects our understanding of the analogy. . . . The subsequently developed orthodox doctrine of the Trinity actually works against the subordinationist implications of Paul's argument about men and women.[8]

Hays ties these two doctrines together so closely that he allows his conclusions about gender in 1 Corinthians 11 to be overturned in some way by his

---

5. Roy E. Ciampa and Brian S. Rosner, *The First Letter to the Corinthians*, Pillar New Testament Commentary (Grand Rapids: Eerdmans, 2010), 511. I infer based on their discussion that Ciampa and Rosner would not support EFS/ERAS.

6. Joseph A. Fitzmyer, *First Corinthians*, Anchor Yale Bible Commentary (New Haven, CT: Yale University Press, 2008), 409. Judith Gundry-Wolf ("Gender and Creation in 1 Corinthians 11:2–16: A Study in Paul's Theological Method," in *Evangelium, Schriftauslegung, Kirche: Festschrift für Peter Stuhlmacher zum 65. Geburtstag*, eds. Jostein Ådna, Scott J. Hafemann, and Otfried Hofius [Göttingen: Vandenhoeck & Ruprecht, 1997], 151–71) likewise does not discuss the implications of her conclusions about gender for the Father-Son relationship, but her position is not strictly hierarchical. I will return to her study below.

7. Richard B. Hays, *First Corinthians*, Interpretation (Louisville: John Knox, 1997), 184.

8. Hays, *First Corinthians*, 192.

understanding about Trinitarian orthodoxy. It is admirable that with this interpretive move Hays prioritizes theology over gender relationships, but a reading of the text that is coherent for both elements is preferable.

Some readings argue for eternal hierarchy in all of the relationships that Paul describes with "head" language. For example, Bruce Ware writes,

> 1 Corinthians 11:3 offers a truth-claim about the relationship between the Father and Son that reflects an eternal verity. That God is the head of Christ is not presented here as an ad hoc relationship for Christ's mission during the incarnation. It is rather an absolute fact regarding this relationship.[9]

Ware claims that this reading is in alignment with the early church which, according to Ware, did not claim any ontological subordination, but still held to the eternal submission of Christ to the Father.[10]

Wayne Grudem also argues for a hierarchical view of 1 Corinthians 11:3[11] and grounds the eternal submission of the Son in the fact that he is "sent" by the Father, concluding: "These relationships are never reversed. The role of planning, directing, sending, and commanding the Son belongs to the Father only."[12] Grudem is right that the *order* never reverses, but what he does not sufficiently demonstrate is an eternal *hierarchy*.[13]

Though a number of other interpreters argue for the eternal submission of the Son, let us conclude with a more extended discussion of one reading of 1 Corinthians in particular—that of Kyle Claunch in *One God in Three Persons*.[14] Claunch's essay aims to show that 1 Corinthians 11:3 "ground[s] gender complementarity in the immanent Trinity"—albeit "indirectly."[15] His essay has three main sections. The first contains Claunch's exegesis. He begins with the meaning of the word *kephalē*, concluding that both "source" and

---

9.   Bruce A. Ware, *Father, Son, and Holy Spirit: Relationships, Roles, and Relevance* (Wheaton, IL: Crossway, 2005), 77. For a more extended critique of Ware, see Scott Harrower's essay in this collection.

10. Ware, *Father, Son, and Holy Spirit*, 80.

11. "[J]ust as the Father has authority over the Son in the Trinity, so the husband has authority over the wife in marriage. The husband's role is parallel to that of God the Father and the wife's role is parallel to that of God the Son" (Wayne A. Grudem, *Systematic Theology: An Introduction to Biblical Doctrine* [Grand Rapids: Zondervan, 1994], 257, 459–60).

12. Wayne Grudem, ed., *Biblical Foundations for Manhood and Womanhood* (Wheaton, IL: Crossway, 2002), 50.

13. "But if we do not have economic subordination, then there is no inherent difference in the way the three persons relate to one another, and consequently we do not have the three distinct persons existing as Father, Son, and Holy Spirit for all eternity. For example, if the Son is not eternally subordinate to the Father in role, then the Father is not eternally 'Father' and the Son is not eternally 'Son'" (*Systematic Theology*, 251).

14. Kyle Claunch, "God Is the Head of Christ: Does 1 Corinthians 11:3 Ground Gender Complementarity in the Immanent Trinity?" in *One God in Three Persons: Unity of Essence, Distinction of Persons, Implications for Life*, eds. Bruce A. Ware and John Starke (Wheaton, IL: Crossway, 2015), 65–93.

15. Claunch, "God Is the Head," 67.

"authority over" are valid, complementary meanings.[16] He demonstrates how each of the three pairings (Christ-man; man-woman; God-Christ) plausibly portrays a relationship of origin. Then, when he turns to argue for "authority" as a meaning of *kephalē*, he offers three pieces of supporting evidence: (1) the lexical attestation for *kephalē* as "authority over"; (2) Pauline use elsewhere; and (3) "the Pauline theology of gender roles in both the home and the church."[17]

After arguing for a typological connection between man-woman and God-Christ relationships, Claunch comes to the issue of most interest to us—the scope of Christ's submission to God. He claims that the "primary"— direct—reference of Paul's three statements in 1 Corinthians 11:3 is the economic Trinity. In other words, the work of Christ in human flesh—during the incarnation—is the explicit reference, which likely limits the subordination of the Son to this stage in the Son's life; however, Claunch suggests that the immanent Trinity must also be in view because, given his understanding of Augustine's theology, "the economic Trinity *reveals* the immanent Trinity."[18] Moreover, "this economic reality reveals something fixed and irreversible about the very eternal triune being of God."[19] This concern is well founded. It indeed would be misguided to say that the Father, Son, and/or Spirit revealed themselves to us in a way that was inconsistent with their essence.

Claunch then parses this relationship further, arguing that the connection between the economic and immanent is "analogical." He supports this with the connection between the sending of the Son (economic) and his eternal generation (immanent)—an example often used elsewhere.[20] The sending is a concrete analogy for the generation of the Son. As he concludes, "The two are not collapsed or identified, but the historical occurrence of the one reveals the eternal reality of the other."[21] Thus, if the Son submits to the Father during the incarnation, then something about his subordination must be reflected in the Godhead. But what?

This brings us to the final stage in Claunch's argument, his discussion of the will of God. Claunch rightly reminds readers that the Father, Son, and Spirit share one divine will; however, he says, in many articulations of an EFS/ERAS position, interpreters appeal to the obedient will of Christ and the authoritative will of God, implying that each person of the Trinity has his own will.[22] Claunch, conversely, looks for a solution to allow the three to remain unified in

---

16.   Claunch, "God Is the Head," 71–75.

17.   Claunch, "God Is the Head," 72. The second and third strike me as circular reasoning.

18.   Claunch, "God Is the Head," 85 (his emphasis).

19.   Claunch, "God Is the Head," 85

20.   See, e.g., Fred R. Sanders, *The Triune God*, New Studies in Dogmatics (Grand Rapids: Zondervan, 2016), 107–18. Here Sanders offers a helpful discussion of the development of this connection.

21.   Claunch, "God Is the Head," 86.

22.   Claunch, "God Is the Head," 88. For examples of those making this error, see Scott Swain and Michael Allen, "The Obedience of the Eternal Son," *International Journal of Systematic Theology* 15, no. 2 (2013): 113, n. 5.

will, but in a way that allows for the eternal submission of the Son to the Father. This portion of Claunch's argument is worth quoting at some length:

> To say that the Son submits eternally to the will of the Father is, I propose, too strong precisely because it implies two distinct wills in relation to one another. It is preferable to say that, in the immanent Trinity, *the one eternal will of God is so ordered that it finds analogical expression in a created relationship of authority and submission: the incarnate Son submits to the will of the Father.*[23]

Here the "will" is for the incarnation. Claunch continues:

> This same model could be applied to any of the works of God in which his will has been revealed to man. Indeed, I propose that this manner of thinking about the one divine will according to an eternal Trinitarian taxis is necessitated by the pro-Nicene categories of Trinitarian theology.[24]

But Claunch has not established why "[t]his same model could be applied to any of the works of God." He shows that his model works once, not that it is a sufficient principle for establishing the eternal subordination of the Son.

This brings me to some problems with Claunch's argument. First, he extrapolates his model to the level of a universal—one that he claims is "necessitated" by "pro-Nicene categories."[25] He has indeed offered one example of how the Son's role in the incarnation is analogically representative of inner-Trinitarian dynamics, but that does not mean the Son's submission to the Father during his earthly life is analogically representative of *eternal* subordination. This leap is certainly problematic, but it is attested elsewhere in Trinitarian theology. Fred Sanders has referred to this argument as a "maximalist" interpretation,[26] which damages our understanding of God "because [his] identity is not established in itself but is utterly dependent on world process as a whole."[27] In other words, Claunch, while trying to reconnect the economic Trinity to the immanent Trinity in Paul's theology, damages the immanent and eliminates the reality of aspects of the Trinity that remain incomprehensible to humanity. Not everything that God does in the world has an obvious correlation to something that God is "in himself" (*in se*; cf. *ad intra*).[28] Moreover, adding to Sanders's concerns, as we shall see, Claunch allows his (and others') interpretation of one aspect of the filial relationship to override traditional understandings of pro-Nicene theology. Ultimately, Claunch advances

23.   Claunch, "God Is the Head," 91 (emphasis his).
24.   Claunch, "God Is the Head," 92.
25.   Claunch, "God Is the Head,"
26.   Sanders, *The Triune God*, 109.
27.   Sanders, *The Triune God*, 111.
28.   Sanders, *The Triune God*, 110–11.

the discussion in offering a more nuanced reading of 1 Corinthians 11. He overcomes some common issues with EFS/ERAS interpretations, but further progress is necessary.

Trinity and *Taxis*

As we have seen, some readings of 1 Corinthians 11 insist upon an eternal relationship between the Father and Son that is characterized by submission and authority, even when comparing their interpretation with the theology of earliest Christianity. In this section, I will introduce another pro-Nicene term, namely *taxis* or "order," and show how this concept is crucial for understanding the Trinity and offers a helpful counterpoint to proposals that argue for EFS/ERAS.[29] For the pro-Nicenes, the Father was "first" among the three persons of the Trinity. He is the one who generates the Son and who "spirates" the Spirit. The Son and Spirit are "second" and "third," respectively. The pro-Nicenes held the three persons to be equal in essence and will, though differentiated by this order and their "origin" of sorts—their "procession." Lewis Ayres summarizes the pro-Nicene view in this way:

> For all pro-Nicenes the Father is presented as first in an order in the Godhead, and as the source of Son and Spirit. It is not surprising that we find this commonality: pro-Nicene formulations of the coequal persons emerged from a context in which the generation of the Son from the Father as equal to the Father was the focus of argument.[30]

---

29. Though I cannot address the discussion here, *taxis* also offers a helpful correction to social models of the Trinity that argue for full mutuality among the persons to an extent that the distinctions among the persons are diminished. Another pro-Nicene concept that has been brought to this discussion is "inseparable operations"—"each of the three are necessarily implicated in the action of any of the other three as a result of their single, simple, divine nature" (Matthew R. Crawford, "Clarifying Nicene Trinitarianism: The Difference between Relations of Origin and Relations of Authority and Submission," Blog, *Euangelion* [June 25, 2016], http://www.patheos.com/blogs/euangelion/2016/06/matthew-crawford-clarifying-nicene-trinitarianism-with-cyril-of-alexandria). There Crawford also shows how Cyril of Alexandria's Trinitarian theology (esp. his understanding of inseparable operations and *taxis*) are incompatible with ERAS. For a more thorough discussion of Cyril's Trinitarian theology, see Matthew R. Crawford, *Cyril of Alexandria's Trinitarian Theology of Scripture*, Oxford Early Christian Studies (Oxford: Oxford University Press, 2014).
30. Ayres, *Nicaea and Its Legacy*, 207. Also, "The pro-Nicenes used the word in the sense of a fitting and suitable disposition, not a hierarchy" (Robert Letham, *The Holy Trinity: In Scripture, History, Theology, and Worship* [Phillipsburg, NJ: P & R Publishing, 2004], 400; see also 399–401 esp. n. 59). Likewise, Kevin N. Giles writes, "[*Taxis*] is a synonym for the word *dispose*, meaning to arrange in a proper, given, or prescribed way. . . . When orthodox theologians affirm divine order they are never endorsing hierarchical order in the Godhead. For them hierarchical ordering in the Trinity in being, work, or function is an Arian error" (*Jesus and the Father: Modern Evangelicals Reinvent the Doctrine of the Trinity* [Grand Rapids: Zondervan, 2009], 49). See also Robert W. Jenson, *The Triune Identity: God according to the Gospel* (Philadelphia: Fortress, 1982), 106–7.

These early Christians recognized an ostensible hierarchy in the Father-Son (later also -Spirit) relationship that they sought to reconcile with their understanding of the unity within the Godhead. What they initially developed was an understanding of *taxis* (Greek and Latin for "order" or "ordering") in which the three are distinguished by their number and sequence but not ranked, so to speak. For example, Gregory of Nyssa discusses the order and equality of the Spirit:

> But we assert that, while [the Spirit] is counted third in sequence after the Father and Son, and third in the order of transmission, in all other things he is in inseparable union [with them], corresponding in nature and in honor and in deity and glory and magnificence and in authority over all things and in godly confession. (*Adversus Macedonianos*)[31]

The order and means of transmission for the Spirit differentiates him from the Father or Son as the Spirit, but this differentiation does not separate him from their "sharing of essence."[32] In seeming contrast to his other statements, Ware also speaks to the remarkable nature of the unity within the Godhead:

> The equality of divine persons, then, is the strongest kind of equality possible and is, in fact, *sui generis* (in a class of its own). . . . Because the Father, Son, and Spirit possess the identically same nature, each then must be understood as fully God— not three gods, but three personal expressions of the one and undivided nature that is commonly, fully, and eternally possessed by each of the divine persons.[33]

This equality "in a class of its own" may well be beyond our comprehension. It may well also be beyond analogy to human relationships. But to determine this, we must return to 1 Corinthians 11:3.

Kephalē and 1 Corinthians 11:3

Interpreters often bring traditional historical-critical methods and pro-Nicene categories to bear on 1 Corinthians 11:3. For those not supporting

---

31. This is my translation of the Greek text found here: Gregory of Nyssa and Friedrich Müller, *Opera Dogmatica Minora*, vol. 3.1 (Leiden: Brill, 1958), 100.

32. For this language and a brief discussion about some later developments or clarifications of *taxis*, see Ayres, *Augustine and the Trinity*, 50–51. Unfortunately, sometimes *taxis* is misunderstood to describe something hierarchical. For example, Ware, importing his understanding of the Trinity into his definition of *taxis*, writes, "A word often used by early church theologians for the evident authority structure of the Father-Son relationship in the Godhead is *taxis*, which means 'ordering.' There is an ordering in the Godhead, a 'built-in' structure of authority and submission that marks a significant respect in which the Persons of the Godhead are distinguished from one another" (*Father, Son, and Holy Spirit*, 72). As Letham points out, this use of *taxis* does not originate with Ware. Arians also used the term in this way (Letham, *The Holy Trinity*, 400; cf. Giles, *Jesus and the Father*, 49).

33. Bruce A. Ware, "Christian Worship and *Taxis* within the Trinity," *The Southern Baptist Journal of Theology* 16, no. 1 (2012): 28, 29.

EFS/ERAS, one strategy might be to restrict Christ's submission in this passage to the incarnation, which suggests that Paul presents Christ, man, and woman—all of humanity—in submission. When Paul refers to Christ in the verse, the incarnation is indeed primarily in view; however, perhaps Claunch is correct, and the humanity of Christ cannot be separated so easily from his divinity.[34] In the following section, I will evaluate proposals for the meaning of the word *kephalē*, arguing that hierarchy is not essential to the term, whereas order is. This word study serves to confirm the viability of *taxis* for understanding 1 Corinthians 11 since parallel meanings may well be operative within the lexical form (*kephalē*) also.

The lexical form *kephalē* is said to have frequent attestation with the meaning "authority over," but authority is not always the key dimension. Two other translations are also convincing to interpreters: (1) "source or origin," or (2) "preeminent, prominent, etc." In the context of 1 Corinthians 11, each of these meanings is more plausible than "authority over."[35] In the discussion that follows, I will show that these definitions, even if they do not rid the passage of hierarchy ultimately, should be considered the more likely meaning(s) of *kephalē* in this context. A focus on "source," for instance, appears elsewhere in the passage:

> 11:8   For man was not made *from woman* (*ek gynaikos*), but woman *from man* (*ex andros*).

> 11:12   for as woman was *made from man* (*ek tou andros*), so man is now [*made through woman*] (*dia tēs gynaikos*). And all things are *from God* (*ek tou theou*).

Prior to 1 Corinthians 11, the source of teaching is significant (1:10–17; 3:1–9),[36] as well as the source of wisdom (1:18–31, esp. 1:30), the source of the Spirit (1:11–16), and the source of the world (8:6). Thus, particularly in the opening chapter, source is an established theme for this correspondence with the Corinthians.

---

34.   See Letham, *The Holy Trinity*, 397–99. Moreover, as Scott Swain and Michael Allen have pointed out, obedience cannot simply be a part of the *forma servi* because in John's Gospel the language used to link the two is also used by the Spirit, who never takes on a human nature ("The Obedience of the Eternal Son," 125).

35.   Anthony Thiselton likewise concludes that "[this verse] does *not* seem to denote a relation of 'subordination' or 'authority over', but he is also wary about defining *kephalē* as source (*The First Epistle to the Corinthians: A Commentary on the Greek Text*, NIGTC [Grand Rapids: Eerdmans, 2000], 815–16, emphasis his).

36.   This facet of the theology of 1 Corinthians is more implicit than the other topics as Paul does not rely on source language (e.g., *ek*, genitives of source), but these passages are commonly interpreted in this way.

Through this "source language" in 1 Corinthians 11, Paul demonstrates a mutual necessity between man and woman.[37] Adam was the only man in history who did not require a woman to enter the world, but God determined that he did in fact need a woman (Gen. 2:8). Thus, source is more central than authority to the argument of the passage as a whole. Additionally, in these later verses equality between man and woman is highlighted, not hierarchy—"*all* are from God." In fact, as Gordon Fee contends, the only clear mention of authority (there *exousia*) is 1 Corinthians 11:10: "For this reason, the woman [is] to have authority over her head because of the angels."[38] Nevertheless, one objection to the "source" interpretation of 1 Corinthians 11:3 is the first pairing: "Christ is the head of man," though, as Fee argues, this could refer to Christ's role in creation (Col. 1:16: "by him all things were created") or redemption ("new creation"), in which Christ is the source of life for all of humanity.[39] These aspects of Christ's relationship with humanity are not explicitly in view, through arguably neither is Christ as humanity's authority. Even so, some studies have questioned the legitimacy of this gloss altogether,[40] though subsequent rejoinders have appeared.[41]

Another view argues that *kephalē* is a living metaphor, and as such has a more flexible meaning. Interpreters who hold this view (e.g., Anthony Thiselton, Gregory Dawes) do reject a definition of *kephalē* that is as restrictive as "authority over" or "source" (or both!).[42] Operating with the assumption that *kephalē* has a broader metaphorical application, A. C. Perriman conducts his own survey of the uses of *kephalē* in Greek literature and concludes that the word has this range of meanings:

> (i) the physical top or extremity of an object, such as a mountain or river; (ii) more abstractly, that which is first, extreme (temporary or spatially); (iii) that

---

37. Gundry-Volf, "Gender and Creation in 1 Corinthians 11:2–16," 163–64. She also notes a degree of mutuality in the pneumatic relationship. Women have authority over men when they prophesy.

38. My translation. The other place where "authority" and gender is brought together is 1 Corinthians 7:4: "For the wife does not have authority over her own body, but the husband does. Likewise, the husband does not have authority over his own body, but the wife does."

39. Gordon D. Fee, *The First Epistle to the Corinthians*, NICNT, rev. ed. (Grand Rapids: Eerdmans, 2014), 556. Claunch cites approvingly, though ultimately he is influenced by the argument of Thiselton cited below ("God Is the Head," 72).

40. For example, A. C. Perriman, "The Head of a Woman: The Meaning of Κεφαλή in I Cor. 11: 3," *Journal of Theological Studies* 45, no. 2 (1994): 602–22. Perriman surveys those studies that predate him as well.

41. Richard S. Cervin, "On the Significance of Kephalē ('Head'): A Study of the Abuse of One Greek Word," *Priscilla Papers* 30, no. 2 (2016): 8–20; Philip B. Payne, *Man and Woman, One in Christ: An Exegetical and Theological Study of Paul's Letters* (Grand Rapids: Zondervan, 2009), 113–40. Cyril of Alexandria also reads this passage in terms of source. See Crawford, "Clarifying Nicene Trinitarianism."

42. Thiselton, *The First Epistle to the Corinthians*, 800–806, 812–22; Gregory W. Dawes, *The Body in Question: Metaphor and Meaning in the Interpretation of Ephesians 5:21–33*, BibInt 30 (Leiden: Brill, 1998).

which is prominent or outstanding; and (iv) that which is determinative or representative by virtue of its prominence. Here, moreover, we remain in sight of the commonest figurative usage of *kephalē* in the LXX, by which the head, representative of the whole person by synecdoche, serves as the locus of a wide range of moral and religious experiences.[43]

Though the glosses derived from Perriman's study (e.g., "prominent, foremost, uppermost, preeminent," via Thiselton) may appear to suggest a strong operative hierarchy,[44] Perriman cautions against reading this into the lexical form itself: "the metaphorical use of *kephalē* cannot be thought to introduce in any *a priori* or necessary manner ideas of authority or sovereignty into the text."[45]

Bringing Perriman's study to bear on 1 Corinthians 11:3, we see that the first meaning ("physical top") is not likely here, but rather that Paul is working with the more metaphorical end of the range of meaning. The third meaning, "that which is prominent or outstanding" is compatible with the context, but its application does not assist us with interpreting the passage because it leaves unanswered a key question, namely: *in what way* is man prominent/outstanding in comparison to woman? This leaves us with meanings two and four, which would suggest that Paul may be describing priority ("temporally or spatially") and/or representation or determination. The latter understanding of *kephalē could* fit each pairing, but since man and woman are two separate categories (and minimizing this would impinge upon Paul's argument for gender distinction/differentiation), it is unlikely that Paul intends for man to be "determinative" or "representative" (i.e., "typical") of woman.[46]

The process of elimination above leaves the final meaning in the semantic range: "that which is first, extreme (temporary or spatially)." This sense of the word *kephalē* is preferred for two reasons: (1) it makes sense in each of

---

43. Perriman, "Head of a Woman," 618; cf. Cervin, "On the Significance of Kephalē ('Head')."

44. Thiselton, *The First Epistle to the Corinthians*, 817. "Preeminence" is also favored by Gundry-Volf; however, she contra Perriman concludes that, even with this meaning in place, *kephalē* still has "patriarchal connotations" ("Gender and Creation in 1 Corinthians 11:2–16," 159–60). Ultimately, she concludes: "The women and men wore the 'hat' of the pneumatic which was 'neither male nor female' and symbolized their equality in the Lord, and at the same time they wore the 'hat' of the first century Mediterranean man or woman which was either masculine or feminine and carried the connotations of traditional gender roles in a patriarchal society" (Perriman, "Head of a Woman," 168).

45. Perriman, "Head of a Woman," 616–17. There he continues: "In very few, if any, of the passages considered does the argument depend on *kephalē* having such a meaning. In none is the word directly linked with ideas of obedience or submission or authority," but he does allow that "the sort of prominence denoted by 'head' will in many instances also entail authority and leadership" (616).

46. Perriman disagrees: "the behavior of the woman reflects upon the man who as her head is representative of her, the prominent partner in the relationship, or that the woman's status and value is summed up in the man" ("Head of a Woman," 621). He does not discuss how that applies to God and Christ.

the three relationships, and (2) it is not mutually exclusive.[47] In other words, other uses within Perriman's (and others') range of meaning could also be operative, even if the primacy of the "head" is the main meaning that Paul intends to convey. Paul's use of *kephalē* here could, for example, also convey "that which is prominent or outstanding." The fact that the entity described as *kephalē* is "first" offers a potential rationale for its prominence. So how might this apply in 1 Corinthians 11:3? How are Christ, man, and God "first"?

Let us first consider a more literal temporal preeminence. Christ is undoubtedly "first" in relationship to man. As Paul says in 1 Corinthians 8:5, we ourselves—indeed all things—exist "through him." Likewise, as previously noted, man came before woman in the garden and is thus first. With the third relationship (God and Christ), the question of temporal primacy is more challenging. If we speak of the incarnate Christ, then God is first, but if the referent is consistent, then the incarnate Christ would not be head of the man. If the reference is Christ without the restriction to the incarnation, a pro-Nicene standpoint, if adopted for this passage, would not allow for temporal primacy. The Son is generated, and yet there was never a time when he was not.

Nevertheless, if we look to *kephalē* as a descriptor of that which is first, but not temporally nor authoritatively, then we find something rather similar to *taxis*—the theological term discussed above that describes an order but not a hierarchy. Anthony Thiselton, without connecting the passage to *taxis*, reaches a similar conclusion:

> The one God, the one Lord, and the one Spirit [12:4–6] exhibit mutuality, oneness, and distinctiveness in a way which is sufficiently close to Paul's dialectic of gender for him to appeal to the nature of God and of Christ in this passage.[48]

If Paul's primary intention is to describe right worship for man and for woman in their distinctiveness, then authority is *not* the primary dynamic at work within the discussion. This is not to say that other Pauline passages do not supplement "order" in the Christ-man/man-woman/God-Christ relationships, particularly with regard to the first pairing. For the relationship between Christ and man, it would not be suitable to speak *only* of Christ as one who is first in order—elsewhere Christ is absolutely an authority over humanity; however, for the purposes of this discussion, man needs a head. Christ serves as one who is of the same kind, who in the fullness of his humanity is equal with humanity, but who remains first—though not just in order.

---

47.   Cynthia Long Westfall argues for a familial understanding of the metaphor, which also coheres well with this: "The ancestor is the head, and the descendants are the seed. . . . Since man is the origin of life for woman, he is her head" (*Paul and Gender: Reclaiming the Apostle's Vision for Men and Women in Christ* [Grand Rapids: Baker, 2016], 84). She later extends this claim to God and Jesus, arguing that this has Christ's sonship (and generation) in view (Westfall, *Paul and Gender,* 89–91).

48.   Thiselton, *The First Epistle to the Corinthians,* 803–4.

Therefore, should we ground our understanding of gender relationships in the "immanent Trinity" (or the relationship between the Father and Son)? No. What Paul offers is one connection between the two relationships. If Paul seeks to establish relative mutuality, but with elements of dissimilarity between the two genders, the relationship between the Father and Son is a helpful image indeed. It is when we draw too strong a connection between the Trinity and gender dynamics that our interpretations become overdetermined, and we imply that an understanding of the triune nature of God is fully within reach.[49] Is that unity not, as Ware says, *sui generis*?[50] Those who think that gender hierarchy is crucial to Paul's theology are served well by a "Trinity with tiers," and those who seek true mutuality may even find an "order" imposing; but the doctrine of God must be the starting point, not the doctrine of gender.

Reading 1 Corinthians 11 with an emphasis on mutuality, not submission, does not prohibit one from reading 1 Timothy 2, for example, in terms of a gender hierarchy. But Paul can describe relationships between men and women outside the framework of authority and submission, too. He can have female coworkers (Rom. 16) and prescribe mutual decision-making about sex in marriage (1 Cor. 7), and he can describe a time (present or future) where gender is without consequence (Gal. 3:28–29). Along the same vein, Paul can place an emphasis on the close unity between the Father and Son (e.g., 8:6), or he can place an emphasis on the distinctiveness of the Father or Son. Some emphasize one aspect or the other, but reading Paul through the lens of later categories reminds us to do both—to balance the emphasis of our preferred reading strategies. Additionally, some of these modern discussions show that aspects of their relationship are not obviously one or the other. Relationship highlights diversity *and* unity.[51]

Relations in Pauline "Subordination" Texts

Wesley Hill, in his recent book *Paul and the Trinity*, argues that "there are tensions in Paul's letters that lead to the construction of Trinitarian conceptualities."[52] In the course of his study, Hill offers readings of three

49. One can find countless discussions about the pitfalls of comparing divine and human relations. This intersects and overlaps with the transcendence of God and apophaticism. For more, see Kathryn Tanner, "The Foolishness and Wisdom of All God's Ways: The Case of Creation Ex Nihilo," in *The Wisdom and Foolishness of God: First Corinthians 1–2 in Theological Exploration*, eds. Christophe Chalamet and Hans-Christoph Askani (Philadelphia: Fortress, 2015), 261–87; Kathryn Tanner, *Jesus, Humanity and the Trinity: A Brief Systematic Theology* (Philadelphia: Fortress, 2001). I am grateful to Benjamin G. White for the connection between my research and Tanner's.

50. Ware, "Christian Worship and *Taxis* Within the Trinity," 28. See above for the context of this quotation.

51. For more on the tensions and paradoxical aspects of Paul's theology of gender, see Gundry-Volf, "Gender and Creation in 1 Corinthians 11:2–16." For her, different aspects or "loci" (such as "culture, eschatological life in Christ, and creation") alter Paul's discussion.

52. Wesley Hill, *Paul and the Trinity: Persons, Relations, and the Pauline Letters* (Grand Rapids: Eerdmans, 2015), 171.

classic "subordination" texts (Phil. 2:6–11; 1 Cor. 8:6; 15:20–28) that utilize two classic tools from Trinitarian theology: relations and *redoublement*—the French word for "repeating" or "doubling."[53] At its most basic, the latter entails reading, and subsequently describing, a text twice, typically in view of the "oneness" and then the "three-ness" of God.[54] Interpreters would first read a passage in search of elements that focused on the unity of the Trinity and then would double back and read the passage in search of elements that focused on one person (e.g., Jesus).[55] A theology of 1 Corinthians or Pauline literature more broadly must attend to both elements if one is to evaluate whether these texts are triune in character.

Redoublement can also be paired with relations in interpretation. One can certainly speak of "Father" and "Son" language as that which identifies God and Jesus as distinct persons. This relationship may also be said to reveal something about their "order"—a son is "from" a father, just as Jesus is generated from God. But when Paul appeals to God's paternity, he does not *only* speak of the Father because this designation necessitates another. In other words, God cannot be a Father without having a child.[56] Each time Paul uses "Father" or paternal imagery, Jesus is also in view. Francis Watson summarizes this mutual necessity well: "the purpose of the father/son language is to indicate that God and Jesus are identified by their relation to each other, and have no existence apart from that relation."[57] Thus one can also speak of this familial language as that which identifies God and Jesus as united, inseparable persons. This paired with God's interactions with Jesus throughout the Pauline corpus[58] shows that Paul's "God-language" reveals mutuality between the two characters, though, as Wesley Hill shows, this mutuality is ultimately asymmetrical.[59] He writes in the conclusion to his study:

> One might think that this asymmetry simply *confirms* subordination; Jesus is subordinate to God, that *that is what* asymmetry *means*. . . . But . . . those differing relations are one perspective on God and Jesus that must be held together with a

---

53. Hill, *Paul and the Trinity* esp. chs. 3–4. See also M. Sydney Park, *Submission within the Godhead and the Church in the Epistle to the Philippians: An Exegetical and Theological Examination of the Concept of Submission in Philippians 2 and 3*, LNTS 361 (London: Bloomsbury T & T Clark, 2007), esp. chapter 4.

54. Hill, *Paul and the Trinity*, 99–100.

55. Lewis Ayres contends that "there are in fact many forms of 'redoublement' to be found in Trinitarian tradition" and that Augustine's primary method was "the interweaving of two strands of exegesis and philosophical reflection" (*Augustine and the Trinity*, 260–61).

56. Hill, *Paul and the Trinity*, 31–35, esp. 32.

57. Francis Watson, "The Triune Divine Identity: Reflections on Pauline God-Language, in Disagreement with J. D. G. Dunn," *Journal for the Study of the New Testament* 80 (2000): 114–15.

58. For example, the frequent description of God as the one who raised Jesus from the dead (1 Cor. 6:14; cf. Rom. 4:24; 8:11; 10:9; 1 Cor. 15:15; 2 Cor. 1:9; Gal. 1:1; Eph. 1:20; Col. 2:12; 1 Thess. 1:10). See also Hill, *Paul and the Trinity*, 52–53.

59. Hill, *Paul and the Trinity*, 80–81.

second perspective which sees them as fundamentally one or unified: God and Jesus share the divine name; they are both together "the Lord."[60]

The unity of Father and Son and their mutual dependence on one another, both in salvation and in the constitution of their identities, disallows subordination within the Godhead.

Conclusion

Although traditional understandings of 1 Corinthians 11 argue that hierarchy is the primary dynamic in the three relationships (Christ-man; man-woman; God-Christ), a critique of previous interpretations paired with a reconsideration of the lexical form *kephalē* and pro-Nicene categories reveal something to the contrary. Paul describes three *ordered* relationships, where one has preeminence over the other, but without the explicit interplay of authority and submission. If Paul indeed describes an ordered, mutual relationship between God and Christ, then this mirrors later Christian articulations of the Trinity in terms of *taxis*. This concept paired with *redoublement* and an understanding of relationality and Pauline God-language reveal unity and yet distinction between Father and Son. With this, Paul seems to describe a Trinity without *tiers*, but not a Trinity without *taxis*.

---

60.   Hill, *Paul and the Trinity*, 170 (emphasis his).

Bibliography

Ayres, Lewis. *Augustine and the Trinity*. Cambridge: Cambridge University Press, 2014.

_____. *Nicaea and Its Legacy: An Approach to Fourth-Century Trinitarian Theology*. Oxford: Oxford University Press, 2004.

Cervin, Richard S. "On the Significance of *Kephalē* ('Head'): A Study of the Abuse of One Greek Word." *Priscilla Papers* 30, no. 2 (2016): 8–20.

Ciampa, Roy E., and Brian S. Rosner. *The First Letter to the Corinthians*. Pillar New Testament Commentary. Grand Rapids: Eerdmans, 2010.

Claunch, Kyle. "God Is the Head of Christ: Does 1 Corinthians 11:3 Ground Gender Complementarity in the Immanent Trinity?" In *One God in Three Persons: Unity of Essence, Distinction of Persons, Implications for Life*, edited by Bruce A. Ware and John Starke, 65–93. Wheaton, IL: Crossway, 2015.

Crawford, Matthew R. "Clarifying Nicene Trinitarianism: The Difference between Relations of Origin and Relations of Authority and Submission." Blog. *Euangelion*, June 25, 2016. http://www.patheos.com/blogs/euange-lion/2016/06/matthew-crawford-clarifying-nicene-trinitarianism-with-cyril-of-alexandria (accessed November 20, 2018).

_____. *Cyril of Alexandria's Trinitarian Theology of Scripture*. Oxford Early Christian Studies. Oxford: Oxford University Press, 2014.

Dawes, Gregory W. *The Body in Question: Metaphor and Meaning in the Interpretation of Ephesians 5:21–33*. BibInt 30. Leiden: Brill, 1998.

Fee, Gordon D. *The First Epistle to the Corinthians*. Rev. ed. NICNT. Grand Rapids: Eerdmans, 2014.

Fitzmyer, Joseph A. *First Corinthians*. Anchor Yale Bible Commentary. New Haven, CT: Yale University Press, 2008.

Giles, Kevin N. *Jesus and the Father: Modern Evangelicals Reinvent the Doctrine of the Trinity*. Grand Rapids: Zondervan, 2009.

Gregory of Nyssa, and Friedrich Müller. *Opera Dogmatica Minora*. Vol. 3.1. Leiden: Brill, 1958.

Grudem, Wayne A. *Systematic Theology: An Introduction to Biblical Doctrine*. Grand Rapids: Zondervan, 1994.

Grudem, Wayne, ed. *Biblical Foundations for Manhood and Womanhood*. Wheaton, IL: Crossway, 2002.

Gundry-Volf, Judith M. "Gender and Creation in 1 Corinthians 11:2–16: A Study in Paul's Theological Method." In *Evangelium, Schriftauslegung, Kirche: Festschrift für Peter Stuhlmacher zum 65. Geburtstag*, edited by Jostein Ådna, Scott J. Hafemann, and Otfried Hofius, 151–71. Göttingen: Vandenhoeck & Ruprecht, 1997.

Hays, Richard B. *First Corinthians*. Interpretation. Louisville: John Knox, 1997.

Hill, Wesley. *Paul and the Trinity: Persons, Relations, and the Pauline Letters.* Grand Rapids: Eerdmans, 2015.

Jenson, Robert W. *The Triune Identity: God according to the Gospel.* Philadelphia: Fortress, 1982.

Letham, Robert. *The Holy Trinity: In Scripture, History, Theology, and Worship.* Phillipsburg, NJ: P & R Publishing, 2004.

Park, M. Sydney. *Submission within the Godhead and the Church in the Epistle to the Philippians: An Exegetical and Theological Examination of the Concept of Submission in Philippians 2 and 3.* LNTS 361. London: Bloomsbury T & T Clark, 2007.

Payne, Philip B. *Man and Woman, One in Christ: An Exegetical and Theological Study of Paul's Letters.* Grand Rapids: Zondervan, 2009.

Perriman, A. C. "The Head of a Woman: The Meaning of Κεφαλή in I Cor. 11: 3." *Journal of Theological Studies* 45, no. 2 (1994): 602–22.

Sanders, Fred R. *The Triune God.* New Studies in Dogmatics. Grand Rapids: Zondervan, 2016.

Swain, Scott, and Michael Allen. "The Obedience of the Eternal Son." *International Journal of Systematic Theology* 15, no. 2 (2013): 114–34.

Tanner, Kathryn. *Jesus, Humanity and the Trinity: A Brief Systematic Theology.* Philadelphia: Fortress, 2001.

_____. "The Foolishness and Wisdom of All God's Ways: The Case of Creation Ex Nihilo." In *The Wisdom and Foolishness of God: First Corinthians 1–2 in Theological Exploration*, edited by Christophe Chalamet and Hans-Christoph Askani, 261–87. Philadelphia: Fortress, 2015.

Thiselton, Anthony C. *The First Epistle to the Corinthians: A Commentary on the Greek Text.* NIGTC. Grand Rapids: Eerdmans, 2000.

Ware, Bruce A. "Christian Worship and *Taxis* Within the Trinity." *The Southern Baptist Journal of Theology* 16, no. 1 (2012): 28–42.

_____. *Father, Son, and Holy Spirit: Relationships, Roles, and Relevance.* Wheaton, IL: Crossway, 2005.

Ware, Bruce A., and John Starke, eds. *One God in Three Persons: Unity of Essence, Distinction of Persons, Implications for Life.* Wheaton, IL: Crossway, 2015.

Watson, Francis. "The Triune Divine Identity: Reflections on Pauline God-Language, in Disagreement with J. D. G. Dunn." *Journal for the Study of the New Testament* 80 (2000): 99–124.

Westfall, Cynthia Long. *Paul and Gender: Reclaiming the Apostle's Vision for Men and Women in Christ.* Grand Rapids: Baker, 2016.

CHAPTER 3

What Does "Father" Mean?

Trinity without Tiers in the Epistle to the Hebrews

AMY PEELER

With its unwavering commitment to Jesus's identity as both Son of God and Son of Man, Hebrews serves as a vital voice in any conversation about the Son and hence the Trinity. In this essay, I aim to contribute to the conversation on the equality of glory, power, and will of the Father and the Son. I do so in three steps. First, I acknowledge the different ways the author uses important terms in his presentation of God the Father, God the Son, and their relationship. In sundry and diverse manners, current debates about the Trinity hinge upon particular meanings of these terms, meanings that are at some times made explicit but at other times just assumed. I aim to show at the outset the complexity Hebrews introduces through its language, and hence the care needed when translating and interpreting these terms. Second, I present an exposition of pertinent passages in Hebrews showing that the Father and the Son possess the same glory, power, and will. Finally, I explore arguments for the eternal relation of authority and submission in God and find them wanting in light of the ways in which Hebrews uses paternal/filial terms and concepts. Hebrews drinks deeply from the fitting language of the family to articulate the mystery of the sovereign and salvific glory of the triune God.[1]

---

1. Due to space constraints and the dominant language of Hebrews, this essay will focus upon the Father and the Son. The Spirit plays a vital role in the relationship of the Father and the Son as well as in the action

Nuances of Theological Language

Because this chapter focuses upon language and meaning of terms, it is vital to address the subject of referents. In other words, when Hebrews utilizes the words *theos, patēr,* and *huios,* what does the author have in view? Hebrews demands clarity in interpretation because the author can use the same terms for different referents.

For example, when the author mentions "God" (*theos*), about whom is he speaking? The word *theos* can signify God the Father, the divine person in relationship with the Son and the Spirit. The clearest examples of this referent in Hebrews occur, unsurprisingly, when *theos* is mentioned in relationship to the *huios*/Son. In 4:14, Jesus is the great High Priest who is the *huios tou theou,* the Son of God. *Theos* here cannot mean the triune God for Jesus cannot be the Son of himself.[2] It is also clear that a personal distinction is at play when the Son who is priest is being anointed by God (1:9), is being called by God (5:5, 10), or is presenting an offering to God, all of which point to the meaning "God the Father" (2:17; 9:14, 24). Finally, it is God the Father at the right of whom the Son as eternal high priest takes a seat (12:2).

On the other hand, the author also uses *theos* to refer to the Son who is God. In the opening catena of Scriptures, God the Father[3] speaks to the Son and addresses the Son as *theos*. The Father clearly does so in Hebrews 1:8, "Your throne, O God, is forever and ever" and likely also in verse 9, "God (*theos* as vocative) your God anointed you."[4]

In a third instantiation, in Hebrews 11:3 the author asserts that he and his readers know by faith that the ages have been created by the word of God (*theos*). Since he has portrayed both God the Father and God the Son as involved in creating (1:2, 10), then this seems to be a multivalent reference to both God the Father and God the Son.[5]

---

of salvation (briefly discussed in the following pages). For further treatment of the Spirit in Hebrews see Jack Levinson, "A Theology of the Spirit in the Letter to the Hebrews," *CBQ* 78 (2016): 90–110; David M. Allen, "'The Forgotten Spirit': A Pentecostal Reading of the Letter to the Hebrews" *Journal of Pentecostal Theology* 18 (2009): 51–66; Stephen Motyer, "The Spirit in Hebrews: No Longer Forgotten?" in *The Spirit and Christ in the New Testament and Christian Theology: Essays in Honor of Max Turner,* eds. I. Howard Marshall, Volker Rabens, and Cornelis Bennema (Grand Rapids: Eerdmans, 2012), 213–27; Matthew W. Bates, *The Birth of the Trinity: Jesus, God, and Spirit in New Testament and Early Christian Interpretations of the Old Testament* (Oxford: Oxford University Press, 2015), especially 41–84 and 157–74.

2. See also 6:6, 7:3, and 10:29.

3. My statement is based upon the argument that *theos* in 1:1 refers to God the Father because that *theos* then speaks in/by the Son (1:2) and to the Son (1:5, 8, 10, 13).

4. In support of verse 9 read as a vocative see Harold W. Attridge, *The Epistle to the Hebrews,* Hermeneia (Minneapolis: Fortress, 1989), 60; Paul Ellingworth, *The Epistle to the Hebrews,* NIGTC (Grand Rapids: Eerdmans, 1993), 124; David Arthur DeSilva, *Perseverance in Gratitude: A Socio-Rhetorical Commentary on the Epistle "to the Hebrews"* (Grand Rapids: Eerdmans, 2000), 99.

5. In my own analysis, I see likely reference to God the Father in 1:1; 2:4*, 9*, 13*, 17; 4:14; 5:4, 10; 6:6; 7:3, 25*; 9:14, 24; 10:29; 12:2; 13:15,* 20* (the asterisk indicates passages that might be God as triune). I see

Kyrios/Lord functions in much the same way. The Father addresses the Son as Lord in 1:10, and it is Jesus who is the Lord who descends from the tribe of Judah (7:14). It is the Lord Jesus who is raised and worthy of glory (13:20). It is quite likely the Lord Jesus in view as the one who articulates the story of great salvation and then gives that message to his messengers (2:3). At the same time, the Father is in view in the citation of Psalm 110:3, where the Lord swears that the Son will be priest forever (Heb. 7:21). The Father God seems also to be the Lord who disciplines his sons (12:5–6). Consequently, respectable arguments are possible for the Father, the Son, or both with the remaining uses of *kyrios* in 8:2, 8, 9, 10, 11; 10:16, 30 and 13:6.

Hence, when one is analyzing Hebrews and comes to the term *theos* or *kyrios*, it is exegetically responsible, even necessary, to inquire which referent—God the Father, God the Son, or the triune God[6]—the author might be invoking.

Interpreters must exercise similar care in the reading of the word *huios*/son. By this term, is the author limiting his comment to the incarnate experience of the Son, when he is on earth as a Son of Man? This is clearly the case when the author mentions the son who makes purification for sins (1:3) since the rest of the letter reveals that this purification happens after his embodiment. Many are the ways in which the Son, in his incarnate state, acts in distinction from the Father and is acted upon by the Father to achieve salvation.[7] He bears the glory and honor of humanity (2:7/Ps. 8:6 LXX). He is lowered, suffers, is perfected, and is exalted by the Father (Heb. 2:8–10). In so doing, he accepts the honor of God's invitation to be a priest in the order of Melchizedek (5:6) where he learns obedience through what he suffered (5:8). Conversely, with *huios* the author could be speaking of the eternal Son, in other words, the son who existed before the ages (1:2, 8) and will exist enthroned forever (1:10, 13; 13:8). Hence, when reading a passage like 3:6, "the son over his house," or 7:28, "the son who has been perfected forever," interpreters must inquire which moment in the life of the Son is in view or, alternatively, if the author is speaking comprehensively of his pre- and post-incarnate life.

The Unreserved Equality of the Son and the Father with Respect to Glory, Power, and Will

With such interpretive options acknowledged, in the following analysis I note the ways in which the author of Hebrews affirms the same[8] glory, power, and will among the distinct persons of the triune God.

---

probable triune references in 1:6; 2:10; 3:4, 12; 4:4, 9, 10, 12; 5:1; 6:1, 3, 5, 7, 10, 13, 17; 7:1, 19; 9:10, 14; 10:7, 12, 21, 31; 11:4, 5, 6, 10, 16, 19, 25, 40; 12:7, 22, 23, 28, 29; 13:4, 7, 16.

6. Since the author of Hebrews asserts that the Holy Spirit speaks the words of God and facilitates the salvation of God, one can make a good argument for the presence of a pneumatological person of *theos* in Hebrews.

7. In other words, this is a way of speaking with reference to the economic trinity.

8. The word "same" demands attention because the following argument hinges upon it. I will argue that the author of Hebrews uses paternity and sonship in such a way that the Christian tradition came to

Glory

It raises little contention to assert that the author of Hebrews presents the Father and the Eternal Son as sharing the same glory. This proclamation begins in his opening exordium. The lodestar of this assertion in Hebrews 1 appears in the center of the author's multiple descriptions of the Son in the first sentence, where he describes the Son as one who is the reflection of his glory and the imprint of his being (*ōn apaugasma tēs doxēs kai charactēr tēs hypotaseōs autou*, Heb. 1:3a). It is worth taking each phrase in turn.

The word *apaugasma* is a *hapax legomena* in the New Testament, and it appears only once in the Septuagint in the Wisdom of Solomon where *Sophia* is the *apaugasma* of eternal light (7:26). Previous to this appearance in Wisdom, the author describes *Sophia* as the emanation (*aporroia*) of the pure glory of the Almighty (7:25), and then as the spotless mirror of God's work (7:27). The word *apaugasma*, similar to the parallel descriptions, conveys that which shows forth an aspect of God.

Philo uses *apaugasma* as a description of the reason of humanity, which is an impression (*ekmageion*), fragment (*apospasma*), or radiance (*apaugasma*) of the blessed nature of divine reason (*Opif.* 146). In *Plant.* 50, he interprets the word *agiasma* as the "*apaugasma* of things that are holy, the imitation (*mimēma*) of the archetype." Philo links the breath of God with *apaugasma* as it applies to creation. When God breathed into the first human, this breath was a ray (*apaugasma*) of God's nature (*Spec.* 4:123).[9]

Hence, although this word can be used for a variety of referents, it communicates trustworthy revelation. That which is faithful to its source is communicated out. The *apaugasma* is not the entity *in toto* but is a trustworthy representation of the entity.[10] In Hebrews, then, it seems fitting to say that the Son is a faithful representation of God's glory. The Son is the outpouring of God's glory, which indicates it is the same glory of the Father.

The author himself illuminates the term *apaugasma* with the next phrase in which he describes the Son as being the *charactēr tēs hypotaseōs*. The word *hypotaseōs* has its own debated meanings,[11] but all of them point toward a

---

assert that the Son shares not a similar but subsidiary glory, power, and will but that the Son and the Father possess and manifest *one shared* glory, power, and will.

9. The word also appears once in the Apocalypse of Abraham, where it describes the way in which Abraham saw a flash of light associated with the figure of death (*Apoc. Abr.* 16:8).

10. ". . . patristic consensus favours the interpretation that Christ is the effulgence of the divine *doxa*" (*TDNT* 1:508, "ἀπαύγασμα").

11. For patristic interpretation of Hebrews on this term, see Rowan A. Greer, *The Captain of Our Salvation: A Study in Patristic Exegesis of Hebrews*, BGBE 15 (Tübingen: Mohr Siebeck, 1973), 92–93, 102–6. For ancient into modern conversation about the Christology reflected here see Jon C. Laansma and Daniel J. Treier, eds., *Christology, Hermeneutics, and Hebrews: Profiles from the History of Interpretation*, LNTS 423 (London: Bloomsbury, 2012).

central aspect of God.[12] The author asserts then that the Son reflects this aspect as a *charactēr*. Another New Testament *hapax, charactēr* in other literature expresses both metaphorical and literal meanings. It can be the scar left by a burn (Lev. 13:28), a written character (Testament of Simeon. 5:4; *Aristeas* 11; Josephus, *Ant.* 12:14–15; 12:36), or that which is engraved (Philo, *Creation* 18; *Alleg. Interp.* 1:61; 3:95; *Worse* 77). It can also indicate the likeness both physical and emotional left by parents on their children, a culture (the Greek one in this instance, 4 Macc. 4:10), or as contemporary language would say, as "characteristic," an element which distinguishes a thing (*Creation* 151; *Opif.* 69; *Alleg. Interp.* 3:97; *Cher.* 4). Josephus makes a similar move associating it with the distinguishing features of someone's face (*War* 2:106; *Ant.* 13:322; 2.97; 10:191. Something's *charactēr* is that which distinguishes and gives identity to that thing. In this instance, the Son bears the character of God's being. The divine Son replicates the central core of who God is. If God the Father has glory the Son radiates it because he has the same nature.

Continuing past this phrase in 1:3, at the culmination of the first sentence, the author asserts that the Son has inherited a better name than the angels. Interpreters of Hebrews have equated this name with the title *huios* because of the citation of Psalm 2:7 which follows.[13] Others, however, see the "name" as a reference to the name of God, which the Son inherits by virtue of the fact that he is Son of God.[14] If this is the case, then this becomes a bold assertion of the glory of the Son because the Scriptures of Israel frequently associate God's name with God's glory.[15]

One of the most stunning displays of that which the Father and the Son share appears in the third citation found in Hebrews 1:6. When God speaks again, according to this author, God speaks the words, "and let all the angels of God worship/bow down to him" (*kai proskynēsatōsan autō pantes angelloi theou*),[16] to the firstborn.[17] A statement that Moses and the

---

12. Harold Attridge notes the related but distinct meanings in Hebrews and collects them under the phrase, "whatever underlies a particular phenomenon, whatever is its actuality or its most basic or fundamental reality or 'essence'" (*Hebrews*, 44).

13. William L. Lane, *Hebrews*, 2 vols., WBC 47a–b (Dallas: Word, 1991), 1:17; David M. Hay, *Glory at the Right Hand: Devotion to Jesus in Earliest Christianity* (Grand Rapids: Eerdmans, 2003), 109–10. See the nuanced discussion in Ellingworth, *Hebrews*, 105–6, 110.

14. Richard Bauckham, "The Divinity of Jesus Christ in the Epistle to the Hebrews," in *Epistle to the Hebrews and Christian Theology*, eds. Richard Bauckham et al. (Grand Rapids: Eerdmans, 2009), 33; D. Stephen Long, *Hebrews*, Belief (Louisville: Westminster John Knox, 2011), 44.

15. Exod. 33:19; Num. 14:21; 1 Chron. 16:29; Neh. 9:5; Pss. 28:2; 71:19; 78:9; 95:8; 101:16; 113:9; Mic. 5:4; Mal. 2:2; Isa. 24:15; 30:27; 42:8; 48:11; 66:19; Dan. 3:43, 52. See also the Apocryphal writings, Jdt. 9:8; 1 Macc. 14:10; 3 Macc. 2:9, 14; Psalms of Solomon. 11:8.

16. The quote from Hebrews closely resembles but does not follow exactly the extant Septuagintal mss of Deuteronomy 32:43 or Psalm 96:7. See discussion in Craig R. Koester, *Hebrews*, AB 36 (New York: Doubleday, 2001), 193.

17. The author notes that God does so when he leads the firstborn into the inhabited realm (*oikoumenē*). Interpreters debate the precise timing of this statement, with the incarnation, exaltation, and second

Psalmist spoke concerning the God of Israel is now specified as a statement
the Father speaks about the Son, commanding that the angelic host give
him obeisance. In the assertions and lived reality of Jewish monotheism,
only God is worthy of worship.[18] Here in Hebrews, the firstborn Son now is
shown to possess that quality fitting only for God.[19]

The fact that the Father and the Son are worthy of equal glory continues
throughout the letter. In the third chapter where the author is showing the
comparative greatness of the Son with respect to Moses, the faithful servant
of God, he asserts that the Son is worthy of more glory than Moses in the
same way that (quite obviously) the one who builds the house has more honor
than the house (Heb. 3:3). The author's comparison is telling here in that
he draws from a striking ontological distinction rather than a difference in
degree. In other words, he could have drawn a comparison between the archi-
tect and the laborer, both humans involved in the building process but with
one having more creative responsibility and therefore more honor. Instead,
he compares the inanimate thing, the house, and its creator for the distinction between Jesus and Moses. He extends the comparison by noting that just
as every house is built by someone, so too everything is constructed by God
(Heb. 3:4). Since he has drawn the Son into the creative sphere of God (1:2,
10) and named him as *theos* (1:8), the glory associated with Jesus here is not
more glory of one important leader as compared with another, but the glory
of the creator, the glory of God, in comparison with one of God's (ontologically different) servants.[20]

At the close of the sermon, both Jesus and God dwell in the heavenly
Jerusalem (12:23–24), a place of glory.[21] In the benediction, the author of

coming suggested as options (see Ellingworth, *Hebrews*, 117–18 for the options). Many conclude
that the exaltation seems the most viable in Hebrews including James W. Thompson, *Hebrews,*
Paideia (Grand Rapids: Baker Academic, 2008), 54; Ben Witherington III, *Letters and Homilies for
Jewish Christians: A Socio-Rhetorical Commentary on Hebrews, James and Jude* (Downers Grove, IL:
InterVarsity, 2007), 128–29; DeSilva, *Perserverance*, 96–98.

18.   "Before the advent of Christianity [I would add: and also after the rise of other exclusive monotheistic
religions like Ilah hag-Gabal in the second century], Judaism was unique among the religions of the
Roman word in demanding the *exclusive* worship of its God. It is not too much to say that Jewish
monotheism was defined in practice by its adherence to the first and second commandments"
(Richard Bauckham, *Jesus and the God of Israel: God Crucified and Other Studies on the New
Testament's Christology of Divine Identity* [Grand Rapids: Eerdmans, 2009], 140).

19.   "We have a good deal of evidence that devout Jews were quite scrupulous in restricting full worship to
the God of Israel alone" (Larry W. Hurtado, *Lord Jesus Christ: Devotion to Jesus in Earliest Christianity*
[Grand Rapids: Eerdmans, 2003], 34).

20.   In the subsection "Christology of Divine Identity," in the chapter "The Divinity of Jesus in the Letter
of the Hebrews," Richard Bauckham provides a lovely articulation of the point I am arguing here:
"Essentially a Christology of divine identity includes Jesus in the unique identity of God as understood
in Second Temple Judaism. It takes up the defining characteristics of Jewish monotheism—the ways
in which the God of Israel was understood to be unique—and applies them also to Jesus" (*Jesus and
the God of Israel*, 233).

21.   Isa. 3:8; 52:1; 60:1; Psalms of Solomon 11:7, Bar. 5:1.

Hebrews proclaims that Jesus Christ is the one through whom God restores his people to do his good will, and then he closes by proclaiming glory to Jesus forever and ever (Heb. 13:21). This is the same type of praise directed toward the God of Israel in the Psalms (Pss. 71:19; 103:31 LXX) and in other writings of Israel's people (Dan. 3:52; 1 Esdr. 5:58; *4 Macc.* 18:24). With direct attribution, as well as associations with God's name and throne and dwelling, the author of Hebrews throughout this letter asserts that the Son possesses the glory the Father also possesses.

Power

As it is with glory so also is it true with power. The author confesses the Son's sovereignty based upon his divine nature as revealed by his relationship with the Father. The author asserts that God the Son is equally as powerful as God the Father; in other words, they both reign supreme over all things.

Such claims begin as soon as the author introduces the Son into his discourse and asserts that God has appointed him, the Son, as heir of all things, *ta panta* (1:2b). Everything is his rightful possession. This inheritance is not entirely a future reality,[22] because the Son also presently upholds his inheritance, *ta panta*, by his powerful word (1:3). Just as the author introduces God as the One who speaks, so too the Son speaks and in so doing expresses his sovereign sustaining power.[23] In addition, as the author first turns his attention to the motif of purification in 1:3c, he foreshadows the Son's priestly role, but he also recalls the divine power expressed in the cleansing from sin (Num. 14:18; Ps. 50:4 LXX; Isa. 53:10; Jer. 40:8). This catena includes as well the Father speaking to the Son not only as the means through which God created, but as the creator: "You, Lord, founded the earth, and the heavens are the works of your hands" (Heb. 1:10/Ps. 101:26). The scriptural catena of chapter 1 closes with an assertion of the Son's sovereignty. God promises that as he takes a seat at the place of the power of God—because God's right hand is frequently noted as the location of his power in judgement or in support[24] —God will subdue his enemies under his feet. Continuing past the first chapter, the Messiah is in a position of power in that he is over his house (3:6), and the author continues to remind his reader of his position at God's right hand.[25]

Closely related, his citation of Psalm 8 in chapter 2 draws upon the same theme of sovereignty. While interpreters have debated whether the author

---

22. Although some of his sovereignty remains promised for the future, see 1:13.
23. The pronoun *autou* at the end of 1:3b is ambiguous and could refer to either God the Father's power or that of his Son. Even if the author has the Father's power in mind here, the Son is clearly the one bearing all things (since the nominative masculine participles refer back to the Son) and does so by his word even if he speaks that word in the power of the Father.
24. From the Septuagint: Exod. 15:6, 12; Deut. 32:40; Pss. 17:7; 18:35; 20:6; 21:8; 44:3; 45:4; 48:10; 60:5; 63:8; 73:23; 76:11; 77:54; 79:16; 88:14, 26; 97:1; 107:7; 109:5; 117:15; 120:5; 137:7; 138:10; Job 40:14; Isa. 41:10; 48:13; 62:8; 63:12; Hab. 2:16; Lam. 2:3–4; Psalms of Solomon 13:1; Wis. 5:16; Sir. 47:5.
25. Heb. 8:1; 10:12; 12:2.

reads the psalm christologically or anthropologically, many, view the psalm functioning in both ways. It describes what is true of Jesus now as the representative human, with both immediate and future implications for other humans.[26] In the author's citation of the psalm, the lines "you have put him over the works of your hands" and "Sheep and Cattle, all together, and further the beasts of the plain, the birds of the air and the fish of the sea—the things that pass through paths of seas" are not cited. If the psalm was praising God for putting humans over the natural world, by eliminating those phrases the author can assert that Jesus's dominion is much more comprehensive, not just over animals, but over humans, angels, the ages, and literally every thing.[27] His comment leaves little doubt in that regard. God has left nothing—*ouden*—that is not subjected to him (2:8).

This sovereignty, however, was hard-wrought. The incarnate Son displays his power by dying, and in so doing, nullifies (*katargeō*) the one who holds the power of death (Heb. 2:14). This allows the Son to rescue those who had been enslaved under the devil by their fear of his power. This is God the Father's power on display as well because God led many children to glory (Heb. 2:10) and he perfects the *archegos*. The power of the Son, as is true of the power of the Father, creates, sustains, cleanses sin, defeats death, and reigns supreme over all things. There is one power of God which the Father and the Son both enact.

Eternality

Before moving to the shared will of the Father and the Son, I wish to note the ways in which Hebrews asserts the eternal nature of the Son along with the Father. This could be a manifestation of either God's glory or God's power. God's speech to the Son includes the royal affirmation that his throne endures forever (Ps. 44:7 LXX/Heb. 1:8a). Affirmations of his eternal nature continue in the following citation of Ps. 101 LXX, where the Father, speaking to the Son, affirms two times that, distinguished over creation that he created, he will, unchanging, endure forever (1:11a, 12c). Finally, in one of the most well-known verses of Hebrews, the author asserts that Jesus is the same yesterday, today, and forever (13:8).

Will

The shared power and glory between the Father and the Son in the opening sentences also point toward the will they both share. Participation of both the Father and the Son in the actions described above suggest that they both willed to create, to sustain the creation, to cleanse sin, and to reign over all

---

26. See discussion in Ellingworth, *Hebrews*, 150–52; David Moffitt, *Atonement and the Logic of the Resurrection in the Epistle to the Hebrews*, NovTSup 141 (Leiden: Brill, 2011), 121–22.

27. Ps. 8:8–9, NETS. See Amy L. B. Peeler, *You Are My Son: The Family of God in the Epistle to the Hebrews*, LNTS 486 (New York: Bloomsbury T & T Clark, 2014), 66–69.

things. There is one will of God which both Father and Son enact, although they enact this one will in different ways.

The focal point for the "will of God" in Hebrews is the bringing of salvation. The author of Hebrews gives indication that both Father and Son will for this redemption and act to make it happen. After hints toward this salvation with the assertion of cleansed sins (1:3) and those who will inherit salvation (1:14), in the section of the sermon marked as the second chapter, the author begins to discuss how God has brought this about. The Lord speaks it (Heb. 2:3); God witnesses to it (2:4), then the citation of Psalm 8 provides the author's launching pad for discussing the "it" of salvation. Jesus, as the one humbled and exalted, tasted/experienced death on behalf of all (2:9). He tasted death (the word for "tasted," *geusētai*, is middle form with an active meaning), suggesting that he willed to die,[28] in a manner that was efficacious for others. If the variant *charis theou* is correct,[29] then God the Father participated in this death by facilitating it through his grace.

In verses 14–18, the author highlights the Son's actions in bringing about salvation. He shared in flesh and blood (2:14); he nullified the devil (2:14b); he rescued (2:15); he aided the seed of Abraham (2:16). He won, through his own death and living offering to God, the human portion of his inheritance that had been enslaved. Then in verse 17, the form becomes passive: He *was made like* his brothers, which interpreters have seen as pointing to the action of God the Father.[30] Both God the Father and God the Son are active in the Son becoming human for the sake of human salvation.

In the center section the author takes up the language of the covenant to describe salvation. The Son mediates the covenant (7:22; 8:6; 9:15; 12:24) that the Lord has promised (8:8–12). The Lord and God who speaks about the covenant in Jeremiah 31 could be God the Father; but because the author has used *kyrios* and *theos* for the Son, because the Son speaks Scripture, and because the Son has been with God since before creation, it very well could be the case that the Son also proclaims the covenant, along with the Father, that his sacrifice will enact. To enact this covenant, he offers his own blood (9:12) to obtain redemption. The author then reiterates this idea with slightly

---

28. One might counter that Hebrews 5:7 describes Jesus as *unwilling* to die since he supplicates God, the one who can save him from death, with tears and great cries. As is the case with the Gethsemane and passion narratives, such emotive expression demonstrates the excruciating nature of the cross, and could even point to the will of the human Jesus to avoid his death (although, it is also possible that he is praying to be saved "out of" rather than "from" death or that "the one who was able to save from death" refers to God and not the content of Jesus's prayers—see Lane, *Hebrews*, 1:120). Even if the human Jesus is praying for an escape, this is the (temporary) will of the human Jesus, for "he remains 'obedient' and actually 'learns obedience' in his historical, fleshly life" (Long, *Hebrews*, 95). The will of the eternal Son is to come to do God's will (Heb. 10:7, 9).

29. This reading has the best manuscript support, but the variant, *chōris theou*, was known by several church fathers.

30. Ellingworth, *Hebrews*, 181; Lane, *Hebrews*, 1:64; Long, *Hebrews*, 60–61.

different words. He offered his own self through the eternal spirit to cleanse and prepare others for service (9:14). He appears before God (9:24) to offer a sacrifice that will remove sins (9:26, 28). The prophet records the divine word that expresses God's desire to be in communion with his people (8:10/Jer. 38:33LXX), and the Son makes that communion possible through his sacrificial offering. By putting the words of Psalm 40 on the lips of Jesus, the author has him assert twice, "I have come to do your will" (Heb. 10:7, 9). This is the will by which the author and his readers are sanctified (10:10), perfected (10:14), and forgiven (10:18) because Jesus offered his body (Heb. 10:10). Finally, if 12:2 should read "for the sake of the joy set before him," then Jesus endured the cross as a good,[31] even joyfully, knowing that it would result in the bringing of many sons and daughters into God's household. The Son's words, actions, and emotions show that both God the Father and God the Son, in addition to willing creation, willed for the redemption of their human creation and worked to achieve that restored covenant relationship.

Distinction among the Persons

Thus far, in an attempt to read Hebrews faithfully, I believe I have articulated theological positions with which few would disagree. God the Father and God the Son share glory and power and will because both are God, yet the author also can describe them as distinct persons who perform distinct actions in the economy of salvation. This is, in fact, the great power of Hebrews for the doctrinal articulation of the church. It proclaims both sameness and distinction, contributing to the doctrine of the Trinity.[32]

Hebrews' differentiates the relationship between God of Israel and Jesus at the outset of his letter using the language of Son and Father. In the author's initial assertion, it is implied that God's speech is that of a Father because God is now speaking in a Son, and it soon becomes clear that this Son is God's. The first citation found in the following sentence confirms this intimation when God first speaks the Scriptures of Israel and proclaims his identity as Father. Twice God affirms each identity: naming the Son, asserting God the Father's own role in begetting, then explicitly affirming his identity as Father and Jesus's as Son.[33]

---

31. Attridge, *Hebrews*, 357; Thompson, *Hebrews*, 248. For the opposite opinion, namely that Jesus chose the cross instead of joy, see Lane, *Hebrews*, 2:413–14 and Chrysostom, *Homilies on the Epistle to the Hebrews* 28.4 (*NPNF*[1] 14:493).

32. See Peter Widdicombe, *The Fatherhood of God in Origen and Athanasius*, OTM (Oxford: Oxford University Press, 2000); Laansma and Treier, eds., *Christology, Hermeneutics, and Hebrews*; Gregory W. Lee, *Today When You Hear His Voice: Scripture, the Covenants, and the People of God* (Grand Rapids: Eerdmans, 2016); Richard Bauckham, ed., *Epistle to the Hebrews and Christian Theology* (Grand Rapids: Eerdmans, 2009).

33. Peeler, *You Are My Son*, 29–42. This has bearing for the Spirit here as well. Since the author believes that God speaks the Scriptures through the Spirit and since the relationship of God here is expressed through speech, hearers can rightly imagine the presence of the Spirit in these words as this relationship is proclaimed.

Related to this relationship, the author asserts that the Son is the heir of God. The first and last thing stated about the Son in the first sentence concerns his inheritance. God has appointed him as heir of all things (1:2), and he has inherited a name more excellent than the angels (1:4), which, as argued above, is responsibly interpreted as God's name. It is fitting that a father would give an inheritance to a son. It is also fitting that a son would bear the name of his father, and participate in the father's vocation, outlined here in chapter 1 as the activities of creating, sustaining, purifying, and reigning.

In the scriptural catena of chapter 1, the author of Hebrews draws from the royal texts that describe God's relationship with the king of Israel to portray God's relationship with the one he has come to know as Jesus, the Messiah. Like every other author of the New Testament, the author of Hebrews has described the God of Israel's relationship with this person with paternal/filial language and has articulated related fields associated with that relationship (inheritance, name, vocation).

Hence it is clear even in the first chapter that Hebrews distinguishes the Father and the Son before, during, and after the incarnation. Before the incarnation, God the Father speaks in the Son, appoints him as heir, and creates through him. God the Son addressed as Lord by God the Father is also proclaimed to the active Creator himself. He has inherited a name that makes him better than the angels because he is the Son. After the incarnation, after making purification for sins, God the Father commands the angels to worship the Son,[34] anoints the Son, and proclaims his eternal throne. The Son takes his seat in sovereignty at God's right hand at the Father's invitation where he intercedes for his followers (see also 7:25). God the Father through the Scriptures of Israel proclaims the Son's existence before creation and after creation is changed. God ever exists as Father and Son and Spirit—one in power, glory, and will—yet it is also the case that the author of Hebrews describes God the Father often as the initiator of divine action.

Without Tiers

If there exists a supra-temporal initiation on the part of the Father, does that mean the Father has authority over the Son? In other words, while those seeking to be aligned with the Scriptures and tradition would affirm the relation of Father, Son, and Holy Spirit in the Trinity, different theological positions arise due to the interpretation of the relation between those persons in salvation history. All agree that the Son and Father share the same glory. All also agree that both have the same power over creation, but disagreement arises in this question: Is there an authority and submission within the Godhead? Put differently, do the different enactments of the one will suggest a distinction in authority?

---

34. The timing of 1:6 is debated, but an exaltational reading seems likely in light of the use of *oikoumenē* in 2:5 and the exaltational setting of several of the quotes in chapter 1. See the options and supporters in Koester, *Hebrews*, 192.

Bruce Ware appeals to Hebrews 1:1–2 in a 2016 blog post to note the divinity of the Son and the Spirit, and the primacy of God the Father. The issue at hand, however, is whether the Father's initiation and the Son's and Spirit's reception implies authority and submission that continues into eternity past and eternity future, in other words, does Hebrews affirm the "eternal relation of authority and submission" (hereafter ERAS)?[35] For Ware, "primacy" becomes evidence of "Fatherly authority," but must it be so? Supporters of ERAS point toward the will of the Father obediently enacted by the sent Son as evidence of the authority and submission within the eternal Father/Son relationship. I would contend that Hebrews does not demand that interpretation, and in fact gives no evidence of a time in which tiers existed in the Trinity. My argument thus far has led to the assertion that Hebrews notes the distinction but equality of the Father and the Son in the enactment of the one divine will, which is the sending of the Son. In other words, the way that Hebrews uses Father/Son language affirms personally distinguishable sovereignty but no eternal submission.

Will

Pertaining to the subject of the will in Hebrews, two questions still need specification. First, whose will is being enacted here? Ware states in an earlier writing, "Yet we have scriptural revelation that clearly says that the Son came down out of heaven to do the will of his Father."[36] Grudem is even more stark. In one of his assessments of Ephesians 1:9–11, which includes the phrase, "who works all things according to the counsel of his will," Grudem states, "But the authority to plan salvation and to decide to send the Son is an authority that Scripture attributes to the Father only."[37] One might imagine that Hebrews 10:7 and 9 would offer support here since the Son says, "I have come to do your will." This is commonly taken as a reference to the human will of the incarnate Son.[38] Even if readers were to imagine a preincarnate conversation here, interestingly, in Hebrews 10, the author, by quoting the psalm, does not

---

35. This is the phrase preferred by its proponents in the online discussion taking place in 2016. See, e.g., Bruce Ware, "God the Son—At Once Eternally God with His Father, and Eternally Son of the Father," posted June 9, 2016, http://www.reformation21.org/blog/2016/06/god-the-sonat-once-eternally-g.php (accessed May 25, 2017).
36. Bruce Ware, "How Shall We Think about the Trinity?," in *God Under Fire: Modern Scholarship Reinvents God*, eds. Douglas S. Huffman and Eric L. Johnson (Grand Rapids: Zondervan, 2002), 275. Because Ware is discussing the differentiation between the Father and the Son on this point, there is little evidence of the unity of the divine will.
37. Wayne Grudem, "Doctrinal Deviations in Evangelical-Feminist Arguments about the Trinity," in *One God in Three Persons: Unity of Essence, Distinction of Persons, Implications for Life*, eds. Bruce A. Ware and John Starke (Wheaton, IL: Crossway, 2015), 39.
38. See, e.g., Maximus the Confessor, *Opuscule* 7: "If then his humanity has a rational soul, then it possesses the natural will. For everything that is rational by nature, certainly also possesses a will by nature. If then, as man, he has a natural will, he certainly wills in reality those things that, as God by nature he has fashioned and introduced naturally into the constitution of [God Incarnate]" (*Maximus the Confessor*, trans. Andrew Louth, The Early Church Fathers [London: Routledge, 1996], 184–85).

employ *paternal* language. In his speech, he says, "I have come . . . to do your will O God (*theos*)." Since the author has named both the Father and the Son as *theos* (Heb. 1:8), Hebrews will not offer unambiguous support for the will being that of the Father's. Similarly, Hebrews 6:17 and 13:21 also discuss the will as that of God (*theos*). If that paternal language is not present, it removes an important support for authority, as Ware understands it, as a "central part of the notion of 'Father.'"[39]

Moreover, there is a departure from tradition in saying that the Son's coming is the eternal purpose of the Father, if by that one means a distinction between the will of the Father and the Son.[40] Augustine states, "The Trinity is proposed to our belief and believed—and even understood by a few saints and holy persons—as so inseparable that whatever action is performed by it must be thought to be performed at the same time by the Father and by the Son and by the Holy Spirit . . . the Son does not do anything which the Father and the Holy Spirit do not do."[41] The redemption of humanity is the eternal purpose of God—God the Father and God the Son and God the Spirit—enacted in creation by the Son's offering and the Spirit's facilitation (Heb. 9:14) through God's grace (2:9). Salvation is not the will of God the Father, but the will of the one triune God.

Let's assume, however, that the author does imagine that *theos* here in Hebrews 6, 10, and 13 is God *the Father*. That would not negate the rest of the letter that shows that the Son desires and acts toward the same will. Gregory of Nyssa in his discussion of the singularity of the actions of God states a distinction in the persons:

> Therefore when we ask from where this good thing came to us, we find through the guidance of the Scriptures that it is from the Father, Son, and Holy Spirit. But

---

39. Ware, "How Shall We Think," 272.
40. In fact the scriptures appealed to by Ware in this essay ("How Shall We Think," 276) do not explicitly say that the Father purposed or destined the Son. I disagree with his argument on Ephesians 1:3–5 for this is about God the Father's election of *humanity* not the Son. Many have written about the compromise of the inseparable operations if salvation is the will of the Father distinct from the Son. Kyle Claunch states concerning the belief in the "submission of the Son to the Father in the eternal preincarnate state" that this "seems to entail a commitment to three distinct wills in the immanent Trinity. . . . [T]hey are making a conscious and informed choice to conceive of will as a property of person rather than essence" ("God is the Head of Christ: Does 1 Corinthians 11:3 Ground Gender Complementarity in the Immanent Trinity?," in Ware and Starke, eds., *One God in Three Persons*, 88). Kevin Giles writes, "For Athanasius the three divine persons are one in being and one in action. *Who they are* and *what they do* cannot [be, sic] separated" (*The Trinity and Subordination: The Doctrine of God and the Contemporary Gender Debate* [Downers Grove, IL: InterVarsity, 2002], 14–15). Concerning Athanasius, Lewis Ayers notes how Augustine received this understanding as part of the tradition: "Augustine does not argue for the doctrine of inseparable operations but states it as an inherited part of tradition, and thus provides us with a key indicator that we must locate his earliest Trinitarian theology within the Latin pro-Nicene tradition" (*Nicaea and Its Legacy: An Approach to Fourth-Century Trinitarian Theology* [Oxford: Oxford University Press, 2004], 369).
41. Augustine, *Letter* 11.2; cited in Ayers, *Nicaea*, 369.

though we presuppose that there are three persons and names, we do not reason that three lives have been given to us—individually one from each of them. It is the same life, activated by the Holy Spirit, prepared by the Son, and produced by the Father's will. Therefore then, the Holy Trinity works every activity according to the manner stated, not divided according to the number of the *hypostases,* but one certain motion and disposition of good will occurs, proceeding from the Father through the Son to the Spirit.[42]

Ware now seems to speak in a very similar way:

I gladly affirm my commitment to the doctrine of the inseparable operations of the Father, Son, and Holy Spirit. . . . There cannot be a separation or division in the work of the One God since each person participates fully in the One nature of God. But this does not preclude each person accessing, as it were, those qualities of the divine nature (e.g., power, knowledge, wisdom) distinctively yet harmoniously, according to their own hypostatic identities as Father, and as Son, and as the Holy Spirit, such that they bring to pass one unified result accomplishing the one work of God.[43]

If there is affirmation of one divine will expressed by the different persons, could that indicate that this author believed the Son was submitting to the authority of the Father before the incarnation in coming to do his will? It is not *necessary* to view obedience to a shared will, even a will initiated by one and enacted by another (although, of course, while these actions of initiation and enactment are appropriated to the person of the Father and the Son, the actions of the Father and the Son are not separated from one another) as authority and submission. Paul Meyer writes, "The correspondence of action between Son and Father has been misunderstood as obedience within a patriarchally structured relationship." John 10:18 is "not the surrender of Jesus's own will to yield to God's but the willing act of Jesus's own initiative and authority . . . which is grounded in the relationship of mutual knowledge and love between Jesus and his Father."[44] I would add my voice to others who have argued that the Son coming to do the will of God, a will he, his Father, and the Spirit share, does not of necessity have to be viewed as an act of authority and submission. He is

42. Gregory of Nyssa, "Concerning We Should Think of Saying That There Are Not Three Gods—To Ablabius," in *Sources of Early Christian Thought: The Trinitarian Controversy,* trans. and ed. William G. Rusch (Philadelphia: Fortress, 1980), 155.

43. Bruce Ware, "Knowing the Self-Revealed God Who is Father, Son, and Holy Spirit," posted July 4, 2016, https://secundumscripturas.com/2016/07/04/knowing-the-self-revealed-god-who-is-father-son-and-holy-spirit (accessed May 25, 2017).

44. Paul Meyer, "The Father: The Presentation of God in the Fourth Gospel," in *Exporing the Gospel of John: In Honor of D. Moody Smith,* eds. R. Alan Culpepper and C. Clifton Black (Louisville: Westminster John Knox, 1996), 260–61; quoted in Christopher W. Cowan, "'I Always Do What Pleases Him': The Father and Son in the Gospel of John," in Ware and Starke, eds., *One God in Three Persons,* 55.

obedient in the flesh to what he willed in eternity with the Father and the Spirit. The interpretation of an obedience to a shared will as "submission to authority" hinges, it seems to me, on the meaning of the terms "Father" and "Son."

Sending

Another argument is that sending and being sent depicts the authority of the Father and the submission of the Son.[45] In Hebrews 3:1, the author refers to Jesus as the *apostolos*, the sent one, of our confession. Sending and being sent *could* be actions of authority and submission, but this too is not necessary. Kevin Giles suggests that what could be in mind with this concept is the Jewish idea of *Shaliach*, in which "the one sent has the same authority as the one who sends him: he is as the sender himself."[46] He refers to Hurtado's *Lord Jesus Christ*, in which Hurtado suggests that John presents Jesus as the agent or representative of God such as the Logos or Sophia. Cowan counters that to focus on the unity denies the subordination present in agents. He suggests that "the idea that the sent one is subordinate to the sender is clearly implied in John's Gospel, whether the sent one is Jesus, John the Baptist, or the emissaries of the Pharisees."[47] Appealing to other humans in the gospel, such as John or the emissaries of the Pharisees, does not support his case because Jesus has a unique relationship to the Father that may *or may not* be like that of other senders and sent ones. Moreover, he assumes what he seeks to prove. Sending and sent "clearly impl[y]" authority and subordination only if one assumes that to be true.

It is not clear that Augustine did so. In *De Trinitate*, he states:

> But if the Son is said to be sent by the Father on this account, that the one is the Father, and the other the Son, this does not in any manner hinder us from believing the Son to be equal, and consubstantial, and co-eternal with the Father, and yet to have been sent as Son by the Father. Not because the one is greater, the other less; but because the one is Father, the other Son; the one begetter, the other begotten; the one, He from whom He is who is sent; the other, He who is from Him who sends. For the Son is from the <u>Father</u>, not the Father from the Son. . . . Because He was not sent in respect to any inequality of power, or substance, or anything that in Him was not equal to the Father; but in respect

---

45. Cowan states, "John show[s] that Jesus assumes a subordinate role to his Father. The first [theme] is John's presentation of the Son as 'sent' by the Father" ("The Father and Son in the Gospel of John," 48). Although he uses the name Jesus here, he does not think this "being sent" only applies to the incarnate Jesus, but prior to the incarnation as well (62). Similarly Ware concludes after surveying verses in Paul, John, and Peter, "This requires, then, an authority-submission relationship in eternity past, one in which the Father chooses and sends, and the Son submits and comes" (*Father, Son, Holy Spirit: Relationships, Roles, and Relevance* [Wheaton, IL: Crossway, 2005], 79).
46. Kevin Giles, *Jesus and the Father: Modern Evangelicals Reinvent the Doctrine of the Trinity* (Grand Rapids: Zondervan, 2006), 119.
47. Cowan, "The Father and the Son in the Gospel of John," 49–50, 54.

to this, that the Son is from the Father, not the Father from the Son; for the Son is the Word of the Father, which is also called His wisdom. What wonder, therefore, if He is sent, not because He is unequal with the Father, but because He is "a pure emanation (*manatio*) issuing from the glory of the Almighty God?" For there, that which issues, and that from which it issues, is of one and the same substance.[48]

It is vital to this essay that Augustine is quoting from the same language as that used in Hebrews 1:3. He clearly affirms that there is not inequality in being sent, only that there are different relations. The debate hinges again on the meaning of Father and Son.

Father and Son

Yet since this sending and being sent is applied to the Father and the Son, I will endeavor to show that roles of authority and submission are not the way in which the author of Hebrews uses the language of Father and Son. Supporters of ERAS seem to assume that the Father and the Son, simply by virtue of being Father and Son, function along the line of authority and submission.[49]

---

48.   Augustine, *On the Trinity* 4.20.27 (*NPNF*[1] 3:83).

49.   One could amass many quotes on this point, but I first select from recent posts from major players. Wayne Grudem wrote, "But what kind of eternal Father-Son relationship is this? That is the point of difference. Bruce Ware and Owen Strachan and I have understood it in terms of *the eternal authority of the Father and the eternal submission of the Son within their relationship*. That seems to us to best account for the very names 'Father' and 'Son' as they would certainly have been understood in the ancient world, and also to best account for multiple passages of Scripture that show a consistent pattern. . . . These activities between the Father and Son are one-directional and they are never reversed anywhere in Scripture" ("Another Thirteen Evangelical Theologians Who Affirm the Eternal Submission of the Son to the Father," posted June 20, 2016, http://www.reformation21.org/blog/2016/06/another-thirteen-evangelical-t.php [accessed May 25, 2017]). The scriptures he puts forth here only work to support authority and submission *if one assumes* that is what Father/Son means. Conversely, one can imagine one-directional movement on a level plane rather than on a tier. In other words, the assumptions one brings to the words used in Scripture determine if one sees authority/submission in the Godhead or not.

   Bruce Ware states on a blog post, "Precisely because the Father eternally begets the Son, the Father, as eternal Father of the Son, has the intrinsic paternal hypostatic position of having authority over his Son; and precisely because the Son is eternally begotten from the Father, the Son, as eternal Son of the Father, has the intrinsic filial hypostatic position of being in submission to his Father. The eternal modes of subsistence, then, ground the eternal distinction between Father and Son (and Spirit), while the eternal relations of authority and submission then flow out from and are expressive of those eternal modes of subsistence. Honestly, eternal (ontological) modes of subsistence, and the eternal (functional and hypostatic) relations of authority and submission work like hand and glove…they function in an eternal Father-Son relationship, in which the Father always acts in a way that befits who he is as Father, and Son always acts in a way that befits who he is as Son. Their Father-Son manner of relating (functioning) is seen (in part) in the authority of the Father and submission of the Son, as is evidenced by the vast array of the biblical self-revelation of the Trinitarian persons. And, since the Father is eternal Father, and the Son eternal Son, this manner of relating is likewise eternal" ("Knowing the Self-Revealed God who is Father, Son, and

Such writers seem to worry that if Father and Son is only about procession and not about authority and submission, a (the?) necessary distinction of the persons, and therefore the Trinity itself, crumbles. Christopher Cowan states, "Such emphasis on their harmony runs the risk of swallowing up any distinction between the two."[50] Moreover, they express a concern that a Trinity without tiers could lead to modalism.[51] Ware suggests, "The egalitarian denial of any eternal submission of the Son to the Father makes it impossible to answer the question why it was the 'Son' and not the 'Father' or 'Spirit' who was sent to become incarnate."[52]

To the contrary, those who would deny eternal authority and submission in the Godhead can affirm the eternal personal existence of God the Father, God the Son, and God the Spirit without knowing *why* it was the Son who came to do the will of *theos*. Kathryn Sonderegger states:

> is it the case, we might ask, that any Person of the Trinity could have been Incarnate? . . . If so, as some modern theologians charge, we have learned nothing about God's Personal Life by the Incarnation. . . . Yet, others say, were we to say that *only* the Son could be incarnate we would affirm a difference, a salient difference, in the Deity of the Son—and that is the ancient and never fully eradicated danger of Arianism in Christology.[53]

This lack in knowing *why* does not deny that it was the Son who came, and moreover will not necessarily devolve into modalism because texts like Hebrews doggedly affirm the eternal personhood of both the Father and the Son which

---

Holy Spirit," posted July 4, 2016, https://secundumscripturas.com/2016/07/04/knowing-the-self-revealed-god-who-is-father-son-and-holy-spirit [accessed May 25, 2017]).

    Michael Ovey finds support for authority and submission in the term Son in *Contra Arianos* by Athanasius, and argues that Athanasius applies servant language to the eternal Son ("True Sonship—Where Dignity and Submission Meet," in Ware and Starke, eds., *One God in Three Persons*, 142–44). Yet it seems to me that Athanasius makes the opposite point than Ovey assumes. The father calling his son "servant" is an example of language used that everyone knows is not true of the "nature" of the Son. This is an example of Athanasius's thesis: "For terms do not disparage His Nature; rather that Nature draws to Itself those terms and changes them. For terms are not prior to essences, but essences are first, and terms second" (*Four Discourses against the Arians* 2.3 [*NPNF*[2] 4:349]). When the Son is called a servant in Scripture, Athanasius says, "and the like, let not any on this account deny that He is proper to the Father and from Him" (*Four Discourses against the Arians*, 2.4 [350]).

50. Cowan, "The Father and the Son in the Gospel of John," 58.

51. Concerning Millard Erikson's rejection of eternal supremacy and eternal subordination, Grudem states, "To say this is actually to obliterate the differences among the members of the Trinity . . . it is hard to distinguish what Erickson says from the ancient heresy of modalism, the view that there is only one person in God who manifests himself in different ways or 'modes' of action" ("Doctrinal Deviations," 25).

52. Wayne A. Grudem, *Biblical Foundations for Manhood and Womanhood* (Wheaton, IL: Crossway, 2002), 248.

53. Kathryn Sonderegger, "The Humility of the Son of God," in *Christology Ancient and Modern*, eds. Oliver D. Crisp and Fred Sanders (Grand Rapids: Zondervan, 2013), 69.

existed before creation.[54] We are not made privy to the decision of why the Son came to be incarnate and not the Father, but the distinctions in the Trinity, and hence the Trinity itself, are not dependent upon the sending because the Father/ Son/Spirit relationship exists eternally.

Father/Son Language

If, then, Father/Son is not necessarily another way of saying "authority and submission,"[55] I suggest alternative ways in which Hebrews fills out the meaning of those terms. The language of Father/Son in and of itself indicates authority and submission in the case of adult fathers and child sons, but not necessarily when it is employed for adult fathers and adult sons. It can be. Cowan brings forth examples, ancient and modern, to answer his question, "How would John's readers have understood a father-son relationship? . . . In the patriarchal culture of first-century Palestine, a father exercised author- ity over his son."[56] Grudem concurs, even as he acknowledges the develop- mental shift that in the Bible sons are not always commanded to obey their fathers.[57] Concerning an objection like mine that authority and submission create a picture of an infantilization of the eternal Son, he states, "The prob- lem with this objection is that it fails to take account of the thought patterns of the ancient world, especially the biblical world. In multiple examples in Scripture, an adult human son is still subject to the authority and leadership role of his human father, at least within the life of the family."[58]

It is possible that this meaning of Father and Son as authority and submission was dominant in the first century, but that seems to introduce another problem. It seems to assume that the authors of the New Testament are beholden to cultural meanings of the day. Is it not the case that they use human language (for what else could they use?) but transform the meaning of that language? God is Father, but that does not mean God is biological

---

54. See my exegetical argument on Hebrews 1:1–5 in *You Are My Son*, 29–50.

55. Ware, "How Shall We Think," 270: "Is not the eternal and inner-Trinitarian Father-Son relationship indicative of some eternal relationship of authority *within* the Trinity itself?"

56. Cowan, "The Father and the Son in the Gospel of John," 52–53. He includes a citation here from Craig Keener's John commentary where he states that "Ancient Mediterranean culture regarded fathers as greater in rank than sons" (*The Gospel of John* [Peabody, MA: Hendrickson, 2003], 2:983). This seems to me precisely the kind of language one would want to avoid if making a comparison to God the Father and God the Son. Is God the Father "greater in rank" than God the Son?

57. Wayne A. Grudem, "Biblical Evidence for the Eternal Submission of the Son to the Father," in *The New Evangelical Subordinationism? Perspectives on the Equality of God the Father and God the Son*, eds. Dennis W. Jowers and H. Wayne House [Eugene, OR: Pickwick, 2012], 230–32. I am indebted to "Daughter of the Reformation" blog for this reference: see Rachel Miller, "Does the Son Eternally Submit to the Authority of the Father?," posted May 28, 2015, https://adaughterofthereformation. wordpress.com/2015/05/28/does-the-son-eternally-submit-to-the-authority-of-the-father (accessed October 5, 2017).

58. Grudem, "Biblical Evidence," 230.

male as all other fathers are. Hence, it is also the case that while Father may have largely meant authority in the first century, it may not be used for God in exactly the same way. Moreover, if God has chosen to reveal himself in the language of Father and Son, does that language only rightly communicate itself in some times and cultures? For today, in my own context, adult sons are to respect their adult fathers, but they are not expected to submit to their authority. In fact, as anyone in the sandwich generation is well aware, sons are often called to care for and make decisions on behalf of their fathers. Authority and submission are not bound up supra-culturally in the relational terms of father/son. Hence for those in cultural contexts like my own, we do not hear the words in the same way. To state it differently, the Greek word *huios* corresponds to the English word *son*, and so it is a fitting translation; nevertheless, the concepts associated with the word *huios/son* are shaped by particular cultures.[59] It seems vitally important to me, then, to allow Scripture and not cultural assumptions—even the assumptions of the culture at the time of the writing of the Scripture—to supply the concepts of the terms. While the author of Hebrews speaks about the growing perfection/maturity of the Son (2:10; 5:9; 7:28), almost all interpreters associate this with his incarnational vocation.[60] Hence, the eternal Father/Son relationship in Hebrews never automatically indicates a distinction in authority/submission.

In fact, the author of Hebrews works against that logic. He states that God appoints this Son as heir of all things. Several fascinating assumptions are at play in this statement. We know not who is writing nor to whom, but it is clear from his text that he adheres to the Scriptures of Israel and builds his argument on the assumption that his readers do the same. These texts affirm that God possesses all of creation.[61] Hence, God who owns all has appointed his Son as the heir of all. The difficulty with this subset of familial relationships, namely inheritance, is that inheritance is built upon death (as the author of Hebrews himself explicitly affirms, 9:16–17). It is also incredibly clear that the Scriptures affirm that God is eternal.[62] How then can the eternal God give everything he possesses to another since he will never cease to possess it due to his eternal nature?

The answer is twofold. First, this is an early indication that this Son is no ordinary king (as the Old Testament witness of sonship might insinuate),[63] but is himself worthy of such an inheritance because he is God. The affirma-

---

59. On the importance of distinguishing between words and concepts, see, classically, James Barr, *The Semantics of Biblical Language* (Oxford: Oxford University Press, 1961), 207–31.
60. David Peterson, *Hebrews and Perfection: An Examination of the Concept of Perfection in the "Epistle to the Hebrews,"* SNTSMS 47 (Cambridge: Cambridge University Press, 1982).
61. Gen. 1–2; Exod. 9:29; Deut. 10:14; Pss. 2:8; 24:1.
62. Exod. 3:15; 15:18; Deut. 32:40; Ps. 9:7.
63. Son of God applied to the nation of Israel (Exod. 4:22) and the king of Israel (Pss. 2:7; 89), neither of which were divinized. See Marianne Meye Thompson, *The Promise of the Father: Jesus and God in the New Testament* (Louisville: Westminster John Knox, 2000), 47–48.

tion of divinity becomes clear in the following sections of the chapter through the association of the divine name, worship, creation, and eternality, as argued in the first section. God is not graciously sharing all that is his with someone who does not deserve it, but appoints the Son as heir because he is God.

Yet there is an appointment, a distinction of persons in which God the Father appoints and God the Son is appointed. "Being appointed as heir" fits within the linguistic schema of Father/Son, yet because this is God and not a human father and son, this inheritance is unlike any other. It could be the case that the author of Hebrews imagines this appointment as applicable to the Incarnate Son. He has introduced the temporal framework of "these last days" and this is the Son who has made purification for sins. On the other hand, this is the same one who images God's (eternal) being and was with God before the creation of all things. All that to say, it is not immediately, nor decisively (in my opinion) clear, if the appointment occurs pretemporally, post-incarnationally, or both.

Even if it is pre-temporal, this aspect—inheritance—of the familial language leaves no indication of authority *and submission*. This is an inheritance retained yet also given. God the Father maintains his authority to be sure, so supporters of ERAS are correct on the first half of the equation. But where is there any submission? The Son possesses all things just as does the Father. God's authority is not a zero-sum equation where only one person can possess it, but instead there seems to be plenipotentiary in which God the Father and God the Son both have authority. If this is an appointment outside of time, then there is no time in which both the Father and the Son did not have equal authority.

If there is a notion of authority inherent in masculine language, as Ware argues,[64] is "son" not also a masculine term? Ware himself then goes on to argue that Christ's maleness shows him to be the authoritative Lord.[65] Then why does authority adhere only in the Father? It is not masculine language that determines authority for Ware but specifically *paternal* language, which reiterates he is using this language as would be applied to an adult/child relationship, or a relationship that is in some way not equal. The Son is less neither in age nor maturity from the Father, and hence has no less authority than the Father as shown by the sovereignty granted him by the Father. Authority applies to both the Father and the Son, but this is an authority of God (God the Father, God the Son, God the Spirit) over all humanity. There is one fulcrum of authority: God over humans, not the Father over the Son.

One may protest, however, that this appointment as heir concerns God's relationship over humanity within which Father, Son, and Spirit share as equally sovereign. What about within Godself? The author builds the descriptions of the Son in verses 1–4 upon the relationship of Father/Son which he

---

64.   Ware, "How Shall We Think," 272.
65.   Ware, "How Shall We Think," 274.

hears articulated by God the Father in the first two citations of Israel's Scriptures. If this is the post-exaltational rearticulation of the relationship that existed eternally, then it provides revelation about the nature of God. What these texts reveal is that this speech-act defines the person of the Father, Son, and Spirit. The eternal begottenness of the Son is also the eternal begetting of the Father. Just as there was no time when the Son was not, there was no time when God the Father was not God the Father. This relationship mutually and equally affects both the Father and the Son. If this is an eternal mutually affecting relationship in which glory and power are equally shared, there is no evidence of any tangible difference in which "Father" means "authority" and "Son" means "submissive one."

As further support, in chapter 5, when the author discusses Jesus's prayer to the One who could save him from death, he asserts that the Son learned obedience through which he suffered (5:9). Again, there is widespread consensus that this pertains to the Son's incarnate experience, either at Gethsemane or on the cross. Pertinent for this discussion is the way in which the author introduces this assertion about learning obedience: *kaiper ōn huios*, "even though being son" (Heb. 5:8). One might expect that were this a human father/son relationship, especially an adult/child relationship, the author would build upon the fact that he was son to make the point about obedience. He could have used a causal term here, being translated, "because he was son, he learned obedience (as all sons do, especially when they are immature (see Heb. 5)." The author, however, with his use of *kaiper*, "even though," seems to be pointing toward some kind of dissonance. It is ill-fitting, he suggests, for such a son *as this*, a Son equally sovereign with his Father, to have to learn obedience.[66] His sonship did not work normally along the lines of authority and submission, command and obedience, but it did during the incarnation.

Finally, it is eminently clear that Jesus sitting at God's right hand is one of the most important tropes throughout the Epistle to the Hebrews. Like other New Testament authors, the author of Hebrews cites and alludes to Psalm 110:1 in reference to Jesus, doing so frequently enough that some have claimed this sermon is a midrash on that text.[67] Ware and Grudem have claimed that this position affirms the Son's submission to the Father because,

---

66. Scott Harrower states, "the work of God the Son in the economy of salvation entails his learning obedience to God the Father in new ways through new challenges. Stated another way, it would be unnecessary for the second person of the Trinity to learn obedience to God the Father in the economy of salvation if within the inner-relational life of God, the eternal Son had always been obedient to God the Father in such a manner" (*Trinitarian Self and Salvation: An Evangelical Engagement with Rahner's Rule* [Eugene, OR: Pickwick, 2012], 93). He calls attention to a similar reading by Paul Ellingworth, "The present verse . . . probably implies a contrast between his eternal status on one hand, and the learning process of christ's earthly life on the other . . . the likely meaning is 'Although he has (eternally) the status of (God's) Son'" (*Hebrews*, 293).

67. George Wesley Buchanan, *The Book of Hebrews: Its Challenge from Zion* (Eugene, OR: Wipf & Stock, 2006), 452.

"In his sitting at God's right hand" this is "a position of authority second to that of the Father himself (Acts 2:32–33; Eph. 1:20–22; Heb. 1:3; Pss. 110:1; 45:9; Rev. 2:26; et al)."[68] If the son's position shows that he is *second* in authority, Hebrews offers no indication of his lower rank. As the previous arguments presented, the Son shares the same glory, power, and supremacy as the Father. The royal language of being at God's right hand functions to differentiate the Son from the Father and indicate the personhood of both. Moreover, "right hand" Psalm 110:1 language in Hebrews applies only to the post-exultation, post-incarnate Messiah. The One who has taken on a body has now presented that body to God. And since he remains embodied,[69] the author must describe him located in reference to God. He is no longer only spirit, but embodied, and therefore takes his session in the most powerful and closest proximity to the Father possible—at his right—yet remains a distinct embodied person.[70] There is no indication of secondary authority, only embodied differentiation.

Ware notes how "egalitarianism . . . seems incapable, logically, to explain this divinely chosen use of masculine language."[71] If the meaning is not paternal authority at the expense of the authority of the Son, and I have endeavored to show that that is not the case in Hebrews, then why is Father/Son appropriate language for two of the persons of God in this sermon? First, sonship conveys an intimacy of relationship with God superior to that of God's servants (which include the prophets, 1:1; angels, 1:7, 14; Moses, 3:5; and the priests, 5:5, 7:28). Second, familial language works incredibly well to convey both sameness (a son bears the name and image and inheritance of his father) at the same time as differentiation of persons.

Conclusion

Hebrews discloses that God the Father and God the Son, distinct persons, are both gloriously sovereign and in their sovereignty have acted out their one will to redeem humanity. The author uses *patēr/huios* language to convey the uniquely intimate relation between distinct persons of God.

ERAS supporters seem to equate the Father's initiation with the Father's authority. I have endeavored to show that there was never a time when the Father's authority was distinct from and supreme to the Son's since Father and Son are mutually dependent upon the other, and upon the Spirit, for the distinction of relationship. In addition, since the Son as God was appointed heir of all things before creation and remains sovereign at God's right hand

---

68. See Andy Naselli, "Live-blogging of Trinity Debate: Ware-Grudem vs. McCall-Yandell," posted October 9, 2008, http://henrycenter.tiu.edu/2008/10/trinity-debate-ware-grudem-vs-mccall-yandell (accessed October 5, 2017).

69. See the argument by David Moffitt for the logical necessity of resurrection in Hebrews in *Atonement and the Logic of Resurrection*.

70. To be seated on the lap of God might better convey the same authority but not only is this image a bit silly but has no scriptural warrant, which the right-hand language offers.

71. Ware, "How Shall We Think," 272.

forever, they share in equal authority. One must also assume that sending and being sent imply the distinction of authority and submission but the Father sending the Son indicates not submission to the will of the Father, but enactment of the will of God. There was and is authority but no submission, for the authority was given by the Father to the Incarnate Son as a reiteration of the equal glory, will, and power of the eternal Son.

In close, *why* does it matter to assert equal authority but no eternal submission? Eternal submission is to misunderstand the Son, and therefore diminish his glory, power, and will. I see no way that a decrease of the divinity of the Son can be avoided when he is portrayed as not just eternally responsive, but eternally submissive.[72] Eternal submission of the Son also misapprehends the Father as a God who retains power rather than shares it, and if there were ever a day when the evangelical church needed a correction on its understanding of power, that day is now.

Such strong words are necessary, as is the recognition that as all of us write on this topic, we are seeking to better understand faithfully the trustworthy revelation of the Holy Scriptures that speak to the mystery of God's being and relations. I view such efforts as a faithful exercise of our giftedness/calling for the edification of the body of Christ, but we must also acknowledge that while we can know truly we cannot know fully. Until the dim mirror be removed, may this exegesis serve to stimulate good thinking about God, deeper love of God, and even in the midst of heated debate, an abiding unity in the body of Christ.

---

72. Karl Barth serves as a formidable conversation partner here, as articulated in *CD* 4.1, "The Obedience of the Son of God." It seems right to check our "all too human" assumptions that for God to be second is "something mean," but Barth is not so easily coopted as a proponent for the eternal subordination of the Son (see Darren O. Sumner, "Obedience and Subordination in Karl Barth's Trinitarian Theology," in *Advancing Trinitarian Theology: Essays in Constructive Dogmatics*, eds. Oliver D. Crisp and Fred Sanders [Grand Rapids: Zondervan, 2014], 130–46).

    Barth does not say that the Scriptures present the revelation of the eternal obedience, submission, and humility of *the Son alone*. Instead, the Son willingly becomes incarnate to enact the one will of the humble triune God. In the assessment of Sumner, "the obedience of the Son *pertains to* God's being. For Barth, obedience indicates not a subordination *of* being, but a subordination *within* the one, undivided, and undimished being of the triune God. It is vital to Barth's presentation that the Son's submission is not the necessary and therefore passive consequence of his being (e.g., by virtue of his eternal procession), but the active consequence of his willing. The Son *chooses* the way of obedience (cf. Heb. 5:8); he does not have it thrust upon him" ("Obedience," 139).

Bibliography

Allen, David M. "'The Forgotten Spirit': A Pentecostal Reading of the Letter to the Hebrews." *Journal of Pentecostal Theology* 18, no. 1 (2009): 51–66.

Athanasius. *Four Discourses Against the Arians.* In vol. 4 of *The Nicene and Post-Nicene Fathers,* Series 2. Edited by Philip Schaff and Henry Wace, 303–447. 1892. Repr. Peabody, MA: Hendrickson, 1994.

Attridge, Harold W. *The Epistle to the Hebrews.* Hermeneia. Minneapolis: Fortress, 1989.

Augustine. *On the Trinity.* In vol. 3 of *The Nicene and Post-Nicene Fathers,* Series 1. Edited by Philip Schaff, 1–228. 1887. Repr. Peabody, MA: Hendrickson, 1994.

Ayres, Lewis. *Nicaea and Its Legacy: An Approach to Fourth-Century Trinitarian Theology.* Oxford: Oxford UP, 2004.

Barr, James. *The Semantics of Biblical Language.* Oxford: Oxford University Press, 1961.

Barth, Karl. *Church Dogmatics.* 4 vols. in 13 parts. Edited by G. W. Bromiley and T. F. Torrance. Edinburgh: T & T Clark, 1956–75.

Bates, Matthew W. *The Birth of the Trinity: Jesus, God, and Spirit in New Testament and Early Christian Interpretations of the Old Testament.* Oxford: Oxford UP, 2015.

Bauckham, Richard. "The Divinity of Jesus Christ in the Epistle to the Hebrews." In *Epistle to the Hebrews and Christian Theology,* edited by Richard Bauckham et al., 15–36. Grand Rapids: Eerdmans, 2009.

_____. *Jesus and the God of Israel: God Crucified and Other Studies on the New Testament's Christology of Divine Identity.* Grand Rapids: Eerdmans, 2009.

Bauckham, Richard, ed. *Epistle to the Hebrews and Christian Theology.* Grand Rapids: Eerdmans, 2009.

Buchanan, George Wesley. *The Book of Hebrews: Its Challenge from Zion.* Eugene, OR: Wipf & Stock, 2006.

Chrysostom, John. *Homilies on the Epistle to the Hebrews.* In vol. 14 of *The Nicene and Post-Nicene Fathers,* Series 1. Edited by Philip Schaff, 335–522. 1889. Repr. Peabody, MA: Hendrickson, 1994.

Claunch, Kyle. "God is the Head of Christ: Does 1 Corinthians 11:3 Ground Gender Complementarity in the Immanent Trinity?" In *One God in Three Persons: Unity of Essence, Distinction of Persons, Implications for Life,* edited by Bruce A. Ware and John Starke, 65–93. Wheaton, IL: Crossway, 2015.

Cowan, Christopher W. " 'I Always Do What Pleases Him': The Father and Son in the Gospel of John." In *One God in Three Persons: Unity of Essence, Distinction of Persons, Implications for Life,* edited by Bruce A. Ware and John Starke, 47–64. Wheaton, IL: Crossway, 2015.

DeSilva, David Arthur. *Perseverance in Gratitude: A Socio-Rhetorical Commentary on the Epistle "to the Hebrews."* Grand Rapids: Eerdmans, 2000.

Ellingworth, Paul. *The Epistle to the Hebrews.* NIGTC. Grand Rapids: Eerdmans, 1993.

Giles, Kevin. *Jesus and the Father: Modern Evangelicals Reinvent the Doctrine of the Trinity.* Grand Rapids: Zondervan, 2006.

_____. *The Trinity and Subordination: The Doctrine of God and the Contemporary Gender Debate.* Downers Grove, IL: InterVarsity, 2002.

Greer, Rowan A. *The Captain of Our Salvation: A Study in Patristic Exegesis of Hebrews.* BGBE 15. Tübingen: Mohr Siebeck, 1973.

Gregory of Nyssa. "Concerning We Should Think of Saying That There Are Not Three Gods—To Ablabius." In *Sources of Early Christian Thought: The Trinitarian Controversy.* Translated and edited by William G. Rusch, 149–61. Philadelphia: Fortress, 1980.

Grudem, Wayne. "Another Thirteen Evangelical Theologians Who Affirm the Eternal Submission of the Son to the Father." Posted June 20, 2016. http://www.reformation21.org/blog/2016/06/another-thirteen-evangelical-t.php (accessed May 25, 2017).

_____. "Biblical Evidence for the Eternal Submission of the Son to the Father." In *The New Evangelical Subordinationism? Perspectives on the Equality of God the Father and God the Son*, edited by Dennis W. Jowers and H. Wayne House, 223–61. Eugene, OR: Pickwick, 2012.

_____. *Biblical Foundations for Manhood and Womanhood.* Wheaton, IL: Crossway, 2002.

_____. "Doctrinal Deviations in Evangelical-Feminist Arguments About the Trinity." In *One God in Three Persons: Unity of Essence, Distinction of Persons, Implications for Life*, edited by Bruce A. Ware and John Starke, 17–45. Wheaton, IL: Crossway, 2015.

Harrower, Scott. *Trinitarian Self and Salvation: An Evangelical Engagement with Rahner's Rule.* Eugene, OR: Pickwick, 2012.

Hay, David M. *Glory at the Right Hand: Psalm 110 in Early Christianity.* SBLMS 18. Nashville: Abingdon, 1973.

Hurtado, Larry W. *Lord Jesus Christ: Devotion to Jesus in Earliest Christianity.* Grand Rapids: Eerdmans, 2003.

Keener, Craig S. *The Gospel of John.* Peabody, MA: Hendrickson, 2003.

Kittel, Gerhard. "ἀπαύγασμα." In vol. 1 of *Theological Dictionary of the New Testament*, edited by Gerhard Kittel, trans. Geoffrey W. Bromiley, 508. Grand Rapids: Eerdmans, 1964.

Koester, Craig R. *Hebrews.* AB 36. New York: Doubleday, 2001.

Laansma, Jon C., and Daniel J. Treier, eds. *Christology, Hermeneutics, and Hebrews: Profiles from the History of Interpretation.* LNTS 423. London: Bloomsbury, 2012.

Lane, William L. *Hebrews.* 2 vols. WBC 47a–b. Dallas: Word, 1991.

Lee, Gregory W. *Today When You Hear His Voice: Scripture, the Covenants, and the People of God*. Grand Rapids: Eerdmans, 2016.

Levinson, Jack. "A Theology of the Spirit in the Letter to the Hebrews." *CBQ* 78 (2016): 90–110.

Long, D. Stephen. *Hebrews*. Belief: A Theological Commentary on the Bible. Louisville: Westminster John Knox, 2011.

Maximus the Confessor. Translated by Andrew Louth. The Early Church Fathers. London: Routledge, 1996.

Meyer, Paul W. "'The Father': The Presentation of God in the Fourth Gospel." In *Exploring the Gospel of John: In Honor of D. Moody Smith*, edited by R. Alan Culpepper and C. Clifton Black, 255–73. Louisville: Westminster John Knox, 1996.

Miller, Rachel. "Does the Son Eternally Submit to the Authority of the Father?" Posted May 28, 2015. https://adaughterofthereformation.word-press.com/2015/05/28/does-the-son-eternally-submit-to-the-authority-of-the-father (accessed October 5, 2017).

Moffitt, David M. *Atonement and the Logic of the Resurrection in the Epistle to the Hebrews*. NovTSup 141. Leiden: Brill, 2011.

Motyer, Stephen. "The Spirit in Hebrews: No Longer Forgotten?" In *The Spirit and Christ in the New Testament and Christian Theology: Essays in Honor of Max Turner*, edited by I. Howard Marshall, Volker Rabens, and Cornelis Bennema, 213–27. Grand Rapids: Eerdmans, 2012.

Naselli, Andy. "Live-blogging of Trinity Debate: Ware-Grudem vs. McCall-Yandell." Posted October 9, 2008. http://henrycenter.tiu.edu/2008/10/trinity-debate-ware-grudem-vs-mccall-yandell (accessed October 5, 2017).

Ovey, Michael. "True Sonship—Where Dignity and Submission Meet." In *One God in Three Persons: Unity of Essence, Distinction of Persons, Implications for Life*, edited by Bruce A. Ware and John Starke, 127–54. Wheaton, IL: Crossway, 2015.

Peeler, Amy L. B. *You Are My Son: The Family of God in the Epistle to the Hebrews*. LNTS 486. New York: Bloomsbury T & T Clark, 2014.

Peterson, David. *Hebrews and Perfection: An Examination of the Concept of Perfection in the "Epistle to the Hebrews."* SNTSMS 47. Cambridge: Cambridge University Press, 1982.

Sonderegger, Kathryn. "The Humility of the Son of God." In *Christology Ancient and Modern*, edited by Oliver D. Crisp and Fred Sanders, 60–73. Grand Rapids: Zondervan, 2013.

Sumner, Darren O. "Obedience and Subordination in Karl Barth's Trinitarian Theology." Pages 130–46 in *Advancing Trinitarian Theology: Essays in Constructive Dogmatics*. Edited by Oliver D. Crisp and Fred Sanders. Grand Rapids: Zondervan, 2014.

Thompson, James W. *Hebrews*. Paideia. Grand Rapids: Baker Academic, 2008.

Thompson, Marianne Meye. *The Promise of the Father: Jesus and God in the New Testament*. Louisville: Westminster John Knox, 2000.

Ware, Bruce A. *Father, Son, Holy Spirit: Relationships, Roles, and Relevance.* Wheaton, IL: Crossway, 2005.

_____. "God the Son—At Once Eternally God with His Father, and Eternally Son of the Father." Posted June 9, 2016. http://www.reformation21.org/blog/2016/06/god-the-sonat-once-eternally-g.php (accessed May 25, 2017).

_____. "How Shall We Think About the Trinity?" In *God Under Fire: Modern Scholarship Reinvents God*, edited by Douglas S. Huffman and Eric L. Johnson, 253–77. Grand Rapids: Zondervan, 2002.

_____. "Knowing the Self-Revealed God who is Father, Son, and Holy Spirit." Posted July 4, 2016. https://secundumscripturas.com/2016/07/04/knowing-the-self-revealed-god-who-is-father-son-and-holy-spirit (accessed May 25, 2017).

Widdicombe, Peter. *The Fatherhood of God from Origen to Athanasius*. OTM. Oxford: Oxford University Press, 2000.

Witherington, Ben, III. *Letters and Homilies for Jewish Christians: A Socio-Rhetorical Commentary on Hebrews, James and Jude*. Downers Grove, IL: InterVarsity, 2007.

CHAPTER 4

The Trinitarian Dynamic in the Book of Revelation

IAN PAUL

The evidence for the oneness and the equality of the Father and the Son and the close association of the Spirit with them is quite compelling and strongly suggests that one of the great permeating themes of the Apocalypse is the Triune nature of the Godhead.[1]

So concludes Woodrow W. Whidden in his survey of key passages in the text, noting the close association of Jesus with God, and the more complex textual evidence for the role of the Holy Spirit.[2] His approach is supplemented by the later survey by Edwin Reynolds, who seeks to explore the language about God, Jesus, and the Spirit more systematically.[3] Though they are both valuable, both need further support at the level of exegesis, since (for example) they assume that the opening epistolary greeting is Trinitarian without further discussion, when this observation has been significantly contested (see section 1b below).[4] In this piece, I hope to combine careful

---

1. Woodrow W. Whidden, "Trinitarian Evidences in the Apocalypse," *Journal of the Adventist Theological Society* 11, nos. 1–2 (2000): 248–60.
2. Whidden, "Trinitarian Evidences in the Apocalypse," 248–60.
3. Edwin Reynolds, "The Trinity in the Book of Revelation," *Journal of the Adventist Theological Society* 17, no. 1 (2006): 55–72.
4. Whidden, "Trinitarian Evidences in the Apocalypse," 248 comments "It is quite evident that the Father, Spirit, and Son are in focus here"; he later notes the contrary view of David E. Aune, *Revelation*

exegesis of the range of titles introduced in chapter 1 with an analysis of the
worship of the Lamb and the "one on the throne," as well as a consideration of
the role of the Spirit throughout the book.

The task of describing the Trinitarian dynamic in the book of Revelation
is fascinating for two main reasons. First, there is an extraordinary diversity
of terms, actions, and ideas deployed in relation to the understanding of God
(the Father), Jesus, and the Spirit and their interrelationship, far in excess of
any other text of comparable length in the rest of the New Testament,[5] and
there is some real diversity and discontinuity with and between these ideas.
Secondly, the complexity and internal self-references within the book create
a sophisticated intratextual web which needs careful exploration if we are to
discern the theological picture that the text is painting.[6]

These dynamics are immediately evident in the opening sentence of the
text, the beginning of the epistolary prologue of 1:1–11, and its complement
in the epistolary epilogue which forms an *inclusio* for the whole book in 22:6–
21. The "revelation of Jesus Christ" can be understood in either an objective
(it is a revelation that comes from Jesus) or a subjective (it is a revelation about
Jesus) sense, and commentators are equally divided—and in fact as John's
vision report unfolds it is clear that both senses are present.[7] But immediately this revelation is said to have its origin in God, who has given it "to him,"
that is, to Jesus. The subject of the following phrase is not immediately clear:
is it God or Jesus who "makes it known by sending his angel to his servant"?
Servants (or slaves, *douloi*) are mentioned fourteen times in the text, and as
a description of God's people are almost always servants "of God" (7:3; 10:7;
15:3; 19:5), though once Jesus calls them "my servants" (2:20) and once the
genitive is either ambiguous or shared (22:3). However, the parallel phrase in
22:6 clarifies the process: It is "the Lord God" who "sent his angel to show his
servants." This implies that "Christ is set within the chain of revelation, so that
he is one of the agents who reveals . . . the chain of communication is from
God to Jesus to an angel to John and finally to Christian 'servants'":[8] Jesus is

---

1–5, Word Biblical Commentary 52 (Dallas, TX: Word, 1997), 34, though without exploring the
    exegetical issues.

5. Loren L. Johns lists no fewer that forty-nine different "titles" for or descriptions of Jesus in Revelation,
    weighted towards the early chapters—though he carefully qualifies what he means by "title." See
    Loren L. Johns, *The Lamb Christology of the Apocalypse of John: An Investigation into Its Origins and
    Rhetorical Force*, reprint ed. (Eugene, OR: Wipf & Stock, 2014), 217–21.

6. I make the case for the unity of the book of Revelation based on the occurrence of words with
    special frequency in "Source, Structure and Composition in the Book of Revelation," in *The Book of
    Revelation: Currents in British Research on the Apocalypse*, eds. Garrick Allen, Ian Paul, and Simon
    Woodman, WUNT II (Tübingen: Mohr Siebeck, 2015), 41–54. For a more general argument, see
    Richard Bauckham, "Structure and Composition," in *The Climax of Prophecy: Studies on the Book of
    Revelation* (Edinburgh: T & T Clark, 1993), 1–37.

7. Translations throughout are my own, though they are quite often similar to that of the NIV.

8. G. K. Beale, *Revelation*, New International Greek Testament Commentary (Grand Rapids: Eerdmans,
    1999), 183.

here distinct from God and functions as his faithful emissary in the task for which God has commissioned him, just as John then does in turn in passing on what has been revealed to him.

But the matching epistolary epilogue paints a rather different picture. Epistolary authorship by John ("I, John, am the one seeing and hearing these things," 22:8) gives way to epistolary authorship by Jesus ("I, Jesus, sent my angel to testify these things to you"[9]) in a way that parallels Paul's personal ending of 1 Corinthians when he takes over writing from his amanuensis:[10]

	1 Corinthians 16		Revelation 22
21	I, Paul, write this greeting	16, 20	I, Jesus . . . bear witness
22a	Let anyone who does not love the Lord be accursed . . .	18	If anyone adds . . . God will add to the plagues . . .
22b	Our Lord, come!	20	I am coming/Come, Lord Jesus
23	The grace of the Lord Jesus be with you	21	The grace of the Lord Jesus be with all

The inclusion of this personal interjection functions in Paul as a guarantee of the authenticity of the letter as his own words (even if actually inscribed by another),[11] and in Revelation the addition of "testimony" echoes a typical Roman witness statement. Jesus displaces both God as the sender of the angelic witness to John *and* John as the author of the text, so that (in effect) John has become an amanuensis not just for the speech of the angel but also for the speech of Jesus, reflecting the importance of the major sections of *audition* (rather than *vision*) which comprise all of chapters 2 and 3 and most of chapters 17–18 and 19:1–10.

This double dynamic—of the introduction of God, Jesus (and the Spirit) as distinct characters and agents within the narrative which is then followed by the merging of role and even identity as the vision report unfolds—is something we will see repeatedly across the text.

---

9. Although the "angel" is sent to testify, it transpires that the testimony is that of Jesus himself ("The one who testifies to these things" in 22:20).

10. See the detailed discussion in Craig R. Koester, *Revelation: A New Translation with Introduction and Commentary* (New Haven, CT: Yale University Press, 2014), 846–47, 855–59. The opening grammar of 1 Corinthians 16:21 is slightly different ("This greeting is in my own hand, Paul")—see Anthony C. Thiselton, *The First Epistle to the Corinthians* (Grand Rapids: Eerdmans, 2013), 1346—but that does not undermine the strength of the parallel.

11. Koester, *Revelation*, 1348.

1. The Titles in the Epistolary Greeting

The extended epistolary greeting in 1:4–8 provides the foundation for John's proto-Trinitarian description of God and introduces titles and ideas that are developed throughout the text. It thus offers a template for exploring a wide range of issues in John's understanding of God, Jesus, and the Spirit and the relationship between them.

The opening form, "John, to the seven assemblies[12] in Asia, grace and peace to you" follows the Pauline adaptation of the standard Greco-Roman epistolary form of: sender; recipient; greeting and wish for divine blessing.[13] Paul consistently includes Jesus with God as the source of divine blessing, which in itself is of enormous theological significance as Bauckham points out:

> It shows how naturally early Christians implicitly included Jesus in the divine
> . . . even if they had no way of conceptualising in ontological terms this rela-
> tion of Jesus to God.[14]

But the greeting in Revelation is unique in having a threefold (rather than twofold) structure, and in using titles and attributes along with (for Jesus Christ) or instead of (for God and the Spirit) names—titles and attributes that draw on Old Testament texts and which develop their theological significance throughout the book.

a. The First Title for God

The threefold title for God as "the one who is, who was and who is to come" is in the nominative, rather than the expected genitive, suggesting that John is using this as an indeclinable title. It derives from the multivalent meaning of the name of Israel's God revealed to Moses in Exodus 3:14, *'ehyeh 'esher 'ehyeh*, rendered in English translations as "I am who I am" or "I was who I was" or "I will be who I will be."[15] John arranges the title in a surprising order, with the present tense first, presumably to emphasize God's living presence and power, and the third term is not a future (as we might expect) but the present participle phrase "the coming one," *ho erchomenos*. This immediately links the distinct identity of the God of Israel with Jesus; it is Jesus who says seven times "I am coming," *erchomai*, twice in a local and immediate sense (2:5 and probably 2:16) and five times in a

---

12.   On the translation of *ekklesiai* as "assemblies" rather than "churches," see Koester, *Revelation*, xx.

13.   On epistolary forms, see Alan Millard, *Reading and Writing in the Time of Jesus* (Edinburgh: T & T Clark, 1964).

14.   Richard Bauckham, *The Theology of the Book of Revelation*, New Testament Theology (Cambridge: Cambridge University Press, 1993), 24.

15.   Theologically, this is connected with the notion of God as *me-'olam ve-ad-'olam*, "from everlasting to everlasting" (1 Chron. 16:36; 29:10; Neh. 9:5; Pss. 41:33; 90:2; 106:48) and Isaiah's description of "the everlasting God" (Isa. 40:28)—though there is no particular *verbal* connection.

cosmic and final sense (probably 3:11, certainly 16:15; 22:7, 12, 20). The future of God's relationship with the created order is made manifest in the coming of Jesus to the world as the consummation of both judgement and redemption. The title is repeated for emphasis in verse 8, and occurs a third time in the heavenly worship of 4:8.

b. The Spirit as "seven[-fold] spirits"

Where we might now expect Jesus to be the second agent in the threefold greeting, we find the "seven spirits before his throne." Craig Koester follows R. H. Charles, E. Schweizer, D. Aune, and others in interpreting these as seven angelic beings (against Bauckham, Beckwith, Bousset, Fee, Keener, Osborne, Sweet and others),[16] since the Dead Sea Scrolls uses "angels" and "spirits" as parallel expressions, and because of the existence of "angelic spirits" before the throne of God in Tobit 12:15 and 1 Enoch 20:1–7.[17] But Bauckham had earlier pointed out that this identification is rare in early Christian literature, and that the description of the seven angels "who stand before God" in 8:2 is in quite different terms. There is a large and varied cast of angels throughout the text (most notably in the six arriving as two sets of three in chapter 14) so there is no reason to think that John would slip a further seven in here "in disguise" as it were. And the insertion of this reference between the titular introductions of God and Jesus, who (as we shall see) converge in title, function, and authority, has the effect of removing any ambiguity, since "grace and peace" as divine blessing flow from all three.[18]

There are two Old Testament springboards for the language of "seven spirits" which occurs here and in 3:1, 4:5, and 5:6. The messianic text Isaiah 11:1–9 begins by describing the "branch of Jesse" as anointed with the Spirit of Yahweh which has six attributes (wisdom, understanding, counsel, might, knowledge, and fear of Yahweh). But the grammatical structure of the LXX puts the opening clause "Spirit of God" as the first of what then becomes *seven* attributes. Combined with the symbolic significance of seven indicating completeness (since in the ancient world there were not only seven days of the week but also seven seas and seven planets), this might lie behind the complex narrative of Zechariah 4. In Zechariah's vision, a golden lampstand has seven lamps on it and stands next to two olive trees, which symbolize the two "sons of oil" (Zech. 4:14), Joshua and Zerubbabel. The meaning of the vision is given as "'Not by might, nor by power, but by my Spirit' says Yahweh

---

16. See the detailed discussion of the main views in Robby Waddell, *The Spirit of the Book of Revelation*, Journal of Pentecostal Theology Supplement Series 30, Blandford Forum (Dorset: Deo, 2006), 9–21.

17. Koester, *Revelation*, 216. Koester also slightly oddly conflates the seven spirits and the seven stars in 3:1 for no obvious reason.

18. See the detailed consideration of the interpretive options in Grant R. Osborne, *Revelation* (Grand Rapids: Baker Academic, 2002), 74. He concludes, "The Zech 4 background makes it probable that John has in mind the Holy Spirit here."

of hosts" (Zech. 4:6), clearly identifying the seven lamps as the Spirit of God, an understanding John deploys in 4:5.[19]

Zechariah's later image, the "seven eyes of Yahweh that range through-out the earth" (Zech. 4:10) are not immediately connected with the (seven) Spirit(s) in that passage, but John fuses this image with the earlier one in 5:6 by identifying the Lamb's "seven eyes" with "the *seven spirits* of God sent out into all the earth." This conjunction has two effects: firstly to iden-tify in some sense the Lamb and Yahweh, since the "eyes of Yahweh" have now become the "eyes of the lamb"; and secondly to place the Spirit in a subordinate position in relation to both God and the Lamb. The situation of the seven lamps "before the throne" is one that is shared by the various members of the assembled throng (including elders, living creatures, and angels) and which signifies worship and obedience. The fact that the throne itself belongs to God, but the lamb then occupies it, and the (seven) Spirit(s) being the eyes of both Yahweh and the Lamb offers a narrative portrayal which might be later expressed in a different register as the Spirit "proceed-ing from the Father and the Son."

c. Titles of Jesus Christ

At first sight, the three titles of Jesus (the only one of the three persons in the greeting who is actually named) in Revelation 1:5 seem to focus on his humanity and do not impinge on the question of divinity, as they all derive from Psalm 89's praise of the Davidic kingship (and lament of its failure). Like the Davidic monarchy, Jesus is a "faithful witness" (*ho martus, ho pistos*) reflecting the permanence of the moon (Ps. 89:37). But both the moon in creation and the Davidic rule in Israel are expressions of the faithfulness of God (Pss. 87:1, 2, 5, 8, 14, and so on). The LXX of the psalm translates the Hebrew *'emunah* with the term *aletheia*, "true," though the participle of the cognate verb *'mn* is rendered by *pistos* in Psalm 89:37. The two terms are closely related in Revelation, with Jesus being "faithful and true" in 3:14 and 19:11 (*pistos kai alethinos*) and the words from God that John has written down being "faithful and true" in 21:5 and 22:6.

However, John transforms the Davidic language of Psalm 89:27 "my firstborn, most exalted of the kings of the earth" in two ways. Firstly, Jesus is now "firstborn *from the dead*," expressing the common New Testament idea of Jesus as the pioneer (Heb. 12:2) or the "firstfruits" of the resurrection (1 Cor. 15:20). But John also shifts Jesus from being preeminent *amongst* the kings of the other nations (as David is) to being ruler *over* the kings of the earth. In making this move, John is putting Jesus on a level with God as the "king of the nations" (15:3–4) to whom all the nations will bow down in

---

19. We should note that the language of "Spirit of God" in the Old Testament does not have the hypostatic connotations that later Christian use assumes, but primarily functions as a metaphor for God's presence amongst his people acting in speech and power.

worship.[20] This universal authority of God is stated in absolute and incomparable terms in these verses, yet the use of the title for Jesus here in the prologue incorporates him within this divine supremacy. This is reflected in the single throne of God being occupied jointly by God and the Lamb from chapter 5 onward, and in the startling use of a singular verb in the proclamation of the reign of "our Lord and his Christ" when "*he* shall reign forever and ever" in 11:16.

> [John] is evidently reluctant to speak of God and Christ together as a plurality. He never makes them the subjects of a plural verb or uses a plural pronoun to refer to them both. The reason is surely clear: he places Christ on the divine side of the distinction between God and creation, but he wishes to avoid ways of speaking which sound to him polytheistic.[21]

The kingly rule of Jesus is expressed most fully in the title "king of kings and lord of lords" in 17:14 and 19:16, a phrase common in Jewish and Christian devotion for God emphasizing his unique and universal authority. It originates in Deuteronomy 10:17 and is reflected in Paul's use in 1 Timothy 6:15. Several texts note the phrase being usurped by other rulers as a sign of their hubris (Dan. 2:37; Ezra 7:12; Ezek. 26:7)—but it is applied to Jesus in Revelation without any sense of irony. There is a parallel here to Paul's ascription of "the name that is above every name" to Jesus in Philippians 2:9–11 leading to devotion ("every knee shall bow and tongue confess") in the phrase that Isaiah records as expressing God's own claim to be without equal ("I am God, and there is no other," Isa. 45:22–24). Jesus, in Philippians and in Revelation, is equal to the one who is without equal.

d. The Doxological Interjection

It is not unusual to include a doxological statement early in a letter (compare 2 Cor. 1:3) but it is characteristic of Revelation's narrative discontinuity for it to form an interjection, after which comes a prophetic pronouncement by God in verse 8, followed by the resumption of the epistolary opening by John in verse 9. The pairing of motivation and action in redemption ("loved us and has freed us . . . by his blood") is not uncommon, occurring in Galatians 2:20 and Ephesians 5:2, and highlights the willing offering by Jesus of himself found in what appear to be catechetical statements such as Mark 10:45 and Matthew 20:28. But this is the only example in the New Testament of doxology directed *to Jesus* rather than to God, and almost unique in Christian devotion, which quite quickly took a threefold,

---

20. The manuscript variant "king of the ages" reflects the ambiguity of the Hebrew phrase *melech 'olam*, which could mean "king of all ages," i.e., king forever, or "king of this age" i.e., king over all other kings.

21. Bauckham, *The Climax of Prophecy*, 139–40.

proto-Trinitarian form in postcanonical writings.[22] The actions of loving, freeing from sin, and making a kingdom of priests are in the Old Testament ascribed to God (Exod. 19:6; Ps. 103:3) and in the New Testament are the actions of God through the agency of Jesus (John 3:16 is typical). But here the actions are presented as Jesus's own accomplishment and performed in his own right. The concluding acclamation ("to him be glory and power") anticipates the exalted worship of chapter 5.

The apocalyptic-prophetic oracle that follows in verse 7 is considered by the majority of commentators to be an anticipation of the *parousia*, Jesus's final return; David Aune is typical when he comments:

> [It] uses a traditional combination of allusions to Dan 7:13 and Zech 12:10 to predict the Parousia ("coming") of Christ as a cosmic event that will be witnessed by all. . . . The imminence of the Parousia and of the end of the world is a central emphasis of Revelation.[23]

The first line, alluding to Daniel 7:13, omits the reference to "one like a son of man," but this lacuna is filled in John's description of his vision of Jesus in verse 13. The combination of allusions, but in reverse order, also occurs in the Olivet Discourse (sometimes called the Little Apocalypse) in Matthew 24:30, where the son of man *is* mentioned, but the quotation from Zechariah is truncated to omit mention of "those who pierced him."[24] Commentators like Aune who take 1:7 as a reference to the Parousia do so on the basis that the same allusions are "clearly" referring to the Parousia in Matthew 24—but R. T. France has demonstrated conclusively that this is not the case.[25] This cluster of predictions in Matthew 24:4–31 is followed immediately by Jesus's emphatic declaration: "Amen I say to you, this generation will certainly not pass away until all these things have come to pass" (Matt. 24:34). Reading this as a failed expectation of Jesus's imminent return does not take into account Matthew's lack of embarrassment at recording such words at the point (by any reasonable reckoning of dating) when "this generation" was indeed passing away,[26] and ignores the consistent use elsewhere in the

---

22. Osborne, *Revelation*, 63, following Aune, *Revelation 1–5*, 46.
23. Aune, *Revelation 1–5*, 59.
24. The parallel in Mark 13:26 includes the citation of Daniel 7:13 but not the citation from Zechariah 12:10. On the similarities and differences between Matthew's use of these texts and Revelation's, see the detailed discussion in Bauckham, *The Climax of Prophecy*, 318–22.
25. R. T. France, *The Gospel of Matthew* (Grand Rapids: Eerdmans, 2007), 889–94 and 923–28. France appears to have been influenced in this by G. B. Caird, *Language and Imagery of the Bible* (London: Gerald Duckworth, 1980) and in turn he influenced N. T. Wright—though, unlike France, Wright does not see the focus switch to the *parousia* from 24:36 onward. N. T. Wright, *Jesus and the Victory of God: Christian Origins and the Question of God: Vol. 2* (London: SPCK, 1996), 339–67.
26. The popular reading of *genea* as "race," referring to the Jews, rather than "generation," indicating timescale, has no lexical foundation. This observation, that the passing of the apostolic generation was the impetus for the writing of the Gospels, is the thesis behind Richard Bauckham's major

gospels and Acts of Daniel 7:13. In the trial narrative in Mark 14:62, Jesus cites Daniel 7:13 with reference to his vindication by God in his resurrection and ascension, and immediately prior to his execution, Stephen has a vision of this fulfilled in Acts 7:56. In all these contexts, "coming" (*erchomenos*) indicates the coming of the Son of Man to the throne, and *not* coming to the earth—the direction of travel is upward, not downward.[27]

So in both Matthew 24 and Revelation 1:7, the use of Daniel 7:13 and Zechariah 12:10 refers to Jesus's exalted status before the Ancient of Days, and his receipt of "authority, glory and sovereign power" and a "kingdom that will not be destroyed" (Dan. 7:14).[28] This understanding fits much better with the immediate context of John's proclamation of Jesus as "ruler" and the language of the doxology, rather than seeing it as an anticipation of his return, which is a minor note (only represented by the third ascription of God "who is to come") in this section. For our purposes, we need to note that, as is common in Revelation, texts where Yahweh is the subject are now applied to Jesus without qualification, so that he becomes the subject and performs the actions that Yahweh performed in the source text. In the oracle in Zechariah 12:10, it is Yahweh who is speaking to his people (Zech. 12:1), and his being "pierced" is a metaphor for the way the people have wounded God by their disobedience (compare the similar metaphor in Luke 2:35). Jesus now becomes the one who is pierced, as he has done in John 19:37 where his crucifixion becomes the "fulfilment" of this text. Although the "mourning" in Zechariah 12:10 suggests fear of judgement, the way that both Revelation and Matthew adapt the LXX suggests recognition and repentance by including allusion to the blessing of the nations in Genesis 22:18.[29] The exaltation of Jesus being seen by "all the tribes of the earth" (rather than the clans of the land [of Israel] in Zech. 12:14) thus anticipates the followers of the Lamb being "redeemed from every tribe, language, people and nation" (5:9; compare 7:9).

So, far from being an unexpected anticipation of Parousia disconnected from the doxological language and the focus on sovereign power in the surrounding verses, this oracle articulates Jesus's exaltation in the presence of God and the consequent recognition of his sovereignty by his followers from every nation. It does so, at least in part, by adapting Old Testament

---

work on *Jesus and the Eyewitnesses: The Gospels as Eyewitness Testimony* (Grand Rapids: Eerdmans, 2008).

27. Aune, *Revelation 1–5*, 53–54 does note that *erchomai* used by Jesus in Revelation generally has the opposite sense, i.e., of his return (but note the qualification to this in 1a. above; the word *parousia* does not occur in Revelation), but the question here is whether the meaning is controlled more by John's later use of the verb or by the Old Testament text and its use elsewhere in the early Christian tradition.

28. As confirmation of this, it is worth noting that in Revelation clouds (*nefelai*) always signify divine presence and power, and form no part of Jesus's return in contrast to Paul's language in 1 Thessalonians 4:17.

29. Bauckham, *The Climax of Prophecy*, 322.

language about Yahweh and making Jesus the subject, as other New Testament writers have done.

e. The Prophetic Oracle: Additional Titles of God

John's language in verse 8, "says the Lord God," appears to be a deliberate echo of authoritative prophetic pronouncements from the Old Testament (for example, Exod. 4:22; 1 Kings 11:31; Jer. 9:22; Isa. 48:17) and forms an *inclusio* with the opening of the greeting in verse 4 by returning to the subject of God. The first part of the statement "I am the Alpha and the O"[30] is unique to Revelation in the New Testament (despite its widespread deployment in Christian worship) and functions both as a counterclaim to that of Zeus to be "the beginning, the middle and the end" and an engagement with Greco-Roman magical cults.[31] Members of these cults were often interested in letters and their repetition, and there is evidence of their interest in the transliteration of the tetragrammaton into Greek as $IA\Omega$. Thus this title in Revelation is specifically connected with the name of Yahweh and the polemical displacement of other gods and their claims to supremacy. It is, then, very striking that this title is repeated in two variant forms, seven times in total, and alternating in ascription to God and to Jesus:

God	1:8	I am the Alpha and the O	1
Jesus	1:17	I am the first and the last	2
God	21:6	I am the Alpha and the O,	3
		the beginning and the end:	4
Jesus	22:13	I am the Alpha and the O,	5
		the first and the last,	6
		the beginning and the end:	7

The first variant "I am the first and the last" in 1:17 is a direct allusion to Isaiah 44:6, and is part of the repeated refrain in this section of Isaiah that "apart from me there is no God," denying the power or even ontological reality of other spiritual powers—and it is this title which is claimed by Jesus in John's opening vision. The second variant "I am the beginning and the end" in 21:6 also derives from Second Isaiah: God is the "first and the last" in Isaiah 41:4, 44:6, and 48:12 in contrast to other powers, and has been speaking and acting "from the beginning" (Isa. 40:21; 41:26). Whilst the characters of Jesus/the Lamb and God/the one on the throne have distinct

---

30. Although "Alpha" is spelled out, spelling out the letter "Omega" does not occur until the sixth or seventh century.

31. On the numerous links between Revelation and the language and ideas of magical cults, see "The Apocalypse of John and Graeco-Roman Revelatory Magic," in David E. Aune, *Apocalypticism, Prophecy, and Magic in Early Christianity: Collected Essays* (Grand Rapids: Baker Academic, 2008), 347–67 and the fuller study by Rodney Lawrence Thomas, *Magical Motifs in the Book of Revelation*, Library of New Testament Studies (London; New York: T & T Clark International, 2010).

titles and roles throughout the narrative, Jesus's claim of the triple title in 22:13 offers the clearest sense of the convergence of his status and identity with that of God. In the end, the fulness of God is found in our encountering him in the person and redemption of Jesus. Bauckham observes:

> This pattern underlines the identification of Christ with God which the use of the titles themselves expresses. . . . It does not designate [Jesus] a second god, but includes him in the eternal being of the one God of Israel who is the only source and goal of all things.[32]

This offers an interesting parallel to Paul's inclusion of Jesus in his citation of the *Shema* (Deut. 6:4) in 1 Corinthians 8:4–6. On this, Gordon Fee uses very similar language to Bauckham's concerning Revelation:

> In the same breath that he can assert that there is only one God, he equally asserts that the designation "Lord" which in the old Testament belongs to the one God, is the proper designation of the divine Son. One should note especially that Paul feels no tension between the affirmation of monotheism and a clear distinction between the two persons of Father and Jesus Christ.[33]

The second part of the prophetic oracle in verse 8 recapitulates the opening threefold title of God (thus also emphasizing the *inclusio* of this short section) and then adds the Old Testament title "Almighty" (*pantokrator*). In conjunction with "Lord God," this appears seven times in the text (here and in 4:8; 11:17; 15:3; 16:7; 19:6; and 21:22) and corresponds to the Old Testament phrase *yhwh 'elohei tsevaot*, "Yahweh God of Hosts." In Revelation it appears in praise and in the context of conflict and victory, and is only ever used of God. There is some connection with the activity of Jesus, in that he "holds fast" (*krateo*, cognate with *pantokrator*) the seven stars in 2:1—but for the most part this title serves to distinguish God from other divine actants, Jesus and the Spirit, in the narrative.[34]

---

32. Bauckham, *The Theology of the Book of Revelation*, 58.
33. Gordon D. Fee, *First Epistle to the Corinthians*, 2nd rev. ed., New International Commentary on the New Testament (Grand Rapids: Eerdmans, 1987), 375.
34. I used the term "actant" from literary theory to indicate someone or something that has an active role in the narrative, rather than the more common "actor," which might imply that one actor could play several roles within a narrative. Simon Woodman does introduce the idea of the persons of the Trinity playing quite different roles in the narrative (Simon Woodman, *The Book of Revelation* (London: SCM, 2008), 63. For most people, Revelation is a book that is either largely ignored, or it is the object of such fanatical study and fanciful interpretation that it passes from the realm of the interesting and helpful into the realm of fantasy and speculation. Much literature has been published in recent years on its interpretation, some of which is scholarly and technical, and some of which is populist and accessible. The problem is that the technical and scholarly material frequently requires careful and detailed study, combined with an advanced level of knowledge, whereas much of the populist material tends toward the fanatical and fanciful. The aim of Woodman's book is to bridge

Detailed consideration of all these aspects of the opening section thus confirm that John's epistolary greeting is indeed proto-Trinitarian, in that it binds together the three characters of God, Jesus, and the Spirit in a way that is reflected in later usage in the book—without losing the distinctive aspects of their identify and action.

2. The Worship of God and the Lamb in Chapters 4–5

There is widespread agreement that the descriptions of worship in Revelation are a central feature of the book. Worship provides a unifying theme to the entire work;[35] it functions as the major source of symbolic persuasion;[36] it provides a series of persuasive artistic descriptions that offers a symbolic alternative to the iconography of pagan worship;[37] its hymns are primary bearers of the theological message of the book;[38] and they continue to provide a theology of both worship and the activity of the Spirit.[39] "There can be no doubting the importance of worship as a theme in the book."[40] As well as including numerous examples of worship in the form of its hymnic sections, Revelation also includes two narrative commentaries on the significance of worship, in the repeated rebuke by an angel of John when he is tempted to "worship" (*proskuneo*) him in 19:10 and 22:9. These episodes function to identify John with his audience in their humanity and fallibility, but they also function clearly to delineate the proper subjects of worship, placing angelic beings with humanity on one side of the dividing line, and God alone on the other side as an appropriate recipient of human worship and obeisance. John's repeated expression "I fell at his feet" recalls his response to the opening encounter with the exalted Jesus (1:17), where he receives no parallel rebuke but only reassurance. Although the technical term *latreuo* is used for the priestly service of God's people in 7:15 and 22:3, *proskuneo* is the principle

---

this gap. It is written with second and third year university students in mind, and would also be helpful for pastors and those in local churches who want to take seriously their study of this often (needlessly complicated) topic, but that is not a point I wish to pursue here.

35.   As argued in Leonard L. Thompson, "Unity through the Language of Worship," in *The Book of Revelation: Apocalypse and Empire* (Oxford; New York: Oxford University Press, 1990), 53–73. This is also the central thesis of the chiastic structure for the book proposed by John Paul Heil, *The Book of Revelation: Worship for Life in the Spirit of Prophecy* (Eugene, OR: Cascade, 2014).

36.   The main thesis of J. Nelson Kraybill, *Apocalypse and Allegiance: Worship, Politics, and Devotion in the Book of Revelation* (Grand Rapids: Brazos, 2010).

37.   Robyn J. Whitaker, *Ekphrasis, Vision, and Persuasion in the Book of Revelation* (Tübingen: Mohr Siebeck, 2015).

38.   So Stephen N. Horn, "Hallelujah, the Lord Our God, the Almighty Reigns: The Theology of the Hymns of Revelation," in *Essays on Revelation: Appropriating Yesterday's Apocalypse in Today's World*, ed. Gerald L. Stevens (Eugene, OR: Pickwick, 2011), 41–54.

39.   Melissa L. Archer, *"I Was in the Spirit on the Lord's Day": A Pentecostal Engagement with Worship in the Apocalypse* (Cleveland: CPT Press, 2015).

40.   James F. McGrath, *The Only True God: Early Christian Monotheism in Its Jewish Context* (Champaign: University of Illinois Press, 2012) 71.

term for worship, and it is unlikely to be a coincidence that it occurs twenty-four times in the text, corresponding to the twenty-four elders who represent the people of God bowing in worship before the throne.[41]

The description and worship of God in chapter 4 has two notable features. The first is that it is suffused with images, ideas, and language of the Old Testament. John's vision of God's throne enabled by transportation "in the Spirit" echoes the visionary experience of Ezekiel (Ezek. 8:3 and 11:5). The rainbow around the throne alludes to God's promise to Noah (Gen. 9:13). The "lightning, rumblings, and peals of thunder" are reminders of the Sinai theophany (Exod. 19:16, recalled in Ps. 77:18). The seven lamps of fire come from Zechariah 4:2. The sea of glass derives from the bronze bath before the temple (1 Kings 7:23–26). The four living creatures come from the beginning of Ezekiel's vision (Ezek. 1:4–14). And the opening trisagion reminds us of the awesome vision of Isaiah 6. This is the God of Israel in all his majesty and power.

And yet equally important elements of John's vision come from a second quite different source—the practices of the imperial cult. The presence of twenty-four elders (rather than priests) within what appears to be a throne room, who wear white (the usual pagan colour of worship) and cast down their golden crowns whilst singing choruses about worth and honor and power all derive from known practices of the cult.[42] In John's dramatic vision report, the God of Israel shares worship with no other: the incorporation of features of the cult is an act of polemical displacement, where

> the sovereignty of God . . . has been elevated so far above all pretentions and claims of earthly rulers that the latter, upon comparison, become only pale, even diabolical imitations of the transcendent majesty of the King of kings and Lord of lords.[43]

Given the implicit denial of anyone else being able to share the worship of the one true God, it is even more extraordinary to observe the way that worship of the Lamb is introduced, developed, and merged with the worship of God in chapter 5.[44]

41. The one exception of *proskuneo* being used in a noncultic sense in 3:9 does not undermine these observations, particularly in the light of the narrative episodes in 19:10 and 22:9, as rightly argued by Brandon D. Smith, "The Identification of Jesus with YHWH in the Book of Revelation: A Brief Sketch," *Criswell Theological Review* 14, no. 1 (2016): 67–84 (82–83) contra McGrath, *The Only True God*, 73.

42. As carefully demonstrated in Aune, "The Influence of Roman Imperial Court Ceremonial on the Apocalypse of John," in *Apocalypticism, Prophecy, and Magic in Early Christianity*, 99–119.

43. Aune, "The Influence of Roman Imperial Court Ceremonial on the Apocalypse of John," 118.

44. This table follows the pattern in Steven J. Friesen, *Imperial Cults and the Apocalypse of John: Reading Revelation in the Ruins* (Oxford/New York: Oxford University Press, 2001), 199.

Verse	Recipient of worship	Offered by	Action of worship	Content
4:8	God	Four living creatures	Ceaselessly saying	Holy, holy, holy is the Lord God Almighty, who was, and is, and is to come
4:11	God	Twenty-four elders	Fall before God, cast crowns down	You are worthy, our Lord and God, to receive glory and honor and power, for you created all things, and by your will they were created and have their being
5:9–10	Lamb	Four living creatures and twenty-four elders	Fall before the Lamb and sing/ chant	You are worthy to take the scroll and to open its seals, because you were slain, and with your blood you purchased for God members of every tribe and language and people and nation. You have made them to be a kingdom and priests to serve our God, and they will reign on the earth
5:12	Lamb	Four living creatures, twenty-four elders, and myriads of angels	Saying with a great voice	Worthy is the Lamb, who was slain, to receive power and wealth and wisdom and strength and honor and glory and praise!
5:13	God and the Lamb	Every creature in heaven, on earth, under the earth, in the sea	Saying	To him who sits on the throne and to the Lamb be praise and honor and glory and power, for ever and ever!

There is clear significance in the Lamb sharing the throne with the One seated there, though this in itself does not provide an *absolute* delineation of these two from the created order, since the followers of Jesus/the Lamb "will reign with him" (20:4, 6; compare 3:21; 5:10; and 22:5). But the incorporation of the Lamb into the monotheistic worship of God does delineate God and the Lamb from the rest of creation.

> The slaughtered Lamb is now not only our central and centering vision, but also the interpretive lens through which we read the remainder of the book. Divine judgment and salvation must be understood in light of—indeed defined by—the reality of the slaughtered Lamb who is worthy of divine worship.[45]

This incorporation is declared so much as developed, and the pattern of worship (set out in the table above) shows three rhythms of progression: in the recipient, which moves from being God, to the Lamb, to God and the Lamb together; in those offering worship, which expands in stages until the final chorus by every creature in the tridecker universe; and in the hymnic expression of worship, ending in the anticipation of eternity.[46] This sense of developing convergence continues through the whole book in a number of different ways. The worship of God by the uncountable multitude in chapter 7, in the interlude between the sixth and seventh seals being opened, includes seven acclamations following the pattern of the worship of the Lamb in 5:12 but incorporating elements from the hymns of 4:11 and 5:13:

4:11	5:12	5:14	7:12
glory	power	praise	praise
honor	wealth	honor	glory
power	wisdom	glory	wisdom
	strength	power	thanks
	honor		honor
	glory		power
	praise		strength

The next interjection of praise comes at the end of the second series, the seven trumpets, in an anticipation of the end when "the kingdom of the world has become the kingdom of our Lord and of his Messiah, and he will reign for ever and ever" (11:15). At this point, convergence of worship is expressed in convergence of grammar, where "the singular [verb] represents the unity

---

45. Michael J. Gorman, *Reading Revelation Responsibly: Uncivil Worship and Witness: Following the Lamb into the New Creation* (Eugene, OR: Cascade, 2011), 115.

46. Friesen, *Imperial Cults and the Apocalypse of John*, 198.

of God and Christ as the 'one' who will rule."[47] Grammatical convergence continues in the second vision of the 144,000 in 14:1; these are the ones distinguished by the "seal of the living God" (7:2) which is a counterpoint to the "mark of the beast" (13:16), and turns out to be comprised of the names of the Lamb and "his Father." But these two names are treated as a single object both here (by means of the singular participle "written") and in 22:4 (by means of the singular pronoun "his"). This second reference comes as part of a series of allusions to God's people in the role of the Aaronic high priest, since they serve him in his temple and see his face. The singular "name" of God and of the Lamb corresponds to the plate of gold on the turban of Aaron inscribed with the name of Yahweh (Exod. 28:36–38).

Though God and the Lamb continue to have distinct narrative identities in the final vision of the New Jerusalem, the language John uses completes this trajectory of convergence. At the opening of the chapter, the holy city comes "from God" (21:2), prepared by him to be a beautiful bride "for the lamb" (21:9), so their narrative roles are distinct. And yet by the second half of the vision, the Lord God Almighty and the Lamb are its (singular) temple (21:22); the glory of God and the Lamb are set in parallel as its (single) light source (21:23); the river of the water of life flows from the (single) throne of God and the Lamb (22:1) before which his priestly people serve (the singular) "him" (22:3). This continued tension between distinction and unity leads Bauckham to observe:

> He wants neither to say that Jesus simply is, without any distinction, the God Jesus called God and Father . . . nor to seem to speak of two gods. . . . The importance of John's extraordinarily high Christology for the message of Revelation is that it makes it absolutely clear that what Christ does, God does. Since Christ shares the one eternal being of God, what Christ is said to do, in salvation and judgement, is no less truly and directly divine and what is said to be done by the one who sits on the throne.[48]

Bauckham's conclusion is contested by two recent studies. First, Adela Yarbro Collins and John Collins explore the imagery of Jesus in Revelation as part of their reflection on the nature of the "son of man" in the Johannine literature.[49] Their central argument is that Jesus is portrayed using angelic imagery, and so is not depicted as fully divine. This is evident in the angelomorphic Christophany of Revelation 1:12–18 and in the depiction of the rider on the white horse as divine warrior in Revelation 19:11–16.

---

47.   Mathewson, Revelation, 152.
48.   Bauckham, The Theology of the Book of Revelation, 63.
49.   Adela Yarbro Collins and John J. Collins, King and Messiah as Son of God: Divine, Human, and Angelic Messianic Figures in Biblical and Related Literature (Grand Rapids: Eerdmans, 2008), 187–203.

> The risen Jesus being seated on the throne certainly implies his exaltation and his sharing in the important activities of God, such as ruling and judgement. Yet divinity admits of different degrees.[50]

This is an odd conclusion in the context of the narrative world of Revelation, which draws a very clear line between the creation and the creator, and puts humanity, the living creatures around the throne, and all angels on one side of the divide, and Jesus (as the Lamb) with God on the other side—indeed, this is a central part of Revelation's polemic against the imperial cult. The distinction between angels (who are not to be worshipped) and Jesus (who is) is reinforced in the repetition of the prohibition by the angel in 19:10 and 22:9, confirmed by the emphatic slogan "Worship only God!"

There are indeed some parallels in some other literature of elements of the portrayal of the messiah as human figure sharing in some divine attributes, such as the depiction of the Son of Man seated on a throne in *1 Enoch* 48.[51] Yet there is no parallel to the multiple symbolic, narrative, and titular ways that the messiah is identified with God in Revelation. Collins and Collins claim that the convergence of the titles "first and last"/"Alpha and Omega"/"beginning and end" do not identify Jesus and God because "It is not necessarily the case that the same attributes have exactly the same significance for Christ as they have for God."[52] It is quite difficult to read this as anything other than an evasion of the evidence of the text.

The second argument is offered by James McGrath in his study of early Christian monotheism in its Jewish context.[53] For McGrath, it counts against the identification of God and Jesus that John apparently "misses many opportunities to make this point in a clear and unambiguous manner," that God is consistently named first of the two in worship, and that the worship depicted "does not incorporate cultic or sacrificial elements."[54] Setting such criteria is an unusual way to read the text, and McGrath does not consider the cumulative narrative impact of the depiction of Jesus in relation to God. He is quite right to note that:

> The depiction of Christ in the Book of Revelation represents a development *within* the context of Jewish monotheism rather than a development *away from* Jewish devotion to only one God.[55]

But this can (and should) be said of all proto-Trinitarian (or proto-binitarian) language in the New Testament; belief in the Trinity is of God as three *in one*.

---

50.   Collins, *King and Messiah as Son of God*, 192.
51.   Collins, *King and Messiah as Son of God*, 206.
52.   Collins, *King and Messiah as Son of God*, 194.
53.   McGrath, *The Only True God*.
54.   McGrath, *The Only True God*, 72, 73.
55.   McGrath, *The Only True God*, 76.

3. The Spirit in Revelatory Action, Divine Speech, and the Eschatological Function

This sense of eschatological convergence between the identity of Jesus and God[56] might lead to a sense that the theology of Revelation is binitarian rather than trinitarian in shape.[57] There are, however, some important elements of the language of the Spirit which question this.

The first is the four occurrences of John being "in the Spirit" (*en pneumati*) at key moments of his vision report.[58] In 1:10, the phrase introduces his opening vision of Jesus and the subsequent audition of the messages to the seven assemblies. In 4:2, the Spirit enables John's vision of worship in heaven, which then leads directly into the seals series. In 17:3, the Spirit transports him (as happened to Ezekiel) to see the visions of revelation and judgement of Babylon. And in 21:10 the Spirit shows John the eschatological goal—the holy city, the New Jerusalem. For John, the revelation of Jesus Christ that comes from God is revealed by the Spirit.

The second element is the key role of the Spirit in speaking the speech of Jesus. Being "in the Spirit," John hears and transmits the prophetic words of Jesus: "Thus says . . ." (*Tade legei* . . . , 2:1, 8, 12, 18; 3:1, 7, 14). But at the end of each message comes the paradoxical slogan "Whoever has ears, let them hear what the Spirit says to the assemblies" (2:7, 11, 17, 29; 3:6, 13, 22). This draws on the solemn prophetic injunction to listen (in the sense of responding in obedient action) to the words of God, expressed in the *Shema* in 6:4 and reiterated by Jesus in its Isaianic form (Isa. 6:9; Mark 4:9, 12). It is also universalised; the words to one assembly are to be heard by *all* the assemblies. But, most striking, the words of Jesus are the words uttered by the Spirit; what Jesus "thus says" is symmetrical to what "the Spirit says." John is here coming very close to Paul, for whom the Spirit enables both right speech about Jesus (1 Cor. 12:3) and the right speech of Jesus through us (Rom. 8:15), and in this sense the "Spirit of God" is "the Spirit of Jesus" (Rom. 8:9; Acts 16:6). This identification of the speech of the Spirit with the speech of Jesus sits in tension with the alignment in 22:17 of the Spirit with "the bride," that is, the people of God, where both together say "Come!"—either

---

56. Though Bauckham, *The Theology of the Book of Revelation*, 58, notes that the convergence of identity expressed in the sevenfold title "first and last" and its equivalents is protological as well as eschatological, there is no sense of adoptionism in the text.

57. A recent example of a binitarian reading is Bogdan G. Bucur, "Hierarchy, Prophecy, and the Angelomorphic Spirit: A Contribution to the Study of the Book of Revelation's *Wirkungsgeschichte*," *Journal of Biblical Literature* 127, no. 1 (2008): 173–94. He can only arrive at his conclusion by eliminating key texts about the Spirit, including the references to the "seven spirits," and even then his conclusion is heavily qualified. He concedes that "certain '(pre)-trinitarian' elements are undeniably present" (193) and concludes: "I have also argued that these views are, by the standards of today's biblical exegesis, legitimate readings of Revelation. Whether they correspond to the intentions of Revelation's author must remain an issue of debate" (194).

58. Comparison with other occurrences of the phrase in the New Testament, and particularly in the gospels (e.g. Matt. 12:28 and pars, Matt. 22:43; see also Rom. 2:29) confirm that there is no significance to "Spirit" being anarthrous, and that there is no reason to think John means "in a [spiritual] trance."

to the coming Jesus, or to those invited to take "the free gift of the water of life," or both. But the identification is supported by the close connection between the "the Spirit of prophecy" and "the testimony of Jesus" in 19:10; the Spirit which animated the Old Testament prophets in carrying God's speech to his people, and now animates John in the writing of this "prophecy" (1:3; 22:7, 10, 18, 19), is the one who speaks in accord with testimony to and about Jesus.[59] John also expresses this by means of his numerical composition, in which "the Spirit" occurs fourteen times:[60] seven times at the end of the messages in chapters 2 and 3; four times in the phrase "in the Spirit" (1:10; 4:2; 17:3; and 21:10); and three times in relation to the Spirit's speech (14:13; 19:10; and 22:17). The testimony of Jesus is in turn connected closely with "the word of God" in 1:2, 9, 6:9 and 20:4, particularly in relation to the suffering of those who remain faithful. God, Jesus, and the Spirit are connected in divine speech by word, testimony, and prophecy.

The third element is the question of the place—or absence—of the Spirit in the New Jerusalem. If the Spirit is the "down payment" of what is to come (2 Cor. 1:22; 5:5; Eph. 1:14) then when that comes, the deposit loses its significance; if the Spirit is the "go-between God,"[61] then what function does the Spirit have in the context of the unmediated presence of God with his people? And yet the full payment completes the deposit rather than displacing it,[62] and the Spirit is not a third party, but the presence of God himself amongst the people of God in anticipation of his fuller manifestation. It is surprising, then, to find no mention of the Spirit within John's report of the eschatological climax from 19:11 to 22:6 (except as the revealer in 21:10) and this gives the final vision a "binitarian" feel, as the convergence of the reigning of the Lamb and God which was introduced in chapters 4 and 5 now reaches its completion. However, it might be possible to understand the Spirit as symbolized in the "river of the water of life" that flows from the throne of God and the Lamb (22:1).[63] In the Johannine tradition, the gift of the water of life (meaning water that is living rather than still, what we might call "running water," and meaning water that

---

59. There is a connection here with John's creative use of the Old Testament; in the process of testifying to Jesus whilst in the Spirit, John feels free to reread the Old Testament texts to authenticate his message to the assemblies to call them to faithful witness. In this sense he is deploying a pneumatic and ecclesiological hermeneutic, as Richard Hays argues Paul is doing in *Echoes of Scripture in the Letters of Paul* (New Haven, CT: Yale University Press, 1993).

60. The number 14 (= 2 x 7) can be understood as signifying complete or faith witness, since two is the number of testimony from Deuteronomy 17:6 and 19:15, and seven the number of completeness. Thus in Revelation both "Jesus" the faithful witness and "saints" who are called to follow his example both occur fourteen times.

61. The title of John V. Taylor's 1975 book on the Spirit and Christian mission.

62. So (to use a slight variation on Paul's metaphor) in Western culture women *add* their wedding ring to their engagement ring rather than *replacing* the one by the other.

63. This was first noticed in modern commentary by Henry Barclay Swete, ed., *The Apocalypse of St John: The Greek Text* (London: Macmillan, 1906), 298 when he comments that "The River of Life which 'gladdens the city of God' is the gift of the Spirit," and he connects this with Andrew of Caesarea's discussion of the Spirit proceeding from the Father *and* the Son.

brings life) is identified with the Spirit (John 4:10, 14, 24), and the Spirit as water flowing from the new temple (in the person of Jesus) fulfils Ezekiel's vision of the temple's restoration (John 7:38; Ezek. 47; John 19:34–35).[64] This connection is alluded to by the echo of Jesus's invitation to the thirsty of John 7:37 in the Spirit's invitation of Rev. 22:17. If the "reward" that Jesus offers is life, and this reward comes "with" him (22.12), this life is received by those who receive the water of life, the outpouring of the Spirit both now and in the age to come.

4. Conclusion

In arguing for theological exegesis within the wider project of the theological interpretation of Scripture, David S. Yeago explores the relationship between doctrine and the text of Scripture:

> [T]he ancient theologians were right to hold that the Nicene *homoousion* is neither imposed on the New Testament texts, nor distantly deduced from the texts, but rather describes a pattern of judgements present in the texts, in the texture of scriptural discourse concerning Jesus and the God of Israel. . . . The New Testament does not contain a formally articulated "doctrine of God" of the same kind as the later Nicene dogma. What it does contain is a pattern of implicit and explicit judgements concerning the God of Israel and his relationship to the crucified and risen Jesus of Nazareth.[65]

Yeago explores this in relation to the "Christ hymn" in Philippians 2:5–11, but in relation to the "pattern of implicit and explicit judgements" within the book of Revelation we need to note three things.

First, where many of the claims about the relation between Jesus and the God of Israel are implicit in other parts of the New Testament, in Revelation they become quite overt and explicit. In relation to the two key texts 1 Corinthians 8:6 and Philippians 2:9–11, we need to read these in the context of the Old Testament texts to which they are alluding (to Isa. 45:23 and Deut. 6:4, respectively) in order to tease out the implications of what Paul is saying. By contrast, John in Revelation actually gives the same titles to Jesus and God the Father quite explicitly, and has them actually perform many of the same actions within the narrative of his vision report.

---

64. Whidden, "Trinitarian Evidences in the Apocalypse," 259–60 supplements these canonical observations with the identification of "the spirit of holiness" with "purifying water" in 1QS 4:21, and evidence from *Pesikta Rabbati* 1:2 and *Odes of Solomon* 6:7–18. He also notes Beale's hesitation about this identification: G. K. Beale, *Revelation*, New International Greek Testament Commentary (Grand Rapids: Eerdmans, 1999), 1104.

65. David S. Yeago, "The New Testament and Nicene Dogma: A Contribution to the Recovery of Theological Exegesis," *Pro Ecclesia* III, no. 2 (1994): 153. Reprinted in Stephen Fowl, *The Theological Interpretation of Scripture* (Oxford: Blackwell, 1997), 87–100. Cited by Smith, "The Identification of Jesus," 71 and by Kevin Giles, *The Rise and Fall of the Complementarian Doctrine of the Trinity* (Eugene, OR: Cascade, 2017), 92.

Secondly, Revelation presents the equality of the persons of the Godhead, particularly the relation between the Father and the Son, much less ambiguously than some New Testament texts.[66] There are no parallels to the language of subordination we find in 1 Corinthians 15:28, the language of dependence in John 5:19, the language of obedience in Romans 5:19, or the language of greater and less in John 14:28. Where other texts consistently depict God as the primary agent of creation, salvation, judgement, reconciliation, calling, and pouring out the Spirit, acting *through* Jesus,[67] in Revelation Jesus is depicted as an agent in his own right—and uniquely in the New Testament as being the object of divine praise in his own right.

Finally, Revelation is distinctive in depicting the Spirit (through a complex set of images) as speaking the speech of both Jesus and the One on the throne, acting for them and with them in revelation and insight, and having a symmetrical relationship (as the eyes of Yahweh who has now become the eyes of the Lamb, as well as possibly being the river of the water of life flowing from the throne of God and the Lamb) with both these other two.

Nicene belief in God as Trinity is the only doctrinal and theological framework which can make sense of the narrative shape and diverse imagery of the book of Revelation in its depiction of the threefold identity of God. Whidden's opening claim that this is a central theological theme of the book is fully justified by careful exegesis of the text.

---

66. For an exploration of the resolution of texts in tension in relation to aspects of the doctrine of the Trinity, see Giles, *The Rise and Fall*, 84–101.

67. See the detailed list of actions and texts depicting the Father acting *through* the Son in Giles, *The Rise and Fall*, 97.

Bibliography

Allen, Garrick, Ian Paul, and Simon Woodman, eds. *The Book of Revelation: Currents in British Research on the Apocalypse*. WUNT II. Tübingen: Mohr Siebeck, 2015.

Archer, Melissa L. *"I Was in the Spirit on the Lord's Day": A Pentecostal Engagement with Worship in the Apocalypse*. Cleveland: CPT Press, 2015.

Aune, David E. *Apocalypticism, Prophecy, and Magic in Early Christianity: Collected Essays*. Grand Rapids: Baker Academic, 2008.

_____. *Revelation 1–5*. Word Biblical Commentary 52. Dallas: Word, 1997.

Bauckham, Richard. *The Climax of Prophecy: Studies on the Book of Revelation*. Edinburgh: T & T Clark, 1993.

_____. *Jesus and the Eyewitnesses: The Gospels as Eyewitness Testimony*. Grand Rapids: Eerdmans, 2008.

_____. *The Theology of the Book of Revelation*. New Testament Theology. Cambridge: Cambridge University Press, 1993.

Beale, G. K. *Revelation*. New International Greek Testament Commentary. Grand Rapids: Eerdmans, 1999.

Bucur, Bogdan G. "Hierarchy, Prophecy, and the Angelomorphic Spirit: A Contribution to the Study of the Book of Revelation's *Wirkungsgeschichte*." *Journal of Biblical Literature* 127, no. 1 (2008): 173–94.

Caird, G. B. *Language and Imagery of the Bible*. London: Gerald Duckworth, 1980.

Collins, Adela Yarbro, and John J. Collins. *King and Messiah as Son of God: Divine, Human, and Angelic Messianic Figures in Biblical and Related Literature*. Grand Rapids: Eerdmans, 2008.

Fee, Gordon D. *First Epistle to the Corinthians*. 2nd rev. ed. New International Commentary on the New Testament. Grand Rapids: Eerdmans, 1987.

Fowl, Stephen. *The Theological Interpretation of Scripture*. Oxford: Blackwell, 1997.

France, R. T. *The Gospel of Matthew*. Grand Rapids: Eerdmans, 2007.

Friesen, Steven J. *Imperial Cults and the Apocalypse of John: Reading Revelation in the Ruins*. Oxford/New York: Oxford University Press, 2001.

Giles, Kevin. *The Rise and Fall of the Complementarian Doctrine of the Trinity*. Eugene, OR: Cascade Books, 2017.

Gorman, Michael J. *Reading Revelation Responsibly: Uncivil Worship and Witness: Following the Lamb into the New Creation*. Eugene, OR: Cascade, 2011.

Hays, Richard B. *Echoes of Scripture in the Letters of Paul*. New Haven, CT: Yale University Press, 1993.

Heil, John Paul. *The Book of Revelation: Worship for Life in the Spirit of Prophecy*. Eugene, OR: Cascade, 2014.

Johns, Loren L. *The Lamb Christology of the Apocalypse of John: An Investigation into Its Origins and Rhetorical Force.* Reprint ed. Eugene, OR: Wipf & Stock, 2014.

Koester, Craig R. *Revelation: A New Translation with Introduction and Commentary.* New Haven, CT: Yale University Press, 2014.

Kraybill, J. Nelson. *Apocalypse and Allegiance: Worship, Politics, and Devotion in the Book of Revelation.* Grand Rapids: Brazos, 2010.

Mathewson, David. *Revelation.* Waco, TX: Baylor University Press, 2016.

McGrath, James F. *The Only True God: Early Christian Monotheism in Its Jewish Context.* Champaign: University of Illinois Press, 2012.

Millard, Alan. *Reading and Writing in the Time of Jesus.* Edinburgh: T & T Clark, 1964.

Osborne, Grant R. *Revelation.* Grand Rapids: Baker Academic, 2002.

Reynolds, Edwin. "The Trinity in the Book of Revelation." *Journal of the Adventist Theological Society* 17, no. 1 (2006): 55–72.

Smith, Brandon D. "The Identification of Jesus with YHWH in the Book of Revelation: A Brief Sketch." *Criswell Theological Review* 14, no. 1 (2016): 67–84.

Stevens, Gerald L., ed. *Essays on Revelation: Appropriating Yesterday's Apocalypse in Today's World.* Eugene, OR: Pickwick, 2011.

Swete, Henry Barclay, ed. *The Apocalypse of St John: The Greek Text.* London: Macmillan, 1906.

Thiselton, Anthony C. *The First Epistle to the Corinthians.* Grand Rapids: Eerdmans, 2013.

Thomas, Rodney Lawrence. *Magical Motifs in the Book of Revelation.* Library of New Testament Studies. London; New York: T & T Clark International, 2010.

Thompson, Leonard L. *The Book of Revelation: Apocalypse & Empire: Apocalypse and Empire.* Oxford; New York: Oxford University Press, 1990.

Waddell, Robby. *The Spirit of the Book of Revelation.* Journal of Pentecostal Theology Supplement Series 30, Blandford Forum. Dorset: Deo, 2006.

Whidden, Woodrow W. "Trinitarian Evidences in the Apocalypse." *Journal of the Adventist Theological Society* 11, no. 1–2 (2000): 248–60.

Whitaker, Robyn J. *Ekphrasis, Vision, and Persuasion in the Book of Revelation.* Tübingen: Mohr Siebeck, 2015.

Woodman, Simon. *The Book of Revelation.* London: SCM, 2008.

Wright, N. T. *Jesus and the Victory of God: Christian Origins and the Question of God: Vol. 2.* London: SPCK, 1996.

Yeago, David S. "The New Testament and Nicene Dogma: A Contribution to the Recovery of Theological Exegesis." *Pro Ecclesia* III, no. 2 (1994): 152–64.

CHAPTER 5

No Son, No Father

Athanasius and the Mutuality of Divine Personhood

PETER J. LEITHART

The recent evangelical brawl about the Trinity has focused on the notion, advanced by Bruce Ware and Wayne Grudem, that the Son is eternally "subordinate" to the Father. It has been a chaotic debate, and less than illuminating. Some critics treated Ware and Grudem as if they were Arians, teaching that the Son is ontologically inferior to the Father, a being somewhat less than fully divine. Both vehemently deny this charge. Ware and Grudem instead argue for a *taxis* of *equally* divine persons, and Grudem has produced an impressive catalog of reliable Protestant theologians who also talk of the eternal "subordination" of the Son.[1] If nothing else, he has demonstrated that his terminology is not novel.

Ware's views on eternal subordination take some odd twists. He has written that it is "not as though the Father is unable to work unilaterally, but rather, he chooses to involve the Son and the Spirit."[2] However it is understood, it is problematic if not worse. If Ware is speaking of God's *ad intra* activity, this

---

1. Wayne Grudem, "Another Thirteen Evangelical Theologians Who Affirm the Eternal Submission of the Son to the Father," *Reformation* 21, http://www.reformation21.org/blog/2016/06/another-thirteen-evangelical-t.php (accessed June 24, 2017).
2. Bruce Ware, *Father, Son and Holy Spirit: Relationships, Roles, Relevance* (Wheaton, IL: Crossway, 2005), 57.

does suggest something like the Arian view that the Father wills to have a Son and Spirit. I assume that Ware is speaking of God's works *ad extra* in creation, providence, and redemption, but even then his position runs contrary to the orthodox (especially Cappadocian) insistence that, in all God's works outside of himself, the Father initiates, the Son executes, and the Spirit perfects. A Father who *chooses* to deploy the Son and Spirit is a Father who chooses to be triune. That is *not* the God revealed in Jesus.

Ware has since clarified by calling his statement a "hypothetical":

> [S]ince the Father is omnipotent, there simply is nothing that could hinder him by nature from doing anything he would choose to do. Of course, this is purely hypothetical, and I acknowledge that my wording here could be made more precise. I did not intend to suggest that the Father ever would act in such an independent manner, or could act independently, strictly speaking, in light of the Trinitarian union of persons.[3]

This is less than satisfactory. The Father is *not*, even hypothetically, omnipotent in himself, because a Father is not and cannot be a Father "in himself." One cannot speculate on what the Father would be like if he had no Son, since without his Son he would not be Father. It is axiomatic to Athanasius, as we will see below: No Son, no Father. Once we start talking about a hypothetical sonless being, we are no longer talking about the Father of the Lord Jesus.

Critics of Ware and Grudem have not always recognized the crucial importance of this point. Some have charged that Ware and Grudem have turned Trinitarian theology into a manifesto for a complementarian view of sexual differences. Some argue, quite rightly, that the triune God is more than a social program, but others, fearing a slip into social Trinitarianism, have argued that Trinitarian theology has *no* implications for our understanding of human relationships.

Jesus would beg to differ. Jesus prays that his disciples would be one as the Father and Son are one (John 17:21). Father and Son are one in a unity of mutual indwelling ("perichoresis"). And Jesus prays that a unity of mutual indwelling would characterize the community of disciples. Jesus wants the church to be an earthly, human analogue of the communion of Father and Son. He wants us to be a communal expression of triune life. Paul would beg to differ too. 1 Corinthians 11:3 lays out three analogous relationships of headship: Christ : every man :: man : woman :: God : Christ. The relation of a man and a woman is analogous to the relationship of God to Christ. To argue that Paul refers to the relation of the Father to the *incarnate* Son implies that the

---

3.   Ware, "An Open Letter to Liam Goligher, Carl Trueman, and Todd Pruitt on Trinitarian Equality and Distinctions," *Biblical Reasoning*, https://secundumscripturas.com/2016/07/08/an-open-letter-to-liam-goligher-carl-trueman-and-todd-pruitt-ontrinitarian-equality-and-distinctions-guest-post-by-bruce-ware (accessed June 24, 2017).

incarnate Son's relation to the Father is something *other* than the *Son's* relation to the Father, and that implies that the incarnate Son is, in his Person,
someone *other* than the eternal Son. To defend a supposed Trinitarian orthodoxy, must we slide toward Christological heresy? One would hope not.

Some critics of Ware and Grudem have argued the dictum that the Trinity
has a "single will" is the touchstone of orthodoxy. I am dubious that this formula
functioned in this way during the patristic period, and the formula itself is
dogmatically indefensible.[4] At a basic level, it violates Gregory of Nazianzus's
claim, which became an axiom of pro-Nicene theology, that we cannot think
of the one without immediately thinking of the three, or of the three without
immediately thinking of the one. If we affirm that God has a single will, we must
at the same time consider how this single will might be differentiated among
three persons. In speaking of God's one will, we must talk, certainly in carefully
nuanced fashion, of a single will that, like *everything else* in the Trinity, exists
only as the one will of three distinct Persons. Unless the Father is capable of
saying "I Father" and the Son capable of "I Son," we are left with the conclusion
that the only "I" in the Trinity is the "I" of the one essence, a conclusion that is
hard to distinguish from modalism. The critics miss the essential mutuality of
the Persons as much as Ware and Grudem do.

One reason for this oversight is some critics' tendency to rely on a one-
dimensional, strictly creedal understanding of patristic orthodoxy. In what
follows, I draw on the work of Michel Rene Barnes to show the variety of positions without the scope of orthodox Trinitarian theology, and follow with a
more detailed examination of some dimensions of Athanasius's Trinitarian
teaching.[5] Substantively, I focus mainly on the various uses made of the key text
of 1 Corinthians 1:24, where Paul identifies Christ as the power and wisdom of
God.[6] This essay aims to demonstrate that a kind of mutual dependence among
the Persons is basic to Athanasius's Trinitarian theology, his account of simplicity, and his very understanding of what it means for God to be God.

Varieties of Patristic Trinitarianism

Michel Rene Barnes has uncovered three distinct theologies of divine
power operating during the Arian controversies of the fourth century.[7] While

---

4. See Khaled Anatolios, "Personhood, Communion, and Trinity in Some Patristic Texts," in *The Holy
    Trinity in the Life of the Church*, ed. Khaled Anatolios (Grand Rapids: Baker Academic, 2014), 147–64.
5. Much of the material on Athanasius is drawn, with additions, reformulations, and modifications,
    from my *Athanasius* (Grand Rapids: Baker, 2011).
6. I have unfortunately been unable to obtain a copy of William McFadden's Pontifical Gregorian
    University dissertation, *The Exegesis of 1 Cor. 1:24, "Christ the Power of God and the Wisdom of God"
    until the Arian Controversy* (1963).
7. Michel R. Barnes, "One Nature, One Power: Consensus Doctrine in Pro-Nicene Polemic," *Studia
    Patristica* 29 (1997): 205–23; more fully, Barnes, *The Power of God: ΔΥΝΑΜΙΣ in Gregory of Nyssa's
    Trinitarian Theology* (Washington, DC: CUA Press, 2001).

Barnes focuses attention on the notion of "power," my interest is in examining how these theologies express the relationship between the Father and Son.

According to fourth-century Arians like Asterius, as well as non-Nicene theologians like Eusebius of Caesarea, there is a power immanent in God that is expressed or imaged in a second power, the Son. This position has roots in Origen, who wrote that "the will of God comes itself to be a power of God. There comes into existence, therefore, another power, subsisting in its own proper nature . . . a kind of breath of the first and unbegotten power of God."[8] According to Athanasius's summary, the "Sophist Asterius" held a similar position. Asterius made much of the grammatical difference between "Christ, of God or the Wisdom of God" and "God's power and God's wisdom." Asterius took from this that Paul teaches that God possesses a "proper power" that is "natural to him, and co-existent in him ingenerately," a power distinct from Christ. This "proper power" was "generative" of Christ and, as generated, created the world, but not identical to Christ. Asterius quoted Romans 1, where Paul speaks of God's "power and Godhead," claiming that "no one would say that the Godhead there mentioned was Christ, but the Father himself." And the same should be true in 1 Corinthians 1:24. Asterius argues further that there are multiple wisdoms and powers, of which Christ is the chief:

> However His eternal power and wisdom, which truth argues to be without beginning and ingenerate, the same must surely be one. For there are many wisdoms which are one by one created by him, of whom Christ is the first-born and only-begotten; all however equally depend on their Possessor. And all the powers are rightly called His who created and uses them: —as the Prophet says that the locust, which came to be a divine punishment of human sins, was called by God himself not only a power, but a great power; and blessed David in most of the Psalms invites, not the Angels alone, but the Powers to praise God.[9]

Asterius operates within an interior/exterior, ungenerate/generate framework. God (or the Father) has an interior wisdom and power, but that is *not* what Paul identifies with Christ in 1 Corinthians 1:24. Rather, Paul identifies Christ with the begotten/generate wisdom and power that come out from God. Asterius makes his case exegetically by pointing out that Paul does not use the definite article with power or wisdom. Christ is not *the* wisdom or *the* power, but the chief of the powers (or wisdoms) generated by God. On this conception, the Father has "his own" proper wisdom and power. Asterius would agree with Ware that the Father can act on his own power if he so chooses.

Barnes labels a second position "pro-Nicene." It maintains the Nicene formula that the Father and Son are 'one substance' and identifies the power

---

8. Origen, *On First Principles* 1.2.9, quoted in Barnes, "One Nature," 211.
9. *Discourses against the Arians* 2.37. Through the remainder of this paper, I cite the Discourses within the text.

(and wisdom) of God as power and wisdom shared by the three Persons. Because there is one nature, there is one power and one wisdom. With roots in the teaching of Tertullian, this position is found in the work of Hilary, Ambrose, Gregory of Nyssa, and Augustine.

Augustine develops his position explicitly in conversation with 1 Corinthians 1:24. He spends two books of *de Trinitate* trying to figure out what Paul means.[10] In Book 6, he tries out the notion that the Father's power and wisdom are simply the power and wisdom that he begets as Son, so that the Father is wise only by virtue of his begotten wisdom, powerful by virtue of begotten power, great by virtue of begotten greatness, etc. In general, he tries out the notion that *all* terms we use to describe God's attributes are relational, inscribed within the Father's begetting of the Son.

Though he finds biblical support for such a view in 1 Corinthians, he rejects this solution in the following book, largely because it seems to violate the axiom of divine simplicity. Being God and being great are not different for God; he is simple. If the Father is great by virtue of the greatness that he begets, then he is God by virtue of the Son, but that would mean that the Father begets his own Godness. Since being God and being *per se* are the same for God, then, on the theory Augustine explored in Book 6, the Father would *be* by virtue of begetting the Son. The Father not only begets his own Godness, but begets his own being, giving birth to his own existence. That, Augustine concludes, is absurd. How, Augustine demands, could the Father do this without having Godness, power, wisdom, being in himself, *originally*, logically though not temporally prior to his begetting? He must *have* it to give it. Finding the strong reading of 1 Corinthians 1:24 absurd, Augustine insists that the Father must have some form of power, wisdom, and all other attributes in himself in order to generate the generated power and wisdom that is the Son. Augustine, like Asterius, ends up with a kind of double-power, double-wisdom theory. God possesses an internal wisdom and power that is the source of the Son who is his wisdom and power.

These are penetrating arguments, but there are conundrums in every direction. Augustine says that "the Father is powerful" is a statement about the *esse* of the Father, rather than a statement *ad Filium relative*. In making that distinction, Augustine seems to threaten simplicity, which he is trying to protect, from another direction. To protect simplicity, he insists that being-God is identical to being-powerful, being-wise, being-great, being-good. But to protect this identity, he must distinguish the Father's being from the Father's being-*Father*. In *himself*, in his substance, the Father is great, wise, powerful; those are descriptions of his being *per se*, rather than descriptions of him as Father. Speaking of the Father's being-wise, powerful, great is not the same as speaking of the Father's being-Father. The former attributes are attributes that the Father has by virtue of divine nature, the latter a personal

---

10.   A lively recent translation is that of Edmund Hill, *The Trinity* (New York: New City Press, 1991).

identification he has only by virtue of his relation to the Son. Apparently in defiance of simplicity, Augustine implies that "being-Father" is *not* identical to the Father's being-God, *not* identical to his being.

Everything, Augustine argues, that is something in relation to another must also be something additional to that relation (*omnis essentia quae relative dicitur est etiam aliquid excepto relativo*). He uses created examples to illustrate, and concludes that "if the Father is not also something with reference to himself, there is absolutely nothing there to be talked of with reference to something else." But that solves a problem at one end only to raise another: How can the *Father* be something *other* than what he is in relation to the Son? Father, as Augustine has said, is a relative term, and it would seem that we cannot even rationally ask, Who or what is the Father *aside from* the relation to the Son? That way lies an abyss, for we cannot help but ask who or what the Father might be when he is not Father, and the answer will be that we simply do not have any idea.

Augustine would answer these queries by appealing again to his distinction between relational and substantive terms. Augustine knows that the Father cannot be Father except by having a Son. He knows that "Father" is a relational term, not a substance term (Books 2–4 are devoted to making this essential anti-Arian argument). Because he is the first Person of the Godhead, the Father is good, just, loving, holy; he is also inherently Father, since, though "Father" is a relational term, he always has a Son. But the way Augustine finally interprets 1 Corinthians 1:24 suggests that the Father has attributes that are *more* proper and natural than the Son, more *intrinsic* to the being of the Father than his being Father, since they are attributes of divine nature itself.[11]

Not only is this theologically questionable, but its proximity to the position of Asterius is worrying. Augustine the pro-Nicene and Asterius the Arian both hold that there is a wisdom and power interior to the Father that is begotten as the Son. Both operate with the same interior-exterior framework. The difference—and it is a radical one, the difference between heresy and orthodoxy—is that Augustine believes that the Father has *always* had his Son, with whom he eternally shares the wisdom and power and other attributes of divine nature. But it is not clear that Augustine has recognized how radically the Trinity alters our conceptions of divine nature and being itself.[12]

---

11. Perhaps this is where the largely misguided criticisms leveled against Augustine hit home, the criticism that he privileges the one essence over the persons. Saying that the Father has "his own" wisdom is not exactly "privileging" unity over plurality, but Augustine leaves open the possibility that the Father has some surplus Godness left over that is not exhaustively poured out in the Son, that is not wholly expressed in his being Father. We can see how the pressure of this argument led Thomas and others to conclude that the Persons simply are their relations, top-to-bottom, the Father Father all the way down, the Son simply and sheerly Son.

12. According to Barnes, Augustine holds that God's power and wisdom are one because they are identical with divine nature, which is one. Ambrose sometimes articulates a similar position. In Barnes's

Augustine's position also fails to take Paul's claim in 1 Corinthians 1:24 at face value. On his reading, Christ is *not* the wisdom and power of God, but receives wisdom and power that the Father possesses in himself. Athanasius offers an alternative view, which Barnes describes as the "Nicene position," that both takes Paul at his word and avoids some of the conundrums of the other positions. Needless to say, it comes with certain conundrums of its own.

Athanasius

Athanasius is no social Trinitarian. Throughout his writings, Athanasius sees Trinitarian theology as simply an elaboration of the ancient confession of the One God. Athanasius confesses that "God is One and Only and First," and yet insists that this is not said to the denigration of the Son. The Son too is "in that One, and First and Only, as being of that One and Only and First the Only Word and Wisdom and Radiance. And he too is the First, as the Fullness of the Godhead (*pleroma tes tou protou kai monou theotetos*) of the First and Only, being whole and full God. This then is not said on his account, but to deny that there is other such as the Father and his Word" (*Discourses* 3.23.6). When Scripture affirms that God is One, it is not a denial of the triad within God, but rather a statement about the true God and a condemnation of all false gods. Since the Son is himself the truth, the Son is not excluded along with idols. When the Scripture records the Lord's "I only," it includes the Son (*hen to mono kai ho tou monou semainetai logos*; *Discourses* 3.24.9). Jesus's claim that "I and the Father are One" (John 17) asserts that the Son is "proper and like the Father's essence"; the Son is not "foreign" to the essence but of the same essence with the Father (*Discourses* 3.25.17). God is one *as Trinity*. Triunity is the shape of the oneness of the living God.

For Athanasius, this means that one cannot, and ought not, develop an understanding of the Father without considering the Son, or of the Son without

---

summary, "Ambrose affirms that neither Word nor Power nor Wisdom can be separated from God the Father because the divine substance is one. . . . The power of one divine person is not increased by the power of another, Ambrose argues, because there are not two powers but one; not two godheads but one. The power of each person of the trinity turns out to be the same, and so their divine nature is the same" (Barnes, "One Power," 218). If Augustine's inner/outer shares a structure with Arianism, the "one power, one nature" position shares structural commonalities with modalism. It is not modalist, but it might blur distinctions among the Persons. After all, if power and wisdom are simply "the same" in the Father and Son, what difference do the Personal distinctions make? It seems that "Father" and "Son" are names, somewhat external labels, for a divine nature that, behind the mask, is wholly indistinguishable, undifferentiated. If one accepts Augustine's argument that the Father has "his own" power and wisdom that are not identical to the Son, one might affirm the reality of the Personal distinctions this way: Perhaps the attributes are "inflected" Personally, such that the Father's power and wisdom is paternal power and wisdom, the Son's filial, the Spirit's Spiritual. The Father's power is unbegotten power, the Son's power is begotten power, the Spirit's is proceeding power. That works within the "one power/wisdom, one nature" paradigm, but so far as I am aware, it is rarely pursued. It seems that something like this is necessary if we want to avoid slippage into modalism.

the Father.[13] To conceive the Father as Father, one must conceive of the Son; to conceive the begotten Son, one must conceive the begetting Father. As John Behr indicates, Athanasius does not formulate a general "immanent Trinitarian theology" which is then "applied" to the economy. his reflections on the intimate relations of the immanent Trinity arise from the confession that Jesus is the eternal Word of the Father. Attempting to isolate a "patrology" or a "Christology" distorts Athanasius's approach, just as it is a distortion to separate Athanasius's teaching on God from his teaching about God's works in creating and, especially, in redeeming humanity. For Athanasius, meditating on the Father, on Christ, on incarnation, on deification is meditation on one multifaceted reality.

The density of Athanasius's treatment of these themes is nicely captured by his paraphrase of Jesus's prayer in John 17. Jesus asks his Father, in effect, "whence is this their perfecting, but that I, Your Word, having borne their body, and become man, have perfected the work, which You gave Me, O Father?," and answers that "the work is perfected, because men, redeemed from sin, no longer remain dead; but being deified, have in each other, by looking at Me, the bond of charity" (*Discourses* 3.23). According to Athanasius, Jesus does his work of perfecting, *telos*-ing, humanity so that humanity reaches its destined end. He "completes" the work, and in so doing "completes" his disciples. This perfection is linked with redemption from sin and death, but also to deification. Man, made in the image of God, was created to be deified, and the contingency of sin and death does not cause God to deviate from that purpose. Deification is closely connected with resurrection, overcoming death. God cannot die, by nature, and, in part, our deification is a participation by grace in the immortality he has by nature.

This perfecting of the human race, though, depends on the incarnation. It is because the Word has borne the body and become man that he can perfect men. he became incarnate to die in the flesh, to overcome death, to grant human beings a share in his own power and wisdom and knowledge and deathless joy. Through the Son, especially in the Son's unity with the Father, believers have a paradigm of charity. And not merely a paradigm: For Athanasius, the contemplative gaze is a transforming gaze. When Jesus says that his disciples will live "by looking at Me," he is not speaking of examining a model, which one then strives to conform to. Conformity comes through the transforming impact of the gaze itself. By looking at Jesus, contemplating his unity with the Father, disciples are bound in charity with one another. When we gaze at the archetype, the archetype impresses himself on us. Even here, when Athanasius is reaching mystical heights, the polemic against the Arians is just below the surface. Only God can make us gods. If the Son brings us to final glory, he must himself *be* eternally glory.

---

13. In much of the later tradition, especially post-Reformation, the doctrine of the Trinity was defended by establishing the deity of each person individually. Scripture teaches that the Father is God, that the Son is God, and that the Spirit is God. There must then be three subsistences or persons in the one God.

Much of Athanasius's argument against the Arians turns on definitions of "Father" and "Son." Human sons are born of the nature and essence of their fathers, not made from external material. So too with divine sonship. Arians emphasized the temporal priority of parents over children, but Athanasius stresses the community of essence. "Those who ask of parents, and say, 'Had you a son before you begot him?' should add, 'And if you had a son, did you purchase him from without as a house or any other possession.' And then you would be answered, 'He is not from without, but from myself.'" There is a difference between possessions and children: "things which are from without are possessions, and pass from one to another; but my son is from me, proper and similar to my essence, not become mine from another, but begotten of me." Human sonship is a perichoretic reality, and a paradigm of divine life. A human father can say, "I too am wholly in him, while I remain myself what I am," a reflection of the relation of the Father with his Son. Thus, "though the parent be distinct in time, as being man, who himself has come to be in time, yet he too would have had his child ever coexistent with him, but that his nature was a restraint and made it impossible" (*Discourses* 1.8.26). There are discontinuities between divine and human begetting, but Athanasius stresses the analogy: "granting the parent had not a son before his begetting, still, after having him, he had him, not as external or as foreign, but as from himself, and proper to his essence and his exact image, so that the former is beheld in the latter, and the latter is contemplated in the former" (*Discourses* 1.8.26).

In other words, the Son is Son by nature and not will (*Discourses* 3.30.59–60).[14] But Athanasius's argument for this is subtle. He claims that the Son cannot be made by will because he himself *is* the good pleasure and will of the Father. "If," Athanasius argues, "in whom he makes, in him also is the will, and in Christ is the pleasure of the Father, how can he, as others, come into being by will and pleasure?" If the Son was not before he was begotten, and if, as Athanasius argues, this can only be understood as a temporal statement, then God willed and determined to beget and to create before the Son was. That is nonsense, since the Son is the Word, and how can God deliberate about anything when he is yet wordless? The Son is the Father's will, and how can the Father will to beget his own will? As Athanasius puts it, planning "goes before things which once were not, as in the case of all creatures. But if the Word is the Framer of the creatures, and he coexists with the Father, how can his counsel precede the Everlasting as if he were not? For if counsel precedes, how through him are all things? For rather he too, as one among others is by will begotten to be

---

14. On the debate about will, see C. Stead, "The Freedom of the Will and the Arian Controversy," in *Platonismus und Christentum: Festschrift fur Heinrich Dorrie*, eds. H.-D. Blume and F. Mann (Munster: Aschendoff, 1983), 245–57. Anatolios (*Coherence*, 121) nicely points out that the issue is not really about the origination (*a quo*) but the termination (*ad quem*) of creation. Being and will are one in God, but this does not mean that being and the *things willed* are one.

a Son, as we too were made sons by the Word of Truth; and it rests, as was said, to seek another Word, through whom he too has come to be, and was begotten together with all things, which were according to God's pleasure" (*Discourses* 3.30.61). Since everything is done by the counsel of the Father with his will, there can be no counsel except the Son. The Son is the "living counsel" of the Father, as well as "power, and Framer of the things which seemed good to the Father." The Son is the "good pleasure of the Father" (*Discourses* 3.30.63), and the "living will" (*zosa boule*) of the Father (*Discourses* 2.14.2). The Son is not made by the good pleasure of God, but is the "object of the Father's pleasure" just as surely as the Father is the "object of the Son's love, pleasure, and honor" (*Discourses* 3.30.66).

Throughout this discussion, Athanasius relies heavily on 1 Corinthians 1:24, which he takes quite straightforwardly. The Father does have "his own" wisdom, word, and power, but that proper (*idios*) wisdom of the Father is not an immanent, unbegotten wisdom. Rather, "his own" wisdom and power *is* the Son himself, a hypostatic word and wisdom, the word and wisdom that is the Father's image. On this basis, he charges that the Arian denial of the Son's eternal nature is a denial of the Father. If the Son is not eternal, then the Father (or the unoriginate) was once without his word and wisdom. Arians insult the Father by implying that he was once fruitless, sonless, and therefore both foolish and mute.

As some scholars have pointed out, it is true that this criticism depends on Athanasius's reading of 1 Corinthians 1:24, but in his defense, Athanasius is merely repeating what Paul says. The logic of his position is:

1. God cannot be without his power and wisdom.
2. Paul identifies this power and wisdom with the Son. "Power" and "Wisdom" are, like "Word," names of the Son.
3. Therefore the Father must never have existed without the Son. To say otherwise is to say the Father was once foolish, mute, and impotent.

This is a direct and conscious assault on the "double" framework shared by the Arian Asterius and the orthodox Augustine. Athanasius firmly denies that the Father has "his own" word or will that, prior to the Son, is the source of the generated word or will. Rather, there is no word or will but the One begotten, who is the Son. On Asterius's view, "there are two 'Wisdoms,' one which is proper to God and exists together with him, and [the other] the Son who has been brought into this Wisdom; only by participating in this Wisdom is the Son called Wisdom and Word. Wisdom came into existence though Wisdom, by the will of the God who is wise" (*Discourses* 1). For Athanasius, this is an error because it implies that the Son is wise by participation in a more original wisdom, in the same way that creatures are capable of being wise.

Barnes argues that Athanasius struggles to explain how the Son's possession of wisdom differs from wisdom by participation. He often uses "radiance" imagery, drawn from Hebrews 1:3: The radiance of a light source is not light by participation in the light, but is an inescapable supplement to the light source. Athanasius does not always describe this source-supplement relation in ontological terms, and so risks offering an equivocal, quasi-subordinationist explanation. In his *On the Synods*, however, Athanasius makes the ontological point clearly:

> The Son is not such [that is, a Son] by participation, but, while all things origi-
> nated have by participation the grace of God, [the Son] is the Father's Wisdom
> and Word of which all things partake, it follows that He, being the deifying and
> enlightening power of the Father, in which all things are deified and quickened,
> is not alien in essence from the Father but coessential. For by partaking of him,
> we partake of the Father; because the Word is the Father's own.[15]

On Athanasius's argument, then, the Father truly *is* nothing without the Son. He certainly is not God without the Son, since God must be wise and powerful. Contrary to Augustine, Athanasius does affirm that the being of the Father depends on the generation of the Son. Of course, since the Son is begotten of the Father, the Son is nothing without the Father either. Athanasius insists, further, that the Father never has been without the Son, who is his own Word, "proper" to his essence, so the Father has never been without his power, wisdom, goodness, being. God is radically dependent *ad intra*. As a human being in time, I was before I was a father; I *am* apart from at least some of my human relations; I am more than my fatherhood. The heavenly Father *is not* before or apart from being Father; the Person Paul calls "God" isn't God except as he is Father of the Son.

In a direct response to Asterius, Athanasius links 1 Corinthians 1:24 with Romans 1:18–20, arguing that the power and Godhead that is seen in the creation *is* the Son (*Discourses* 1.4.12: *idios autou dunamis kai theiotes, hina ton uion semane*). Since the Son is *idios* to the Father, he is as "proper" to the Father as any of the Father's "attributes." Augustine agrees that there is not the slightest sliver of a gap between the Father and Son, just as he would not allow the slightest sliver of space between the Father and his attributes. But for Athanasius, those two statements are identical: there is not the slightest sliver of a gap between the Father and his attributes *because* the Father has all that he has *in the Son*, who is proper to his essence. Augustine believes as strongly as Athanasius in an eternal radiance from the light of the Father. Yet, Augustine is still capable of *conceiving* an unsupplemented origin: a Father "in himself" having attributes "in himself," the light without radiance, the fountain without the stream. Augustine leaves a small crack open for thinking that the Father has something that is "his own," something that appears more intimate and intrinsic to his being than the Son. Athanasius says that

---

15.   Quoted in Barnes, *Power of God*, 147–48.

the Scriptures entail the conclusion that *"the Son is the Father's All*; and nothing was in the Father before the Word" (*Discourses* 3.30.67). Trinitarian theology is not a gloss on theology per se. It is theology proper. No Son, no Father. No Son, indeed, no *God*.

From this, it is evident that Athanasius is as committed to the axiom of simplicity as Augustine. It is equally evident that Athanasius has modified simplicity in accord with Paul's claims about the Son as the wisdom, power, and Godhead of God. For Athanasius as for Augustine, God *is* his attributes, but Athanasius makes it clearer that the God who is his attributes is the Father, Son, and Spirit. And Athanasius makes it clear that simplicity has to be construed within a triune frame. One ought not even ask, Is the *Father*, considered in himself, identical to his attributes? The question itself is absurd, and admits of no truthful answer. The question cannot be answered affirmatively, since the Father does not exist at all except as Father of the Son. He is only conceivable as one who cannot be "considered in himself." The question cannot be answered negatively either, since, by the axiom of simplicity, we cannot affirm that the Father is different from his power and wisdom. We can ask and answer questions of simplicity properly only with Trinitarian elaboration. God is his power because the Father has proper power of his own that *is* the Son begotten by the Spirit. God is identical to his wisdom because the Father has eternally begotten a Son through the Spirit, a Son who *is* his word and wisdom.

Conclusion

Athanasius's use of 1 Corinthians 1:24 highlights a central danger in contemporary Evangelical talk of intra-Trinitarian "hierarchy": Its uni-directionality obscures the mutuality and dynamism of the relations among the Persons. Relations constitute each Person as the Person he is, and so mutual relations constitute the Trinity as Trinity. Mutuality could not be more fundamental to the life and being of God. Suppose, for the sake of argument, that the Father, as "first" Person, has *some* sort of primacy ("made of none; neither created, nor begotten," as the Athanasian Creed puts it). Even if we accept that "primacy" is a felicitous formula, the Father's precedence is immediately destabilized, because the Father is "first" only by begetting a "second." He is source only because there is a supplement.

A Sonless Father is as impossible as a Fatherless Son. As Athanasius insisted, if we deny the Son we deny the Father: No Son, no Father. Only by having a Son is the Father *eternally* Father, as opposed to a faceless Somesuch who *becomes* Father. The personal identity of the Father is as eternally "dependent" on the Son's sonship as the Son's identity as Son is eternally "dependent" on the Father's begetting. Whatever "hierarchy" exists within the Trinity has a self-cancelling quality, a quality that reverberates in human experience. As any attentive parent will tell you, the inversion of hierarchy is the arc of family history: long before children become parents themselves, they remake their parents. Wordsworth was talking about something else, but his line captures the point: "the [C]hild is father of the [M]an."

In the economy, the eternal mutuality among the Persons manifests itself in a dynamic mutual glorification. "Glorify thy Son together with Thyself, Father," Jesus prays, "with the glory which I had with Thee before the world was" (John 17:5). Jesus asks the Father to glorify him with pre-creation glory, now as God-*man*, Logos-made-*flesh*. But Jesus prays for the Father to glorify him so that "the Son may glorify Thee" (17:1). Given the scriptural connection between the Spirit and glory, we may say that, in the economy, the Father and Son glorify one another in and by the Spirit. If the Father is glorious, it is with the glory by which the Son glorifies him; if the Son is glorified, it is because the Father has glorified him in the Spirit. There is not even a slightest sliver of a crack of an opening to begin speculating about whether each has glory "in himself." Asking such "in himself" questions sets our theology askew from the get-go. Athanasius poses the radical claim that a sonless God cannot be *God*, since such a God would be fruitless, barren, foolish, impotent, and wordless.

The consequences are soul-altering. On any account of Trinity, the Son *who is fully divine* receives from the Father, which means that there is such a thing as *divine* receptivity. God has and bestows glory, but when that truth is refracted Trinitarianly, we discern that God has, bestows, *and receives* glory. If we may, with caution, introduce "subordination" into our account of the immanent Trinity, there is such a thing as *divine* subordination, and we may follow Barth in concluding that *humility* is a divine attribute. Current debates aside, it is hard to see how we can say anything less, once we affirm that Jesus reveals the Father: If you have seen Me, he tells Philip, you have seen the Father, because the Son does nothing except what he sees the Father doing. If the Son humbles himself, it can only be because he has taken cues from his Father (John 5).

The difference between the triune God and the multiple gods of polytheism is not mathematical. Trinitarian theology does not distribute standard-issue Unitarian attributes among three divine persons. Christians worship and declare a God unlike any God human beings have or could conceive. As N. T. Wright has said, to say that Jesus of Nazareth is God is to say something remarkable about Jesus. It is also to make an astonishing claim about God. It's not merely that Jesus is God or Godlike. The momentous truth is that God is like Jesus. The momentous truth is that the Father is Father by begetting a Son, powerful by the eternal power he generates, wise by a wisdom that is at once his own and another.

Bibliography

Anatolios, Khaled. "Personhood, Communion, and Trinity in Some Patristic Texts." In *The Holy Trinity in the Life of the Church*, edited by Khaled Anatolios, 147–64. Grand Rapids: Baker Academic, 2014.

_____. *Athanasius: The Coherence of His Thought*. London: Routledge, 1998.

Barnes, Michel R. "One Nature, One Power: Consensus Doctrine in Pro-Nicene Polemic." *Studia Patristica* 29 (1997): 205–23.

_____. *The Power of God: ΔYNAMIΣ in Gregory of Nyssa's Trinitarian Theology*. Washington, DC: CUA Press, 2001.

Hill, Edmund. *The Trinity*. New York: New City Press, 1991 Stead, Christopher. "The Freedom of the Will and the Arian Controversy." In *Platonismus und Christentum: Festschrift fur Heinrich Dorrie*, edited by H. D. Blume and F. Mann, 245–57. Munster: Aschendoff, 1983.

Leithart, Peter J. *Athanasius*. Grand Rapids: Baker, 2011.

Ware, Bruce. *Father, Son, and Holy Spirit: Relationships, Roles, Relevance*. Wheaton, IL: Crossway, 2005.

CHAPTER 6

Beholding the Beholder

Precision and Mystery
in Gregory of Nyssa's *Ad Ablabium*

AMY BROWN HUGHES

This essay focuses on Gregory of Nyssa's specific contribution to the Trinitarian speaking of God that characterized the thought of Nicene Cappadocians such as Gregory of Nazianzus and Basil of Caesarea. Gregory played an important role in the establishment of theological language and thought that locates the unity at the level of being while preserving the distinction of the Trinity from all other being. During the volatile period of Trinitarian deliberation that was the late fourth century, the overarching question for Gregory was how to conceive of God as one undivided essence as well as three distinct persons. His theological method allows for a speaking of God that both resists hierarchical notions of God that lead to the subordination of the Son and the Holy Spirit and provides the church with a meaningful way to speak of God.

Modern theology has had ample opportunity in recent years to rethink, reimagine, and reevaluate received Trinitarian tradition. Within that larger frame, evangelical theology is experiencing a particular moment of refinement in our understanding of the Trinity. At stake in the discussion of speaking of God is certainly a concern for proper terminology and the theological undergirding of Trinitarian discourse; but also the weighty question of how humans relate to this God. How we speak of God shapes the human experience of God. Gregory of Nyssa's articulation of the economic and the imma-

nent Trinity buys him the ability to speak of God with a kind of specificity
and diversity that we aim for but are often unable to attain. In works like
Ad Ablabium, we see Gregory workshop his ideas about unity and distinction—what works, what does not.[1] He tackles difficult ideas with nuance and
elegance, distinguishing himself as a synthetic thinker who is able to speak
with precision while also reveling in mystery.

As theologian, philosopher, and bishop, Gregory seamlessly weaves
together the confessional with learned philosophical accuracy. Speaking of
God is a science or art, but it is also a practice. His project in *Ad Ablabium* is
thus a deeply theological one. Recent work on *Ad Ablabium* as well as other
works by Gregory exhibits a shift in scholarship that better reflects the Nyssian
bishop's distinctive approach to theology and articulates his contributions in
all of their richness and fondness for paradox.[2] In this essay I will focus on
Ad Ablabium in particular because of its vast influence and its specific contribution to the methodology of speaking of God. *Ad Ablabium* is also distinct
from other works by Gregory because he approaches unity and distinction
in a "consciously non-philosophical, popular way."[3] However, Sarah Coakley's admonition that this short treatise has a "stranglehold" on treatments
of Gregory's Trinitarian thought is well taken.[4] Therefore, I will draw upon
other works by Gregory to highlight out the rich colors that mark the theological landscape of his Trinitarian thought, such as *Contra Eunomium, Ad
Petrum*, and *In illud: Tunc et ipse filius*.

My primary aim is to show that Gregory's Trinitarian paradigm correctly
understood lays a foundation for speaking of God that helps address the

1. Gregory of Nyssa, *Ad Ablabium quod non sint tres dei,* in *Gregorii Nysseni Opera,* ed. F. Mueller
(GNO) 3.1 (Leiden: Brill, 1958), 37–57, Thesaurus Linguae Graecae Digital Library, http://stephanus.
tlg.uci.edu.proxy.gordonconwell.edu/Iris/inst/csearch.jsp#doc=tlg&aid=2017&wid=003&q=GRE
GORIUS%20NYSSENUS&dt=list&st=all&per=50 (accessed October 2016); for a translation see
William G. Rusch, trans., "Gregory of Nyssa's Concerning We Should Not Think of Saying That There
Are Not Three Gods: *To Ablabius* in *The Trinitarian Controversy,* Sources of Early Christian Thought
(Philadelphia: Fortress, 1980), 149–61.

2. For a recent reception history that covers key arenas of scholarship on Gregory of Nyssa, see
Morwenna Ludlow, *Gregory of Nyssa, Ancient and (Post)Modern* (Oxford: Oxford University
Press, 2007). Ludlow helpfully elucidates why there is such a variety of interpretations of Gregory's
Trinitarian theology.

3. Johannes Zachhuber, *Human Nature in Gregory of Nyssa: Philosophical Background and Theological
Significance* (Leiden: Brill, 2014), 114. This is not to diminish the contribution of this letter, however.
As Lenka Karfíková notes, *Ad Ablabium* represents a synthesis of many of the themes of Gregory's
Trinitarian theology we find in his other works. While we cannot be certain, this suggests a later date
for its composition, perhaps sometime near the end of the 380s ("*Ad Ablabium, quod non sint tres
Dei,*" in *Gregory of Nyssa: The Minor Treatises on Trinitarian Theology and Apollinarism, Proceedings
of the 11th International Colloquium on Gregory of Nyssa [Tübingen, 17–20 September 2008],* ed.
Volker Henning Drecoll and Margitta Berghaus, *Supplements to Vigiliae Christianae* 106 [Leiden:
Brill, 2011], 132).

4. Sarah Coakley, "Introduction—Gender, Trinitarian Analogies, and the Pedagogy of *The Song,*" in *Re-
Thinking Gregory of Nyssa,* ed. Sarah Coakley (Oxford: Blackwell, 2003), 3.

perennial problem that is the automatic assignment of hierarchical notions
to God. While Gregory's audience and challenges were different, his approach
is coherent, cohesive, and remarkably beautiful. Gregory's love for God and
concern for the church that courses through his work offers us much more
than just theological boundaries that mark orthodoxy from heresy. For Gregory, we can and must speak of God. In this essay I will examine Gregory's
articulation of the economic and the immanent Trinity, specifically how
Gregory's Trinitarian theology speaks of distinction without subordination.
This will lead to a consideration of Gregory's understanding of the diversity
of names for God, and, finally, how apophaticism, as a theological and confessional method, lays out a map of how then to speak of God.

On Communion and Submission:
Gregory of Nyssa and the Trinity

Packaged in Gregory's response to Ablabius is a dizzying combination of
conceptions of God's nature, how God relates to the world, and then, more
specifically, how a triune God relates and operates. A central contribution of
the Cappadocians was the innovation—and it was a true innovation—that
one could speak of God in distinction without compromising the simple
divine essence.[5] In addition, for Gregory there is no "starting from" the unity
or from distinction in our speech about God; God is a unity and is known
in distinction.[6] Explaining how to go about this kind of speech was one of
Gregory's central themes that we find throughout many of his works.

In *Ad Ablabium*, Gregory's challenge is to explain how Christians can
hold to a compelling articulation of unity and distinction in the Trinity and
not fall into tritheism or some version of Arianism. He begins with what does
not work: explaining unity and distinction in the Trinity via comparison with
three men (Peter, James, and John) who share a common human nature but
who are distinct persons.[7] The collections of properties that are individuals
(Peter, James, and John) can be counted, but there is no unity in activity that
human nature holds in common, unlike the Trinity.[8] Gregory bemoans the

---

5. According to Zachhuber, crediting the Cappadocians with true originality is valid because "it is one
   thing to use *hupostasis* for the Trinitarian Person, quite another, to give it the particular definition it
   received in the Cappadocians' writings" (*Human Nature in Gregory of Nyssa*, 57).
6. See Sarah Coakley, *God, Sexuality, and the Self: An Essay "On the Trinity"* (Cambridge: Cambridge
   University Press, 2013), 268–73 for a discussion of the interpretive issues resulting from Théodore
   de Régnon's persistent and misleading construct from the late nineteenth century that the East
   "starts from the three and moves to the One" while the West "starts from the One and moves to the
   three" ('Etudes de *théologie positive sur la Sainte Trinité*, 4 vols. [Paris: Victor Retaux, 1892–1898],
   1:428–35). As Coakley notes, de Régnon himself would say that this contrast did not apply to the
   Cappadocians and Augustine.
7. Gregory of Nyssa, *Ad Abl.* 38.7–18.
8. Lucian Turcescu notes that Gregory sees each person as a "unique collection of properties that in
   themselves are not unique" (*Gregory of Nyssa and the Concept of Divine Persons* [Oxford: Oxford
   University Press, 2005], 65).

customary speech that counts human individuals by referring to the problematic plurality "many human natures" that makes expressing the inability to
enumerate natures—divine or otherwise—more difficult.[9] Of course, Gregory
recognizes that his huffing at grammatical bad habits will get him nowhere,
so he steps off his semantic soapbox and declares that, however we speak of
humanity, such sloppiness cannot invade speech with reference to the divine
nature.[10] Obviously, appealing to human nature or human persons to speak of
divinity is insufficient as neither the unity of human nature nor the distinction of persons is comparable to the divine nature and persons.

How, then, can we even begin to speak about the unity of the divine
nature? For Gregory, in speaking of God we find ourselves at the edge of our
finitude, a hard boundary marked by *diastema*, that is, temporality.[11] This
boundary between Creator and creation preserves the transcendence of God,
and only God incarnate can traverse that "barrier which separates uncreated
nature from created being."[12] Strikingly, Gregory does not see butting up to
this limitation as stricture but an indication of proper, creaturely self-knowl-
edge. We have great freedom as diastemic creatures to consider who God is
and to speak of God but we can never cross that boundary and access the
adiastemic; this traversal is not the purview of the created order.

Since adiastemic divine nature does not admit division and is not circum-
scribable how, then, do we speak of distinction of the divine persons? In *Ad
Ablabium* Gregory speaks of hypostatic difference according to "relations of
origin," that is, the Father who is "the cause" (*to aition*), the Son who is "from
the cause" (*ek tou aitiou*) or "directly from the first" (*prosechōs ek tou prōtou*),
and the Holy Spirit who is "by that which is directly from the first" (*dia tou
prōsechōs ek tou prōtou*).[13] He therefore uses causal language to express distinct
relations according to origin without compromising unity of the divine nature
or operation. For Gregory, the terms "caused" or "uncaused," or "unbegotten"

---

9.   Gregory of Nyssa, *Ad Abl.* 40.5–9.
10. Gregory of Nyssa, *Ad Abl.* 41.12–42.3. As some have noted, Gregory's argument is not completely
     convincing or consistent. See Turcescu, *Gregory of Nyssa*, 66 and Zachhuber, *Human Nature in
     Gregory of Nyssa*, 118.
11. According to Vladimir Cvetkovic, Gregory's arguments with the Anomeans precipitated his
     articulation of the "adiastemic" nature of God, and his contribution to the debate was distinctive
     ("St Gregory's Argument Concerning the Lack of ΔΙΑΣΤΗΜΑ in the Divine Activities from *Ad
     Ablabium*," in Drecoll and Berghaus, eds., *Gregory of Nyssa: The Minor Treatises*, 369–82).
12. Gregory of Nyssa, *Contra Eunomium* 2.67, "Gregory, Bishop of Nyssa: The Second Book Against
     Eunomius," trans. Stuart George Hall, in *Gregory of Nyssa, Contra Eunomium II: An English Version
     with Supporting Studies: Proceedings of the 10th International Colloquium on Gregory of Nyssa
     (Olomouc, September 15–18, 2004)*, eds. Lenka Karfíková, Scot Douglass, and Johannes Zachhuber,
     Supplements to Vigiliae Christianae 82 (Leiden: Brill, 2007), 74; See Hans Boersma, "Overcoming
     Time and Space: Gregory of Nyssa's Anagogical Theology" *Journal of Early Christian Studies* 20
     (2012): 584.
13. Gregory of Nyssa, *Ad Abl.* 56.1–10. Turcescu notes that we should not identify this language with the
     filioque (*Gregory of Nyssa*, 68).

or "begotten" do not define the divine nature and do not encapsulate divine distinction either.[14] However, as Lucian Turcescu observes, Gregory's articulation of Trinitarian relations indicates true communion (*koinōnia*) among divine persons that is "more than simply ontological causality."[15] This communion does not admit a diastemic gap, divergence of will, or delay in operation.

Building upon his brother Basil of Caesarea's (d. 379 C.E.) work against Eunomius,[16] Gregory takes issue with the Eunomian insistence on hierarchical distinction between Father and Son that introduces a diastemic gap between them.[17] Gregory writes in *Contra Eunomium* about the distinction between creature and Creator: "One is finite, the other infinite; the one is confined within its proper measure as the wisdom of its Maker determined, the limit of the other is infinity. One stretches out in measurable extension, being bounded by time and space, the other transcends any notion of measure, eluding investigation however far one casts the mind."[18] According to Gregory, instead of preserving divine simplicity, Eunomius's version actually violates true divine simplicity because it predicated that confessing God as ungenerated or unbegotten defines God's substance.[19] Eunomius assumes that the begotten one is "necessarily inferior to the Maker himself in power, rank and nature, in temporal precedence and all honors" and, if that is indeed the case, he questions how one worships the inferior as God.[20] Gregory counters that simplicity cannot admit division or grow or "suffer what we conceive as diminution."[21] Thus, there is no inferiority at all. Gregory insists that the Trinity is simple in substance and wholly other than creation and that the real distinction of divine persons does not jeopardize that simplicity. For Gregory, the Eunomian claim that the Son is not substantially like the Father causes two major problems: First, it collapses the distinction between Creator and creation; and second, it compromises God's salvific activity in the economy.

Around the same time that Gregory was working on the latter part of *Contra Eunomium*, he wrote a letter to his brother Peter, bishop of Sebaste, in which Gregory articulates the decisive standard Trinitarian formula of speaking of unity and distinction.[22] This epistolary treatise *Ad Petrum* (*To Peter his own*

---

14. Cvetkovic, "St Gregory's Argument," 381.

15. Turcescu, *Gregory of Nyssa*, 117.

16. Nyssen wrote the three books of his *Contra Eunomium* between the summer of 380 and 383 C.E. (Turcescu, *Gregory of Nyssa*, 80).

17. Boersma, "Overcoming Time and Space," 582.

18. Gregory of Nyssa, *Contra Eunomium* 2.70 (Hall, 74).

19. According to Zachhuber, for Eunomius, "God *qua* substance is absolutely simple, any term indicating his substance must indicate it entirely; it is therefore impossible to say that the Son and the Father have only certain properties in common while other properties maintain their difference" (*Human Nature in Gregory of Nyssa*, 45).

20. Gregory of Nyssa, *Contra Eunomium* 2.54–55 (Hall, 71).

21. Gregory of Nyssa, *Contra Eunomium* 2.70 (Hall, 75).

22. Because this letter is found among Basil's works, there was an assumption among scholars that he was the author (*Ep. 38* or *To his brother Gregory on the difference between ousia and hypostasis*). Determining the

brother on the divine ousia and hypostasis) followed the synod in Alexandria in 362 C.E., where the gathered bishops worked out the Nicene confusion over the term *hypostasis*, and the Council of Constantinople of 381.[23] Key for Gregory in *Ad Petrum* (as it was in the *Contra Eunomium*) is that triune communion is not like human communion. Between the Father and the Son and the Holy Spirit, "[t]here is no void of some interstice, lacking subsistence, which could cause the harmony of the divine substance with itself to fissure, by breaching the continuity through the insertion of a void."[24] We approach the Trinity and behold a communion that includes no intrusion of space or possibility of division or imposition by an outside force, because no such reality exists.[25]

For Gregory, *hypostasis* allows us to speak of distinction without baldly assuming division of what is not divisible: "This therefore is the hypostasis: not the indefinite notion of the substance, which finds no instantiation because of the commonality of what is signified, but that conception which through the manifest individualities gives stability and circumscription in a certain object to the common and uncircumscribed."[26] A thought about the Father is a thought about the Son is a thought about the Holy Spirit but our thoughts ultimately fail to grasp the ineffable triune communion.[27] The Trinity admits no separation even if our thoughts assign disjuncture; our conception does not dictate or fully access triune reality.

In Gregory's determination to express unity and distinction in the Trinity, he must deal with questions of how that real distinction does not compromise the real oneness. In *Il illud: Tunc et ipse filius* Gregory concentrates on a particularly thorny question about the equality of the Father and Son provoked by 1 Corinthians 15:28 (NRSV): "When all things are subjected to him, then the Son himself will also be subjected to the one who put all things in subjection under him, so that God may be all in all."[28] What does Paul mean when he

---

composition date (key for confirming authorship) is made more difficult as it seems the original opening of the treatise has dropped out. More recently, however, a consideration of its inclusion in Gregory's works as well as the likely context has led the majority of scholars to the conclusion that Gregory is indeed the author (Anna M. Silvas, *Gregory of Nyssa, The Letters: Introduction, Translation and Commentary*, Supplements to Vigiliae Christianae 83 [Leiden: Brill, 2007], 247–48); see also Turcescu, *Gregory of Nyssa*, 47.

23. Silvas, *Gregory of Nyssa, The Letters*, 249.

24. Gregory of Nyssa, *Ad Petrum* 4i (Silvas, 254); here Gregory describes what would later be called perichoresis among the divine persons: contemplating one leads to contemplation of the other two and confessing one requires confessing the other two as well (Turcescu, *Gregory of Nyssa*, 59).

25. In *Ad Petrum*, we see Gregory use the familiar analogy of the common and particular found in Aristotle and the Stoics and that he will employ later in *Ad Ablabium* (if we go with a later date for the latter treatise): the distinction between a noun that expresses the common nature of things that are "plural and numerically diverse" ("man") and nouns that signify individuality or "a circumscription of some reality" instead of common nature ("Paul or Timothy") (*Ad Petrum* 2a–2b [Silvas, 250]). See also Turcescu, *Gregory of Nyssa*, 48.

26. Gregory of Nyssa, *Ad Petrum* 3b (Silvas, 251).

27. Gregory of Nyssa, *Ad Petrum*, 4m (Silvas, 255).

28. Lucas Francisco Mateo-Seco observes that 1 Corinthians 15:28 is central to Gregory's eschatology and shapes its decisively optimistic vision ("Eschatology," in *The Brill Dictionary of Gregory of Nyssa*,

says the Son will "be subjected"? Gregory rejects the Eunomian idea that Paul infers filial subordination and spends the entire treatise exploring the Trinitarian and eschatological implications of 1 Corinthians 15:28.[29]

While our participation in salvation and all of the good things of God as mutable humans comes at the behest of a willing subjection to an immutable God, Gregory does not broker any kind of subjection in the unity of that immutable God.[30] Indeed, the Son's incarnation requires subjection to progress, parents, and the Father; this is appropriate and a good. However, mutability and subjection to the Father is not predicated of the preexistent Word. Christ's submission to his parents found in Scripture indicates the reality of his irrevocable humanness. His progression and obedience is understood as absolute identification with humanity and pedagogical advocacy for all humans unto their flourishing in union with God.[31]

For Gregory, Christ is irrevocably linked to us, and our *telos* as humans is irrevocably linked to Christ; thus, his resurrection and ours must be true in order for the salvific project to exist and succeed.[32] This irrevocable link, our participation in Christ, and our subsequent eschatological union with God explain how it could be that the Son could be eschatologically "subjected." When God is "all in all," Christ's body (i.e., those who irrevocably linked with Christ in the resurrection, the church) will be subjected.[33] Instead of a Eunomian subordination of the Son based on his eschatological subjection to the Father, Gregory reads 1 Corinthians 15 not as the "Son's inferiority to the Father, but the salvific submission of all humans, which constitute 'the body of Christ.' It is Christ's humanity that will submit to the Father, not Christ's divinity."[34] The subjection of the Son does not indicate inferiority but is

---

eds. Lucas Francisco Mateo-Seco and Giulio Maspero, trans. Seth Cherney, Supplements to Vigiliae Christianae 99 [Leiden: Brill, 2010], 275).

29. For Gregory, these "cheating dealers" impose their heresy on the Scriptures to claim that "the apostolic word was composed for them in order to bring down the glory of the Only Begotten God" (*Tunc et ipse* 4 in "On '*Then Also the Son Himself Will be Subjected to the One Who Subjected All Things to Him*' (*In illud: Tunc et ipse Filius*, GNO 3.2)," in Rowan A. Greer (assisted by J. Warren Smith), *One Path for All: Gregory of Nyssa on the Christian Life and Human Destiny* [Eugene, OR: Wipf & Stock, 2015], 118); Morwenna Ludlow points out that while Gregory responds to Eunomius's subordination of the Son and to Marcellus of Ancyra's eschatology, the treatise is probably not intended for those opponents but to work through his views among his neo-Nicene peers, "*In illud: Tunc et ipse filius,*" in Drecoll and Berghaus, eds., *Gregory of Nyssa: The Minor Treatises*, 413, 424.

30. Gregory of Nyssa, *Tunc et ipse* 7 (Greer, 120).

31. Ludlow, "*In illud,*" 416.

32. Gregory of Nyssa, *Tunc et ipse* 11–13 (Greer, 122–23).

33. Gregory of Nyssa, *Tunc et ipse* 16–19 (Greer, 125–26). Gregory makes reference to Colossians 1:24–25, 1 Corinthians 12:27, and Ephesians 4:15–16.

34. Ilaria Ramelli, "Gregory of Nyssa's Trinitarian Theology in *In illud: Tunc et ipse filius*. His Polemic Against 'Arian' Subordinationism and the ΑΠΟΚΑΤΑΣΤΑΣΙΣ," in Drecoll and Berghaus, eds., *Gregory of Nyssa: The Minor Treatises*, 446.

contextualized in eschatological order.[35] In short, Gregory reads Paul's use
of subjection in 1 Corinthians 15:28 eschatologically and ecclesiologically as
predicated by Christology. *In illud: Tunc et ipse filius* is certainly about the
doctrine of the Trinity but its discussion of unity and distinction comes with
an eschatological parallel. As Morwenna Ludlow notes, "Gregory starts with a
Trinitarian question, but ends up with an eschatological answer."[36]

In *Contra Eunomium*, *Ad Petrum*, and *In illud: Tunc et ipse filius*, as in *Ad
Ablabium*, Gregory articulates what speech about God is out of bounds: First,
predicating *diastema* of the adiastemic God, that is, anything that violates the
Creator-creation boundary; second, assuming simplicity of God and yet arguing for the inferiority of the Son; third, admitting any division of operation or
will; and fourth, brokering any subordination of the Son that is not appropriate to his salvific project in the Incarnation. As a brief treatment of each of
these works demonstrates, Gregory offers us much by way of rich theological
grounding for how not to speak of God alongside his innovative articulation of
how to speak of God in unity and distinction. Now we return to *Ad Ablabium*
for a deeper look at Gregory's methodology for speaking of God.

In the Eye of the Beholder:
What God Is and What God Is Not

As we have seen, for Gregory, the inability to circumscribe or define God's
nature is as a result of the Creator-creation distinction. This does not, however,
portend an epistemological or confessional brick wall; there are ways to know
and to speak of God. Lewis Ayres says it well:

> Gregory's statements about the irreducibility and yet unity of the divine person
> can only be approached through first exploring his account of the nature of human
> speech and about the cosmology that grounds that account. Only when we see
> how this account of divine creative power and ontological difference grounds a
> vision of human speech about God will we begin to see what it means for Gregory
> to confess the incomprehensible and yet irreducible distinct divine persons.[37]

In other words, not only does method matter, so do the conceptual pillars
supporting it. In *Ad Ablabium*, we learn that Gregory takes his cues for thinking of and speaking about God's nature from Scripture. Gregory writes, "We
say that every name, whether invented from human custom or handed down

35. Ludlow, "*In illud*," 419. Within the context of his focus on the resurrection (Christ and humans), Ludlow
    notes that Gregory's discussion of the eradication of evil is one of the most explicit articulations of his
    doctrine of universal salvation in his corpus. See also Mateo-Seco, "Eschatology," 275–76.
36. Ludlow, "*In illud*," 422. Ramelli delves deeper into Gregory's connection between his Trinitarian
    polemic against the subordination of the Son and his eschatology (*apokatastasis*). This connection,
    she argues, derives directly from Origen. See "Gregory of Nyssa's Trinitarian Theology," 445–78.
37. Lewis Ayres, "On Not Three People: The Fundamental Themes of Gregory of Nyssa's Trinitarian
    Theology as Seen in *To Ablabius: On Not Three Gods*," in Coakely, ed., *Re-Thinking Gregory of Nyssa*, 16.

from Scripture, is an *interpretation* of the things thought about divine nature and does not comprehend the signification of the nature itself."[38] Gregory acknowledges a diversity of ways of describing or naming God (even those not based directly in Scripture), but is careful to note that they are interpretations of the "perceived properties," not definitive statements that grasp the essence of God.[39] The beauty of these interpretations is that they allow for true things to be said in a human way about God and about God's relation to the world.

Recognizing God as adiastemic does not, in Gregory's purview, diminish God's engagement with the world. In fact, God is the one who sees or beholds all and humans image this quality by beholding God's activities and speaking of God. We are the beholders of the Beholder's beholding of us. Ours is an imperfect beholding, however. According to Gregory, humans engage in *epinoia*, a mental beholding that is akin to seeing "in a mirror, dimly" (1 Cor. 13:12, NRSV). This mirror, however, is not a funhouse mirror that distorts reality; it is the only seeing that a finite mind can accomplish when considering the infinite. Thus, this imperfect beholding is still movement toward knowledge of the infinite, without the expectation of ever reaching it, but with the delight of constantly desiring more. In our capacity as finite beings, our eschatological *telos* is that of union with the infinite who draws our resurrected and desiring selves into ever deeper knowledge of and union with the infinite. For Gregory, this "epistemological ascent" is not a movement driven toward the brightness of knowing, but instead a pilgrimage fueled by the deepest desire into the darkness of unknowing.[40] Beholding the glimpses that are dimly portrayed in the mirror becomes our undoing and our remaking.

The activity of God's beholding is an interpretation of the God-world relation—the God who sees us and knows us. This epistemic activity indicates God's unity and perceived distinction. God (the Father) protects—a beholding activity that results in knowing human situations and acting on their behalf.[41] Christ sees thoughts and thus knows sinful hearts—a beholding activity that results in God as human knowing humanity's sin. The Spirit witnesses—a beholding activity that results in God as Spirit revealing God-knowledge of one human's secret to another. God's beholding activity is not a passive quality but an intimate triune engagement with humanity. The Beholder is with us and invites the interpretation and the participation of humans in this activity of beholding. Yes, God's substance is not definable by creatures, but the with-ness of God and God's advocacy for the flourishing of creation quells any fear that it is improper to speak of God. Instead, all of creation is compelled to speak.

---

38.   Gregory of Nyssa, *Ad Abl.* 42.19–43.2. Emphasis added.
39.   ἐνθεωρουμένας ἰδιότητας 40.24–41.2.
40.   Martin Laird, "Gregory of Nyssa and the Mysticism of Darkness: A Reconsideration," *Journal of Religion* 79 (1999): 597.
41.   Gregory of Nyssa, *Ad Abl.* 44.6–46.2.

Our beholding and speech, however, have a limited referent: activity, not nature. And that limited referent is a unity of activity that starts from the Father (*ek patrōs aphōrmati*), proceeds through the Son (*dia tou huioō proēsē*), and is completed by the Holy Spirit (*en tō tō hagiō teleioutai*).[42] There is no action if it did not start or proceed or if it is not completed: the one action enacted in diverse unified activity, one divine life, "activated by the Holy Spirit, prepared by the Son, and kindled by the Father's will."[43] Gregory continues: "Therefore, then, the holy Trinity works every activity according to the manner already stated, not separately according to the number of the hypostases, but one motion and production of goodwill occurs, and the exchange proceeding from the Father through the Son to the Spirit."[44] This unity of activity speaks to the economic Trinity as well as the immanent relationship within the Godhead. Unity indicates interrelatedness as well as how Trinitarian distinction is understood and perceived as not three gods, but one. Describing God's activity shows the perceived distinction in relation to the world and humanity and how this activity has a definitive origination, procession, and completion, as reflected in Trinitarian distinction. In the Trinity, distinction is located in dependence: "For there is the one which depends upon the first, and there is that one which is through that one which attends upon the first."[45]

Gregory understands, however, that our reflex to subordinate the Son (and the Holy Spirit) is strong, especially as Scripture seems to challenge our speaking of unity of substance and meaningful distinction without admitting division or confusion. In *Ad Petrum* Gregory considers one such passage, Hebrews 1:3, in which the Son is described as "the brightness of his [the Father's] glory and the impression of his hypostasis" and argues that the Son's brightness results from simultaneity and no interval.[46] He draws upon passages such as John 14:9 and Colossians 1:15 to articulate that the Son as image does not distinguish him from the archetype "with regard to the principle of invisibility and goodness."[47] Further, in beholding this image one comes to know that invisible and good archetype: "Indeed one who conceives in thought the form, as it were, of the Son, forms an image of the impress of the Father's hypostasis, beholding the latter through the former, not beholding the unbegottenness of the Father in the copy (for this would be complete identity and no distinction), but discerning the unbegotten beauty in the

---

42.   Gregory of Nyssa, *Ad Abl.* 48.1–2.
43.   Gregory of Nyssa, *Ad Abl.* 48.17–19.
44.   Gregory of Nyssa, *Ad Abl.* 48.20–49.1.
45.   Gregory of Nyssa, *Ad Abl.* 56.5–6.
46.   Gregory of Nyssa, *Ad Petrum* 7c–d (Silvas, 257); As Turcescu notes, modern biblical and patristic scholars do not read Hebrews 1:3 as Nyssen does, as Pauline evidence for an established scriptural difference between *ousia* and *hypostasis* (*Gregory of Nyssa*, 51).
47.   Gregory of Nyssa, *Ad Petrum* 8a (Silvas, 259).

begotten."[48] Certainly we do see in a mirror dimly, but to behold the Son is to behold in a pure mirror a reflection that accesses "vivid knowledge of the face represented" because everything the Father has is beheld in the Son and everything the Son has is the Father's: "the Son abides wholly in the Father and in turn has the Father wholly in himself."[49] For Gregory, the *hypostasis* of the Son "becomes as it were the form and face of the knowledge of the Father, and the hypostasis of the Father is known in the form of the Son, while the individuality which is contemplated in them remains as the clear distinction of the hypostases."[50] Gregory is careful not to collapse the triune God into a monad to preserve distinction. He also qualifies his description of the interrelatedness of the Trinity in order preserve unity. In other words, holding onto the transcendence of God does not come at the expense of perceiving God's activity in the world.

Creativity Speaking: Names of God

Building upon his elucidation of the human capacity to behold God's unified activity, Gregory carefully delineates the limits of naming or describing God. Each name for God holds specific and appropriate meaning that illustrates something about deity. Divine nature itself, however, cannot be circumscribed by the names. God's transcendence is describable, but not definable, so the significance of the names is in either "their rejection of incorrect knowledge with reference to the divine nature or in their teaching that which is correct."[51] No name can in any way encapsulate deity. According to Gregory, those names "invented from human custom" demonstrate something important about God: God's desire for humanity to behold and name divine activity.[52] No doubt, Gregory expects names for God to be congruent with accepted custom, but humans who behold God will be compelled to speak of God in any case, meeting mystery with a sense of discovery and delight at the possibilities.

The Cappadocian innovation in Trinitarian language included both the precise language of the formula of one *ousia* and three *hypostases* and the broader methodology for speaking of mystery that we find exemplified in *Ad Ablabium*. Scot Douglass posits that the Cappadocian linguistic repertoire did more than attempt to provide systematic orthodox speech: "they consciously entered into the very sources of the limitations of language, into that which simultaneously created and compromised language, in order to utilize the creative characteristics of the limitations of language in the name of

---

48. Gregory of Nyssa, *Ad Petrum* 8b (Silvas, 259).
49. Gregory draws on John 16:15 and John 14:10 in addition to the passages already mentioned (*Ad Petrum* 8c [Silvas, 259]).
50. Gregory of Nyssa, *Ad Petrum* 8d (Silvas, 259).
51. Gregory of Nyssa, *Ad Abl.* 44.4–6.
52. Gregory of Nyssa, *Ad Abl.* 42.20–22.

a mediated detour—a never ending, never stable, never unified, fragmented discourse."[53] Language provided the theoretical, rhetorical, and theological framework for their method for their speaking of God. Ludlow summarizes Gregory's embrace of the limits and the fitness of language: "Language is, then, one might say, both imperfect and appropriate."[54] In other words, the innovation here is largely about embracing our human limits so we can humble ourselves rightly before the limitless God who embraces us.

The human capacity to behold offers epistemic, linguistic, and experiential access to God that allows us to draw names together into coherent speech about God. For example, based on scriptural precedent of the Son and Spirit "overseeing," Gregory's summation assumes that such a name is properly ascribed to all persons of the Trinity.[55] There are also names that gesture toward distinction without division in the Godhead: "The Father is God, the Son is God, [we can safely add 'the Spirit is God'] but by the same proclamation God is one, because neither with regard to nature nor activity is any distinction beheld."[56] If the names do not intend to encompass God's substance or imply plurality, one can freely name aspects of God in the singular. Gregory gives some examples—good, holy, savior, judge—and leaves the list open for an undetermined number of names, as long as those names are derived from beholding God's activity.

Gregory does not allude to any sort of hierarchy of names since every name that humanity ascribes is ever limited by finitude. A finite mind cannot comprehend the infinite; human speech cannot touch what is beyond words; and the immaterial cannot be defined by materiality. The immaterial will always slip through material fingers, and all attempts to grasp it will end in futility. This does not mean, however, that we are left with an unnamable and inaccessible God. On the contrary, Gregory strongly affirms a God who welcomes the participatory and experiential act that is naming. Scripture's authority and invented custom's ability to speak meaningfully about God is not questioned.

Even the basic name of "deity," which would seem to have epistemic priority over other, perhaps "lesser," names, is not given such status:

> "Therefore that which is outside of limit is not at all defined by a name. Thus, in reference to the divine nature, in order that the concept of the indefinable might remain, we affirm that the divine is above every name, and one of the names is deity. Therefore the same thing is not able to be a name and to be thought customarily to be above every name."[57] Any name is ranked along with every

53.   Scot Douglass, *Theology of the Gap: Cappadocian Language Theory and the Trinitarian Controversy*, AUS 235 (New York: Peter Lang, 2005), 8.
54.   Ludlow, *Gregory of Nyssa*, 235.
55.   Gregory of Nyssa, *Ad Abl.* 44.11–16.
56.   Gregory of Nyssa, *Ad Abl.* 55.7–10.
57.   Gregory of Nyssa, *Ad Abl.* 52.15–53.3.

other name that humanity can offer in worship to God. In addition, when such terms as "power" or "wisdom" or "sovereign" are ascribed to God, it must be noted that our understanding of the fullness of how such names represent God is beyond human capacity as well. Circumscription is always required. Naming God "wisdom," for example, does not indicate that we have grasped in full what that means. Otherwise we would be treading upon the territory of circumscribing nature (of any kind), for which Gregory faulted Eunomius and worked to eliminate from our *modus dicendi*.

Conclusion: Compelled to Speak in the Lucid Darkness of Apophaticism

While apophaticism can tend to be caricatured as a philosophical and terminological removal from practicality, this is not what Gregory has in mind.[58] Gregory's apophaticism is a particularly timely contribution in the continuing discussion about how to speak of God in modern theology: "Negation . . . has captured something basic to the spirit of the times, reflecting reality as process, which is disjunctive, fissured and ultimately resistant to any schematisation."[59] Gregory's apophaticism is more nuanced than a drawing of boundaries or a retreat into an amorphous "mystery" with believers "languishing in pious agnosticism."[60] Semantically taking up residence in the negative realm contradicts Gregory's amplification of the call to speak of God. Instead, Gregory's approach propels Trinitarian discourse into the realm of the actual act of a human speaking of God: "[I]n his [Gregory's] very act of negating the possibility to express the divine nature with language, he affirms the possibility to investigate the mode of being of the Persons and attests to the value of human knowledge and science."[61] For Gregory, human naming of God illustrates our finite capacity for, desire to participate in, and our perpetual movement into the infinite (*epektasis*). If, as David Bentley Hart posits, the premise of any sound epistemology is delight, then Gregory's approach is definitely a journey of delight that undoes and remakes the human beholder in the process of beholding the Beholder.[62] For Gregory, apophaticism is a map that defines the boundaries in such a way as to illuminate the practically

---

58. See Lewis Ayres and Andrew Radde-Gallwitz, "Doctrine of God," in *The Oxford Handbook of Early Christian Studies*, eds. Susan Ashbrook Harvey and David G. Hunter (Oxford: Oxford University Press, 2008), 864–85 on negative theology and the shape of contemporary feminist scholarship in this vein; and on Gregory's use of "negative theology" specifically, see Ari Ojell, "Apophatic Theology," in Mateo-Seco and Maspero, eds., *The Brill Dictionary*, 68–73; Douglass, *Theology of the Gap*, 154.

59. Oliver Davies and Denys Turner, eds., *Silence and the Word: Negative Theology and Incarnation* (Cambridge: Cambridge University Press, 2002), 2.

60. Paul M. Blowers, "Beauty, Tragedy and New Creation: Theology and Contemplation in Cappadocian Cosmology," *International Journal of Systematic Theology* 18 (2016): 10.

61. Giulio Maspero, *Trinity and Man: Gregory of Nyssa's Ad Ablabium*, Supplements to Vigiliae Christianae 86 (Leiden: Brill, 2007), 110.

62. See David Bentley Hart, *The Beauty of the Infinite: The Aesthetics of Christian Truth* (Grand Rapids: Eerdmans, 2003), 253.

infinite range of naming and human participation while also retaining God as distinct from creation.[63] Apophaticism is Gregory's theological, hermeneutical, and confessional methodology.

In our consideration of any name, we cannot say something about God that is contrary to God's being, of course. We also must take care that we do not get too restrictive and allow some names to dominate (and perhaps oust others) by sheer ubiquity. As we have seen, Gregory places all naming attempts at the same distance from God's essence. With names that are employed more often in Scripture (Father and Son, for example) it is all the more important to be wary of our own impositions on these names. Thus, the church as a naming community is vital. As Gregory demonstrates, traditional Trinitarian discourse properly understood has the ability to hold the weight of creativity and new customs. It also has the ability to throw that substantial weight behind a call for greater circumspection and humility with regard to how humans engage with God and each other. When Gregory speaks of naming according to custom, he is speaking of human beholdings as communally invented and engaged. Speaking of the triune God is a participatory act, where humanity communally and individually engages with Scripture, invented custom, and the experience of God interacting with the world and with the life of the mind and heart. Gregory understood the breadth of Trinitarian discourse, its irreducible embrace with Christology, and the import it carries for confession and practice. The Creator-creation distinction is the safeguard that allows humans agency with which to behold and name God.

Drawing upon Gregory's example, apophaticism, then, is a posture of generosity toward the diversity of beholdings that can result from human experience. Apophaticism also chastens our impulse to turn these historically and culturally constituted experiences into unassailable representations of truth. It is important to listen Gregory's contribution to Trinitarian discourse in order to chasten our own because, as Coakley observes, even the most basic point of *Ad Ablabium* has been greatly misunderstood and in turn has caused some serious consequences, not the least of these with regard to the matter of gender.[64] Replacing one dominant discourse with another that seeks to supplant it is not the answer. Thus, the apophatically shaped human activity of naming God builds the unity of the church by fueling our generosity, and preserves our distinctive contributions by helping us to resist our domination of one another.

For Gregory, we are compelled to speak of God and with this imperative to speak comes the creative and communal freedom to do so within Trinitarian discourse. Speaking of God and recognizing the finitude and circum-

---

63. The Creator-creation distinction preserves difference in the best sense, not as distance, but as a journey into difference (Hart, *Beauty of the Infinite*, 194).

64. See Coakley, "Introduction," 1–14 and *God, Sexuality, and the Self*, esp. 73–81.

scription of our names for God is not a wild shot in the dark at a distant God. Transcendence is not distance, and reveling in mystery need not lack creativity or precision. Gregory of Nyssa's articulation of unity and distinction in the Trinity draws us into participation in Christ and into eschatological union with God. We behold God even as God beholds us.

Bibliography

Primary Sources

Gregory of Nyssa. *Ad Ablabium quod non sint tres dei.* In *Gregorii Nysseni Opera*, edited by F. Mueller, 37–57 (GNO) 3.1. Leiden: Brill, 1958. Thesaurus Linguae Graecae Digital Library. http://stephanus.tlg.uci.edu.proxy.gordon-conwell.edu/Iris/inst/csearch.jsp#doc=tlg&aid=2017&wid=003&q=GREG ORIUS%20NYSSENUS&dt=list&st=all&per=50 (accessed October 2016).

_____. *Contra Eunomium.* Translated by Stuart George Hall under the title "Gregory, Bishop of Nyssa: The Second Book Against Eunomius." In *Gregory of Nyssa, Contra Eunomium II: An English Version with Supporting Studies: Proceedings of the 10th International Colloquium on Gregory of Nyssa (Olomouc, September 15–18, 2004)*, edited by Lenka Karfíková, Scot Douglass, and Johannes Zachhuber, 53–201. Supplements to Vigiliae Christianae 82. Leiden: Brill, 2007.

_____. *In illud: Tunc et ipse Filius.* Translated by Rowan A. Greer in "On 'Then Also the Son Himself Will be Subjected to the One Who Subjected All Things to Him' (In illud: Tunc et ipse Filius, GNO 3.2)." In Rowan A. Greer and J. Warren Smith, *One Path for All: Gregory of Nyssa on the Christian Life and Human Destiny.* Eugene, OR: Wipf & Stock, 2015.

Blowers, Paul M. "Beauty, Tragedy and New Creation: Theology and Contemplation in Cappadocian Cosmology." *International Journal of Systematic Theology* 18 (2016): 7–29.

Boersma, Hans. "Overcoming Time and Space: Gregory of Nyssa's Anagogical Theology." *Journal of Early Christian Studies* 20 (2012): 575–612.

Coakley, Sarah. *God, Sexuality, and the Self: An Essay "On the Trinity."* Cambridge: Cambridge University Press, 2013.

Coakley, Sarah, ed. *Re-Thinking Gregory of Nyssa.* Oxford: Blackwell, 2003.

Davies, Oliver, and Denys Turner, eds. *Silence and the Word: Negative Theology and Incarnation.* Cambridge: Cambridge University Press, 2002.

Douglass, Scot. *Theology of the Gap: Cappadocian Language Theory and the Trinitarian Controversy.* American University Studies 235. New York: Peter Lang, 2005.

Drecoll, Volker Henning, and Margitta Berghaus, eds. *Gregory of Nyssa: The Minor Treatises on Trinitarian Theology and Apollinarism, Proceedings of the 11th International Colloquium on Gregory of Nyssa (Tübingen, 17–20 September 2008).* Supplements to Vigiliae Christianae 106. Leiden: Brill, 2011.

de Régnon, Théodore. *Etudes de théologie positive sur la Sainte Trinité.* 4 vols. Paris: Victor Retaux, 1892–1898.

Hart, David Bentley. *The Beauty of the Infinite: The Aesthetics of Christian Truth.* Grand Rapids: Eerdmans, 2003.

Harvey, Susan Ashbrook, and David G. Hunter, eds. *The Oxford Handbook of Early Christian Studies*. Oxford: Oxford University Press, 2008.

Laird, Martin. "Gregory of Nyssa and the Mysticism of Darkness: A Reconsideration." *Journal of Religion* 79 (1999): 592–613.

Ludlow, Morwenna. *Gregory of Nyssa, Ancient and (Post)Modern*. Oxford: Oxford University Press, 2007.

Maspero, Giulio. *Trinity and Man: Gregory of Nyssa's Ad Ablabium*. Supplements to Vigiliae Christianae 86. Leiden: Brill, 2007.

Mateo-Seco, Lucas Francisco, and Giulio Maspero, eds. *The Brill Dictionary of Gregory of Nyssa*, translated by Seth Cherney. Supplements to Vigiliae Christianae 99. Leiden: Brill, 2010.

Rusch, William G. trans. "Gregory of Nyssa's Concerning We Should Not Think of Saying That There Are Not Three Gods: *To Ablabius*. In *The Trinitarian Controversy*, 149–61. Sources of Early Christian Thought. Philadelphia: Fortress, 1980.

Silvas, Anna M. *Gregory of Nyssa, The Letters: Introduction, Translation and Commentary*. Supplements to Vigiliae Christianae 83. Leiden: Brill, 2007.

Turcescu, Lucian. *Gregory of Nyssa and the Concept of Divine Persons*. Oxford: Oxford University Press, 2005.

Zachhuber, Johannes. *Human Nature in Gregory of Nyssa: Philosophical Background and Theological Significance*. Leiden: Brill, 2014.

CHAPTER 7

Dominium naturale et oeconomicum

Authority and the Trinity

TYLER R. WITTMAN

I: Introduction

Ever since Karl Barth's influential extension of nineteenth-century reformulations of traditional approaches to the divine names, the topic of
the Son's eternal obedience to the Father has been on the agenda of
evangelical theology.[1] In more recent decades, this debate has taken a variety
of turns both within and without those camps adhering to Barth's legacy. For
some, the Son's obedience in time reveals an activity that is eternally constitu-

1. Karl Barth, *Church Dogmatics*, vols. I–IV, eds. Geoffrey W. Bromiley and Thomas F. Torrance, trans.
Geoffrey Bromiley et al. (Edinburgh: T & T Clark, 1956–75), IV/1, 192–210. A sensitive appreciation of
Barth's position within a more traditional framework is offered by Scott Swain and Michael Allen, "The
Obedience of the Eternal Son," *International Journal of Systematic Theology* 15, no. 2 (2013): 114–34.
Similar entries from Roman Catholic theologians include Guy Mansini, "Can Humility and Obedience
be Trinitarian Realities?," in *Thomas Aquinas and Karl Barth: An Unofficial Catholic-Protestant Dialogue*,
eds. Bruce L. McCormack and Thomas Joseph White (Grand Rapids: Eerdmans, 2013), 71–98; Thomas
Joseph White, *The Incarnate Lord: A Thomistic Study in Christology* (Washington, DC: The Catholic
University of America Press, 2015), 277–307.

tive of the identity of the Logos as such.[2] For yet others, the Son's obedience in time discloses that submission is already true of the Son's eternal identity, some even going so far as to make all the Trinity's mutual relations characterized by a genteel hierarchy of differentiated authority.[3] Behind all these views are convictions about how we confess the inner-Trinitarian relations, and how language of authority and therefore obedience has a place in such acts. What follows sets forth an alternative to these revisionist convictions about such matters, though one that is by no means original. Given its intellectual debts, the argument proceeds by way of critical retrieval.

To this end, we explore some relevant aspects of a broadly Thomist, contemplative approach to discourse about God's inner life and external works, specifically as they bear upon our understanding of the relations between the divine persons. Specifically, we are interested in what can and cannot be said about these relations and whether there is room for distinctions in role, function, or authority within them. This will involve first an analysis of how Thomas Aquinas characterizes our knowledge of the divine persons, which attends not only to the structural features of his account but also to the posture of his inquiry and the movements of thought it licenses. We will then examine how such an inquiry might understand the function of "authority" in Trinitarian discourse through the distinction between theology and economy. Reading beyond Aquinas into the early modern period, a different approach comes into view that offers a set of criteria that may be counterintuitive for some dominant modes of contemporary theological reflection. But precisely in these criteria we find a critical salve to contemporary debates.

II: Aquinas on Knowledge of the Divine Persons

For Aquinas, the Trinity "is known according to the properties by which the persons are distinguished. When these are known, the Trinity in God is really known."[4] What are personal properties, how do we discern them, and how are they revelatory of the persons' distinctions? Aquinas's discussion of personal properties comes near the beginning of his treatise on the Trinity in the *Summa theologiae* (Ia.32), and informs his subsequent discussion of the names proper to the divine persons (Ia.33–38). Investigating the persons' names extends the analysis of the divine names already elaborated in his discussion of God's unity of essence (Ia.3–26). Aquinas opens his treatise on

---

2.   Most notably Bruce McCormack in a variety of essays, including "Processions and Missions: A Point of Convergence between Thomas Aquinas and Karl Barth," in McCormack and White, eds., *Thomas Aquinas and Karl Barth*, 99–126.

3.   See select essays in the following volumes: Dennis W. Jowers and H. Wayne House, eds., *The New Evangelical Subordinationism? Perspectives on the Equality of God the Father and God the Son* (Eugene, OR: Pickwick, 2012); Bruce A. Ware and John Starke, eds., *One God in Three Persons: Unity of Essence, Distinction of Persons, Implications for Life* (Wheaton, IL: Crossway, 2015).

4.   Aquinas, *De veritate* 10.13.corp (ET: *The Disputed Questions on Truth*, 3 vols., trans. R. Schmidt [Chicago: Henry Regnery, 1954]).

the Trinity with what is most fundamental, but also what is most formal: the divine processions (Ia.27). From there he proceeds to discuss the other formal concepts of relation and person (Ia.28–29), and then after addressing some matters of logic concerning the coexistence of unity and plurality in God's life (Ia.30–31), he turns to the question of how we know the divine persons (Ia.32). God's revelation is the exclusive means of our knowledge of the divine persons, and this arrives in the form of their several names. Though Aquinas's treatise builds up to its zenith in the concluding question on the divine missions, these are properly understood only in light of the personal names and so Aquinas devotes most of his space to an analysis of names "proper" to the persons (proper in the sense of *proprius*, genuine and particular to the reality in question). In this section, we explore the revelatory character of the names and the manner in which Aquinas pursues his inquiry.

The Orientation of Aquinas's Inquiry

Something of the wider setting within which Aquinas's inquiry operates is visible in his commentary on Pseudo-Dionysius's *De divinis nominibus*, two aspects of which stand out. First and foremost, the inquiry is aimed at the proper reading of Holy Scripture. God's revelation through the prophets and apostles is the authorized speech with which we learn how to praise God.[5] Consequently, "we desist from examining divine things according to our reason, and instead cling to holy Scripture, in which are handed down to us the divine names, which themselves manifest to us God's gifts and the principle of those gifts."[6] Faithfulness to Scripture arbitrates our use of reason in Trinitarian discourse: "[R]eceiving the manifestation of God from holy Scripture, we must *preserve* the things set down in holy Scripture, as (one might say) the best rule of Truth, such that we neither multiply those things by adding to it, nor minimalize them by taking away from it, nor pervert them by interpreting it wickedly."[7] To the extent that we keep to the truth found in Scripture, the truth itself keeps us.

Clinging to the truth of Scripture involves a chastening of reason: "[W]e do not extend ourselves to acknowledge divine things more than the light of holy Scripture extends itself."[8] Those "holy minds who are stretched out towards God . . . throw themselves upon Him, in accordance with what God permits them and what accords with their peculiar condition" to know.[9] The measure of God's condescension and the creature's intellect both require a corresponding intellectual disposition before Scripture—one that ultimately comes from

---

5. Aquinas, *In librum beati Dionysii de divinis expositio* [*DDN*], ed. Ceslai Pera (Turin and Rome: Marietti, 1950), II.4.172.
6. Aquinas, *DDN* I.2.45.
7. Aquinas, *DDN* II.1.125.
8. Aquinas, *DDN* I.1.16.
9. Aquinas, *DDN* I.1.39.

God.[10] Chief among the requisite intellectual virtues are the temperance and magnanimity befitting our response to God's revelation. Temperance answers to the fact that it is the *incomprehensible God* who reveals himself, and magnanimity answers to this incomprehensible God's *self-revelation*. Intellectual virtue demands that we beware of saying too much or too little; either excess is pride and sickness of soul.[11] It is in this sense that the "temperate" theologian neither adds to nor multiplies "the things set down in holy Scripture." But they must confess what is taught them with humble magnanimity: failure to confess the truth at this point disparages "God's gifts and the principle of those gifts."[12]

Second, the sanctified humility requisite for the proper interpretation of Scripture results in an inquiry that is neither overly cautious nor presumptuous. On the one hand, the procedure is apophatic: "we do not know this principle just as he is through the divine names, for this is ineffable and inscrutable, but we know Him as principle and as cause."[13] Aquinas shares this Pseudo-Dionysian apophaticism, but on the other hand he shies away from its excesses with an equal emphasis on positive theology.[14] Just because we do not know God "as he is," or according to the irreducibly unique manner in which God is and knows himself, this does not mean that we cannot say anything about God's inner life. Indeed, some names force us to do just that. Some divine names are "absolute and affirmative," and as such "signify the divine substance, and are predicated substantially of God, although they fall short of a full representation of him."[15] This answers to the first stage through which theological discourse must proceed as it carries out its responsibilities, in material order: First, it speaks about God absolutely, or in himself, "in terms of his own being"; second, it speaks about God "as he is one"; third, it speaks about God's power to act and cause effects; and finally, it speaks about God "in relation to his effects."[16] Theology is inadequate to revelation if it does not attend to all these stages. Not only God's external and internal operations, but God's unity of persons and being must be discussed and confessed dialectically because the latter ground the former's intelligibility. Moreover, when Aquinas attends to names signifying God's inmost being he does not instrumentalize them as but lofty statements about the economy. Absolute names do not merely tell us that God is the cause of something;

10. Aquinas, *DDN* II.4.177.
11. Aquinas, *DDN* I.1.16, 39.
12. Aquinas, *DDN* I.2.45.
13. Aquinas, *DDN* I.2.45.
14. See Gregory P. Rocca, *Speaking the Incomprehensible God: Thomas Aquinas on the Interplay of Positive and Negative Theology* (Washington, DC: The Catholic University of America Press, 2004); Fran O'Rourke, *Pseudo-Dionysius and the Metaphysics of Aquinas* (Leiden: Brill, 1992).
15. Aquinas, *Summa theologiae* [*STh*] Ia.13.2.*corp* (ET by English Dominican Province [New York: Benziger Brothers, 1947]).
16. Aquinas, *STh* Ia.39.8.*corp*.

when we say that "God is good," we mean something more than "God is the cause of goodness" or "God is not evil." God's goodness is not dependent on his external works, but is the fullness of self-communicating perfection proper to God's life alone. So on the contrary, we maintain that "God is good" because God possesses in himself antecedently in an eminent manner whatever goodness we discern in the works of his hands.[17] It is because God is good that he does what is good, not vice versa: act follows being (*operari sequitur esse*).

Theology proceeds through a dialectic between negation and affirmation, positive and negative theology (the *via eminentiae* and *remotionis*, respectively).[18] This interplay between positive and negative theology arises from two modes of predication in Scripture, whose authors attribute one and the same thing to God abstractly and concretely. Thus, God is "life" and "living," "wisdom" and "wise," "love" and "loving," and so forth.[19] Because God possesses in himself the fullness of every perfection communicated in his works, we attribute things to him concretely; God is good, God loves, God is wise. However, these same predicates are identical with God on account of his divine simplicity, for which reason God is his own goodness, love, and wisdom.[20] Both forms of predication are necessary, and the dialectic between them is also the dialectic between temperance and magnanimity. Given this interplay, Aquinas's procedure is a kind of chastened realism—neither a mere play of interchangeable names, nor a storming of heaven's gates with univocalist zeal. Theology is a mediate knowledge, dependent on the Spirit's illumination and the teaching of Christ. All of theology's propositions are therefore but means to the end of knowing and loving the *res* itself: "[T]he act of a believer does not terminate in a proposition, but in a thing."[21] The mediate character of our knowledge means we do not know the *res* as he knows himself.[22] Since the *res* is God the Trinity, then how does all of the preceding bear upon our knowledge of the divine persons?

17. Aquinas, *STh* 13.2.*corp.*
18. Rudi A. te Velde, *Aquinas on God: The "Divine Science" of the* Summa Theologiae (Farnham: Ashgate, 2006), 77–90. The *viae eminentiae et remotionis*, together with the *via causalitatis* constitute the Pseudo-Dionysian "threefold way" (*triplex via*) to the knowledge of God: knowing God through his works (causation), through his transcendent possession of all perfections manifest in those works (eminence), and through the exclusion of anything falling short of that transcendent difference (negation). For a contemporary restatement of this approach, see Scott R. Swain, "On Divine Naming," in *Aquinas Among the Protestants*, eds. Manfred Svensson and David VanDrunen (Oxford: Wiley-Blackwell, 2017), 207–27.
19. cf. Aquinas, *STh* Ia.3.3; Ia.4.
20. On divine simplicity, see Serge Thomas Bonino, "La simplicité de Dieu," in *Istituto San Tommaso: Studi 1996*, ed. Dietrich Lorenz (Rome: Pontificia Università San Tommaso, 1997), 117–51; Tyler Wittman, "'Not a God of Confusion But of Peace': Aquinas and the Meaning of Divine Simplicity," *Modern Theology* 32, no. 2 (2016): 151–69.
21. Aquinas, *STh* IaIIae.1.2.*ad* 2.
22. Aquinas, *STh* Ia.12.7.

The Divine Names and the Trinity

We need now to look at the role positive names play in Aquinas's theology of the Trinity, and particularly in how they enable an apprehension of the persons' distinctiveness. The point of departure here owes to a pro-Nicene commonplace: Scripture delivers some truths that pertain to the Trinity "commonly," and some that pertain to the divine persons "distinctly." This results in a twofold classification of divine names pertaining to God's essence and the persons, respectively.[23] Within the *Summa theologiae*'s treatise on the distinction of persons in God, Aquinas discusses personal names as the primary means of grasping their distinct relations of origin. Again it is only through revelation that the Trinity is made known, and this puts a premium on the role and function of Scripture in Trinitarian discourse. Natural knowledge is of no use in knowing the Trinity because this doctrine concerns relations "through which the persons are related not to creatures, but to one another."[24] The relations signified by the names Father, Son, and Holy Spirit are relations internal to God's life; they concern realities only the Son can reveal (Matt. 11:27). What is revealed is quite minimal, and Aquinas's procedure internalizes this fact; he wishes neither to say more nor less than is warranted by Scripture. The initial questions in the *Summa*'s treatise on the Trinity establish that the relations within God's life concern two processions among three persons. But what makes the persons distinct? Whatever makes them distinct it cannot be anything they have in common (like divinity, or personhood), so what is it?

Aquinas's answer follows a precedent he cites in John of Damascus, who maintains that the three persons of the Trinity are "one in all things except . . . the properties of fatherhood, and sonship, and procession only."[25] Aquinas thus looks to the names of the Father, Son, and Holy Spirit as designating what is distinct about the persons in their mutual relations. Biblical names like "Father," "Son," and "Holy Spirit" signify the persons and help us to grasp their personal properties, which are the means by which we understand their intrinsic distinction. Though Scripture nowhere mentions personal properties, they are implicit within the personal names themselves, as abstract terms embedded within concrete names.[26] Within names like "Father" and "Son" there are the abstract characteristics of paternity and filiation that help us grasp why they are named "Father" and "Son." We name someone a father properly only because they bear a relation of paternity to someone, and so unless there was really a relation

23.   Aquinas, *DDN* II.1.126–27; *STh* Ia.39.5.
24.   Aquinas, *De veritate* 10.13.*corp.*
25.   John of Damascus, *De fide orthodoxa* I.8, in *Saint John of Damascus: Writings*, trans. Frederic H. Chase, Jr. (Washington, DC: The Catholic University of America Press, 1958); Aquinas, *STh* Ia.32.2.*sed contra.*
26.   Aquinas, *STh* Ia.32.2.*ad* 1. Likewise Bonaventure, despite their differences otherwise: "the three names, Father, Son, and Holy Spirit, convey the personal properties of the three persons" (*Breviloquium* I.3.9, in *Works of St. Bonaventure*, vol. 9, ed. Dominic V. Monti [Saint Bonaventure, NY: Franciscan Institute, 2005], 36).

designated by paternity within God's innermost reality, then God would properly be neither Father nor Son *in se*. The resultant teaching would be modalist, for God would only be called Father or Son on account of God's acts toward us.[27] But since these names reveal distinctive features of God's innermost reality, then there is paternity, filiation, and spiration in God.[28]

These personal properties are that "by which" we distinguish the persons' relations of origin: "the proper name of any person signifies that whereby the person is distinguished from all other persons. . . . [I]t is paternity which distinguishes the person of the Father from all other persons."[29] As a personal name, "Father" designates positively a forward relation to the Son.[30] Negatively, we say the Father is "innascible" or "unbegotten" because the name does not in its essential intelligibility presuppose a source-relation from which it derives.[31] Hence, the Father is the principle in the Trinity without a principle: one from whom others proceed, but who himself proceeds from no one.[32] Taken on its own, the name "Son" signifies only a backward, paternal relation. Together, the divine names Father and Son designate a particular relation of opposition, in which the Son's procession from the Father is intelligibly distinct from the Holy Spirit's procession from the Father and Son.

We may conclude our analysis of Aquinas by attending to how he understands personal names to illuminate the character of the inner-divine relations. If theology nominalized the personal names, the result might at best be a barren account of procession or threeness within God's life. Talk of personal properties not only helps solidify our understanding of the Trinitarian *taxis* established in the doctrine of the divine processions, but it also textures our understanding of those processions and thereby "ensures that conceptual articulation of the faith echoes the scriptural economy of revelation in the evangelists."[33] The example of the Father-Son relation is a case in point.

Considering the Son's relation to the Father involves Aquinas in an intensifying analysis of the personal properties of the Father and the Son, paternity and filiation. Here we find expressed inchoately the doctrine of the Son's eternal generation, a doctrine about which Aquinas becomes increasingly apophatic across the course of his career. In his youthful commentary

27. Aquinas, *STh* Ia.28.*sed contra*.
28. Aquinas, *STh* Ia.27.1; Ia.32.2–3.
29. Aquinas, *STh* Ia.33.2.*corp.*
30. Aquinas, *STh* Ia.33.2.*ad* 4; 33.3.
31. Aquinas, *STh* Ia.33.4.
32. Paternity is the Father's "personal property" (*proprietas personalis*), whereas innascibilty is what the later tradition would call a "property of a person" (*proprietas personae*)—a notion belonging to the Father, but not itself designating any exclusive relation. On the nuances of *innascibilitas*, see John Baptist Ku, *God the Father in the Theology of St. Thomas Aquinas* (New York: Peter Lang, 2013), 73–140.
33. John Webster, "Eternal Generation," in *God without Measure: Working Papers in Christian Theology*, vol. 1, *God and the Works of God* (London: Bloomsbury, 2016), 32.

on Lombard's *Sentences*, Aquinas depicts the Son's begetting from the Father
in somewhat isomorphic categories drawn from too tight an analogy with
human activity, and especially the relationship between essence, power, and
operation.[34] The trouble he encounters is with doing justice to the sheer
absence of any transitivity in God's life, which is one of pure act without any
potentiality for becoming: properly speaking, the power to generate (*potentia generandi*) is not even conceptually a mean between the Father's being
and the notional act of begetting. In his mature thought, especially in the
Summa theologiae, we find all such transitivity removed, and this improve-
ment comes alongside an enlarged appreciation for the psychological analogy
and the biblical name "Word" for Trinitarian discourse.[35] Setting aside the
psychological analogy, it suffices for our purposes to examine the function
of "Word" as a proper name among others. Although "Son" designates the
personal property of filiation, it is insufficient alone for our understanding
of that property. More than one name is necessary for whatever understanding we may have of the Son's eternal generation: "no mode of the procession
of any creature perfectly represents the divine generation. Hence we need to
gather a likeness of it from many of these modes, so that what is wanting in
one may be somewhat supplied from another."[36] Due to this need for more
than one name, Aquinas appeals to many other biblical designations for the
Son: Word, Image, and Radiance (cf. John 1.1–14; Col. 1.15; Heb. 1.3). He
explains,

> In the term "Word" the same property is comprised as in the name Son. . . . For
> the Son's nativity, which is his personal property, is signified by different names,
> which are attributed to the Son to express his perfection in various ways. To show
> that he is of the same nature as the Father, he is called the Son; to show that he is
> co-eternal, he is called the Radiance; to show that he is altogether alike, he is called
> Image; to show that he is begotten immaterially, he is called the Word. All these
> truths cannot be expressed by only one name.[37]

---

34.   Emmanuel Perrier, *La fécondité en Dieu: La puissance notionelle dans la Trinité selon saint Thomas
      d'Aquin* (Paris: Parole et Silence, 2009), especially chapters 1 and 3.
35.   On the psychological analogy, see Aquinas' place in the wider history provided by Russell L.
      Friedman, *Intellectual Traditions at the Medieval University: The Use of Philosophical Psychology in
      Trinitarian Theology among the Franciscans and Dominicans, 1250–1350*, 2 vols. (Leiden: Brill, 2012),
      1:49–89. On the development of Aquinas' theology of the Word, see Bernard Lonergan, *Verbum:
      Word and Idea in Aquinas*, eds. Frederick E. Crowe and Robert M. Doran (Toronto: University of
      Toronto Press, 1997); Harm Goris, "Theology and Theory of the Word in Aquinas: Understanding
      Augustine by Innovating Aristotle," in *Aquinas the Augustinian*, eds. Michael Dauphinais, Barry
      David, and Matthew Levering (Washington, DC: The Catholic University of America Press, 2007),
      62–78.
36.   Aquinas, *STh* Ia.42.2.*ad* 1.
37.   Aquinas, *STh* Ia.34.2.*ad* 3.

Now among these names Aquinas assigns a privileged place to "Word," drawn from the prologue to John's Gospel. Above all the different names we use to understand the Son's eternal generation, "the procession of the word from the intellect represents it more exactly; the intellectual word not being posterior to its source except in an intellect passing from potentiality to act; and this cannot be said of God."[38] When properly understood, *Verbum* designates an internal, and not external procession from a source or principle. This lack of transitivity in the essential intelligibility of an interior word issuing forth from the mind is what helps Aquinas improve his own articulation of the Son's immaterial, immanent generation by the Father. Since the name "Son" alone is open to easy distortion, Aquinas coordinates it with Jesus's other scriptural names to illuminate the *res* of his relation to the Father. The result is an account of "generation" that says neither more nor less than needs to be said: the Son is "begotten" of the Father in the sense that he shares the same nature, eternality, likeness, and perfection as the Father by virtue of their relative opposition. To say "eternally begotten" is thus to designate what is unique about the Son's relation to the Father.

However, despite this centrality accorded "Word," the name "Son" retains a more fundamental place in the economy of signs. Aquinas privileges "Son" as the focal point of the other names, for they all serve to illuminate the meaning of filiation. We have just seen how he privileges "Word" in particular as affording the most precise metaphysical intelligibility to our understanding of the Son's immaterial procession from the Father. Aquinas will privilege the personal name "Love" in a similar way when rendering the Holy Spirit's procession intelligible in its distinctiveness from the Son's generation. Both Word and Love reflect privileged means of intelligibility. These decisions reflect Aquinas's confidence in the psychological analogy for the Trinity as most capable of enabling the appropriate insight into the mystery, showing not only how it is rational to believe in two distinct processions in God but also how these processions relate immaterially to our own processes of knowing and love.[39] Beset as our understanding of created paternity and filiation is with creaturely associations, the biblical pattern of naming enjoins us to read Scripture patiently enough that we allow all the biblical names—both essential and personal—for the Son or Spirit to inform dogmatic formulations. It is when these names are all situated alongside one another with ample room to inform our account without losing sight of the other names that no single name becomes overgrown.[40]

38. Aquinas, *STh* Ia.42.2.*ad* 1.
39. See here Aquinas, *STh* Ia.93. Informative studies on Aquinas' theology of the *imago Dei* include D. Juvenal Merriell, *To the Image of the Trinity: A Study in the Development of Aquinas' Teaching* (Toronto: Pontifical Institute of Mediaeval Studies, 1990); Daria Spezzano, *The Glory of God's Grace: Deification according to St. Thomas Aquinas* (Ave Maria, FL: Sapientia, 2015).
40. The details of Aquinas' account are masterfully examined elsewhere: Gilles Emery, *The Trinitarian Theology of St Thomas Aquinas*, trans. Francesca Aran Murphy (Oxford: Oxford University Press,

All the same, the proper names of Father, Son, and Holy Spirit retain a privileged place because the mystery of the Trinity is inseparable from the mystery of salvation. The name of the Father, the Son, and the Holy Spirit is the name into which we are baptized (Matt. 28.19), and fittingly so: In regeneration we are adopted as sons through the natural Son, by the Spirit of adoption, to the Father who predestines us for this grace.[41] This inseparability of the mysteries of the Trinity and salvation reflects the revelatory significance of the visible missions of the Son and Spirit, but it also helps explain the summit of Aquinas's teaching on the doctrine of God in questions 26 and 43 of the *Prima pars* of the *Summa theologiae*. Question 26 concerns God's beatitude and stands at the head of "what belongs to the unity of the divine essence."[42] Since theology aims at knowing and loving God in anticipation of the blessed vision of God, then God's own beatitude exercises an exemplary function (among other things) for theology's contemplation of God in grace. As the God whose life is perfect beatitude in himself, God alone is the object of that knowledge that terminates in beatitude.[43] Similarly, question 43 on the divine missions, those miraculous prolongations in time of the eternal relations of the Son and Spirit to the Father, stands at the head of the treatise on the distinction of persons.[44] Whether we are concerned with creation, humanity created in the *imago Dei*, the moral life and the gifts of the Spirit, or the history of Christ (*acta et passa Christi*), we are concerned with the visible missions of the incarnation and Pentecost, or the invisible missions of the Son and Spirit in which the Trinity indwells believers in grace. In this soteriological respect, the proper names of Father, Son, and Holy Spirit retain a priority amongst other names within holy teaching (*sacra doctrina*)—an inquiry with explicitly soteriological aims.

Through his focus on personal names to convey knowledge of the relations within the Trinity, Aquinas achieves an inquiry that enables him to say what he must about the relations between the persons without saying too much. We have focused on the relation between the Father and Son, and seen that Aquinas understands this positively in such a way that respects God's incomprehensibility. Whatever else might be true of the eternal depths of the Father's relation to the Son, it is not revealed to us. Such an inquiry leaves little

2007), 151–268; Matthew Levering, *Scripture and Metaphysics: Aquinas and the Renewal of Trinitarian Theology* (Oxford: Blackwell, 2004), 165–96.

41. Aquinas, *In Matt.* 28.1.2465, in *Commentary on the Gospel of Matthew*, Latin/English Edition of the Works of St. Thomas Aquinas [WTA], vol. 34, trans. Jeremy Holmes and Beth Mortensen (Lander: The Aquinas Institute for the Study of Sacred Doctrine, 2013).

42. Aquinas, *STh* Ia.26.4.*ad* 2.

43. Aquinas, *STh* Ia.26.3.

44. On the importance of the divine missions for Aquinas' theology, see again Gilles Emery, "Missions invisibles et missions visibles: le Christ et son Esprit," *Revue Thomiste* 106 (2006): 51–99; Emery, "*Theologia* and *Dispensatio*: The Centrality of the Divine Missions in St. Thomas's Trinitarian Theology," *The Thomist* 74 (2010): 515–61.

room for differentiations of authority, or any command-obedience structure within that relation—and this is inseparable from the inquiry's orientation and principles. We will return to this insight in our conclusion, but first we must examine how "authority" does and does not function in Trinitarian formulations. After all, despite the apophatic tenor of Aquinas's inquiry, he still finds room to affirm "the authority of the person sending with regard to the person who is sent."[45] How is that so, and what does it mean?

III: The Trinity and Authority

Various sayings in the church fathers, particularly in Hilary of Poitiers, bequeathed to the Latin tradition the terminology and conceptuality of "authority" (*auctoritas*) in the doctrine of the Trinity.[46] Preserved as these sayings were in Peter Lombard's *Sentences*, they were the subjects of respect and close scrutiny. Consequently, this tradition often defended its use of *auctoritas* to depict the Father's paternity in relation to the Son, and likewise, the Father and Son's active spiration of the Spirit. However, this defense always came with the important caveat that "*auctoritas*" represented only the sense of "authorship" implicit in being a "principle." *Auctor* is therefore little more than another way of saying "principle" (*principium*). Indeed, where the issue is discussed at all one finds the explicit denial that "authority" can bear any other associations when used to speak of the Trinity. This section briefly looks at how Aquinas and others treat authority in regard to its wider associations, before turning to examine more broadly how authority functions within the distinction between theology and economy.

God's Authority ad intra

For Aquinas, the "authority" any person has vis-à-vis another person within God's life is solely the "authorship of origin" (*auctoritatem originis*).[47] Hence, "*auctoritas* of one divine person with respect to another obtains only inasmuch as one is from another eternally."[48] With this in mind, Aquinas still speaks of the Father's authorship of the Son: "although we attribute to the Father something of authority by reason of his being the principle, still we do not attribute any kind of subjection or inferiority to the Son, or to the Holy Spirit, to avoid any occasion of error."[49] He explains that "authority" therefore belongs equally to the Father and the Son, their order being preserved: "If everything which is the Father's is also the Son's, then neces-

---

45. Aquinas, *Contra errores Graecorum ad Urbanum papam*, in *Sancti Thomae de Aquino Opera Omnia iussu Leonis XII*, vol. 40A (Rome: Leonine Commission, 1967), I.14.

46. For example, Hilary of Poitiers, *De trinitate* 9.54: "By authority (*auctoritas*) of the giver, the Father is greater; nevertheless, the Son is not less, to whom oneness of being is given" (cited in Aquinas, *STh* Ia.33.1.*ad*2; cf. Lombard, *Sentences* I.16).

47. Aquinas, *Contra errores Graecorum* I.2.

48. Aquinas, *Contra errores Graecorum* II.23

49. Aquinas, *STh* Ia.33.1.*ad* 2.

sarily the Son also has the Father's authority according to which he is the principle of the Spirit."[50] It follows that the relation between the Father and Son as such may not be characterized by any command-obedience structure: "the relations of lord and father must differ according to the difference of filiation and servitude."[51] This usage suggests that "authority" is devoid of all associations with dominion and commanding power. The Father-Son relation is established on the basis of the opposition entailed by paternity and filiation, not by any opposition between dominion and servitude. Adherence to the strictures of knowing the persons on the basis of their revealed names precipitates a subordination of all conceptualities, like authority or obedience, to the personal properties contained in those names.

Lest he leave any room for doubt, Aquinas explicitly faces the question of whether there is a differentiation of authority among the divine persons, for authority can suggest a difference in dignity or rank.[52] In response, he notes that the latter associations are inapplicable, presumably because they are not included within the essential intelligibility of any of the personal names attributed to the Trinity: "[A]uthority in the Father is nothing but the relation of principle."[53] Since *auctoritas* only designates relations of origin generically, then the "authority" of the sender is implicit in the act of sending another person. What is neither implicit nor explicit is any hint of a differentiation of commanding power (*potestas*) or dominion (*dominium*): "[T]he Son has an authority with respect to the Holy Spirit—not, of course, that of being master or being greater, but in accord with origin alone";[54] "the Holy Spirit is given by the Father and Son alone, inasmuch as they have the authority not of dominion but of origin, because He proceeds from both."[55] Such discriminations become all the more salient when we see that Aquinas is unafraid to use "authority" in the sense of dominion elsewhere in his Trinitarian theology. For example, he interprets the Spirit blowing where he wills (John 3.8) as referring to the Spirit's spontaneous freedom and authority.[56] Indeed, on

50. Aquinas, *Contra errores Graecorum* II.3.
51. Aquinas, *STh* Ia.32.2.*corp.*
52. Aquinas, *De potentia* 10.1.*obj* 17 (ET English Dominican Province [Westminster, MD: Newman, 1952]).
53. Aquinas, *De potentia* 10.1.*ad* 17.
54. Aquinas, *Summa contra Gentiles* IV.24.3 (ET Charles J. O'Neil [South Bend, IN: University of Notre Dame Press, 1975]).
55. Aquinas, *In Gal.* 3.2.127, in *Commentary on the Letters of Saint Paul to the Galatians and Ephesians*, WTA 39, trans. Fabian R. Larcher and Matthew Lamb, eds. John Mortensen and Enrique Alarcón (Lander, WY: The Aquinas Institute for the Study of Sacred Doctrine, 2012). Further analyses of Aquinas's use of authority are provided in Ku, *God the Father*, 149–69; Dominic Legge, *The Trinitarian Christology of St Thomas Aquinas* (Oxford: Oxford University Press, 2017), 96–101.
56. Aquinas, *In Ioan.* 15.5.2059, in *Commentary on the Gospel of St. John*, 3 vols., trans. Fabian R. Larcher and James A. Weisheipl, ed. Daniel Keating and Matthew Levering (Washington, DC: The Catholic University of America Press, 2010); Ku, *God the Father*, 168. Such use is found in the fathers, as well. Interpreting 1 Cor. 12.11—"All these are the work of one and the same Spirit, and he distributes them to each one, just as he determines"—Basil of Caesarea says that even though he is sent by the Father

his reckoning, part of what it means for persons to be rational substances of an individual nature is to "have dominion over their acts, and not only to be acted upon like other things, but to act through themselves."[57] When speaking about the Trinity, *auctoritas* designates for Aquinas a relation of origin, but not any mastery, dominion, or commanding power of one person over another.

Consider as a further example the early modern Jesuit Dionysius Petavius, whose massive *De theologicis dogmatibus* remained influential well into the nineteenth century. After defending the use of *auctoritas* in Trinitarian discourse, and its equivalence to common Greek terms, he nevertheless recommends caution on account of the word's extended associations: "For instance, one is sometimes said to be an authority who precedes [others] by law and dignity; it belongs to such a one to have power [*potestas*] over another, as a guardian is in charge of their minors and has authority over them." Petavius appeals to examples of authority in this sense across various levels of society, from the home to the Church. "In these cases," he concludes, *auctores* are "leaders and standard bearers, [for] others are inferior to them. Certainly in this sense the Father may not be called *auctor* of the Son."[58] What about instances in the tradition where various "old sayings" (*veterum sententia*) attribute to the Father an authoritative supremacy in relation to the Son? In these cases, authority is always understood in the sense of origin: "[T]he Son is from the Father, not the Father from the Son."[59] Since the Father begets the Son and is not himself begotten, then it is legitimate to maintain that "Auctor" is particularly appropriate to the Father.[60] "Author" thus agrees with the Father's personal property of paternity like other terms such as "root, fount, and head."[61] Despite the appropriateness of "author" designating the Father's personal property, however, this cannot be confused with the kind of authority that would mean dominion over the Son and Spirit precisely because this would wed inferiority to procession and superiority to paternity.[62] What we

---

and Son, the Spirit acts *autezousiōs*—on his own authority (Basil, *De fide* 3, in *St Basil the Great: On Christian Doctrine and Practice*, trans. Mark DelCogliano [Yonkers, NY: St Vladimir's Seminary Press, 2012], 239). For another, christological example, see Augustine, *Tractate* 21.10, in *Tractates on the Gospel of John 11–27*, trans. John W. Rettig (Washington, DC: The Catholic University of America Press, 1988).

57. Aquinas, *STh* Ia.29.1.*corp.*

58. Dionysius Petavius, *Theologicorum Dogmatum*, vol. 2, *In quo de Sanctissima Trinitate agitur* [*De trinitate*] (Lutetiae Parisiorum: Cramoisy, 1644), V.5.11 (p. 505). Among the many examples Petavius proceeds to cite, see in particular Augustine, *Contra Maximinum Arianum* II.14.6, in *Patrologia Latina* vol. 42.773–74; Cerealis Castellensis Episcopi, *Libellus contra Maximinum Arianum* 9, in *Patrologia Latina* vol. 58.761–62.

59. Petavius, *De trinitate* V.5.13 (p. 506).

60. Petavius, *De trinitate* V.5.14 (p. 507).

61. Petavius, *De trinitate* V.5.15 (p. 507).

62. Diego Ruiz de Montoya, a famous commentator on Aquinas' doctrine of the Trinity, agrees: "Quoniam authoris nomine, denotatur sola ratio principij sine superioritate, inaequalitate aut

see in these examples is that where authority is used to refer to God's inner life, it is shorn of its common associations with *potestas*, *dignitas*, and *dominium*, such that it implies nothing more than a relation of origin. Authority is not a personal name, and so anything it says about the Trinitarian relations is subordinate to the intelligibility of the personal names as such. Since the names identify the Father-Son relation by eternal generation, then theologians like Aquinas and Petavius relativize the utility of authority in theological discourse about God *in se*. Whether they go sufficiently far is another question, one to which we will return below.

God's Authority ad extra

The examples of Aquinas and Petavius suffice to demonstrate how traditional language of authority has been interpreted with reference to the internal relations of the Trinity. But how does authority figure into those relations as they are extended into the economy? Christ claims not to speak on his own authority, but on the authority of the one who sent him (John 8:28). More pointedly still, the risen Christ tells his disciples that he has been given "[a]ll authority in heaven and on earth" (Matt. 28:18, NRSV). This same line of thought finds its denouement in the Son's eschatological subjection of the kingdom to the Father, upon which "the Son himself will also be subjected to him who put all things in subjection under him, that God may be all in all" (1 Cor. 15:28, NRSV; cf. Ps. 8:6). All these passages suggest the very differentiation in the authority of dominion that Aquinas and Petavius deny obtains between the persons in God's eternal life. So how does the Son's obedience to the Father's authority, and his reception of authority from the Father, cohere with such denials? And how does it connect to God's inner life?

As it respects the economy, the relevant questions of "authority" are typically located within the subject of divine sovereignty or dominion. And since God's sovereignty comes from his omnipotence and lordship, God's authority over all things is equally attributed to the whole Trinity.[63] Central to the best discussions of this material is the distinction between theology and economy, that which belongs to God's being and that which is proper to God on account of his condescension to creatures. Some sixteenth- and seventeenth-century Protestant scholastic theologians illustrate this well. For example, Francis Turretin, in his *Institutio theologiae elencticae*, discusses God's dominion and sovereignty (*dominio et potestate Dei*) as an implication of his power. From God's omnipotence follows his "*sovereignty* [*Potestas*], from which the right and authority of doing what he does belongs to him."[64] On account

distinctione essentiae" (*Commentaria ac Disputationes in primam partem Sancti Thoma De Trinitate* [Lyon: Prost, 1625], d. XLIX, sec. I, p. 421, col. 2.6).

63. Aquinas, *In Gal.* 1.1.13; Ku, *God the Father*, 165.
64. Francis Turretin, *Institutio theologiae elencticae* (New York: Robert Carter, 1847), III.xxii.i; ET George

of the economy, several distinctions become pertinent. The foundation of God's dominion is twofold, respecting his nature and his will. First and foremost, God's dominion is based upon his *"eminence of nature"* or superiority (*huperochē*) by virtue of his divinity with regard to everything that exists.[65] Second, it is based on God's "excellence and *amplitude of beneficence*," or the character of God's rule over his creation.[66] Since God's *potestas* concerns his divinity and the exercise of his kingly rule, Turretin draws a series of distinctions between the authority belonging to God naturally within the economy and that which belongs to Christ peculiarly on account of the economy. The latter is implied in those texts suggesting Christ's reception of authority and power (Phil. 2:9; Matt. 28:19). The key lies in distinguishing between the two senses of dominion. First, natural dominion belongs to Christ on several accounts: his divinity he shares equally with the Father and Holy Spirit, and the consequent providence, universal rule, and administration he exercises indivisibly with the Father and Spirit as God.[67] All the effects the Trinity causes by virtue of their common divine essence belong to him, and so too does the eternal duration of that authority that is Christ's according to his divinity (*kata phusin*): "Thy kingdom is an everlasting kingdom, and thy dominion endures throughout all generations" (Ps. 145:13, KJV). To say anything less would be to deny Christ's full divinity. However, second, there is also an authority that is Christ's according to his particular station within the economy (*kata thein*). This authority he receives from the Father, has its foundation in predestination, its exercise in the kingdom of grace, and its effects in that kingdom's saving benefits; it is "exercised by him as Mediator and *thēanthrōpō* [God-man], whence it is called *personal* because it pertains to the person of the Son and is appointed to his economy," and it will "have an end, at least as to mode, because he will deliver up the kingdom to God the Father (1 Cor. 15:24)."[68] This interpretation of 1 Corinthians 15:24–28 thus draws upon the eighth psalm's eschatological portrait of the son of man having dominion over all creation, humanity's original vocation, showing that this dominion is fulfilled in Christ and nevertheless subordinate to that dominion belonging to the undivided Trinity (cf. Heb. 2:5–9).[69] All through-

---

Musgrave Giger, ed. James T. Dennison, Jr (Phillipsburg, NJ: P&R, 1992), 1:250. On Protestant scholastic views of dominion more generally, see Richard A. Muller, *Post-Reformation Reformed Dogmatics: The Rise and Development of Reformed Orthodoxy, ca. 1520 to ca. 1725*, vol. 3, *The Divine Essence and Attributes* (Grand Rapids: Baker Academic, 2003), 537–39.

65. Turretin, *Institutio* III.xxii.ii (1:250).

66. Turretin, *Institutio* III.xxii.ii (1:250).

67. Turretin, *Institutio* III.xxii.iii (1:250–51).

68. Turretin, *Institutio* III.xxii.iii (1:251). So too Amandus Polanus, *Syntagma theologiae Christianae* (Hanoviae, 1615), III.10, 230 (col. 2i-k), commenting on 1 Cor. 15:24 (cf. also II.29, 188 [col. 1a]). The whole of Polanus' *Syntagma* III.10 addresses texts suggesting an inequality among the divine persons (e.g., John 14:28; 1 Cor. 11:3; 15:24, 28; Prov. 8:22; Col. 1:15; John 5.19; et al.).

69. Thus also Aquinas, *In I Cor.* 15.3.937–49, in *Commentary on the Letters of Saint Paul to the Corinthians*. The distinction between theology and economy is implicit: "He will deliver [the kingdom] up in such

out his discussion, Turretin consistently distinguishes between the authority over creation that the Son has equally with the Father and Holy Spirit as fully God, and the authority that is granted him by and subject to the Father as fully man.

Particularly as it concerns the Father giving all authority in heaven and on earth to the Son (Matt. 28:18), the distinction between theology and economy is essential to the fundamentally Cyrilline character of Reformed Christology. Amandus Polanus notes that the Father giving the Son "all authority" (*pasa exousia*) does not mean that the Father communicated the divine omnipotence to the Son, much less to the Son's humanity. This might suggest either that the Son somehow did not yet fully possess the divine nature, or that the divine omnipotence was communicated directly to his human nature. Polanus explains, "[T]his *exousia* or sovereignty [*potestas*] is not the eternal omnipotence which he possessed before the created world, but rather it is the Mediator's own dominion and command, which he exercises according to both natures as LORD and King of the church, and as judge of the world; it is given to him by the Father in time."[70] Considered economically (*kata oikōnōmian*), the Son has a mediatorial authority subject to the Father. But considered theologically (*kata theologian*), the Father and Son share the same authority: "the Father acts through the Son, not as though by an instrument or attendant of the operation, but as it were by sharing simultaneously the same wisdom, will, power, and authority in acting."[71] Indeed, it is because the Son's authority is identical with the Father's that the Son's teaching encounters us with irreducible force and validity. Any differentiation of sovereign authority between the Father and the Son therefore arises on account of God's economic condescension.

John Owen makes a similar point when commenting on the familiar distinction, drawn from Philippians 2:6–7, between the Son's divine nature (*forma Dei*) and servant nature (*forma servi*). In the form of God, the Son "had dominion over all, owed service and obedience unto none, being in the 'form of God,' and equal unto him."[72] In this state, the Son "was God, participant in the divine nature, for God hath no form but that of his essence and being; and hence he was equal with God, in authority, dignity, and power. Because he was in the form of God, he must be equal with God; for there is *order* in the Divine Persons, but no *inequality* in the Divine Being."[73] When he assumed human flesh and took on the form of a servant, this was "his condescension." The Son assumes the servant form of human flesh without surrendering any of the authority, dignity, and power he has with the Father:

a way that He does not take it from Himself; indeed, He, the one God with the Father and the Holy Spirit will reign" (*In Cor I* 15.3.937).

70. Polanus, *Syntagma* II.29, 187 (col. 2i-k).
71. Polanus, *Syntagma* IV.3, 237 (col. 1h).
72. John Owen, *Christologia*, in *The Works of John Owen*, 16 vols. (Edinburgh: Banner of Truth, 1968), 1:207.
73. Owen, *The Glory of Christ*, in *Works*, 1:326.

"[H]e became what he was not, but he ceased not to be what he was."[74] The logic here is act follows being, the mode of acting follows the mode of being, and so the Son acts from the Father and is sent by the Father in time. For this reason the Father "sent the Son, as he gives the Spirit, by an act of sovereign authority."[75] This authority is understood economically, though, with reference to the voluntarily assumed offices: "It is the office of the Holy Ghost to be an advocate for us, and a comforter to us; in which respect, not absolutely, he is thus sent authoritatively by Father and Son."[76] To reinforce his point, Owen invokes the axiom: "inequality of office does not abrogate equality of nature" (*inaequalitas officii non tollit aequalitatem naturae*).[77] Note well that Owen locates inequality in the voluntarily assumed office, not in an intrinsic function or role of the person considered absolutely. The difference between the two conceptions is significant: One suggests a contingent act of will, the other a necessary act of nature; one refers to mission, the other to procession. The complex discourses of "authority" in Scripture are readily intelligible within a two-natures Christology attentive to the distinction between theology and economy. When thus understood, the Son is both equal to the Father in authority, and subject to the Father's authority: the former is natural and eternal, the latter is voluntary and dispensatory; the former is and remains his as the eternal Word of the Father, the latter is his as the appointed Mediator (*Logos incarnandus*).

Language of "authority" in Trinitarian theology requires considerable reserve, in light of its extended associations with notions like commanding power, superior dignity, and dominion. Aquinas and many scholastics are a sure guide when they explicitly refute the idea that any differentiated authority characterizes the Father-Son relation as such. Reflection on the Father's eternal relation to the Son is exhausted in consideration of the Son's eternal generation, which is disclosed through contemplative reflection on the divine names. In his divinity, the Son exists from the Father (*ex Patre*). Yet, recognizing this does not prevent us from affirming the differentiated authority characterizing this relation as it extends into time on account of the economy's unique circumstances: The Son assumes human nature, offers up the perfect obedience that Adam did not, and lives and reigns as the royal man whose kingdom is ordered to the glory of the Father. As man, the Son receives an authority economically from the Father without abdicating the same authority he shares with the Father as God. To be sure, the Son receives this authority in accordance with his mode of being from the Father; his human nature

74. Owen, *The Glory of Christ*, in *Works*, 1:326.
75. Owen, *Christologia*, in *Works*, 1:219.
76. Owen, *Of Communion with the Father, Son, and Holy Ghost*, in *Works*, 2:229. The theologoumenon of the *pactum salutis* is the background to Owen's formulation, on which see Timothy Baylor's contribution to this volume.
77. Also Turretin, *Institutio* XIV.ii.xvii, xxiii (2:383, 384).

and activity conforms to his personal property of filiation *ex Patre*. But the opposite is not true: The differentiation in authority of dominion between the Father and the Mediator is strictly economic. The point of correspondence between the Son's procession and mission is his filial being and activity; the point of divergence is that the authority of dominion only characterizes the Father's relation to the Son on account of the Son's voluntarily assumed mediatorial office he executes in our flesh.

IV: Conclusion

Traditional approaches to the internal relations of the Trinity privilege the signifying power of God's revealed personal names, which in turn reveal personal properties by which the persons' distinctions are intelligible. The example of Aquinas shows how this approach is couched within an inquiry whose requisite virtues are impressed upon it by the demands of its object. God's incomprehensibility and revelation dictate that theological inquiry operate within the confines of a dialectic between positive and negative theology, which is therefore also a dialectic between boldness and fear, speech and silence. Any distinction we posit between the persons in terms other than those strictly necessary to the revealed names risks unwarranted curiosity. Wishing to say neither too much nor too little, Aquinas follows a precedence of privileging God's names as guides to reasoning about Trinitarian relations. The names are not sundered from the visible missions of the Son and Spirit, for the latter deliver the former to us. Nevertheless, there are things we attribute to the persons on account of their missions that are not constitutive of their eternal identities. Names help us keep procession and mission distinct by pointing us to the infinite fullness of perfection anterior to the missions. This is because names reveal the character of eternal relations "when they are said by themselves."[78] Aquinas and others see in the essential intelligibility of "names that have reference to procession" the best means of understanding the internal relations of the Trinity.[79] As the foregoing examples illustrate, this essential intelligibility includes everything pertaining to the divine nature except the oppositional structure of the persons' relations. The example of authority illustrates how personal names are privileged over other conceptualities, which might threaten to introduce elements into God's internal relations that are either inappropriate to God's eternal perfection or unnecessary to posit because they are accounted for on some other basis (like God's condescension in his economy). Indeed, on this basis we might question whether

---

78. Basil of Caesarea, *Against Eunomius* 2.22, trans. Mark DelCogliano and Andrew Radde-Gallwitz (Washington, DC: The Catholic University of America Press, 2011). Basil differs from Aquinas in important respects. See especially Andrew Radde-Gallwitz, *Basil of Caesarea, Gregory of Nyssa, and the Transformation of Divine Simplicity* (Oxford: Oxford University Press, 2009), 5–6, 113–74; Mark DelCogliano, *Basil of Caesarea's Anti-Eunomian Theory of Names: Christian Theology and Late-Antique Philosophy in the Fourth Century Trinitarian Controversy* (Leiden: Brill, 2010), 153–260.

79. Aquinas, *STh* Ia.27.1.*corp.*

there is any need for language of authority in reference to God's inner life. Where must authority be predicated of the persons' mutual relations beyond the economy? The qualification and retention of *auctoritas* by Aquinas and Petavius seems more traditionalist than necessary, and even then its abiding validity depends upon peculiarities of the Latin. In view of the inseparable connotations authority has in English with dominion and political supremacy, it is best dropped altogether when referring to the divine processions.

The details with which this alternative approach has been supported traditionally are not immune to critique; one could question the exegesis, dialectical tools, metaphysics, or the operative notion of perfection. And indeed many do. On just such grounds, some contemporary theologians have added to the personal properties of the Son on the basis not of his names, but of his activity. Bruce McCormack argues approvingly that Barth's mature Christology entails two significant changes to the doctrine of the Trinity: The first is that he refuses any straightforward equation of God's essence with "hiddenness," and the second is that he adds to the personal properties of the Father, Son, and Spirit. To the Son are added the personal properties of "humility" and "obedience," to the Father "commanding in majesty," and to the Spirit "binding together the Father and Son" in their opposition of majesty and humility.[80] These two positions have the net effect of relating the personal properties (matter of revelation) more closely to their economic forms (manner of revelation). Somewhat similarly, Bruce Ware argues that "submission to the Father" is a personal property of the Son.[81] One might wonder if this implicitly attributes a property of commanding authority to the Father as well, somewhat like McCormack's reading of Barth. Such proposals posit humility, obedience, and submission as constitutive of the Son's relation to the Father in eternity. It follows that what we see in time—even the Son's obedience to the Father—is but an extension of what already takes place in eternity: dominion and servitude, command and obedience, and the unfathomable unity of both in the depths of God. These less circumspect uses of "authority" language to refer to the inner-Trinitarian relations mark a departure from traditional uses of such language. Minimally, this disparity should lead us to ask why that is the case.

Without essaying a genealogy of this disparity, I conclude with two exegetical questions. First, what function do the divine names play in contemporary accounts privileging a conceptuality of the "immanent" and "economic" Trinity over the traditional distinction between the processions and missions?[82]

---

80. Bruce L. McCormack, "The Doctrine of the Trinity after Barth: An Attempt to Reconstruct Barth's Doctrine in Light of His Later Christology," in *Trinitarian Theology After Barth*, eds. Myk Habets and Phillip Tolliday (Eugene, OR: Wipf & Stock, 2011), 111–12.

81. Bruce Ware, "Does Affirming an Eternal Authority-Submission Relationship in the Trinity Entail a Denial of *Homoousios*?," in Ware and Starke, eds., *One God in Three Persons*, 242–5.

82. Some searching criticisms of this conceptuality are provided by Bruce D. Marshall, "The Unity of the Triune God: Reviving an Ancient Question," *The Thomist* 74, no. 1 (2010): 1–32. Further illuminating

Does this conceptuality tend to exalt external activity over personal names as privileged paths of disclosure? The concern here is that zeal for the way of causality (*via causalitatis*) in the traditional "threefold way" may, and sometimes does, diminish how the ways of eminence and negation (*viae eminentiae et remotionis*) chasten the understanding of faith. In other words, do names tell us anything about processions that missions do not? Second, what is gained by adding to the density of personal properties that is not already secured in traditional language of the offices of the Son and the Spirit? More importantly, what is lost? Put differently: what grounds are there for projecting the Son's obedience onto his eternal relation to the Father, which are not already exhausted in reflection on the Son's *forma servi*? However one answers these questions, the contemplative approach to the divine names and the distinction between theology and economy offers a set of principles and warrants that discipline us to say only as much as necessary. The wisdom here is: "God is in heaven and you are on earth, so let your words be few" (Eccl. 5:2). May it be so with us all.

---

criticisms are offered by Jeremy D. Wilkins, "Method, Order, and Analogy in Trinitarian Theology: Karl Rahner's Critique of the 'Psychological' Approach," *The Thomist* 74.3 (2010): 563–92. Wilkins raises the question about whether the economic/immanent conceptuality presupposes a greater affinity to "necessary" reasoning, rather than arguments *ex convenientiae* (an important subject I have left to the side in the present discussion). Fred Sanders is critical, but more sanguine about the conceptuality's possible value (*The Triune God* [Grand Rapids: Zondervan, 2016], 144–53. This cautious optimism is interesting to note alongside the privileged function of missions over names in Sanders's proposal (*The Triune God*, 122–29); nevertheless, his use of the conceptuality avoids its typical pitfalls. For an alternative (yet in many ways complementary) account that accords more weight to the function of names, see Scott Swain, "The Trinity," in *Christian Dogmatics: Reformed Theology for the Church Catholic*, eds. Michael Allen and Scott R. Swain (Grand Rapids: Baker, 2016), 78–106.

Bibliography

Augustine of Hippo. *Tractates on the Gospel of John 11–27*. Translated by John W. Rettig. The Fathers of the Church 79. Washington, DC: The Catholic University of America Press, 1988.

Aquinas, Thomas. *Commentary on the Gospel of Matthew*. In *Latin/English Edition of the Works of St. Thomas Aquinas*, vols. 33–34. Translated by Jeremy Holmes and Beth Mortensen. Edited by The Aquinas Institute. Lander, WY: The Aquinas Institute for the Study of Sacred Doctrine, 2013.

_____. *Commentary on the Gospel of St. John*. 3 vols. Translated by Fabian R. Larcher and James A. Weisheipl. Introduction and Notes by Daniel Keating and Matthew Levering. Washington, DC: The Catholic University of America Press, 2010.

_____. *Commentary on the Letters of Saint Paul to the Corinthians*. In *Latin/English Edition of the Works of St. Thomas Aquinas*, vol. 38. Translated by Fabian R. Larcher, Beth Mortensen, and Daniel Keating. Edited by John Mortensen and Enrique Alarcón. Lander, WY: The Aquinas Institute for the Study of Sacred Doctrine, 2012.

_____. *Commentary on the Letters of Saint Paul to the Galatians and Ephesians*. In *Latin/English Edition of the Works of St. Thomas Aquinas*, vol. 39. Translated by Fabian R. Larcher and Matthew Lamb. Edited by John Mortensen and Enrique Alarcón. Lander, WY: The Aquinas Institute for the Study of Sacred Doctrine, 2012.

_____. *Contra errores Graecorum ad Urbanum papam*. In *Sancti Thomae de Aquino Opera Omnia iussu Leonis XII*, vol. 40A. Rome: Leonine Commission, 1967.

_____. *The Disputed Questions on Truth*. 3 vols. Translated by R. Schmidt. Chicago: Henry Regnery, 1954.

_____. *In librum beati Dionysii de divinis expositio*. Edited by Ceslai Pera. Turin and Rome: Marietti, 1950.

_____. *On the Power of God*. Translated by the English Dominican Province. Westminster, MD: Newman, 1952.

_____. *Summa Theologica*. Translated by the English Dominican Province. New York: Benziger Brothers, 1947.

_____. *Summa contra Gentiles*. 4 vols. Translated by A. Pegis, J. Anderson, V. J. Burke, and C. J. O'Neil. South Bend, IN: University of Notre Dame Press, 1975.

Barth, Karl. *Church Dogmatics*, vols. I-IV. Edited by Geoffrey W. Bromiley and Thomas F. Torrance. Translated by Geoffrey W. Bromiley, et al. Edinburgh: T & T Clark, 1956–75.

Basil of Caesarea, *Against Eunomius*. Translated by Mark DelCogliano and Andrew Radde-Gallwitz. The Fathers of the Church 122. Washington, DC: The Catholic University of America Press, 2011.

_____. *St Basil the Great: On Christian Doctrine and Practice*. Translated by Mark DelCogliano. Yonkers, NY: St. Vladimir's Seminary Press, 2012.

Bonaventure. *Works of St. Bonaventure*, vol. 9. Edited by Dominic V. Monti. Saint Bonaventure, NY: Franciscan Institute, 2005.

Bonino, Serge-Thomas. "La simplicité de Dieu." In *Istituto San Tommaso: Studi 1996*, edited by Dietrich Lorenz, 117–51. Rome: Pontificia Università San Tommaso, 1997.

DelCogliano, Mark. *Basil of Caesarea's Anti-Eunomian Theory of Names: Christian Theology and Late-Antique Philosophy in the Fourth Century Trinitarian Controversy*. Leiden: Brill, 2010.

Diego Ruiz de Montoya. *Commentaria ac Disputationes in primam partem Sancti Thoma De Trinitate*. Lyon: Prost, 1625.

Dionysius Petavius. *Theologicorum Dogmatum*, vol. 2, *In quo de Sanctissima Trinitate agitur*. Lutetiae Parisiorum: Cramoisy, 1644.

Emery, Gilles. "Missions invisibles et missions visibles: le Christ et son Esprit." *Revue Thomiste* 106 (2006): 51–99.

_____. "*Theologia* and *Dispensatio*: The Centrality of the Divine Missions in St. Thomas's Trinitarian Theology." *The Thomist* 74 (2010): 515–61.

_____. *The Trinitarian Theology of St. Thomas Aquinas*. Translated by Francesca Aran Murphy. Oxford: Oxford University Press, 2007.

Friedman, Russell L. *Intellectual Traditions at the Medieval University: The Use of Philosophical Psychology in Trinitarian Theology among the Franciscans and Dominicans, 1250–1350*. 2 vols. Leiden: Brill, 2012.

Goris, Harm. "Theology and Theory of the Word in Aquinas: Understanding Augustine by Innovating Aristotle." In *Aquinas the Augustinian*, edited by Michael Dauphinais, Barry David, and Matthew Levering, 62–78. Washington, DC: The Catholic University of America Press, 2007.

John of Damascus. *Saint John of Damascus: Writings*. Translated by Frederic H. Chase, Jr. The Fathers of the Church 37. Washington, DC: The Catholic University of America Press, 1958.

Jowers, Dennis W., and H. Wayne House, eds. *The New Evangelical Subordinationism? Perspectives on the Equality of God the Father and God the Son*. Eugene, OR: Pickwick, 2012.

Ku, John Baptist. *God the Father in the Theology of St. Thomas Aquinas*. New York: Peter Lang, 2013.

Levering, Matthew. *Scripture and Metaphysics: Aquinas and the Renewal of Trinitarian Theology*. Oxford: Blackwell, 2004.

Legge, Dominic. *The Trinitarian Christology of St Thomas Aquinas*. Oxford: Oxford University Press, 2017.

Lonergan, Bernard. *Verbum: Word and Idea in Aquinas*. Collected Works of Bernard Lonergan 2. Edited by Frederick E. Crowe and Robert M. Doran. Toronto: University of Toronto Press, 1997.

Mansini, Guy. "Can Humility and Obedience be Trinitarian Realities?" In *Thomas Aquinas and Karl Barth*, edited by Bruce L. McCormack and Thomas Joseph White, 71–98. Grand Rapids: Eerdmans, 2013.

Marshall, Bruce D. "The Unity of the Triune God: Reviving an Ancient Question." *The Thomist* 74 (2010): 1–32.

McCormack, Bruce L. "The Doctrine of the Trinity after Barth: An Attempt to Reconstruct Barth's Doctrine in Light of His Later Christology." In *Trinitarian Theology after Barth*, edited by Myk Habets and Phillip Tolliday, 87–118. Eugene, OR: Wipf & Stock, 2011.

_____. "Processions and Missions: A Point of Convergence between Thomas Aquinas and Karl Barth." In *Thomas Aquinas and Karl Barth*, edited by Bruce L. McCormack and Thomas Joseph White, 99–126. Grand Rapids: Eerdmans, 2013.

McCormack, Bruce L., and Thomas Joseph White, eds. *Thomas Aquinas and Karl Barth: An Unofficial Catholic-Protestant Dialogue*. Grand Rapids: Eerdmans, 2013.

Merriell, D. Juvenal. *To the Image of the Trinity: A Study in the Development of Aquinas's Teaching*. Toronto: Pontifical Institute of Mediaeval Studies, 1990.

Muller, Richard A. *Post-Reformation Reformed Dogmatics: The Rise and Development of Reformed Orthodoxy, ca. 1520 to ca. 1725*. 4 vols. Grand Rapids: Baker, 2003.

O'Rourke, Fran. *Pseudo-Dionysius and the Metaphysics of Aquinas*. Leiden: Brill, 1992.

Owen, John. *The Works of John Owen*. 16 vols. Edinburgh: Banner of Truth Trust, 1968.

Perrier, Emmanuel. *La fécondité en Dieu: La puissance notionelle dans la Trinité selon saint Thomas d'Aquin*. Paris: Parole et Silence, 2009.

Polanus, Amandus. *Syntagma theologiae Christianae*. Hanoviae, 1615.

Radde-Gallwitz, Andrew. *Basil of Caesarea, Gregory of Nyssa, and the Transformation of Divine Simplicity*. Oxford: Oxford University Press, 2009.

Rocca, Gregory P. *Speaking the Incomprehensible God: Thomas Aquinas on the Interplay of Positive and Negative Theology*. Washington, DC: The Catholic University of America Press, 2004.

Turretin, Francis. *Insitutio theologicae elencticae*. 3 vols. New York: Robert Carter, 1847.

_____. *Institutes of Elenctic Theology*. 3 vols. Translated by George Musgrave Giger. Edited by James T. Dennison, Jr. Phillipsburg, NJ: Presbyterian & Reformed, 1992.

Velde, Rudi A. te. *Aquinas on God: The "Divine Science" of the* Summa Theologiae. Farnham: Ashgate, 2006.

Sanders, Fred. *The Triune God*. New Studies in Dogmatics. Grand Rapids: Zondervan, 2016.

Spezzano, Daria. *The Glory of God's Grace: Deification According to St. Thomas Aquinas*. Ave Maria: Sapientia, 2015.

Swain, Scott, and Michael Allen. "The Obedience of the Eternal Son." *International Journal of Systematic Theology* 15, no. 2 (2013): 114–34.

Swain, Scott R. "On Divine Naming." In *Aquinas Among the Protestants*, edited by Manfred Svensson and David VanDrunen, 207–27. Oxford: Wiley-Blackwell, 2017.

———. "The Trinity." In *Christian Dogmatics: Reformed Theology for the Church Catholic*, edited by Michael Allen and Scott R. Swain, 78–106. Grand Rapids: Baker, 2016.

Ware, Bruce A. "Does Affirming an Eternal Authority-Submission Relationship in the Trinity Entail a Denial of *Homoousios*?" In *One God in Three Persons*, edited by Bruce A. Ware and John Starke, 242–45. Wheaton, IL: Crossway, 2015.

Webster, John B. *God without Measure*. 2 vols. London: Bloomsbury, 2016.

White, Thomas Joseph. *The Incarnate Lord: A Thomistic Study in Christology*. Washington, DC: The Catholic University of America Press, 2015.

Wilkins, Jeremy D. "Method, Order, and Analogy in Trinitarian Theology: Karl Rahner's Critique of the 'Psychological' Approach." *The Thomist* 74. no. 3 (2010): 563–92.

Wittman, Tyler R. "Not a God of Confusion but of Peace: Aquinas and the Meaning of Divine Simplicity." *Modern Theology* 32, no. 2 (2016): 151–69.

CHAPTER 8

"He Humbled Himself"

Trinity, Covenant, and the Gracious Condescension of the Son in John Owen

T. ROBERT BAYLOR

Introduction

One of the central concerns that has motivated modern theology has been the relationship between theology and economy.[1] How can we reason from the contingent facts of history to necessary and eternal truths, such as the nature and existence of God? This concern is represented in many modern attempts to configure Christian teaching on the doctrine of the Trinity so that the inner life of God is regulated through and more fully determined by the form of God's revelation within the economy of grace—hence Rahner's Rule that the immanent Trinity is the economic Trinity, and vice versa. This is the basic logic informing much of the revival of Trinitarian theology over the better part of the last century.[2] And that includes more

1. I would like to thank Steve Holmes, Tyler Wittman, Jared Michelson, and Kendall Cleveland for their comments on an earlier version of this essay. I would also like to thank the students and faculty in attendance at the University of Aberdeen's Systematic Theology Seminar. They provided some very helpful feedback after I presented a version of this essay in November of 2017.
2. Barth, von Balthasar, Rahner, and Moltmann are all notable examples.

recent attempts to posit an eternal, functional subordination in the Godhead between the persons of the Father and the Son.

These accounts have typically pleaded their case on the basis of those scriptural texts that speak of the Son's submission to his Father, e.g., "the Father is greater than I" (John 14:28). Traditionally, passages like these have been interpreted using a kind of Chalcedonian logic, such that the Son's subordination to the Father is understood as part of that *status exaninitionis*, or "state of humiliation," which Christ elected in the assumption of flesh. As such, the Son's subordination to the Father is not understood as a necessary condition of the Son as he is a divine person. Rather, it is a condition belonging only to the Son's temporal mission, one which he has voluntarily (and therefore, freely and contingently) taken upon himself for the purpose of our redemption. This is the meaning of the apostle's words where he calls us to imitate the mind of Christ: "he humbled himself" (Phil. 2:8).

In contrast with these readings, however, advocates of the eternal, functional subordination of the Son read such biblical texts as referring also to the Son's *divine* person. In that respect, they posit an identity between the Son's mission in time and his relation to the Father in eternity. That submission to the Father's authority which marks the Son's work within the economy of grace is, itself, integral to the *filiation* of the Son. The subordination of the Son to the Father is thus *eternal* in the sense that it is a natural and necessary property belonging to the Son as he is the second person of the Trinity, who is eternally "from the Father."[3] It is also *functional*, in the sense that this subordination determines all acts of the Son, and is discerned on the basis of the Son's temporal mission within the economy of grace. In other words, this subordination is the substance and content of the Son's filiation, defining the *mode* under which the Son (as a divine person) acts in unison with the Father.

It is, perhaps, unsurprising that Reformed theology should be somewhat sympathetic to such an account. In contrast with many of the most venerable Catholic thinkers who restricted Christ's work of mediation to his human nature, the Reformed maintained that Christ is Mediator on behalf of the elect in both his divine and human natures. It is not only as he is human that Christ is "for us," but also as he is God. This is precisely the interest that led a Reformed theologian of no less stature than Karl Barth to affirm that there is a kind of obedience in God.[4] How else could we possibly come to grips with the mission of the Son as a truly *divine* work—as a work elected by God, which is truly a revelation of God?

---

3.   Though they would no doubt hasten to add that this should be understood as a *personal* property, rather than an *essential* property. The Son is not of a different essence than the Father, but obedience to the Father's authority is said to be a personal property of the Son.

4.   Karl Barth, *Church Dogmatics*, Study Edition, vol. IV/1, eds. G. W. Bromiley and T. F. Torrance (London: T & T Clark, 2009), 209.

Yet, historically, Reformed theology has understood the Son's subordination to the Father in different ways. One of the most influential and controversial of those has been through the doctrine of the *pactum salutis* or the covenant of redemption. Though the initial concept is simple enough to grasp—that Christ's redemption of lost sinners in time is grounded in a covenant between the Father and the Son in eternity—this is a very powerful and deceptively complicated doctrine. As one begins to unwind its various stands in the doctrines of God, the Trinity, Christology, or the nature of salvation and its application, the more it becomes clear how ideas buried deep within this concept carry wide-reaching systematic implications for the whole structure of Christian teaching.

What I intend to do in this article is to examine how the doctrine of the *pactum salutis* shaped some Reformed accounts of the Son's humiliation. I will argue that the formulation attempts to identify the basis of the Son's subordination to the Father in the inner life of God, and so in that respect attempts to understand the humiliation of the Son as eternal, in the sense at least that it is eternally *willed* by God, and functional, in that this purpose determines the whole of the Son's activity within the economy of redemption. Nevertheless, one of the principal interests guaranteed by speaking of an eternal "pact" between the Father and the Son was to ground the *status exaninitionis* of the Son in a free and voluntary act of God's will. In this way, the Reformed depicted the humiliation of the Son as an act of *grace* undertaken for our sake, and not as a natural or necessary property of the Son's life as he is the second person of the Trinity. In other words, though eternally willed by God, the humiliation of the Son was nonetheless regarded as a fully *contingent* aspect of the Son's mission, and not as a personal property constitutive of his divine person. And this was for the simple reason that the Reformed wished to maintain that the Son's mission was a *gracious* act, and therefore an act of divine freedom.

I will make this case largely by drawing on the seventeenth-century Reformed thinker, John Owen. Owen's writings in particular have recently been cited as offering historical precedent for contemporary accounts of the eternal, functional subordination of the Son.[5] By examining these figures, I will show why the Reformed have traditionally rejected accounts of the Son's humiliation which take his subordinate status as being a property proper to him as the second person of the Trinity, in the manner that contemporary accounts of eternal, functional subordinationism maintain. And I will show that they did this precisely by means of the *pactum salutis*.

I should state here that the following should not be read as an endorsement of the *pactum salutis*. Though I do not have space here to articulate them, I think there are good reasons not to endorse the notion of an intra-

---

5. See the essay by New York City Pastor John Starke: "Augustine and His Interpreters," in *One God in Three Persons: Unity of Essence, Distinction of Persons, Implications for Life*, eds. Bruce Ware and John Starke (Wheaton, IL: Crossway, 2015), 164.

Trinitarian covenant, or, at the very least, to be dubious about the project. My objective here is not to demonstrate the truthfulness or even the internal consistency of the doctrine. I intend only to demonstrate how Reformed theologians who do hold to this doctrine make use of the concept in order to avoid some of the exact conclusions that have recently been reached by those endorsing eternal functional subordination. My hope is that, in doing so, I might be able to offer some assistance to those indebted to this kind of covenant theology, by pointing them to those ways in which their own tradition sought to be faithful to Nicene Christian teaching on the nature of God and the doctrine of the Trinity.

A number of really excellent pieces have already been written narrating the tradition-history of the *pactum salutis*,[6] assessing its basis in exegesis,[7] or attempting a contemporary dogmatic reconstruction,[8] so I will not dwell at length on these issues here. Instead, I will focus my exposition on how the covenant frames the nature of the Son's *status exinanitionis*. I will do this, first, by surveying the dogmatic function of the covenant of redemption, before moving on to explore the intra-Trinitarian dynamics of covenant-making. The latter will require four parts. The first will describe the general nature of a covenant. In the second part, I will examine the coherence of the *pactum salutis* with teaching on the unity of the divine will. The third part will focus on Owen's readings of several scriptural texts to ascertain how this eternal covenant is manifested within the temporal mission of the Son, and what exactly it says about the nature of Christ's obedience. Finally, we will examine the freedom of the Father and the Son in the making of this covenant, along with its significance for understanding the Son's eternal relation to the Father.

I. The Covenant of Redemption and the Free Grace of God

Though it is often panned as an overly "speculative" doctrine, constructed remotely from the revelation of Christ within the economy of grace, from its very inception, the burden of the *pactum salutis* was to articulate a distinctly Calvinistic vision of the work of the Mediator, one that takes full account of his substitutionary work and the unconditional nature of his grace. This is evident from the very earliest articulation of the doctrine in David Dickson's 1638 address to the General Assembly of the Church of Scotland. The address

---

6. See J. V. Fesko, *The Covenant of Redemption: Origins, Development, and Reception* (Göttingen: Vandenhoeck & Ruprecht, 2010).

7. Richard Muller, "Toward the Pactum Salutis: Locating the Origins of a Concept," *Mid-Western Journal of Theology* 18 (2007): 11–65.

8. Scott R. Swain, "Covenant of Redemption," in *Christian Dogmatics: Reformed Theology for the Church Catholic*, eds. Michael Allen and Scott R. Swain (Grand Rapids: Baker Academic, 2016), 107–25; see also John Webster, "It Was the Will of the Lord to Bruise Him: Soteriology and the Doctrine of God," in *God of Salvation: Soteriology in Theological Perspective*, eds. Murray Rae and Ivor Davidson (New York: Routledge, 2010), 15–34.

consists largely in a polemic against Arminianism, arguing that the Armin-
ians compromised the nature of Christ's redeeming work by reducing the efficacy of Christ's blood to the purchasing of a mere "possibility of some man's
salvation." Dickson links this reduction of the saving efficacy of Christ's death
to conditional election and the correlative claim that, through the universal
grace of Christ, humankind is once again restored to the position of Adam,
capable of striking a "bargane betwixt God and man." The "maine errour" of
this position, he claims, is that it fails to attend to the eternal "Covenant of
redemption betwixt God and Christ."[9]

Dickson goes on to sketch what this covenant consists in:

(1) A pretemporal covenant between God and Christ, the "second persone"
who is "designed Mediatour betwixt God and Man," such that Christ
himself forms the "ground" of all God's actions toward the believer in the
covenant of grace.

(2) The "number and names" of the elect for whom Christ would offer himself,
along with the "gifts and graces" to be bestowed on them, as well as the
"tyme and means" in which they would be bestowed.

(3) The "pryce of the redemption" is also fixed here, such as, "how lang he
should be holden captive of death."

(4) By this covenant, Christ was also "made sure of success before he [put his]
hand to the making of the world," because "all power in heaven and earth
[was] given to him to bring it to pass."

(5) Finally, it was determined that the covenant would be administered in
such a way that it still requires our personal holiness, but nonetheless
excludes any reason for the sinner to despair of acceptance with God, as
Christ himself is the guarantor of our justification.[10]

The function of the doctrine for Dickson is to reduce the covenant of
grace to the administration of an earlier covenant made between the Father
and the Son in eternity. By grounding the former in the latter, Dickson can
secure both the definitiveness of Christ's death as well as the unconditional
nature of his grace. This is why Dickson roots the whole of his discourse in

---

9. Dickson, "Arminianism Discussed," in *Records of the Kirk of Scotland, containing the Acts and Proceedings of the General Assemblies, from the Year 1638 Downwards*, ed. Alexander Peterkin (Edinburgh: Peter Brown, 1845), 156. See also Carol A. Williams, "The Decree of Redemption Is in Effect a Covenant: David Dickson and the Covenant of Redemption" (PhD Diss., Calvin Seminary, 2005), 171–75.

10. "Arminianism Discussed," 159.

the teachings of Isaiah 52:13 and John 6:37, two texts which treat the *reward* which Christ receives upon the completion of his work, namely, the salvation of a people for the sake of his name. The certainty of Christ's reward as represented in these texts implies that Christ's work is preceded and commissioned by a divine promise given to the Son, which indicates that the salvation of the church is conditioned solely upon the work of the Mediator.

The *pactum salutis* has this function thanks to a series of important (though sometimes implicit) commitments about the nature of divine righteousness. I cannot explore them here, but in many Reformed accounts, God's promise was regarded as an act of divine condescension in which God freely obligates himself to reward the work of Christ, who is appointed as our Surety (or legal substitute) and Head, with the benefits of grace and salvation for his elect upon his fulfilment of the work of redemption. The nature of Christ's office as a *surety* who stands in our place, bearing our punishment and meriting the benefits of salvation on our behalf, along with the manner of his installation to this office by means of the covenant, is absolutely critical, here. Christ is the *proton dektikon*—the "seed of Abraham" and principal of the covenant, to whom all its promises and benefits radically accrue.[11] This guarantees that all the benefits of redemption are purchased solely by Christ without respect to any prior condition in us.

Essentially, the covenant serves to guarantee the *unconditionally gracious* character of Christ's work. In accounts where the concept of "divine obligation" features prominently, this point can sometimes be formally occluded. But materially, the function is much the same. This can be seen, for example, in Owen's famed "double payment" argument in *The Death of Death*.[12] God has covenanted with Christ in the *pactum salutis*, having completed his work, and Christ has a *right* to his reward which God has obliged himself to grant. For as it would be unjust for a merchant to require payment twice for the same thing, so also it would be unjust for God to require satisfaction for sin at the hands of Christ and those for whom Christ has died. In his justice, God cannot fail to deliver to Christ all those benefits for which he died. And Scripture teaches that God does, in fact, require satisfaction for sin from all of the damned. Since not all partake of Christ's benefits, and since it would be unjust for God to deny the elect any of the benefits which Christ has purchased, it must therefore be that Christ died only to purchase the redemption of his elect.

By reducing the covenant of grace to an administration of the covenant of redemption, Owen can argue here that the extension of divine grace to the elect is not a merely *arbitrary* act, one that is performed in pure freedom and over which God has "absolute dominion" either to give or not to give.[13] On

11.   *Works of John Owen*, 24 vols., ed. W. H. Goold (Edinburgh: T & T Clark, 1850–1855), 1:146.
12.   *Works of John Owen*, 10:288.
13.   "Absolute dominion" was a semitechnical term for the scholastics. It stands in contrast to an

the contrary. Having given his promise, God's righteousness and justice are engaged such that he cannot deny the gift of grace to the elect without breaking faith with Christ, and in so doing, denying his very nature. In essence, this means that the administration of the covenant of grace is grounded in divine justice[14]—that righteousness by which God keeps faith with the Mediator in the salvation of his elect.

But while this covenant may be administered according to strict justice, this does not mean that it is not also a free act of divine mercy and grace. God's promise and election are free. If they were not free, then grace would not be the free gift of God that it is. For this reason, God's grace must be an act of his "absolute dominion."[15] That is, he must have the right and power *not* to give it. If he were somehow naturally *obliged* to grant his grace to sinners, then grace would not be grace. Now, while God is obliged to keep his promise to us in Christ, and so extend his grace to all those for whom Christ died, he was by no means obligated to make this provision for our forgiveness in the *pactum salutis*. It is an act of the highest freedom.

Owen has a variety of ways of expressing this. He speaks, for instance, of the freedom of God's judgment and punishment apart from the covenant. He also speaks of the act of entering into a covenant with us as an act of God *binding* himself. This indicates that God's dealings with us by the covenant are a contingent arrangement. Perhaps the most evocative image is his comparison of the freedom of God in covenant to that of the creation of the world. Just as God is perfect in himself, and so had no need to create the world but did so out of sheer generosity, so also God had no obligation or need in himself to extend his grace to sinners, but did so out of his sheer love and mercy.[16]

II. Trinity and the Covenant of Redemption

It should be apparent, then, that for Reformed theologians like Owen and Dickson who ground the administration of the covenant of grace in a prior covenant between the Father and the Son, a great deal of their soteriology hangs on the coherence of the concept of an intra-Trinitarian covenant. Of course, in some contemporary theology, the notion of an intra-Trinitarian covenant does not register as an especially unusual idea. This is due, no doubt, to the fact that the concept has been commonplace in some traditions of Christian theology for several hundred years now. But early attempts to expound the nature of the *pactum salutis* found navigating the relevant Trinitarian dogmas to be a first-order concern in establishing the soundness and

---

inclination of will or a necessity of nature, and it indicates the full and absolute freedom of God either to act or not to act in some particular matter, e.g., as in the creation of the world.

14. Note that not all Reformed thinkers held to this point. Many argued that the extension of the *beneficia Christi* to the elect was an act of God's dominion, and so cannot properly be regarded as an act of "justice."

15. *Works*, 6:470–71.

16. *Works*, 19:86.

coherence of the doctrine. The relationship between the divine missions and processions, the inseparability of operations, the will as a property of the divine nature, and the divine nature as being singular, concrete and common to the three persons of the Trinity—these doctrinal interests had to be carefully negotiated in order to demonstrate the companionability of the *pactum salutis* with traditional Trinitarian teaching. The fact that many contemporary Reformed thinkers no longer see some of the difficulties that such a covenant might pose to the doctrine of the Trinity is probably an indication of the degree to which we have witnessed the erosion of those concepts which once formed the core of Trinitarian teaching for the patristics and medievals, and, indeed, for many Reformed thinkers as well.

Owen, for example, addresses the Trinitarian dimensions of this doctrine directly in an exercitation of his Hebrews commentary entitled "The Federal Transactions between the Father and the Son" (1668).[17] This exercitation follows a series of chapters exploring the office of the priesthood in general, the origin of Christ's priesthood in particular—specifically as it relates to the place of the incarnation within God's purposes in creation and redemption, and finally, "the original" or basis of Christ's priesthood in the purposes of God. The material progression of these chapters moves from below to above, attempting to "trace those discoveries which God hath made of his eternal counsels in this matter."[18] As such, Owen's discussion of the *pactum salutis* is an attempt to integrate a number of theological judgments about the work of Christ and the dispensation of his grace with traditional teaching on the Trinity and the counsels of the divine will as the ground of all God's works within the economy of redemption.

In his catechism, Owen classifies the divine counsels as part of the "internal works" of God.[19] They are "works" of God, in the sense that they are contingent divine acts that concern things which are *ad extra* to the divine nature. Yet, unlike God's "external works," which all have some created reality as their term, the "internal" works of God are acts which remain immanent within God himself, such as his counsels and decrees. As such, they do not yet have any extrinsic objects to which they are directed. The purpose of this distinction is essentially to register a modal difference in the way that the divine counsels exist within God. God's purposes are necessary, but they are not necessary in the way that God's existence is necessary. The existence of the one divine nature in the eternal processions of the Father, Son, and Holy Spirit is *absolutely* necessary—it could not be otherwise. But all the purposes of God, which are fixed in the internal works of his counsels and decrees, are

---

17. *Works*, 19:77–97. Owen also has a chapter discussing the *pactum salutis* in his *Vindiciae Evangelicae* (*Works*, 12:496–508). However, this chapter will look predominantly at the Hebrews commentary since its Trinitarian commitments are more fully developed.

18. *Works*, 19:15.

19. *Works*, 1:473.

only *hypothetically* necessary. They are not necessary *in themselves*, because they are by nature such things as might have been otherwise. Accordingly, the necessity of their existence stems from the divine will. They are necessary *only because God has willed them so to be.*

Of course, this is not to suggest that God's will was ever in doubt. Though Scripture speaks of God's purposes as being established in divine "counsels" (Ps. 55:14; Zech. 6:13; Eph. 1:11), unlike the counsels of men, the counsels of God are not discursive. They involve no deliberation or debate. They are rather eternal and immutable. In his perfection, God possesses immediate and intuitive knowledge of all things, including those plans which he purposed in himself from all ages. But Owen thinks that the contingent nature of the divine counsels is best articulated by observing a distinction between the activity of the divine intellect and will. It is the role of the intellect to weigh the various courses of action available to any agent, and it belongs to the will to determine which course of action to take. Similarly, according to his intellect, God has an immediate knowledge of all things that he has power to do (his *potentia absoluta*), and so of all courses that his will might take (his *potentia ordinanda*). But it is by means of his *will* that God determines which course he *shall* in fact take.[20] And since God's will is most free, although he has eternal knowledge of all his own purposes and plans, these purposes are absolutely contingent upon the freedom of his will and are elected solely because they serve the divine purpose. So, when Scripture speaks of God's will being established in "counsels," Owen thinks it primarily indicates that the purposes of God are established in perfect wisdom and freedom.[21]

The language of "counsels" also carries, to Owen's mind at least, an intimation of the Trinitarian nature of God and God's works. In this way, it is intended to signify the mutual concurrence of the Father, Son and Holy Spirit in the determination of the divine will.[22] In a lengthy examination of Genesis 1:26 and Proverbs 8:22–31, Owen argues that this language establishes distinct "transactions" between the persons of the Trinity within the eternal counsels of God, particularly with respect to humankind and the manner in which their creation and redemption would redound to the glory of God as he is triune.[23] It is the covenantal nature of these Trinitarian "transactions," as expressed within the *pactum salutis*, which Owen aims to demonstrate in this exercitation. He proceeds by first asserting the covenantal nature of these transactions, then moves on to describe the nature of covenants in general (along with the particular *kind* of covenant in which the *pactum salutis* ought to be classed) before, finally, correlating these judgments with one another, to demonstrate that the will of God in this matter is properly covenantal in nature.

---

20. *Works*, 11:142–43.
21. *Works*, 18:143.
22. *Works*, 19:49.
23. *Works*, 19:58.

Moving in this manner from a general moral theory of covenants to the nature of the *pactum salutis* and the divine decrees is something of a treacherous path. It runs the risk of drawing the analogy between God and creatures too closely by imposing some highly formalized concepts, which were developed for very particular moral settings, onto the inner life of God. Owen shows some awareness of this possible danger throughout his treatment, and at a few points, this leads him to make refinements to these concepts in their application to the divine life. But on the whole, this does not lead him to adjust his basic commitments regarding the nature of covenants in general. More frequently, the course of Owen's argument endeavours to show how a right understanding of the divine life is in fact accommodating of a proper covenant. There is an important material reason for this. Owen wishes to affirm that salvation is grounded in a real and proper covenant between the Father and the Son so that he can argue that the dispensing of Christ's benefits is administered according to divine *justice*. This, as we saw above, supports his account of definite atonement. Now, if the covenant of redemption is not a *proper* covenant, but only *improperly* a covenant— if it is only a "covenant" or covenant-like—then it cannot be maintained that Christ's benefits are dispensed to the elect by divine *justice*, and Owen's argument for definite atonement is substantially weakened. Accordingly, it is important that Owen draw the analogy between creaturely and divine covenants as closely as possible.

A. Covenants, Covenantal Relation, and the Covenant of Redemption

For the most part, seventeenth-century moral debates regarding the nature of contractual agreements were developed in reference to the concept of natural law. That is because the rights and obligations which arise from any voluntary agreement are guaranteed by more fundamental moral principles inscribed upon the law of nature by our Creator. Nature logically precedes act. So, voluntary agreements can formalize a new kind of relation between covenanting parties, in which the agreed rights and obligations of the covenant accrue to each party by virtue of their voluntary participation in the covenant. But since any covenantal relation is *voluntary* in character, it must ultimately supervene upon those relations (along with their attending rights and obligations) that the covenanting parties maintain by the law of nature. It was therefore the operative presupposition that any account of the proper nature of a covenant must be consonant with (or at the very least, not contradictory to) the wider dictates of the law of nature. Indeed, where a covenant explicitly stands in contradiction to the order of nature, there cannot be a covenant. As we will see below, this point will be relevant for our understanding of the *pactum salutis* and the mission of the Son.

With respect to the general nature of a covenant, Owen argues that a covenant is "complete" or "equal," that is, a legitimate and true covenant, if it meets the conditions below. Owen justifies some of these conditions biblically, but it would be a mistake to assume that the necessity of these claims is primarily exegetical. The biblical justifications here are relatively thin and, in any event, these conditions were fairly common tropes in seventeenth-century philosophical and legal texts treating the nature of contracts. As such, their necessity is likely as much indebted to local convention and wider forms of moral reasoning as it is to any strictly biblical consideration. Of course, Owen does not take these to be mutually exclusive, either—indeed, to his mind, the moral universe forms the broader context of the biblical narrative, and so he expects the two to be mutually reinforcing. Nevertheless, it is worth remembering that the following conditions are supported and informed by a wider network of biblical, theological, and moral judgments. They are as follows:

(1) A covenant must be between distinct persons. Owen bases this judgment, formally at least, on Galatians 3:20, which claims that "a mediator is not of one," and so suggests that there must be diverse parties between which Christ mediates. The implicit assumption is that, as Christ acted on behalf of his people in the formalising of the covenant, the covenant of redemption must be between distinct parties.[24]

(2) It must be a voluntary agreement. Owen's stated reason for this is that the biblical term for covenant (*berith*) derives from a root meaning "to choose." Accordingly, a proper covenant is one in which both parties enter freely into an agreement, without coercion and unconstrained, but with a "due consideration and right judgment" of its terms. There cannot be a proper covenant where one party is forced to accept the terms, e.g., in the way that a captive might offer consent to his captor under duress. Such circumstances invalidate the nature of a covenant, because they are inconsistent with its nature as a voluntary agreement.

(3) It must pertain to things (e.g., goods or services) under the power of those persons. That is to say, there can be no proper covenant where one or more of the covenanting parties does not have a right over those things to which the covenant pertains. So, for example, a child has no power to enter into a proper covenant since they are not yet under their own power, but by the law of nature, remain under the power of their parents. Until they have a right and power over their own affairs, they cannot enter into a legitimate, binding covenant.[25]

(4) Finally, it must be to the "mutual content and satisfaction" of all persons involved. In other words, if either party is absolutely disad-

---

24.   Owen denies the possibility of making a covenant, "properly so called," with oneself (*Works*, 19:82).
25.   *Works*, 19:82–83.

vantaged by it, then it does not have the character of a complete covenant, because it is not fully voluntary and free.

A proper covenant must meet all of the above conditions, and where any
are absent, the covenant cannot be considered equal and may therefore be
annulled. Owen will go on to demonstrate just how the covenant of redemption meets each of these conditions—in some instances more convincingly
than others. But first, he observes that, if the election of Christ did take the
form of a covenant, then it must be classed as belonging to a particular *kind*
of covenant, namely, one "depending solely on the personal undertakings and
services of one party."[26] This is, after all, the nature of that work which Christ
undertook on behalf of his people as their surety. He took it upon himself to
fulfil the just demands of the law in their stead. Accordingly, there are three
additional factors which condition the character of this type of covenant:

(5) It involves a proposal of service. In the covenant of redemption, this
proposal is made by the Father, who is the "Author" of this covenant,
to the Son, detailing the nature of his proposed service within the
terms of the covenant, particularly, that he should redeem the elect by
means of his obedient life and sacrificial death.

(6) It also involves a promise of reward. The Father extends a promise to
the Son that he would not only deliver the elect from their sin, but also
that he would support Christ's earthly ministry with grace, and glorify
Christ's human nature upon the completion of his work.[27]

(7) Finally, it involves an acceptance of the terms of the stated proposal.[28]
The covenant is formally enacted with the Son's willing acceptance of
the Father's promise and his commitment to perform the work which
the Father has proposed.

B. *The Covenant of Redemption and the Unity of the Divine Will*

As there is one God, and not three gods, the conditions outlined above
raise a question as to whether the notion of an intra-Trinitarian covenant is
fully compatible with traditional convictions about the unity of the Trinitarian persons within the one divine essence.[29] Owen anticipates this problem,

---

26. *Works*, 19:83.
27. *Works*, 19:93–94.
28. *Works*, 19:83.
29. For the relation of this aspect of Trinitarian dogma to the current subordination debates, see D.
Glenn Butler Jr.'s article, "Eternal Functional Subordination and the Problem of the Divine Will," *ETS*
58, no. 1 (2015): 131–49. To my mind, Butler's line of critique is one of the more perceptive.

raising the critique that the divine counsels "cannot be properly federal" for the simple reason that a covenant requires the consent of two or more parties, while the counsels of God are "single acts of the same divine understanding and will."[30] This particular challenge to the covenant of redemption is rooted in the doctrine of divine simplicity. Traditionally, the intellect and will of God were regarded as being properties of the divine *nature*. A "nature," here, is what underwrites the activity of any particular agent—it is *that by which* the agent acts. And since, as Scripture declares, there is only *one* God (Deut. 6:4), there is only one divine nature. Thus, while affirming the full deity of the Father, the Son, and the Holy Spirit, classical Trinitarian theology also maintained that the divine nature is undivided, singular, and common to the Trinitarian persons. "I and the Father are one" (John 10:30).

In order to keep faith with this tradition, when speaking of the agency of the persons of the Trinity, older theologians often invoked the principle that the *opera Trinitatis ad extra indivisa sunt*—the works of the Trinity *ad extra* are indivisible. The rule functions to maintain the unity of the works of God by reminding us that the principle of all divine activity in any of the Trinitarian persons is always the simple, undivided divine essence which is common to each person. "[T]he Son can do nothing by himself; he can do only what he sees the Father doing, because whatever the Father does the Son also does" (John 5:19). This is true in all divine acts of any kind. In the incarnation, for example, the power by which the Son takes up his human nature is the power of his divine nature, which he shares in common with both the Father and the Holy Spirit. In that respect, therefore, it can truly be said that the work of the incarnation is indivisibly also the work of the Father and the Holy Spirit, even though the Son, and not the Father or the Holy Spirit, became incarnate.[31] The logic of this doctrine insists on the unity and coherence of God's works *ad extra* in respect of their emergence from a common principle of activity, even as it discerns within these works a distinction between the action of some particular Trinitarian person and the common principle of that person's action. In that sense, the incarnation is both a "common work" (*opus commune*) of the Trinity and also a "proper work" (*opus proprium*) of the Son. Owen recalls this tradition here in order to challenge an overly simplistic or anthropomorphic account of what it must mean for the persons of the Trinity to covenant together with one another.

In what sense, exactly, is it possible for the Father and the Son to covenant together when they are one in essence? As we noted above, covenanting requires an act of "voluntary agreement" among the parties involved. But the will is a natural faculty, and so in God is a property belonging to the common divine essence. There are in God not three wills in agreement, but one will only which

---

30. *Works*, 19:77.
31. For more on this point, see Tyler R. Wittman, "The End of the Incarnation: John Owen, Trinitarian Agency, and Christology," *IJST* 15, no. 3 (2013): 284–300.

is common to the Father, the Son and the Holy Spirit. So, if it is in fact the case that there is only one divine will, then in what sense can we regard the Father and the Son as offering a distinct "voluntary agreement" in this covenant? Can there be a real "agreement" between the Father and the Son where their consent arises not from distinct wills, but from one common will?

As we have said, a considerable amount of Owen's soteriology hangs on the intelligibility of an intra-Trinitarian covenant,[32] so how does he respond to this critique? In keeping with the older tradition, Owen acknowledges that the faculty of the will is proper to the divine essence and as such is undivided and common to both the Father and the Son. This is a point he makes fairly routinely in his Trinitarian writings:

> The Father, Son, and Spirit have not distinct wills. They are one God, and God's will is one, as being an essential property of his nature; and therefore are there two wills in the one person of Christ, whereas there is but one will in the three persons of the Trinity.[33]

Still, Owen maintains that this does not exclude the possibility of an agreement of wills. For since the divine will in this matter is "acted distinctly" in the persons of both the Father and the Son, it nonetheless has the nature of a proper covenant on that account.[34] He explains:

> such is the distinction of the persons in the unity of the divine essence, as that they act in natural and essential acts reciprocally one towards another,—namely, in understanding, love, and the like; they know and mutually love each other. And as they subsist distinctly, so they also act distinctly in those works which are of external operation. And whereas all these acts and operations, whether reciprocal or external, are either with a will or from a freedom of will and choice, the will of God in each person, as to the peculiar acts ascribed unto him, is his will therein peculiarly and eminently, though not exclusively to the other persons, by reason of their mutual *in-being*. The will of God as to the peculiar actings of the Father in this matter is the will of the Father, and the will of God with regard unto the peculiar actings of the Son is the will of the Son; not by a distinction of sundry wills, but by the distinct application of the same will unto its *distinct acts* in the persons of the Father and the Son. And in this respect the covenant whereof we treat differeth from a pure decree; for from these distinct actings of

---

32. This is particularly important in Owen's context, where he is attempting to consolidate the catholic Trinitarian tradition against the anti-Trinitarianism of the Socinians. If he cannot demonstrate the consonance of the covenant of redemption with traditional affirmations of the Trinity, he would be attempting a revision not only of the doctrine of salvation, but also the doctrine of the Trinity.
33. *Works*, 19:87; cf. 12:497.
34. *Works*, 19:77.

the will of God in the Father and the Son there doth arise a new habitude or relation, which is not natural or necessary unto them, but freely taken on them.[35]

Owen's intention in this paragraph is to clarify the sense in which the
internal works of the Father and the Son are both common and distinct in the
covenant of redemption. To do this, Owen draws an analogy to the essential
acts of the Trinity. "Natural and essential acts" here are to be distinguished
from what are sometimes called "notional acts." "Notional acts" refer to those
acts, such as "generation" and "spiration," that constitute the relations between
the Trinitarian persons, and so distinguish them according to their personal
properties. These are not the acts Owen has in mind here, for these acts are
not reciprocal. "Essential acts," on the other hand, are the necessary acts of the
one divine nature, such as knowledge, love, will, etc. Inasmuch as these are
acts of the divine nature, they are acts common to the Father, Son, and Holy
Spirit. But because the persons of the Trinity subsist distinctly, acts common
to the Trinity can also be considered distinctly in the persons according to the
order of their subsistence. And because the persons of the Trinity can themselves be the object of the essential acts of the divine nature, these acts have
a reciprocal character.[36] So, for example, love is an essential divine act. But
because essential acts can be considered distinctly in the persons, and since
the persons are also objects of these acts, it can truly be said that the Father
loves the Son and Spirit, that the Son loves the Spirit and the Father, and that
the Spirit loves the Father and the Son. In this sense, God's inner life admits of
infinite reciprocal acts by virtue of the "mutual in-being" of the Father, Son,
and Holy Spirit in the one divine essence.

What Owen is doing in the paragraph above is comparing the *essential*
acts of the Trinity, as they are *common, distinct,* and *reciprocal* acts, with the
internal works of the Father and the Son in the covenant of redemption. Like
love, the will is also a property of the divine nature, and as such, it is enacted
commonly. Therefore, the willing of a "covenant" between the Father and the
Son, like God's essential acts, must be a work common to the Trinity. But
essential acts of the Trinity, while common to the persons, can also be considered *distinctly* in the persons. And if this is the case in essential acts, then it
must be no less true in the internal works of God, which find their principle

---

35. *Works*, 19:87–88; cf. 12:497.
36. Owen classifies these internal acts of the persons as being "*ad invicem*," that is, "alternating" or
     "reciprocal" acts. "And these acts *ad invicem* . . . are natural and necessary, inseparable from the being
     and existence of God. So the Father knows the Son and loveth him, and the Son seeth, knoweth, and
     loveth the Father. In these mutual actings, one person is the object of the knowledge and love of the
     other" (*Works*, 3:66–67). Owen cites John 3:35, Matthew 11:27 and Proverbs 8:22–31 for support.
     As I have noted above, Owen treats this last text thoroughly in his Hebrews commentary to provide
     biblical warrant for the concept of the *pactum salutis*. For a helpful summary of Owen's classification
     here, see Kendall Beau Cleveland, "The Covenant of Redemption in the Trinitarian Theology of John
     Owen" (PhD diss., University of St. Andrews, 2016), 74–78.

in the essential property of the divine will. Accordingly, the acts of will in the covenant of redemption can be considered distinctly in both the Father and the Son, without undermining the unity of the divine will. And because the persons of the Trinity can themselves be the objects of these acts of willing, they also have a *reciprocal* character.

Of course, God's essential acts and his internal works are *different* from one another as well. While God's *works* are contingent, his *essential* acts are necessary—he cannot be without them. Moreover, this particular internal work of God, the covenant of redemption, is reciprocal in a unique sense. For thought all essential acts of the Trinity are reciprocal, in that they are equally the acts of the Father, Son, and Holy Spirit and have the Trinitarian persons as their objects, some works of God belong "distinctly and eminently" to partic- ular persons of the Trinity. As we said above, the power by which the Son assumes human nature is common to the Father, Son, and Holy Spirit. And yet, neither the Father nor the Holy Spirit took on flesh and became incarnate, but only the Son. This is because the incarnation is the *opus proprium* of the Son, for it is in the person of the Son that this act of divine power reaches its "term."[37] Owen appears to regard the works of the Father and the Son in the covenant of redemption similarly. The covenant of redemption is a common act of the Trinity in the sense that it proceeds from a common principle of activity—namely, the divine will. But the "commissioning" of the Son in this covenant is the *opus proprium* of the Father, and the "acceptance" of the cove- nant, the *opus proprium* of the Son.[38] In contrast with God's essential acts,

---

37.   "The incarnation, considered 'inchoatively' or from the perspective of its inception, as one of the works of the Godhead *ad extra*, must be an undivided or common work (*opus commune*) of all persons in the Trinity. However, considered 'terminatively' or from the perspective of its completion, it is a divine work that concludes in the person of the Son with the assumption of human nature and is, therefore, the *opus proprium* of the Son. Thus, 'after a certain manner' (*certo modo*) the incarnation is a personal work belonging to the economy of the Godhead *ad extra*, not an essential or common work" (Richard Muller, *Post-Reformation Reformed Dogmatics*, 4 vols. [Grand Rapids: Baker, 2003], 4:272). Cf. Wittman, "End of the Incarnation," 297–98.

38.   It would be tempting to construe these as "appropriated acts" since it would reduce the strictness of the analogy between divine and human covenants on the one hand, and simplify the nature of the internal works of God on the other. But I take it that Owen does not regard these as appropriations for the following reasons. First, as I will demonstrate below, Owen's intention here is to explain the sense in which the Son has an *obligation* to the Father. To do this, Owen needs to show that there is a proper covenant between the Father and the Son, which requires a voluntary agreement of two persons. That means his burden here is to demonstrate the personal *distinctness* that obtains between these acts of willing. Second, the *pactum salutis* is the basis of the Son's *opus proprium* within the economy of grace. Owen argues that the graciousness of Christ's work consists in the fact that it manifests the love of the eternal Son as he freely and voluntarily assumed this work by means of the covenant. This argument makes the most sense if Owen regards Christ's work within the economy of grace to be expressive of the *opus proprium* of the Son within the *pactum salutis*—namely, the act of his consenting to become our Mediator. Finally, Owen does not employ the language of appropriation here in his Hebrews commentary. One might read Owen's claim in *Vindiciae Evangelicae*, that the divine will is "appropriated" to the persons (*Works*, 12:497), as explaining the covenant in terms of

then, the covenant of redemption is an internal work of God that also admits of *proper* and *distinct* acts that reach their term peculiarly in the persons of the Father and the Son.

Because the will of God in this matter is comprehensive of all parts and dimensions of the covenant of redemption, it includes those *opera propria* that are peculiar to the Father, such as commissioning and sending, and those that are peculiar to the Son, such as accepting and being sent. These distinct acts of the persons are themselves included in the divine will, so that the wills of the Father and the Son in the *pactum salutis* are identical with respect to the matter or object of the divine will. Yet, with respect to their proper acts in the *pactum salutis*, the will of the Father and the Son remain personally distinct. Owen chooses his grammar very carefully here: "The will of God as to the peculiar actings of the Father in this matter *is* the will of the Father, and the will of God with regard unto the peculiar actings of the Son *is* the will of the Son."[39] So then, the substance of those acts of will that are peculiar to the Father and the Son in the covenant of redemption are themselves commonly willed by the Trinity, and so do not materially differ from the content of the divine will in any of the Trinitarian persons. They are merely *acted* distinctly. In the same way that the persons of the Trinity can commonly will the salvation of lost sinners, while also willing distinct and peculiar acts for themselves and each other in the work of salvation, so also here, the Father, Son, and Holy Spirit can will commonly to covenant for the salvation of the elect, even as the Father and the Son have their own proper and distinct acts in the internal work of covenanting. In a manner of speaking, then, we might summarize Owen's argument here by saying that the Father and the Son will *commonly* to will a covenant *distinctly*.

As an explanation for the sense in which there can be "agreement" in the one, undivided divine will, this is plausible. There is, to be sure, a long and venerable tradition that assigns a prominent place to mutually reciprocal acts of love within the communion of the Trinity. Most notably, we might think of the Trinitarian theology of Richard of St. Victor and the legacy he left in the thought of many subsequent Franciscan theologians through Bonaventure. God's life is a communion of love, composed in the eternal processions of the Father, Son, and Holy Spirit and in their relations of origins, but in such a way as to be inclusive of infinite acts of mutual fellowship and delight. If we are

---

the doctrine of the appropriations (Wittman, 292). However, it seems clear to me that Owen is using this word in a less technical sense there, as he goes on to say that the works that God wills distinctly in the covenant are "distinctly carried on" by the persons in their missions "so that the same God judges and becomes surety, satisfieth and is satisfied, in these distinct persons." The works mentioned here—the act of judgment and of making satisfaction—are not mere appropriations, but are what Owen elsewhere describes as works proper to the Father and the Son in the economy of grace. It thus seems more natural to read Owen's claim in *Vindiciae* that the divine will is "appropriated" to each as being nontechnical in nature. Cf. K.B. Cleveland, "Covenant of Redemption", 73, n. 63.

39. Emphasis mine.

willing to acknowledge such transactions in the eternal, immanent life of the persons of the Trinity, then there is little reason to object to Owen's account of the covenant of redemption on these grounds.

However, it is more than a little unusual to have to speak of the Father and the Son as "willing commonly to will a covenant distinctly and properly." It makes you wonder why one has to speak this way at all. Older Reformed theologians founded Christ's election on a divine decree, which in many ways seems much more straightforward. Why not relax the language of "covenant" here by eliminating the notion of any proper and reciprocal internal works between the persons Trinity in this work, and simply ground the work of Christ in a divine decree that is commonly willed by the Father, Son, and Holy Spirit? Owen tells us explicitly: "in this respect the covenant whereof we treat differeth from a pure decree; for from these distinct actings of the will of God in the Father and the Son there doth arise a new habitude or relation, which is not natural or necessary unto them, but freely taken on them."[40] In other words, it is important that we speak of a *covenant* here, and not simply a decree, in order to explain the existence of a "new habitude or relation" that obtains between the Father and the Son, which was not "natural or necessary" but was "freely taken on them." As we shall see, this new relation consists in an *obligation* of the Son to obey the Father, which would indeed be difficult to explain in a manner consistent with Nicene Trinitarianism without invoking the concept of a covenant.

C. The Submission of the Son and the Covenant of Redemption

The covenant, once accepted, formalises a "new habitude or relation" between the Father and the Son. But because of the nature of this particular kind of covenant, in which one party proposes and prescribes the services to be rendered by the other party, Owen argues that, when formalized, it necessarily results in a kind of *inequality* between the parties involved.

> And this [acceptance of the proposed terms of the covenant] indispensably introduceth an inequality and subordination in the covenanters as to the common ends of the covenant, however on other accounts they may be equal; for he who *prescribes* the duties which are required in the covenant, and giveth the promises of either assistance in them or a reward upon them, is therein and so far superior unto him, or greater than he who *observeth* his prescriptions and *trusteth* unto his promises. Of this nature is that divine transaction that was between the Father and Son about the redemption of mankind. There was in it a prescription of personal services, with a promise of reward; and all the other conditions, also, of a complete covenant before laid down are observed therein. And this we must inquire into, as that wherein doth lie the foundation and original of the priesthood of Christ.[41]

---

40.   *Works*, 19:88.
41.   *Works*, 19:83–84.

This is a critical element of Owen's account of the *pactum salutis*, and it is one that deserves careful attention, especially given its possible implications for the doctrine of the Trinity. We ought to observe immediately that Owen's quote above is careful to limit the nature of the inequality in question to the "common ends of the covenant," acknowledging that the covenanting parties might be equal in all other respects. But what exactly is the purpose of affirming a kind of "inequality" between the Father and the Son in virtue of this covenant? How should this covenantal relation be understood relative to traditionally pro-Nicene commitments regarding the coequality of the Son with the Father—commitments which Owen has so ardently defended elsewhere? And how do these various commitments present themselves at the level of an exegesis of the biblical texts?

It is clear from the surrounding context that Owen here introduces the concept of "inequality" as a way of accounting for the distinct form of the Son's mission within the economy of grace.[42] For Christ's earthly ministry is characterized, above all, by his unwavering obedience and submission to the Father's will. But Owen thinks that the nature of this submission is best explained with reference to an eternal covenant between the Father and the Son. This, he suggests, is the significance of those biblical texts like Matthew 27:46 (which quotes Psalm 22:1), John 20:17, or Hebrews 10:9 (which quotes Psalm 40:8), where Christ is depicted as referring to the Father as "my God." According to Owen, the appropriation of God's name with the possessive pronoun echos the language of the new covenant in Jeremiah 31:33, "I will be their God, and they will be my people." Owen deems such language to be "declarative of a covenant." "For God, declaring that he will be a God unto any, engageth himself unto the exercise of his holy properties, which belong unto him as God, in their behalf and for their good; and this is not without an engagement of obedience from them." This engagement of the divine properties for the benefit of another is, for Owen, the entire purpose of the covenant; but the covenant also brings with it certain duties and obligations on the side of the creature. In the case of Christ, that involved obedience to the law of the Mediator as stipulated in the covenant of redemption—a meritorious fulfilment of the moral law, and the satisfaction of the punishment due to the elect. Accordingly, Owen judges these kinds of expressions to "argue both a covenant and a subordination [of the Son] therein."[43]

---

42. Some interpreters have leveled critiques of Owen (or defended him from critiques) that his account of the *pactum salutis* is functionally "binitarian" because of the relative absence of the Holy Spirit. But this concern (on the one side or the other) reveals a misunderstanding of both the function of the doctrine and its place in God's inner life. The doctrine is not intended to be a gloss on nor an augmentation to the Trinitarian processions and relations. It is rather an attempt to explain the *form* of the Son's mission as a *surety* who stands in the stead of sinners by grounding it within the internal works of God. One should not therefore expect the *pactum salutis* to have a proportionate emphasis on the Holy Spirit, because the primary purpose of the doctrine is to explain the form of God's saving work in the mission of the *Son*.

43. *Works*, 19:84.

Owen takes a similar reading of John 14:28—"the Father is greater than I." Though he acknowledges that virtually all of the church fathers attributed the subordination in this passage to Christ's *human* nature alone so that they might avoid the Arian reading that the Son is not coequal with the Father, Owen argues that such a reading is too obvious. "[T]he inferiority of the human nature unto God or the Father is a thing so unquestionable as needed no declaration or solemn attestation, and the mention of it is no way suited unto the design of the place."[44] It is clear, then, that the "inequality" that arises between the Father and the Son is not simply a function of the inferiority of Christ's human nature to his divine nature. Rather, Owen understands it as reflective of the Son's obligation to be obedient to the Father's will. Consequently, he sees it as revelatory of "the covenant engagement" between the Father and the Son in eternity. "[F]or therein . . . the Father was the prescriber, the promiser, and lawgiver; and the Son was the undertaker upon his prescription, law, and promises."[45]

Notably, Owen reflects further on this point, as to whether the subordination of the Son to the Father revealed in such passages might in fact be proper to the Son *qua* Son by virtue of his eternal generation from the Father. In other words, might we read passages like John 14:28 as a statement of the Son's eternal and necessary relation to the Father in virtue of the communication of the divine essence? Might it be that the Father is said to be greater than the Son—that he is the "God" of the Son—because the Son eternally receives his being from the Father? Owen denies this. Christ is truly confessed to be "God of God" in virtue of his divine sonship and his eternal generation from the Father. And the communication of the divine essence from the Father to the Son is depicted in passages like Psalm 2:7[46] or Proverbs 8:25.[47] But Owen maintains that the Father is not said to be the "God" of Christ on account of the Son's eternal generation. When Scripture speaks of God being a "God unto" Christ or being "his [Christ's] God," it implies two things. First, it implies an "acting of divine properties on [Christ's] behalf," which Owen has already suggested is the very substance of a covenant. And secondly, it implies "a dependence on the other side [that is, on Christ's side] on him [Christ] who is so a God unto him." In other words, to claim that the Father is the "God" of Christ must imply the dependence of Christ upon the Father as his God.

Yet, *for this very reason*, Owen draws the opposite inference—namely, that this scriptural idiom *does not* refer to the eternal generation of the Son from the Father. Owen's reason for doing this is certainly biblical. He thinks it misses the allusion to the language of Jeremiah. But that consideration

---

44. *Works*, 19:84.
45. *Works*, 19:85.
46. *Works*, 12:189.
47. *Works*, 19:68.

cannot explain why Owen excludes the possibility that this covenantal relation is itself an effect of the Son's eternal procession from the Father. Unless,
of course, Owen thinks that such an explanation would entail an ontological
subordination that is inconsistent with the Son's natural coequality with the
Father. This is why Owen places the covenant and the Son's relation of origin
in opposition to one another.[48] The Son's subordination to the Father is not
to be grounded in the Son's relation of origin. Instead, the subordination of
Christ in the economy refers us to a dependence that the Son has upon the
Father in virtue of that "new habitude and relation" established within the
covenant. According to Owen, it is the covenant, and not the processions,
which form the "sole foundation" of the Son's dependence upon the Father.[49]

Again, the covenantal relation between the Father and the Son is further
explored in an interpretation of Zechariah 6:12–13 (KJV):

> Thus speaketh the LORD of hosts, saying, Behold the man whose name is The
> BRANCH; and he shall grow up out of his place, and he shall build the temple of
> the LORD: Even he shall build the temple of the LORD; and he shall bear the glory,
> and shall sit and rule upon his throne; and he shall be a priest upon his throne:
> and the counsel of peace shall be between them both.

Christian readings of the Hebrew Bible have long seen "the Branch" as
a prophecy about Christ and his gathering of the church. But unlike those
Christian interpreters who take "the counsel of peace . . . between them both"
as a reference to the new covenant ministry which Christ inaugurated, Owen
interprets this instead as referring to a pre-temporal covenant between Jehovah and "he who was to be . . . 'The Branch.'"[50] It is, in other words, an explicit
statement about the Covenant of Redemption between the Father and the Son
in eternity. Owen thus denies that this counsel might have taken place with
Christ "as he was a man, or was to be a man." For, there cannot possibly be any
proper "counsel" between God and man, as Romans 11:34 (KJV) teaches—
"For who hath known the mind of the Lord? or who hath been his counsel-
lor?" In his human nature, therefore, Owen claims that Christ was merely "the
servant of the Father to do his will" (citing Isaiah 42:1). "God takes counsel

---

48. Owen does not deny that there is an *analogy* between the filiation of the Son in eternity and the
obedience of the Son in time. In fact, this analogy illumines for Owen the nature of the church's own
adoption, as well as its spiritual duty to love and worship Christ (e.g. *Works*, 1:144–146; 9:612–615).
What is denied here, however, is that the filiation of the Son is itself the *basis and ground* of the Son's
obedience to the Father. Were this the case, the Son's obedience to the Father would be necessary
rather than free, undermining both the coequality of the Son with the Father and the gracious nature
of the Son's mission.

49. *Works*, 19:85. Cf. *Works*, 12:497, where Owen says that this "new habitude and relation" is "new" in
the sense that it is in God "freely, not naturally."

50. *Works*, 19:85.

with [Christ]," he argues, "as he was his *eternal Wisdom*, only with respect unto his future incarnation."[51]

It should be clear from the foregoing that the "inequality" that manifests itself in the Son's submission to the Father in the economy of grace is his obligation to obey the Father in all things. And this is not rooted merely in the Son's assumption of flesh. For Owen, its ground must be sought in the inner life of God. At the same time, however, Owen also resists grounding the Son's submission in his eternal generation from the Father, instead identifying the covenant of redemption as the "sole foundation" of the Son's obligation. This is the source of that "new habitude or relation" between the Father and the Son, which is not "natural or necessary" but was "freely taken on them."[52] In order to understand the nature of the Son's submission to the Father, then, we must therefore inquire into the status of the covenant of redemption within the divine life. And this requires us to examine Owen's theology of the freedom of the divine will.

D. The Freedom of the Covenant and the Condescension of the Son

We said above when considering the conditions of a proper covenant that a covenant must be a voluntary agreement between distinct persons pertaining to goods or services under their power and to the mutual satisfaction of both parties. Having looked briefly above at the nature of the divine will, we have seen something of what it means for the Father and the Son to act as "distinct persons" in the covenant.[53] And it is beyond dispute that the Father and Son have a right over their missions in the work of redemption, or that this covenant fully conduces to their mutual satisfaction in the display and communication of their glory. It is, however, a matter of crucial importance for us to understand the sense in which the covenant is a *voluntary* agreement. This is crucial, as we have seen, because it is integral to the equity and justice of the agreement, without which it cannot be considered a proper covenant. And one of Owen's central objectives here is to demonstrate that the *pactum salutis* is, in fact, a proper covenant. Accordingly, he needs to demonstrate that the covenant of redemption rests eternally on the concurrent wills of both the Father and the Son.

According to Owen, Scripture denominates the *voluntary* nature of this covenant in various ways. As I have shown in the previous section, Scripture represents the Son as rendering willing obedience to the Father, as when the author of Hebrews quotes Psalm 40 in reference to Christ: "Lo, I come to do thy will, O God" (Heb. 10:9, KJV). As we have seen, Owen takes this obedi-

---

51. *Works*, 19:85.
52. *Works*, 19:88.
53. We might complicate this picture by probing what the term "persons" means in this context, but given constraints of space, we have had to leave this issue to one side.

ential disposition as a sign of the covenant between the Father and the Son. Christ's mission is portrayed in this manner because he is in covenant with the Father, who is the "original," or "principle," or "author"[54] of the covenant, and as such, is the One "whose will in all things is to be attended unto."[55]

Scripture speaks directly to the will of the Father in proposing this covenant by addressing his sovereignty and authority in the "giving" or the "sending" of the Son. "God so loved the world that he gave his only begotten Son" (John 3:16, KJV). This act of "giving" and "sending" the Son attests the will of the Father as the "enjoiner, prescriber, and promiser" of the covenant.[56] But in these texts, the Father's work in sending the Son is depicted, above all, as being *gracious*. And as Owen is quick to point out, such a work could not be gracious if it were not also *free*.

> [The Father's] will was *naturally* at a perfect liberty from engaging in that way of salvation which he accomplished by Christ. He was at liberty to have left all mankind under sin and the curse, as he did all the angels that fell; he was at liberty utterly to have destroyed the race of mankind that sprang from Adam in his fallen estate, either in the root of them, or in the branches when multiplied, as he almost did in the flood, and have created another stock or race of them unto his glory. And hence the acting of his will herein is expressed by *grace*,—which is free, or it is not grace,—and is said to proceed from love acting by choice; all arguing the highest liberty in the will of the Father.[57]

Owen's point here is, quite clearly, to ensure the *graciousness* of the covenant by guaranteeing its *freedom*. He thus denies that the Father entered into the covenant out of any cause in the creature. It is not true to say that the covenant was necessary even on the grounds that, as the Creator, God is inclined by his nature to alleviate the miserable condition of his creatures. For if such were the case, God's grace would not be *free*. And Scripture itself abundantly attests that God had the right and liberty to pass over the entire human race in judgment, just as he did with the angels. The fact that he has not done so, but has entered into a covenant with Christ for our redemption does not speak to a putative inclination of his nature that necessitates him being merciful to creatures. On the contrary. Owen thinks it reveals the full *freedom* of the Father's will. This freedom is, in fact, *natural* to God in the sense that it is inextricable from his being—the simple entailment of his utter perfection and absoluteness. For this reason, Owen here draws an analogy between the freedom of the Father in making the covenant and the freedom of God in creating the world:

54.   Cf. *Works*, 12:501; 20:380; 1:225.
55.   *Works*, 19:86.
56.   *Works*, 19:86.
57.   *Works*, 19:86.

Let none, then, once imagine that this work of entering into covenant about the salvation of mankind was any way necessary unto God, or that it was required by virtue of any of the essential properties of his nature, so that he must have done against them in doing otherwise. God was herein absolutely free, as he was also in his making of all things out of nothing. He could have left it undone without the least disadvantage unto his essential glory or contrariety unto his holy nature. Whatever, therefore, we may afterwards assert concerning the necessity of satisfaction to be given unto his justice, upon the supposition of this covenant, yet the entering into this covenant, and consequently all that ensued thereon, is absolutely resolved into the mere will and grace of God.[58]

In the two quotations above, Owen thus defines the covenant of redemption as being *absolutely* contingent, in the sense that its existence depends entirely on a contingent act of the divine will. This was a fairly standard commitment among the Reformed scholastics. The covenant of redemption is one of God's internal works. And what makes the internal works of God *works* of God is the fact that they are *contingent* acts of the divine will. Moreover, Owen further specifies the nature of this contingency by denying that the Covenant was *naturally necessary* to God. That is to say, there is nothing in the divine nature which either *requires* or *disposes* the Father toward giving the covenant.[59] On the contrary, it was an act of his absolute dominion—an expression of his "perfect liberty"—and as such, must be resolved into his "mere will and grace."[60]

Since Owen's understanding of the freedom of the covenant stands here in direct relation to his account of divine grace, it is important that we take stock of Owen's claim at this point. The entire purpose of the covenant of redemption was to ensure the fully gracious character of Christ's work. If we neglected Owen's account of divine freedom, therefore, we might miss what is one of the most integral elements of his account of the work of Christ—that which makes it an unconditional *gift*—namely, its *voluntary* character. This touches directly on our question about the nature of Christ's humiliation since, as Owen argues, the "sole foundation" of Christ's obligation to the Father is established in the covenant.

Now, it is a constant refrain in Owen's works that Christ's love for sinners is demonstrated by the willing and voluntary assumption of his office in the covenant. Positively, Owen makes this point by speaking of Christ's "susception" of his office as an act of "infinite condescension." Since the Creator is

58. *Works*, 19:86.
59. This is a broader theme in Owen's theology of grace and divine perfection, though we cannot explore it here.
60. For more on this issue in Reformed theology generally, see Richard Muller, *Divine Will and Human Choice: Freedom, Contingency and Necessity in Early Modern Reformed Thought* (Grand Rapids, MI: Baker, 2017).

infinitely above his creatures, Scripture states that God "humbleth himself to behold the things that are in heaven, and in the earth" (Ps. 113:5–6, KJV). Every act in which God turns to the creature is therefore a movement of divine condescension and humility. But if, as Owen says, "it is an act of mere grace in him to take notice of things below,"[61] how much more is it an act of grace that the Son of God should take our very nature upon himself and subject himself to life under the law? This, Owen writes, is "the most ineffable effect of the divine wisdom of the Father and the love of the Son," it is "the highest evidence of the care of God towards mankind . . . the glory of Christian religion, and the animating soul of all evangelical truth."[62]

The glory of this divine condescension consists precisely in its freedom. Christ had nothing to gain from this act, nor was he in any way bound to do it. It was an act of free mercy—a course elected by love. This is why the apostle depicts the Son as voluntarily electing to take on flesh when he says that Christ "humbled himself" (Phil. 2:8). According to Owen, Scripture speaks in this manner for two reasons: "First, to demonstrate that the things which he underwent in his human nature were . . . voluntarily consented thereunto. Secondly, to manifest that those very acts which he had in command from his Father were no less the acts of his own will."[63] In other words, the submissive posture with which Christ is characterised in the biblical text attests the *freedom* of the Son in his obedience, not its natural necessity.

> Wherefore, as it is said that the Father loved us, and gave his Son to die for us; so also it is said that the Son loved us, and gave himself for us, and washed us in his own blood. These things proceeded from and were founded in the will of the Son of God; and it was an act of perfect liberty in him to engage into his peculiar concernments in this covenant. What he did, he did by choice, in a way of condescension and love. And this his voluntary susception of the discharge of what he was to perform, according to the nature and terms of this covenant, was the ground of the *authoritative mission*, sealing, and commanding, of the Father towards him. See Ps. 60:7, 8; Heb. 10:5; John 10:17, 18. And whatever is expressed in the Scripture concerning the will of the human nature of Christ, as it was engaged in and bent upon its work, it is but a representation of the will of the Son of God when he engaged into this work from eternity.[64]

So, then, the humility of the Son in his earthly obedience is a representation of the condescension of the Son in offering his consent to the covenant. We should note here that Owen describes the Son as having a "perfect liberty" in this matter, the same term Owen uses to describe the freedom of the Father

61. *Works*, 1:324.
62. *Works*, 1:330.
63. *Works*, 19:87.
64. *Works*, 19:87.

either to offer or not to offer the promise of the covenant. This implies that the Son enjoys no less freedom than the Father in this act of covenanting. Moreover, it should be observed that Owen here identifies the will of the Son as the "ground" of the Father's "authoritative mission, sealing and commanding." By grounding the Father's authority over the Son in an act of the Son's own "perfect liberty," Owen is able to resolve the Son's subordination to the Father entirely into the covenant itself. While this locates the basis of the "inequality" between the Father and the Son in the inner life of God, it does so at the level of God's *internal works*, which we have said are *contingent*. This is absolutely critical, because it ultimately allows Owen to distinguish the obligation that Christ bears before the Father in his servant-form, from the Son's natural coequality with the Father in their immanent triune life. The Christ's obedience to the Father is thus represented as a contingent aspect of the Son's mission, rather than as a necessary property of his divine person.

The suggestion that obedience is a property natural to Christ's divine person would in fact seriously undermine Owen's argument here by subverting the free and voluntary character of the covenant. Moreover, it would also deprive him of an important aspect of his atonement theology, as he regularly appeals to Christ's voluntary assumption of the covenant in order to explain how it is both "just and equal" that the Son should suffer in our place in the manner that he does. This is a point of some immediate significance to Owen. One of the regular challenges levelled against Reformed doctrines of the atonement was that it was unjust for God to punish the sins of the elect in the person of Christ. By reading Christ's obedience to the Father as a sign of his free condescension in the covenant, however, Owen can argue strongly for the voluntary character of Christ's mission, and on that basis, for the justice of the Father's demands:

> for this mind was in him, that whereas he was in the form of God, he humbled himself unto this work, Phil. 2:5–8, and by his own voluntary consent was engaged therein. Whereas, therefore, he had a sovereign and absolute power over his own human nature when assumed, whatever he submitted unto, it was no injury unto him, nor injustice in God to lay it on him.[65]

Because Christ had the liberty to *refuse* the covenant, but nonetheless voluntarily assumed it, the hardships of his mission were neither improper nor unjust. In this way, the freedom of Christ's will in the covenant serves to protect the substitutionary nature of his work.

Owen also defends the voluntary character of Christ's obedience negatively, as well. He does this by arguing the inverse of the point above, namely, by upholding the Son of God's natural freedom from the law. Typically, Owen makes this point in connection with Paul's teaching in Galatians 4:4—"God

---

65. *Works*, 19:87.

sent his Son, born of a woman, born under the law." Christ's submission to divine law is here represented as a consequence of his mission in the Father's "sending." And because that mission is contingent, Owen consistently reads this passage as implying the Son's natural freedom from the law as he is divine. So, for example, reflecting on the nature of Christ's obedience in his *Meditations on the Glories of Christ*, Owen writes:

> From the very constitution of our natures we are necessarily subject unto the law of God. All that is left unto us is a voluntary compliance with unavoidable commands; with him it was not so. An act of his own will and choice preceded all obligation as unto obedience. He obeyed because he would, before because he ought. He said, "Lo, I come to do thy will, O God," before he was obliged to do that will. By his own choice, and that in an act of infinite condescension and love, as we have showed, he was "made of a woman"; and thereby "made under the law." In his divine person he was Lord of the law,—above it,—no more obnoxious unto its commands than its curse. . . . This was the original glory of his obedience. This wisdom, the grace, the love, the condescension that was in this choice, animated every act, every duty of his obedience,—rendering it amiable in the sight of God, and useful unto us.[66]

Though humankind is subject to the law of God by nature, the eternal Son was subjected to it by *grace*. For in his divine nature he was "Lord of the law." Owen thus concludes that all Christ's "obligation" to the Father is radically preceded by an "act of his own will and choice." Here again, the consent of the Son in the Covenant of Redemption functions as the *ground* of the Father's authority: "He obeyed because he would, before because he ought." And in this way, the covenant distinguishes between the natural coequality of the Father and the Son, on the one hand, and the subordination of the Son to the Father in the economy of grace, on the other. For being "in the form of God," Christ is "a participant of the divine nature," and so "equal with God, in authority, dignity, and power." Indeed, this is entirely necessary. "Because he was in the form of God, he must be equal with God; for there is *order* in the Divine Persons, but no *inequality* in the Divine Being."[67] The evident inequality between the Father and the Son in the Son's earthly ministry is therefore an attestation of the Son's willing condescension to this work by means of a covenant.

In other words, Owen thinks that the obedience of Christ to the Father is every bit as much evidence of his *sovereign freedom* as it is of his humility and love. And just as before, this point has immediate relevance in securing the substitutionary nature of Christ's work. The Socinians often rejected the notion that Christ's obedience could be imputed to others on the grounds that, as Christ was a man, he was naturally obligated to obey the Father's will.

---

66. *Works*, 1:339.
67. *Works*, 1:326.

Owen's response is that the obedience which Christ renders is not merely that of his human nature, but of his whole person, which is both human and divine. And as he is God, Christ is Lord over the law, and so in no way naturally obligated to obey it. Christ's assumption of this work is thus testament that the whole of his life and obedience to the Father is an act of sheer *grace*. And consequently, he has the power to donate his merit to others, since he has no need of it for himself.[68]

The absolute freedom of the Son in the covenant of redemption thus forms the proper backdrop for understanding the nature of his humiliation in the economy of redemption. His obligation to obey the law is actually grounded in his supreme right. His submission to the Father's authority is, in all reality, an expression of his own sovereign freedom. And his evident inequality with the Father throughout his earthly mission actually has its foundations in an act of unparalleled equality and liberty. In short, all contingent acts of the Son within history are antecedently conditioned by the freedom and independence of his divine nature. But if Christ's humiliation is not set in relief against the background of his absolute sovereignty and freedom, then the gracious character of Christ's condescension to us cannot fully emerge.

Conclusion

From what we have seen in the foregoing, it should now be clear that, for Owen, one of the primary purposes of the *pactum salutis* is precisely to avoid the conclusion that advocates of eternal, functional subordination of the Son wish to defend, namely, that subordination to the Father is a personal property of the Son. Owen thinks the subordination of the Son has its basis in the inner life of God, and he can affirm that it is "eternal" in the limited sense that it is eternally willed by God. But it is fundamental to Owen's whole manner of reading Scripture that the subordination of the Son to the Father in the economy of grace must have its basis in a free and voluntary covenant between the persons of the Trinity in eternity. The claim that the Father has some natural authority over the Son, as to his divine person, would disrupt the entire logic of Christ's mission. For on that account, Christ's obedience to the Father would arise as a matter of necessity, rather than as a free act of the Son. Such a claim inevitably reduces the gratuity of Christ's mission, and so fails to grasp the full extent of Christ's love for us. The humiliation of the Son was not finally a matter of necessity. It proceeded rather from the Son's own infinite blessedness, self-sufficiency, and freedom. And it is precisely in this freedom that the mystery of Christ's condescension and the example of his love are so compelling—not in the fact that he was humbled, but in the fact that "he humbled himself."

---

68. *Works,*   5:255–56.

Bibliography

Barth, Karl. *Church Dogmatics*. Study Edition. Volume IV/1. Edited by G. W. Bromiley and T. F. Torrance. London: T & T Clark, 2009.

Butler Jr., D. Glenn. "Eternal Functional Subordination and the Problem of the Divine Will." *Evangelical Theological Journal* 58, no. 1 (2015): 131–49.

Cleveland, Kendall Beau. "The Covenant of Redemption in the Trinitarian Theology of John Owen." PhD Diss., The University of St Andrews, 2016.

Dickson, David. "Arminianism Discussed." In *Records of the Kirk of Scotland, containing the Acts and Proceedings of the General Assemblies, from the Year 1638 Downwards*, edited by Alexander Peterkin, 156–59. Edinburgh: Peter Brown, 1845.

Fesko, J. V. *The Covenant of Redemption: Origins, Development, and Reception*. Göttingen: Vandenhoeck & Ruprecht, 2010.

The Holy Bible: King James Version, Electronic Edition of the 1900 Authorized Version. Bellingham, WA: Logos Research Systems, Inc., 2009.

Muller, Richard. *Divine Will and Human Choice: Freedom, Contingency and Necessity in Early Modern Reformed Thought*. Grand Rapids: Baker, 2017.

Owen, John. *Works of John Owen*. 24 vols. Edited by W. H. Goold. Edinburgh: T & T Clark, 1850–1855.

Starke, John. "Augustine and His Interpreters." In *One God in Three Persons: Unity of Essence, Distinction of Persons, Implications for Life*. Edited by Bruce Ware and John Starke, 155–72. Wheaton, IL: Crossway, 2015.

———. *Post-Reformation Reformed Dogmatics*. 4 vols. Grand Rapids: Baker, 2003.

———. "Toward the Pactum Salutis: Locating the Origins of a Concept." *Mid-Western Journal of Theology* 18 (2007): 11–65.

Swain, Scott W. "Covenant of Redemption." *Christian Dogmatics: Reformed Theology for the Church Catholic*, edited by Michael Allen and Scott R. Swain, 107–25. Grand Rapids: Baker Academic, 2016.

Webster, John. "It Was the Will of the Lord to Bruise Him: Soteriology and the Doctrine of God." In *God of Salvation: Soteriology in Theological Perspective*, edited by Murray Rae and Ivor Davidson, 15–34. New York: Routledge, 2010.

Williams, Carol A. "The Decree of Redemption Is in Effect a Covenant: David Dickson and the Covenant of Redemption." PhD Diss., Calvin Seminary, 2005.

Wittman, Tyler R. "The End of the Incarnation: John Owen, Trinitarian Agency, and Christology." *International Journal of Systematic Theology* 15, no. 3 (2013): 284 300.

CHAPTER 9

Protestant Scholastics on Trinity and Persons

JEFF FISHER

This chapter further clarifies the theology of the eternal relationship between the Father and the Son by providing a historically accurate portrait of post-Reformation teaching. It specifically considers what several of the most significant Protestant scholastics, from Peter Marty Vermigli in the 1550s to Francis Turretin in the 1680s, articulated about possible forms of subordinationism regarding the Trinity. Six characteristic themes consistently emerge from their writings. Among these themes is the repeated contention that going beyond what Scripture reveals about the mystery of the Trinity has resulted in many errors and heresies. In their pursuit of countering heresy, they developed several explanations to rule out any conclusion that the Son was eternally subordinate or inferior to the Father.

Building upon Nicene orthodoxy, they developed the view that, although he is begotten of the Father, the Son has the attribute of aseity, and therefore is *autotheon* ("God of himself"). They articulated that the deity, or divine essence, is "communicated" to the Son by the Father so that the personhood of the Son is generated, but not his deity. The Reformed orthodox made this distinction in order to reject any implication of eternal hierarchy or subordination in the divine nature. They explained that any Scripture passages that taught the subordination of the Son exclusively corresponded to the functional or economic implementation of the divine plan. While they acknowledged that this "order of operations" followed the "order of subsisting," they adamantly insisted that the numbering of first, second, and third persons could not refer to chronology, hierarchy, or authority. This chapter substantiates that there is effectively no historical support for Reformed orthodox theologians affirming that the Son is relationally subordinate or submissive to the Father in eternity, because they considered that to be too closely associated with heretical views they were combatting.

Although the current debates regarding the Trinity often skip over the period immediately after John Calvin, the scholarly writings of Protestant theologians during this time provide significantly helpful language, categories, and clarifications for theological topics.[1] Current scholars frequently refer to this era, spanning from around 1560 to 1725, as "Reformed Orthodoxy," "Protestant Scholasticism," or "Reformed Scholasticism."[2] These terms are generally synonymous and refer to the academic theology that resulted from the use of a scholastic method to facilitate academic argument with the purpose of reaching defensible doctrinal conclusions based on Scripture and bound by the Reformed confessions.[3] While this method utilized human reason and deductive logic, its focus was to ground theological conclusions on biblical interpretation. In a specific discussion that requires as much nuance as the subordination or submissiveness of the Son, the writings of these theologians prove to be particularly useful.[4]

Our attention will center around the period identified as "early" Reformed orthodoxy (ca. 1560–1640).[5] However, for this particular theological topic, a

---

1. As examples of recent works which give little attention to or entirely skip this era, see Gregg Allison, *Historical Theology: An Introduction to Christian Doctrine* (Grand Rapids: Zondervan, 2011), 246–49; Stephen D. Kovach and Peter R. Schemm, Jr., "A Defense of the Doctrine of the Eternal Subordination of the Son," *Journal of the Evangelical Theological Society* 42, no. 3 (1999): 461–76; Wayne Grudem, *Evangelical Feminism and Biblical Truth* (Wheaton, IL: Crossway, 2012), 415–22; Millard Erickson, *Who's Tampering with the Trinity? An Assessment of the Subordination Debate* (Grand Rapids: Kregel, 2009), 139–68; and Kevin Giles, *The Eternal Generation of the Son* (Downers Grove, IL: InterVarsity, 2012), 186–90.

2. See, for example, Willem J. Van Asselt, *Introduction to Reformed Scholasticism*, trans. Albert Gootjes (Grand Rapids: Reformation Heritage, 2011); Carl Trueman and R. Scott Clark, eds., *Protestant Scholasticism: Essays in Reassessment* (Eugene, OR: Wipf & Stock, 2007); Richard Muller, *Post-Reformation Reformed Dogmatics: The Rise and Development of Reformed Orthodoxy, ca. 1520 to ca. 1725*, 4 vols. (Grand Rapids: Baker, 2003). Hereafter PRRD 4.

3. See the summary in Van Asselt, *Introduction*, 9 and "Protestant Scholasticism: Some Methodological Considerations in the Study of its Development," *Nederlands Archief Voor Kerkgeschiedenis* 81, no. 3 (2001): 265–74. For explanation of each component, see *Introduction*, 1–3, 57–62, 80–83, 196–201.

4. After the writing of this chapter, Kevin DeYoung posted on his blog a summary of views in the Reformed tradition, which includes a few from this time period. Notably, he independently reached very similar conclusions on the contributions of post-Reformation theologians to this debate. See his "Distinguishing Among the Three Persons of the Trinity within the Reformed Tradition," posted September 27, 2016, https://blogs.thegospelcoalition.org/kevindeyoung/2016/09/27/distinguishing-among-the-three-persons-of-the-trinity-within-the-reformed-tradition/ (accessed September 28, 2016).

5. On the division of these time periods see Richard Muller, *After Calvin: Studies in the Development of a Theological Tradition* (New York: Oxford University Press, 2003), 4–7. For an excellent summary of the overall continuity and discontinuity between the Reformation and this time period, see Richard Muller, *Calvin and the Reformed Tradition* (Grand Rapids: Baker, 2012), 13–50.

slightly earlier starting point and a slightly later ending point will prove beneficial. As is the case with most theological developments, the controversies and debates of their time shaped the writings about the Trinity among the Protestant scholastics.[6] During the early decades of the Reformation, most writings on the doctrine of the Trinity focused on refuting the ancient and classic heresies. These writings were often relatively brief, highly scriptural, and not overly technical.

With the rise of Renaissance humanism came an increased interest in original languages, which facilitated the Reformation insistence on the primacy of Scripture over church tradition and a greater emphasis on biblical exegesis.[7] However, these interests also brought attention to text-critical problems with certain biblical passages which had been traditionally understood as "proving the Trinity" (e.g., 1 John 5:7; 1 Tim. 3:16). These emphases also raised questions about the "non-biblical" language that had been used to articulate the doctrine of the Trinity.[8] A resulting problem emerged when others began to argue that Scripture alone could not lead to the traditional Trinitarian doctrine.

Among the most famous of these were the anti-Trinitarians Michael Servetus (1509–1553) and Faustus Socinus (1539–1604).[9] The influence of their works offers us a useful timeframe for situating the Protestant scholastic articulations of the Trinity. Servetus published his first book, *De Trinitatis Erroribus* ("*On the Errors of the Trinity*"), already in 1531, but it became most controversial in the 1550s.[10] On the other end of the timeframe, the most universally accessible publications of the Socinians appeared in the 1650s and 1660s.[11] Richard Muller distinguishes "an early Reformation phase, extending as far as 1535 or 1540" and "a later stage, beginning around 1540, during which the rise of anti-Trinitarian teachings demanded response from the Reformers."[12] He later notes that Trinitarian controversies during the period of high orthodoxy (ca. 1640–1725) had a different tone and different emphases based on newer forms of heresy and additional questions.[13]

---

6. For a summary of Trinitarian debates and conclusions regarding the person and deity of the Son, PRRD 4:83–91, 275–88, 299–301. See also Benjamin Merkle, *Defending the Trinity in the Reformed Palatinate: The Elohistae* (New York: Oxford University Press, 2015), 22–32, 47–62 for additional examples. While many of these were disputes with those rejecting Trinitarian doctrine, others were among those embracing orthodox Trinitarianism (e.g., Christological debates regarding the Lord's Supper and the self-existence of the Son).

7. PRRD 4:62, 196–99; Merkle, *Defending the Trinity*, 26–32.

8. PRRD 4:62, 91. For the specific discussions on the terms and texts, see 4:167–89.

9. PRRD 4:75–76, 91–99 for brief summaries of their views and impact.

10. Servetus was executed for heresy in Geneva on October 27, 1553.

11. PRRD 4:91–99. Muller specifically identifies the publication of the *Bibliotheca Fratrum Polonorum* (1656) as "a significant point in the development of seventeenth-century antitrinitarianism" (93).

12. PRRD 4:60. See pp. 65–74 for some background on this development into the time of Calvin and p. 83–103 on Trinitarian developments from 1565–1640.

13. PRRD 4:61–62. Muller specifically observes a shift when "the language and conceptual framework of Christian Aristotelianism was no longer universally accepted, even among the orthodox writers."

Focus and Aim of the Chapter

For our purposes, then, we will consider the teachings of some of the most significant Protestant scholastic theologians from around 1550 to 1680 in order to see the shifts and similarities that span multiple disputes, debates, and heresies. As Muller observes, "theologians of the age of orthodoxy found it increasingly necessary to develop trinitarian arguments both polemically and positively," which resulted in writings that had a "far more organized, articulate, and exegetically sophisticated form than was found in the sixteenth century."[14] Their conclusions frequently fell in line with the teachings of the earlier Reformers. Yet their scholastic approach enabled them to provide clarifications and distinctions that previous theologians had not addressed.

This chapter aims to provide a historically accurate portrait of the Protestant scholastics' views on the persons of the Trinity. Since many of these theologians spent hundreds of pages articulating and defending numerous aspects related to the Trinity, this chapter cannot address all that they said. Therefore, our focus will center on the ways they articulated the relationship between the Father and the Son in their theological and exegetical works. In particular, this chapter presents what several of the most significant Protestant scholastics wrote about the eternal relationship between the Father and the Son with specific attention given to concerns they expressed about erroneous forms of subordinationism during their respective time periods.

Protestant Scholastic Scholars

Based on the timeframe identified above, we will explore the writings of several Reformed orthodox theologians who influenced the dissemination and development of the doctrine of the Trinity.[15] The earliest theologian included in this study is Peter Martyr Vermigli (1499–1562), who though not technically considered a Protestant scholastic, had a definitive influence on the development of theology among the Reformed orthodox, particularly through the posthumous publication of his *Loci Communes*— first in 1576 and then at least ten more times until 1624.[16] Among those

---

14. PRRD 4:91. Muller states, "With specific reference to the Trinity, the Reformed orthodox consistently raised broader doctrinal questions in their exegesis of texts that had, in the Christian tradition, become the basis for trinitarian formulation" (89).

15. In addition to several of the theologians included here, Richard Muller also draws from Gulielmus Bucanus (d. 1603), William Perkins (1558–1602), Amandus Polanus (1561–1610), Henry Ainsworth (1569–1622), Johannes Wollebius (1589–1629), and Johann Heinrich Alsted (1588–1638) in PRRD 4. Brannon Ellis focuses on later Reformed scholastics such as Bartholomaeus Keckermann (1572–1609), Lucas Trelcatius, Jr. (1573–1607), Gisbertus Voetius (1589–1676), Johannes Maccovius (1588–1644), and Bernhardinus De Moor (1709–1780) in *Calvin, Classical Trinitarianism, and the Aseity of the Son* (Oxford: Oxford University Press, 2012).

16. Peter Martyr Vermigli, *Loci Communes* (London: John Kyngston, 1576), 78–86. These were assembled from his *loci* in his biblical commentaries published in the 1550s and 1560s, including his *In selectissimam D. Pauli priorem ad Corinthios Epistolam* (Zurich: Christoph Froschouer, 1551) with republications in 1567 and 1572.

shaped by Vermigli's preaching was Girolamo Zanchi (1516–1590), who lectured on the Old Testament for the academy in Strasbourg and wrote *De tribus Elohim* (1572).[17] Muller refers to Zanchi's volume as "perhaps [the] most elaborate formulation" of the positive development of the doctrine of the Trinity.[18] Two others from that generation included here are Theodore Beza (1519–1605), the successor to Calvin in Geneva and the head of the Academy there, and Zacharias Ursinus (1534–1583), the primary author of the Heidelberg Catechism.[19] As representatives of those in the early seventeenth century, we will consider the writings of Francis Gomarus (1563–1641), professor at Leiden and the leading voice against the Remonstrants at the Synod of Dort, and William Ames (1576–1633), a student of William Perkins who ministered in Holland and authored the influential *Medulla Theologica* (*"The Marrow of Theology,"* 1623).[20] Finally, we will incorporate perhaps the most famous of all Reformed scholastics, Francis Turretin (1623–1687), professor at the Academy of Geneva for thirty years and author of *The Institutes of Elenctic Theology* (1679–1685), as the representative for the developments and ongoing issues regarding the Trinity into the late seventeenth century.[21] Each of these theologians formulated specific theological explanations about the eternal relationship between the Father and the Son in ways that sought to maintain both the unity of God and the distinction of persons without falling into heretical or erroneous forms of subordinationism. Six characteristic themes emerge from their writings, which aid us in clarifying key issues related to the eternal relationship between the Father and the Son.

---

17. Jerome Zanchi, *De tribus Elohim, aeterno patre, filio, et spiritu Sancto, uno eodemque Iehova* (Neustadt an der Haardt: Harnisius, 1597). This work is also found in *Operum theologicorum D. Hieronymi Zanchii, Vol. I* (Heidelberg: Stephanus Gamonetus and Matthaeus Berjon, 1605) and *Operum theologicorum D. Hieronymi Zanchii Vol. 9* (Geneva: Samuel Crispin, 1617–1619). The English translation is Girolamo Zanchi, *On the Triune Elohim: Eternal Father, Son, and Holy Spirit, One and the Same Jehovah*, 2 vols., ed. Ben Merkle (Moscow, ID: Wenden House, 2016).

18. PRRD 4:84. Muller specifically notes that this work had a greater interest than many previous works in establishing a correct use of terminology and the theological tradition.

19. Theodore Beza, *Propositions and Principles of Divinitie Propounded and Disputed in the University of Geneva*, trans. John Pentry (Edinburgh, 1595); *Confession Christiane fidei, et eiusdem collation cum Papisticis Haeresibus* (Geneva, 1560); *Tractationes theologicae* (Geneva, 1570–1582). Zacharias Ursinus, *The Commentary of Dr. Zacharias Ursinus on the Heidelberg Catechism*, trans. G. W. Williard (Grand Rapids: Eerdmans, 1954).

20. Francis Gomarus, *Disputationum theologicarum quarto repetitarum quarta de trinitate personarum in una Dei essentia* (Leiden: Ioannis Patii, 1605); William Ames, *The Marrow of Theology*, trans. and ed. John D. Eusden (Durham, NC: Labyrinth, 1983). This volume is a translation of the third Latin edition published in 1629. Ames had a significant impact on English Protestantism and Puritanism in New England.

21. Francis Turretin, *Institutes of Elenctic Theoloy*, trans. George Musgrave Giger, ed. James T. Dennison, Jr. (Phillipsburg, NJ: P & R Publishing, 1992). "Elentic" refers to a logical refutation of an opposing view, often in the form of a syllogism, which leads to a positive statement of a truth.

Terminology and Mystery in the Trinity

In nearly all their writings, the Protestant theologians of the generation after Calvin felt compelled to address questions related to whether the Trinitarian terms formulated in the early church were biblical and still useful for the church. They all affirmed that although key doctrinal terms, such as *essentia* and *ousios* ("essence"), *substantia* ("substance"), *natura* and *physis* ("nature"), *persona* and *hypostasis* ("person"), *subsistentia* ("subsistence"), and *Trinitas* ("Trinity") were not all found in Scripture, they were rightly developed and should be retained for use in the church.[22] As one example, Zanchi stated:

> Although these expressions, about which there is a question, do not appear sylla-
> ble by syllable in Scripture, nevertheless they are not alien to Scripture, since not
> only do we have the thing itself in Scripture, but also there are terms in Scripture
> from which these expressions are derived by true and necessary consequence.[23]

These theologians defined and explained each of these terms with little change in their already existent usage.[24] In fact, they reiterated and appealed to much of what had been taught previously by Augustine and other church fathers.[25] They consistently maintained that the triune God exists as one single shared divine essence, subsisting as three persons, each distinguished from the other by their unique incommunicable properties based on their relations as persons, such that each person is *homoousion* ("of the same essence"), coessential, and consubstantial with the others.[26] Following Nicene-Constantinopolitan orthodoxy, they rejected all forms of "similar" essence or substance as a reiteration of the Arian heresy that made the Son ontologically or "essentially" less divine than the Father.[27]

In addition to clarifying their terms, these theologians repeatedly acknowledged that the Trinity was an unsearchable mystery to be embraced by faith.[28] Ursinus specifically stated that all the orthodox fathers had acknowledged that the eternal generation of the Son and the procession of the Holy Spirit

22. For example, see Beza, *Propositions and Principles*, 4 [2.2–3]; Ursinus, *Commentary*, 127–28, 132; Zanchi, *On the Triune Elohim*, 24–36; Turretin, *Institutes*, 253–60.
23. Beza, *Propositions and Principles*, 24. See very similar statements in Beza, *Propositions and Principles*, 8–9 and Turretin, *Institutes*, 257–60 [23.XVI-XXX]. For an analysis of Zanchi's interaction with the anti-Trinitarians on the use of extrabiblical terminology, see Merkle, *Defending the Trinity*, 111–15.
24. See van Asselt, *Introduction*, 126, 197; PRRD 4:208–14, 417–18.
25. Maarten Wisse, "The Teacher of the Ancient Church: Augustine," in *Introduction to Reformed Scholasticism*, ed. Willem J. van Asselt (Grand Rapids: Reformation Heritage Books, 2011), 50.
26. See Vermigli, *Loci Communes*, 78, 82–83; Beza, *Principles and Propositions*, 4–5 [2.7–9]; Ursinus, *Commentary*, 134; Zanchi, *On the Triune Elohim*, 13–14, 22–23, 28–36, 50–53; Ames, *Marrow*, 83–87; Gomarus, *Disputationum theologicarum*, 2–10; Turretin, *Institutes*, 181–83, 191–94, 265–72.
27. See, for example, Vermigli, *Loci Communes*, 78, 83. Zanchi articulated, "'the entire, infinite essence of God is in each divine person, and therefore the same essence is fully in each" (*On the Triune Elohim*, 30).
28. For example, see Beza, *Propositions and Principles*, 4 [2.1–2]; Zanchi, *On the Triune Elohim*, 14–15; Ames, *Marrow*, 89; Turretin, *Institutes*, 261–65, 292, 302.

are inexplicable and beyond our comprehension.[29] Zanchi declared that "no man, no matter how holy and wise, has ever been able to, or ever will be able to, understand by his own intelligence, what God is."[30] However, this did not mean that nothing could be said about the Trinity, but rather that the Trinity could not be fully explained and only what Scripture reveals should be utilized when formulating doctrine about God. They expressed that errors easily and readily arise when one seeks to go beyond what Scripture says. Zanchi even contended that all heresies resulted from only two possibilities:

> [E]ither they have not restrained themselves within the limits of holy Scripture, but driven by curiosity they desired to search out that which God has not revealed; or, that which he revealed, they carefully studied, but they then failed to interpret according to the analogy of faith.[31]

The Reformed orthodox insisted that their Trinitarian theology derived from and was bounded by what God revealed about himself in Scripture. A major feature of their definition and articulation of the Trinity, which they maintained was derived from Scripture, was the "eternal generation—or the divine begetting—of the Son."[32]

Eternal Generation of the Son

As adherents to Nicene orthodox Christianity, all the Reformed orthodox defended the notion of the Son's eternal generation based on passages of Scripture, such as Hebrews 1:5 quoting Psalm 2:7, Colossians 1:5, and John 1:14, 1:18, and 15:18. They observed that many of these passages indicated that Christ previously existed before his birth and possessed something more than a human nature. They appealed to multiple Old Testament and New Testament texts to "prove his divinity and eternal perpetual nature."[33] They specified that the Father is "father" because the Son is begotten.[34] Gomarus contended that the generation of the Son is proven by all the Scriptures where the Father is called Father, since

---

29. Ursinus, *Commentary*, 132. See also a summary of others confessing the same thing in PRRD 4:146 and 4:151–54.

30. Zanchi, *On the Triune Elohim*, 14. See also comments by sixteenth-century interpreters in Graham Tomlin, ed., *Philippians, Colossians*, Reformation Commentary on Scripture, NT XI (Downers Grove, IL: IVP Academic, 2013), 46.

31. Zanchi, *On the Triune Elohim*, 14. For an analysis of Zanchi on the mystery of the Trinity, see Merkle, *Defending the Trinity*, 117.

32. See PRRD 4:86, 4.145–50, 275.

33. For example, see Vermigli, *Loci Communes*, 78–79; Ames, *Marrow*, 88–91; Turretin, *Institutes*, 283–91, 294–302. Zanchi includes 56 passages from the Old Testament alone to prove Christ's deity (*On the Triune Elohim*, 60–121).

34. Zanchi, *On the Triune Elohim*, 56–57, 168–69; Ames, *Marrow*, 88. See also Zanchi's comments in Tomlin, *Philippians, Colossians*, 46 quoting from Girolamo Zanchi, *De religion Christiana fides—Confession of Christian Religion*, eds. Luca Baschera and Christian Moser, 2 vols. (Leiden: Brill, 2007), 1:201–3.

"from the filiation is that which by generation is understood."[35] Zanchi insisted that those who deny eternal generation not only rob the Son of his deity, but they also "deny that the Father is the Father when they deny that the Son was truly begotten from Him."[36] He, like others, affirmed that always and from eternity, the Son was the Son of God the Father—and not just at the incarnation.[37]

When Vermigli addressed why the Spirit is not called a "son," since he too "proceeds from the Father and does not have an origin from himself," he responded simply that Scripture never refers to the Spirit as begotten or as a son, but uses the term "procession" to refer to the "emanation" of the Spirit.[38] He acknowledged that it is difficult to discriminate between "procession" and "generation," but appealed to Augustine and other fathers to explain that "the Holy Spirit is neither begotten nor unbegotten," because "if we say 'unbegotten,' we seem to make him the Father, and if we decide 'begotten,' we seem to say he is the Son."[39]

Turretin's summary articulates the way many phrased the eternal relationship between the Father and the Son: "So the Son is said to be from the Father by generation; not with respect to essence and absolutely as God, but with respect to person and reduplicatively as Son."[40] These theologians reasoned that since both the Father and the Son are divine, they must share the same essence or nature and have both existed in and from all eternity. By utilizing the terms from the creeds, the church fathers, and their Latin Bibles, they maintained that the Son is "eternally begotten," not created, or made, or adopted.[41] They saw this as the means to uphold the personal distinctions between Father and Son while also sustaining that each is fully God.

The Aseity of the Son

While universal agreement existed on the eternal generation of the Son, one of the most significant intra-orthodox disputes during this period addressed the question of whether or not the begotten Son was *autotheon* (self-existent God).[42] They debated whether the Son had the attribute of

---

35.   Gomarus, *Disputationum theologicarum*, 4.

36.   Zanchi, *On the Triune Elohim*, 9.

37.   Zanchi, *On the Triune Elohim*, 41, 44–45, 123–30. Ames utilized this reasoning to affirm *theotokos*, since there were not two sonships of Christ, but rather because Christ was always the Son of God, "it may truly and rightly be said that Mary was the mother of God" (*Marrow*, 137–38).

38.   Vermigli, *Loci Communes*, 84–85.

39.   Vermigli, *Loci Communes*, 85. He noted the problem that one would have either two Fathers or two Sons, which Scripture never indicates. He further observed that for the Holy Spirit to be "begotten" of the Father and the Son would make them parents and contradict Scripture's teaching that the Son is the "*only* begotten."

40.   Turretin, *Institutes*, 281.

41.   For example, Zanchi reasoned that "there is a sameness of essence, since the Son is from the Father, not fashioned by command, but begotten from his nature, not divided from the Father, remaining complete, perfectly emanating" (*On the Triune Elohim*, 31–32). See also Gomarus, *Disputationum theologicarum*, 2.

42.   PRRD 4:87–89.

aseity, subsisting "from himself" (Lat. *à se*), or if his subsistence was from the Father. Affirming the eternal generation of the Son seemed to generate two opposing but equally problematic conclusions. On the one hand, if the Son is derived from the Father, as begetting would imply, then some argued, he must be inherently subordinate to the Father, and not have the same divine essence. On the other hand, if the Son is *autotheon,* then some argued he must not be begotten of the Father—and therefore either there is no distinction between the persons or one must affirm tritheism with three "self-existent" Gods.[43]

The Reformed orthodox wanted to maintain both the eternal generation and the *aseity* of the Son. They insisted:

> [A]ll three divine persons need to share all the divine attributes in the same way, not as accidental attributes that are distinct from their divine essence, but as defining characteristics that each of them has in Himself.[44]

They were concerned that saying the Son obtained his "existence as God" from the Father would affirm a kind of subordination among the persons or a unidirectional dependence. Since a frequently recurring anti-Trinitarian argument was that in order to maintain both the personal distinctions and monotheism one had to conclude some form of subordination of the Son and the Spirit to the Father, they wanted to avoid that deduction.[45]

When John Calvin was forced to deal with this question in an earlier controversy, he defined "the generation of the Son from the Father as origination of sonship, not divinity," since it could not be "an origin in time nor an origin of being."[46] He insisted that for the Son to be fully divine, he must possess the divine attribute of self-existence (aseity). Calvin further contended for the Son's *absolute* aseity. However, this became a minority view among later Reformed theologians.[47]

The solution for most of the Reformed orthodox was to affirm that the *aseity* of the Son was due to "an eternal and incomprehensible *communication of the unitary divine essence*" from the Father to the Son and the Spirit.[48] Ursinus, for example, explained that "essence" is "a thing subsisting by itself—not sustained by another, although it may be *communicated* to more."[49] Since

---

43. For example, Arminius argued that identifying each of the persons as having the essence *a se ipso* lost the unity of the Godhead and lapsed into tritheism (see PRRD 4:328–29).

44. Wisse, "The Teacher of the Ancient Church: Augustine," 46, 50–52.

45. See PRRD 4:191, 300–301. Muller explains, "Not only was the denial of aseity a characteristic of Arminius' theology, it became in the seventeenth century a subordinationistic problem associated with the antitrinitarianism of the age" (329).

46. PRRD 4:324–25. See also Giles, *Eternal Generation,* 172–85.

47. See especially Ellis, *Calvin, Classical Trinitarianism, and the Aseity of the Son,* 3, 169–96. Muller cites Polanus and Bucanus as two of the few who followed Calvin's view (PRRD 4:326–27).

48. PRRD 4:287–88, see also 324–32. Emphasis mine for clarity.

49. Ursinus, *Commentary,* 129–30. See also Turretin, *Institutes,* 256, 270–72, 278, 291–93, 298, 308–9.

the divine essence is "communicable individually," it may be shared by more than one person.[50] Ursinus summarized:

> For the Father is, and exists of himself, not from another. The Son is begotten eternally from the Father, that is, he has *his divine essence communicated to him* from the Father in a way not to be explained. The Holy Spirit proceeds eternally from the Father and the Son, that is, has *the same divine essence communicated to him* from the Father and the Son, in an inexplicable manner.[51]

These theologians repeatedly explained that the eternal generation of the Son was a "communication of the divine essence" in which the whole and entire essence is communicated to (or shared with) the Son, yet also retained by the Father.[52] Ursinus again specified:

> It is proper to say, the divine essence is communicated, but not to say, the divine essence is begotten or proceeds, because to be communicated and to be begotten are not the same thing; for . . . that is begotten to which the substance of him that begets is communicated.[53]

In terms of essence, each person of the Trinity is "of himself and God himself."[54] Yet that essence itself is not generated (since it is eternal), but the *personhood* of the Son is generated in eternity with the communication of the divine essence. Turretin sought to further clarify these distinctions:

> Although the Son is from the Father, nevertheless he may be called God-of-himself (*autotheos*), not with respect to his person, but essence; not relatively as Son (for thus he is from the Father), but absolutely as God inasmuch as he has the divine essence existing from itself and not divided or produced from another essence (but not as having that essence from himself). So the Son is God from himself although not the Son from himself.[55]

---

50. Ursinus, *Commentary*, 130. See also the discussion of this in PRRD 4:282.

51. Ursinus, *Commentary*,   135. Emphasis mine.

52. See Urisnus, *Commentary*, 126–27, 131, 136–37; Gomarus, *Dipustationum theologicarum*, 2, 4–5, 10; Zanchi, *On the Triune Elohim*, 32, 42; Vermigli, *Loci Communes*, 79; Aegidius Hunnius, in his comments on John 5 (Craig Farmer, ed., *John 1–12*, Reformation Commentary on Scripture, New Testament IV [Downers Grove, IL: IVP Academic, 2014], 178–79). Beza's students were expected to articulate, "God the Father after an unspeakable manner of generation begat his only Son, by communicating his whole essence with him" (*Propositions and Principles*, 5–6 [3.3]).

53. Ursinus, *Commentary*, 136–37. Turretin later sought to clarify the distinction that the Father begat the Son as "coexisting" such that the "divine essence is communicated to the begotten, not that it may exist, but subsist" (*Institutes*, 301).

54. PRRD 4:209, 212. Ames specified, "As far as essence is concerned, therefore, the single subsistences are rightly said to exist of themselves" (*Marrow*, 88).

55. Turretin, *Institutes*, 291–92. Turretin commented on the charge against Calvin by Gentilis which sparked this entire discussion.

For the Protestant scholastics, this explained how the Father is not the Son nor the Spirit, but each person still eternally shares the same divine essence. Since the Son and Holy Spirit always exist and subsist just as much as the Father, this communication of essence did not happen in time, but is eternal.

As Gomarus articulated, the reason for making this form of explanation was to demonstrate that the divine begetting is not opposed to the unity of the essence and that what is communicated should not be understood as "either *more superior or inferior,* or cause to its effects, or as a container to its contents, or a whole to the part," but rather as each person subsisting from oneself (*à se*) and "in all things at the same time and entirely indivisible and singular."[56] This solution enabled the Protestant scholastic theologians to maintain Nicene-Constantinopolitan distinctions of the persons without implying hierarchy or a form of subordination among the persons. Muller summarizes Zanchi's explanation by stating, "even though the Son receives all from the Father insofar as he is generated or begotten, this Sonship implies no subordination: the Son is not a dependent essence."[57] By affirming the aseity of the Son by means of the communication of the divine essence, the Reformed orthodox attempted to remove any implication that the Son was in some way eternally inferior or subordinate to the Father.

Functional Economic Subordination because of the Incarnation

While the Protestant scholastics ardently maintained that the Son was equal in his divinity and in no way subordinate to the Father in his essence, they did acknowledge that there were passages of Scripture that taught some kind of subordination of the Son. They consistently attempted to explain that any subordination was "economic" or "functional" and by no means "ontological," since that was a heresy long rejected by the church fathers. The Swiss Reformed theologian Benedict Pictet captured this perspective:

> Again, if the Son is said in any passage to be inferior to the Father, and to work by the Father, such passage only shows that there is something in Christ besides the divine nature, namely the human nature, according to which he is inferior to the Father, and also that there is a certain order of operation between the Father, Son, and Holy Ghost, and a kind of economy; but it by no means proves that Christ, as God, is inferior to the Father.[58]

---

56. Gomarus, *Disputationum theologicarum,* 10. Emphasis mine.
57. Richard Muller, *Christ and the Decree* (Grand Rapids, MI: Baker Academic, 2008), 113. Muller cites Zanchi, *De Incarnatione filii Dei* in *Opera,* VIII, col. 31.
58. Benedict Pictet, *Christian Theology,* trans. Frederick Reyroux (Philadelphia: Presbyterian Board of Publication, 1876), II.xvi.9. The original work is *Theologia christiana* (Geneva: 1696).

Gomarus also utilized the terminology of "divine economy" to explain that there is a kind of sequence in which the works of the persons *ad extra* follow the works of the persons *ad intra*.[59] These theologians specified that the properties of the person (paternity of the Father, filiation of the Son, and procession of the Spirit) corresponded to the "external operations" so that the Father acts in creation, the Son in redemption, and the Spirit in sanctification and vivification.[60] They identified that there was "an order of operating," which "follows the order of subsisting."[61] As Turretin stated, the execution of the divine mission followed the order of subsisting, but only "with respect to office and economy, not in relation to essence."[62] Once again, they did not want to imply that the Son (or the Spirit) was in some way inherently subordinate or inferior to the Father because of his particular role in carrying out the divine plan.

To substantiate their insistence that the Son's role did not imply any inferiority, the Reformed orthodox appealed to Scripture passages, including where Jesus says he does the work his Father is doing, to show that all three persons of the Trinity are always working together in agreement, even though one person may be more prominently credited with a particular action.[63] They argued that the triune cooperative action proves their equality and ensures that there is no sense in which the Son is inferior to the Father with regard to his divine nature.[64] Vermigli, for example, made the distinction that "although those works are common to the three persons, nevertheless they are separately and singularly ascribed to the Son."[65] He specified that this cooperation among the Trinity should be used "to refute the Arians in the highest" and disprove anyone who would say "the Son was either a creature or less than the Father."[66] Similarly, Ames affirmed, "There is no preeminence of dignity in this working together, but the greater unity and identity in one and the same cause."[67] While acknowledging an "order of operations" among

---

59.   Gomarus, *Disputationum theologicarum*, 3. See also Ursinus, *Commentary*, 137.
60.   For examples, see Gomarus, *Disputationum theologicarum*, 7; Ames, *Marrow*, 93–94; Turretin, *Institutes*, 281. Ames summarized that in the "usual appropriation, creation is attributed to the Father, redemption to the Son, and sanctification to the Spirit."
61.   Turretin, *Institutes*, 280, 281–82.
62.   Turretin, *Institutes*, 269.
63.   Vermigli, *Loci Communes*, 80; Turretin, *Institutes*, 270; *Marrow*, 91–93. Muller summarizes that "the *opera ad extra* are understood as the indivisible work of the entire Trinity, working as one God, but 'according to the order of the persons,' and according to the special economy or arrangement of the divine work as it terminates upon an individual divine person'" (PRRD 4:170–71).
64.   Vermigli, *Loci Communes*, 80; Zanchi, *On the Triune Elohim*, 64–65.
65.   Vermigli, *Loci Communes*, 78. As one example, Vermigli appealed to 1 Corinthians 10:3, where Paul ascribes to Christ the role of liberating the people of Israel. See also Zanchi, *On the Triune Elohim*, 43, 45 for similar arguments.
66.   Vermigli, *Loci Communes*, 78. In his Corinthians commentary, Vermigli cited Augustine, *De Trinitate* 1.8 and 1.10 where he states that the common work of the Trinity is from all the persons, so that "not only the Father subjects all things to the Son, but the Son likewise subjects all things to himself" (*Corinthios*, 415a).
67.   Ames, *Marrow*, 93.

the persons of the Trinity, they intentionally resisted any notion that the Son could be divinely inferior or subordinate to the Father.

Instead, they acknowledged that any subordination of the Son was because of his humanity and entirely corresponded to Christ's work as mediator, which required that he assume a human nature.[68] The Reformed orthodox utilized this form of "functional subordination" of the Son to maintain the equality in essence of the Son and the Father by connecting any Scripture passages about the Son's "lesser" status entirely to the incarnation. They pointed back to Hilary, Augustine, and Athanasius to explain that subordinationist passages in the New Testament did not refer to the Son in his divinity, but according to the "economy of his humanity."[69] Vermigli expressed, "Since Christ, by which he was man, was less than the Father, for that reason he was able to become the interceder."[70]

They appealed to passages like Philippians 2:5–7 and John 17:5 to argue that before he humbled himself in the incarnation, God the Son equally possessed the same majesty, glory, and authority as the Father.[71] Zanchi specified that although it was after the resurrection that Christ as a man "returned to heaven and sits at the right hand of the Father with the same majesty and dominion as the Father," he previously possessed these attributes from all eternity before the incarnation.[72] Vermigli explained the implication of the Son's subordination in 1 Corinthians 15:27–28:

> It ought to be seen that we do not consider this subjection of the Son toward the Father to be either forced or reluctant. It should be thought of as voluntary, deliberate, and exceedingly willing. Those who refer to it according to the divine nature wish to take this less properly and by the subjection, they understand it to be obedience (*obsequiam*) and most perfect consent. Another [interpretation] is more expeditious: we understand this to be about the human nature.[73]

He rejected the idea that the Son was subject to the Father by obedience and consent in his divine nature. Rather, the Son's subjection to the Father was because of the incarnation.[74] Turretin likewise observed that it was Christ's

---

68. See PRRD 4:279–80.
69. PRRD 4:331.
70. Vermigli, *Loci Communes*, 84.
71. See, for example, Zanchi, *On the Triune Elohim*, 160 and the exegetical comments in Tomlin, *Philippians, Colossians*, 44–45.
72. Zanchi, *On the Triune Elohim*, 160.
73. Vermigli, *Corinthios*, 415a. Vermigli appealed to Augustine where he articulated that Christ was subjected to the Father according to humanity when he became one of us.
74. Vermigli, *Corinthios*, 415a. Vermigli even addressed the possible objection that 1 Corinthians 15:28 seems to imply that Christ is not presently subjected to the Father even though he is still incarnate. He explained that the incarnate Christ *is* presently subject to the Father because of his incarnation, but that this passage is saying Christ will be *acknowledged as* subject to the Father at the final resurrection.

incarnation that made him "not to be everywhere present and to be less than the Father. . . . He is so less than the Father by reason of voluntary humiliation (*exinanitionis*) and assumed flesh as nevertheless to be equal to him with respect to eternal deity communicated to him from eternity."[75]

However, not all Reformed orthodox theologians restricted this subordinate mediatorial function of the Son to the *time* of the incarnation. While the "subjection" of the Son happened at his incarnation, the plan for him to become incarnate happened before creation. Zanchi, for example, reasoned that since Christ "is the same yesterday and today and forever" (Heb. 13:8), he has to be the only one who "saved, reconciled, justified, regenerated, all who are saved from the earth's foundation all the way to the end of the world."[76] Even before his incarnation, "He is the same one who does this duty, always himself saving the faithful. For he always is, was, and will be the same mediator Christ and high priest." [77] They acknowledged a way in which the preincarnate Son was subject to the Father—but still *only* with respect to the mutually determined redemptive plan that the Son would become the incarnate mediator. Ames specified that it was not even with regard to the *person* of Christ the Son, but rather the Father "bound his Son to *this office* through a special covenant."[78] By specifying that any "eternal" subordination was only related to the future mediatorial role or office in the incarnation, they intended to resist any sense of divine subordination of the Son. In a similar way, they insisted that the Spirit was not subordinate to the Father or the Son, even though he too is sent by them according to the divine plan.[79]

This theme is evident in Vermigli's explanation for what 1 Corinthians 11:3 means by saying that God is the head of Christ.[80] By following the parallel between Christ and the husband, he observed that Christ is not head of the husband because of his divine nature, since that would obviously be infinitely greater, but rather is "our head, by which he is God and man. For in that manner, he is partly equal and partly superior to us."[81] He then observed:

> Likewise, God is the head of Christ, not so much as to his divine nature, because there is the highest equality among them; nor also so much as to his human nature—since he received it separately, he is infinitely different from the Father.

75.   Turretin, *Institutes*, 292.

76.   Zanchi, *On the Triune Elohim*, 45.

77.   Zanchi, *On the Triune Elohim*, 45. Zanchi made a similar argument that Christ has to have been "head of the church" from the foundation of the world to the present time (158).

78.   Ames, *Marrow*, 132.

79.   PRRD 4:372. In his *Loci Communes*, Vermigli observed that Constantinople added "Lord and lifegiver" to reinforce the equality of the Spirit with the Father and the Son. Any notion of a hierarchical ordering among the persons he categorized with Arianism (83).

80.   Vermigli, *Corinthios*, 282b–84a. This section is labeled "How God is the head of Christ" (Quomodo deus capus Christi).

81.   Vermigli, *Corinthios*, 283a. Vermigli argued that even where Christ is "head" with regard to his human nature surpassing ours, that is "all on account of his divinity."

> Consequently, God will be the head of Christ on *account of which his human and divine nature is held together at the same time*; since then he is partly equal and partly inferior to the Father. Nor does Christ have the Father as head so much as to his divine nature, unless perhaps you want to understand head as fount and origin, from which he is perpetually generated.[82]

Vermigli noted that the Arians used this passage to argue "that the Son is less than the Father" and that there is "some superiority (*excellentiam*) of the Father over the Son, so that one of them presides (*praesit*) and the other truly is subjected (*subiiciatur*)."[83] Vermigli explicitly stated, "But we reject this."[84] He did not want to grant that there is any way that the Son in his divine nature is subject to or inferior to the Father.

As he explained how the parallel of the husband as head of the wife related to God as the head of Christ, he raised the question whether the subjection of the woman referred to the "untainted woman" (*integris mulier*) or was because of the first sin. He observed that "clearly no mention of subjection" is found in Scripture when the woman was created, but that only *after* the first sin "was the turning to your husband and 'he will be your master' added."[85] He reasoned that sin had corrupted humanity so much that "it was necessary for stricter rule (*dominatu*) of the husband."[86] Vermigli's exegesis on the husband-wife relationship here reveals that he did not see an inherent, created subjection of wives to husbands, because he did not want to allow for a parallel inherent, eternal subjection of Christ to God. He explicitly stated this reasoning:

> For whatever subjection or obedience is attributed to the Son towards the Father, it is *all assumed according to the incarnation and his human nature* and matters on account of our salvation. For Christ, to the extent as man, was obedient to the Father all the way to death, was afflicted, prayed, and suffered much, by which he declared him to be inferior to the Father.[87]

---

82. Vermigli, *Corinthios*, 283a. Emphasis mine.

83. Vermigli, *Corinthios*,, 283a. For a similar defense, see his comments on 1 Corinthians 15:27–28, where Vermigli also noted that a heretical view "viciously picks this for the subjection of the Son to the Father" and treats the persons of the Trinity like the Greeks do Jupiter and Saturn (415a).

84. Vermigli, *Corinthios*, 283a. He appealed to Chrysostom's "double reason" why this passage actually proves the opposite and confirms *homoousion*. He explained that "because the head and the rest of the body retain the same nature or kind even though they exercise different offices or services," God and Christ must share the same divine nature, just as Christ and man share a human nature.

85. Vermigli, *Corinthios*, 283a. Vermigli here is referring to Genesis 3:16. He maintained that Paul was teaching that "the gospel does not overthrow politeness," so the traditions should continue since "there are others who are subject," even if wives are not inherently subject to husbands (282b).

86. Vermigli, *Corinthios*, 283b. Vermigli also pointed to Ephesians 5 as illustrating that "the best rulers are those who follow the same [example as Christ]—and do not do violence to the other" (283b–84a).

87. Vermigli, *Corinthios*, 283b. In his later comments that 1 Corinthians 15:27–28 implied a kind of subordination, he declared, "the Apostle does not want to dream such at all about Christ towards the Father" (415a).

As Vermigli demonstrates, the Protestant scholastics consistently endeavored to clarify that any implication that Christ was inferior, subject, submissive, or subordinate to the Father was exclusively because of his incarnation.[88]

The Reformed orthodox did not utilize the current terminology, "eternal functional subordination of the Son" or "eternal relationship of authority and submission"; and they likely would not have affirmed either. They did not identify the plan of the incarnation as "eternal" in the same sense that each divine person's existence is eternal. Rather, the plan of the triune God is "eternal" only in the sense that it is before creation. Any sense in which the Son was subordinate to the Father had to be considered only in relationship to the plan before creation that the Son would become incarnate in the economic implementation of that plan. In their words, the Protestant scholastics allowed for subjection of the Son in "the order of the operation of the persons."[89] But the eternal relationship between Father and Son had to be one of total equality in authority.

Order in Existence of Persons without Inferiority

The same conclusion is evident from the way the Reformed orthodox allowed for a kind of subordination in the "order of procession."[90] It is essential to recognize what the Reformed orthodox mean by the use of the term "order" here. They understood "order" as referring to the *numbering* of the persons—which could not be chronological because that would imply that one or more members of the Trinity was not eternal and therefore, not fully divine.[91] They also did not want to insinuate that this "order" had any form of hierarchy. The Protestant scholastics identified that Christ's sonship was because of his begetting, but they consistently argued that this begetting did not (and could not) imply a subordinate or submissive relationship to the Father.

They specified that the properties of each person are distinguished such that none of the persons can be the other, but by their shared substance or essence, each person had the same equality, glory, perfections, honor, worship, and authority.[92] The Reformed students at Geneva were expected to articulate, "Amongst these persons, distinguished indeed, by their respective properties, although there be an order; yet is there *not any degree*, whence either *any inferiority,* inequality, or confusion may arise."[93] The summary from Ursinus clearly identifies what the Protestant scholastics meant by "order of the persons."

---

88. See also Muller, *Christ and the Decree*, 87–93, 109–14, 156.
89. Muller summarizes that the Reformed orthodox "assume the essential equality of the divine persons, double procession, and the removal of all subordination except in the order of the procession and operation of the persons" (PRRD 4:84). See also Muller, *Christ and the Decree*, 30.
90. PRRD 4:84.
91. See PRRD 4:276.
92. Beza, *Propositions and Principles*, 4 [2.7]; Ursinus, *Commentary*, 128, 134; Gomarus, *Disputationum theologicarum*, 10; Ames, *Marrow*, 90; Zanchi, *On the Triune Elohim*, 152–53; Aegidius Hunnius in Farmer, ed., *John 1–12*, 171–72, 322, 394–95, 398–99. See also PRRD 4:300.
93. Beza, *Propositions and Principles*, 5 [2.10]. Emphasis mine.

> This is, therefore, the order, according to which the persons of the Godhead exist: The Father is the first person, and as it were, the fountain of the divinity of the Son and Holy Spirit, because the Deity is communicated to him of no one; but he communicates the Deity to the Son and Holy Spirit. The Son is the second person, because the Deity is communicated to him of the Father, in the eternal generation. The Holy Ghost is the third person, because the Deity is communicated to him from the Father and the Son, in the eternal spiration or procession.
>
> And yet the Father is not prior in time to the Son and Holy Ghost; nor is the Son before the Holy Ghost, but only in the *order of existing*; for no person of the Godhead is before or after the others in time, or *dignity, or degree*, but only according to the *order in which they exist*.[94]

Repeatedly they rejected the notion that this "order of existing" indicated any kind of degree, inferiority, submission, or subordination. Turretin even made the charge that the Remonstrants deny "the consubstantiality (*homoousian*) of the Son with the Father and maintain that the Son (not only in order, but also in dignity and power) differs from the Father and is not coordinate and consubstantial with him, but only subordinate."[95] In this way, they differed little from John Calvin. Muller summarizes Calvin's view:

> Calvin certainly allowed some subordination in the order of the person—but in order *only*, as indicated by the generation of the Son from the Father and by procession of the Spirit from the Father and the Son, but he adamantly denied any subordination of divinity or essence.[96]

The position of the Protestant scholastics is far different from a view that uses "order" to imply rank or status. The Reformed orthodox rejected any notion that the Father as "first" in subsistence implied that the Son or the Spirit was relationally lesser in status, rank, or authority. For them, there could not be an eternal subordination of the preincarnate Son that corresponded to his divine nature at all. In fact, claims that the Father had authority over the Son was at the core of so many of the anti-Trinitarian errors they were trying to eradicate.

Unparalleled Mystery with regard to Human Relations

Finally, because of the forms of heresies espoused during these time periods, another recurring theme among the Protestant scholastics was their warnings that attempting to make parallels between human relationships and the ineffable mystery of the Trinity was unwise and dangerous. Some even criticized Origen,

---

94. Ursinus, *Commentary*, 135. Emphasis mine. For a similar summary, see Ames, *Marrow*, 88. See also Turretin, *Institutes*, 280–81, 293, 309.
95. Turretin, *Institutes*, 283.
96. PRRD 4:80. See also PRRD 4:81–82, 324; Calvin, *Inst.* I.xiii.17–18.

Augustine, Hilary, and other church fathers for attempting to draw analogies from humanity or nature to explain the Trinity. Vermigli warned that interpretations of 1 Corinthians 11:3 "ought to take up a comparison rightly."[97] Following Chrysostom, he commented that if one makes the wrong comparisons, it will lead to an "immense difference" or an "infinite gap," and result in absurd deductions, "since not all things can be compared."[98] He stated, "Because if you do not accept the right analogy which is compared, you will easily err."[99]

Drawing comparisons or parallels with particular details of the Trinity had opened the door to too many errors and heresies, because it confused the finite with the infinite and used categories and terms that do not apply in the same way to God as they do to humans.[100] Many of these theologians pointed out that one could not speak in terms of begetting, essence, and persons with the same understanding as that of humans without resulting in error.[101] They often used "as if" or "so to speak" or "as an illustration" in their own analogies so as not to imply any kind of direct correlation between the nature, essence, or social relationship of the Trinity and humanity.[102] If, for example, one would attempt to use aspects of the divine relationship between the Son and the Father to determine what a human father-son (or husband-wife) relationship should look like, then one must either be subjectively selective in what gets included or one opens the door to all kinds of absurdities and even heretical conclusions, because only certain things are analogous in certain ways, as revealed by Scripture.[103]

Conclusion

These Protestant Scholastic theologians consistently maintained the uniqueness of the eternal Father-Son relationship within the Trinity. In particular, they sought to qualify and clarify nearly every instance or every potential instance where the charge of the Son's subordination to the Father could arise. They upheld the historical, orthodox distinctions between the persons of the Trinity, including the eternal generation of the Son. They developed the explanation that for the Son to be *homoousion* with the Father, he must be *autotheon*, and therefore in the eternal generation of the Son as person, the divine essence is "communicated" to the Son. The purpose for this clarification was to avoid and resist any implication that the Son in his divine nature is inferior or subordinate to the Father. Rather, they continually reiterated that the Son was only "operationally subordinate" in his office as incarnate mediator.

97. Vermigli, *Corinthios*, 283a.
98. Vermigli, *Corinthios*, 283b.
99. Vermigli, *Corinthios*, 283b.
100. See, for example, Zanchi, *On the Triune Elohim*, 35, 50.
101. Zanchi, *On the Triune Elohim*, 32, 35, 50; Gomarus, *Disputationum theologicarum*, 7–8; Turretin, *Institutes*, 298.
102. For example, see Beza, *Propositions and Principles*, 4, 5 [1.5–6, 2.2, 3.4]; Ames, *Marrow*, 85.
103. Zanchi, *On the Triune Elohim*, 7, 141–43, 156–58; Vermigli, *Loci Communes*, 85.

The only way any would consider the Son as "functionally subordinate" to the Father was exclusively related to the triune plan that the Son would become the incarnate Christ. These theologians would reject any sense that the Son's subordination corresponded with his eternal divinity or even his personhood. They adamantly insisted that the "order of subsisting" as first, second, and third persons did not refer to chronology or hierarchy or authority.

There is effectively no historical support for Reformed orthodox theologians who would say that the Son is relationally subordinate or submissive to the Father eternally. To put it in the terms they used, the Son is only subordinate or submissive to the Father in the order of operations of the divine economy (which follows the ordering of the persons), but not subordinate or submissive in his divinity, his person, his relationship with the Father, and certainly not in his essence or ontology.

Bibliography

Allison, Gregg. *Historical Theology: An Introduction to Christian Doctrine.* Grand Rapids: Zondervan, 2011.

DeYoung, Kevin. "Distinguishing Among the Three Persons of the Trinity within the Reformed Tradition." *The Gospel Coalition.* https://blogs.thegospelcoalition.org/kevindeyoung/2016/09/27/distinguishing-among-the-three-persons-of-the-trinity-within-the-reformed-tradition/ (accessed September 28, 2016).

Ellis, Brannon. *Calvin, Classical Trinitarianism, and the Aseity of the Son.* Oxford: Oxford University Press, 2012.

Erickson, Millard. *Who's Tampering with the Trinity? An Assessment of the Subordination Debate.* Grand Rapids: Kregel, 2009.

Farmer, Craig, ed. *John 1–12.* Reformation Commentary on Scripture, New Testament IV. Downers Grove, IL: IVP Academic, 2014.

Giles, Kevin. *The Eternal Generation of the Son.* Downers Grove, IL: InterVarsity, 2012.

Grudem, Wayne. *Evangelical Feminism and Biblical Truth.* Wheaton, IL: Crossway, 2012.

Kovach, Stephen D., and Peter R. Schemm, Jr. "A Defense of the Doctrine of the Eternal Subordination of the Son." *Journal of the Evangelical Theological Society* 42, no. 3 (1999): 461–76.

Merkle, Benjamin. *Defending the Trinity in the Reformed Palatinate: The Elohistae.* New York: Oxford University Press, 2015.

Muller, Richard. *After Calvin: Studies in the Development of a Theological Tradition.* New York: Oxford University Press, 2003.

_____. *Calvin and the Reformed Tradition.* Grand Rapids: Baker, 2012.

_____. *Christ and the Decree.* Grand Rapids: Baker Academic, 2008.

_____. *Post-Reformation Reformed Dogmatics: The Rise and Development of Reformed Orthodoxy, ca. 1520 to ca. 1725.* 4 vols. Grand Rapids: Baker, 2003.

Tomlin, Graham, ed. *Philippians, Colossians.* Reformation Commentary on Scripture, New Testament XI. Downers Grove, IL: IVP Academic, 2013.

Trueman, Carl, and R. Scott Clark, eds. *Protestant Scholasticism: Essays in Reassessment.* Eugene, OR: Wipf & Stock, 2007.

van Asselt, Willem J. *Introduction to Reformed Scholasticism.* Translated by Albert Gootjes. Grand Rapids: Reformation Heritage, 2011.

_____. "Protestant Scholasticism: Some Methodological Considerations in the Study of Its Development." *Nederlands Archief Voor Kerkgeschiedenis* 81, no. 3 (2001): 265–74.

Wisse, Maarten. "The Teacher of the Ancient Church: Augustine." In *Introduction to Reformed Scholasticism.* Edited by Willem J. van Asselt. Grand Rapids: Reformation Heritage Books, 2011.

Primary Sources

Ames, William. *The Marrow of Theology*. Translated and edited by John D. Eusden. Durham, NC: Labyrinth, 1983.

Beza, Theodore. *Propositions and Principles of Divinitie Propounded and Disputed in the University of Geneva*. Translated by John Pentry. Edinburgh, 1595.

_____. *Confession Christiane fidei, et eiusdem collation cum Papisticis Haeresibus*. Geneva, 1560.

_____. *Tractationes theologicae*. Geneva, 1570–1582.

Gomarus, Francis. *Disputationum theologicarum quarto repetitarum quarta de trinitate personarum in una Dei essentia*. Leiden: Ioannis Patii, 1605.

Pictet, Benedict. *Christian Theology*. Translated by Frederick Reyroux. Philadelphia: Presbyterian Board of Publication, 1876.

Turretin, Francis. *Institutes of Elenctic Theology*. Translated by George Musgrave Giger. Edited by James T. Dennison, Jr. Phillipsburg, NJ: P &R Publishing, 1992.

Ursinus, Zacharias.*The Commentary of Dr. Zacharias Ursinus on the Heidelberg Catechism*. Translated by G. W. Williard. Grand Rapids: Eerdmans, 1954.

Vermigli, Peter Martyr. *Loci Communes*. London: John Kyngston, 1576.

_____. *In selectissimam D. Pauli priorem ad Corinthios Epistolam*. Zurich: Christoph Froschouer, 1572 [1551].

Zanchi, Jerome. *De tribus Elohim, aeterno patre, filio, et spiritu Sancto, uno eodemque Iehova*. Neustadt an der Haardt: Harnisius, 1597.

_____. *On the Triune Elohim: Eternal Father, Son, and Holy Spirit, One and the Same Jehovah*. Translated by Michelle Bollen, Angela Filliceti, Rachel Jo, and Sam Taylor. Edited by Ben Merkle. Wenden House, 2016. http://www.nsa.edu/wp-content/uploads/2015/09/OnTheTriuneElohimBks1-3.pdf.

CHAPTER 10

There Is a Method to the Madness

On Christological Commitments of Eternal Functional Subordination of the Son

JULES A. MARTÍNEZ-OLIVIERI

"Though, this be madness, yet there is method in it." Polonius's proverbial declaration to Hamlet serves as a literary warning to our reflective naiveté. For communicative actions can be strange, but we can find logic and purpose in them. Theology is served by method, even though at times theology's product, doctrines, can seem strange. Method in theology can facilitate the elucidation of the faith by helping the church conceptualize its dogma and praxis, confession and life.

The Nicene Creed is a confession that communicates the life of the God of the gospel. It is a dogmatic formulation that, methodologically, uses Christological categories within a Trinitarian framework. It confesses God as Father, Son, and Spirit in the eternality of intra-divine communication, with the Son, the "Lord Jesus," as the *personae salutis*. A more explicit confession on the divinity of the Holy Spirit would wait until the Council of Constantinople (ca. 381). Nevertheless, Nicaea's Christological articulation is the first dogmatic definition of the church that makes explicit the Christian conception of God as Trinity, and especially, confessing the Son as consubstantial with the Father. The Son's relation to God is defined as coeternal, filial, unbegotten from the

Father. Christological reflection benefits from this terminology which conceptualizes the Gospels' testimony regarding Jesus, the Son, and God. Terms like *ousía* (substantia), *hypostasis* (persona), *and physis* (natura) were strategically employed. The clarity of relationship formulated in the Nicene tradition made it unthinkable to conceive of the Son without the Father, the Father without the Son, and the Father and Son without the Holy Spirit. Trinitarianism provided intelligibility to the claims of Christology and vice versa.

Faithfulness to the Nicene symbols has long been a criterion for orthodoxy. The church receives its language and categories, and enlists it to ensure doctrinal fidelity. In recent times, there have been new debates which employ argumentation based on the nature of the Trinity and the Son's filial obedience. As a result, we are forced to reexamine how these arguments come from (or betray) our ancient creeds, namely, the Nicene Creed and its theological rule. Some evangelicals are purporting that it is precisely the Nicene Creed that invites the church to envision the Son as eternally subordinate to the Father. For example, Wayne Grudem offers this summary:

> Paul makes the parallel explicit when he says, "I want you to understand that the head of every man is Christ, the head of woman is her husband, and the head of Christ is God. Here is a distinction in authority. . . . Just as God the Father has authority over the Son, though the two are equal in deity, so in marriage, the husband has authority over his wife, though they are equal in personhood. In this case, the man's role is like that of God the Father, and the woman's role is parallel to that of God to the Son.[1]

Others find this *theologoumen* an innovation that is highly problematic and a breach of the historic consensus of the church. Millard Erickson summarizes a counter argument:

> The problem is this: If authority over the Son is an essential, not an accidental, attribute of the Father, and subordination to the Father is an essential, not an accidental, attribute of the Son, then something significant follows. Authority is part of the Father's essence, and subordination is part of the Son's essence, and each attribute is not part of the essence of the other person. That means that the essence of the Son is different from the essence of the Father. . . .That is equivalent to saying that they are not *homoousios* with one another.[2]

In order to approach this discussion, I will attend to the task of Christology, its method, and the kind of decisions that are involved in the theological

---

1. Wayne A. Grudem, *Systematic Theology: An Introduction to Biblical Doctrine* (Downers Grove, IL: InterVarsity, 1994), 459–60.
2. Millard Erickson, *Who's Tampering with the Trinity? An Assessment of the Subordination Debate* (Grand Rapids: Kregel 2009), 172.

judgments sustaining the thesis of the eternal functional submission (hence-forth, EFS) of the Son.

Christology: Access to the Triune Land

Christology is the dogmatic locus that seeks to provide an account of the significance and relevance of Jesus of Nazareth as the Son of God through the conceptualization of his life acts, death, resurrection, ascension, and session. Christology attends to the exposition of the reality of Christ, fully God and fully human, exploring how in him God, humanity and the world are implicated. Christology, as a discipline, offers an additional lens to evaluate the current debate.

Every attempt at doing systematic Christology must deal with the issue of method. Theological method is important to our discussion, because it helpfully reveals certain "precommitments" that give rise to and persuade our conclusions. So, for example, it is no secret that supporters of EFS are seeking to make explicit connections between Trinitarian relations and anthropology in an effort to anchor a complementarian ecclesiology as deriving from God's internal life.[3] Nevertheless, a desire to maintain a complementarian theology by appealing to divine ontology is problematic. Method and Christology will surface some of these maneuvers.

Paying attention to methodological decisions is helpful because it reveals presuppositions that are logically prior to the articulation of doctrine. This is true in virtually all theological and biblical themes, but most crucially with regards to certain topics such as the two natures of Christ, the resurrection, the Trinity, or the nature of the church. The choice of method always reveals the concerns of debaters. For example, when reviewing two plausible alternatives, our context creates a confirmation bias that moves us towards conclusions that are amiable to our concerns. After all, methodology is not devoid of the concerns, culture, and conditions that shape the life of theologians.[4] We are helped when we understand (and even trace) our cultural and local concerns which drive our methodology.

Methodologies in the discipline of Christology are diverse. For instance, one can (a) begin with the historical dimension—the personal history of Jesus of Nazareth, attending to chronological developments that will lead to the confession that Jesus is the Christ and Son; or (b) begin explicitly with the mystery of Christ as the eternal Son of God made flesh in the person of Jesus. In the latter, a Christology "from above" begins from the identification of Jesus

---

3. There is no logical or necessary connection between EFS, Trinitarian theology, and complementarianism. That is to say, one could hold to ecclesial complementarianism and still not appeal to any thesis argued by EFS.

4. Parts of this essay are summaries of a broader argument in Jules A. Martínez-Olivieri, *A Visible Witness: Christology, Liberation and Participation*, Emerging Scholars (Minneapolis: Fortress, 2016), Chapter 5.

as the second person of the Trinity, with the incarnation and the revelation of his origin, redemptive mission, and relationship with the Father and Spirit. The christologies of St. Athanasius, St. Cyril, Thomas Aquinas, Karl Barth, and Urs von Balthazar are prime examples of the "from above" approach. His divinity is assumed.

With a Christology "from below," the starting point is the humanity of Jesus, paying attention to the acts (*facta*) and discourse (*verba*) of Jesus's life. Here, reflection assumes his humanity and moves toward the eventual confession of his divinity. The focus on Jesus's humanity is one of the distinctive methodological contributions of contemporary christologies. Among those who have used this starting point, we find Theodore Mopuesia, John Chrysostom, and contemporaries like Wolfhart Pannenberg and Jürgen Moltmann.[5]

In both methodological movements, there is an inherent relational tenor. We must pay attention to how the relationship of the Son to the Father is conceptualized. God the Father as frame of reference is nearly always the ultimate horizon of Jesus's faithfulness. That is, the Son is the definitive example of how to live before the Father, and the life lived in the Holy Spirit of Jesus is the configuration of Christian praxis.

For our purposes, an explicit Trinitarian Christology is under review. It should be stated upfront that faithful Christology is based on the depiction of God's hypostatic activity in the economy of redemption, concurring with the creedal confessions of Nicaea and Chalcedon. As Robert Letham states in the tradition of the Nicene consensus (further affirmed at Council at Constantinople in 381), "Father and the Son are one in being, equal in power and glory, possessing all God's attributes."[6] The persons in the Godhead are of the same essence, coeternal, coequal, co-powerful, and differentiated by their relations of origin. And the Westminster Confession 2.3 explains, "The Father is of none, neither begotten nor proceeding; the Son is eternally begotten of the Father; the Holy Ghost eternally proceeding from the Father and the Son."

The present discussion arises in response to evangelicals that are making theological judgements regarding the metaphysics of those divine relations,

---

5.   Modern and contemporary Christology has largely preferred an *ascending* method. There are at least two versions of the *von unten* or ascending approach. One is a *progressive approach* that affirms that from the origin there are biblical affirmations and ecclesial experiences that at least contain the realities that later would develop into christological affirmations. The other is the *evolutionary-genetic approach*, which affirms that Jesus as the Christ and divine Son is a created reality under the influx of a myriad of mythological and philosophical ideas. This version is theologically unattainable. The former takes seriously the historicity of Jesus, the *facta* of his life or the historical experience of the apostles in the resurrection. Cf. Wolfhart Pannenberg, *Jesus—God and Man*, 2nd ed. (Philadelphia: Westminster, 1977), 158–87; Leonardo Boff, *Jesus Christ Liberator: A Critical Christology for Our Time* (Maryknoll, NY: Orbis, 1978), 182–85.

6.   Robert Letham, "Eternal Generation in the Church Fathers," in *One God in Three Persons: Unity of Essence, Distinction of Persons, Implications for Life*, eds. Bruce A. Ware and John Starke (Wheaton, IL: Crossway, 2015), 121, 123.

but in a way that revises earlier creedal consensus.[7] This is based on methodological decisions, not necessarily ones that are immediately obvious from the biblical text. One might describe it as an attempt to do high Christology *"from below."* Jesus must be understood in constitutive relationality with the Father. By his trust in his Father, obedience to his mission, and in death and resurrection, the Son realizes his filial role.

We will examine this in more detail soon. Suffice it to say, there may be a hasty urgency of this task, one which lies in contextual ecclesial concerns rather than theological concerns. The particular concern for proponents of EFS of the Son is to demonstrate how to order human gendered relations under a hierarchical framework that finds origin in the Trinity. They do so by not only appealing to scriptural complementarity patterns of relationships between men and woman, but by grounding those in God's life in himself. In this view God's relational life becomes a prototype that should structure gendered relationships.

We enter this discussion noting that here evangelical theologies are symbiotic with other traditions. In their optimism for finding in the doctrine of God a model for social and political configuration, the proponents of EFS *de facto* join a movement in modern theology, which for a myriad of reasons considers the Trinitarian relationality a metaphysical archetype for a "social program," or "egalitarian society," or "democratic society," or "a queer community," or a "socialist utopia."[8] This, not by virtue of their conclusions, but rather by their methodological maneuvering. Each of these as its own plausibility structures, and they have in common a confidence that God's life *ad intra*, apart and independent from the created order, can in fact direct human relationality.

---

7. By "consensus," I do not mean that Nicaean theologians use the same terminology or instrumental conceptuality to arrive at the same conclusions. Their agreement does not necessarily lie in the concepts used throughout the centuries, but in the theological judgements that present a synthesis of God's dramatic speech and acts in the canonical witness regarding the Son Jesus. David Yeago has argued for the important differentiation between concepts and judgements. For example, Yeago observes that Athanasius's use of the concept of *homoousios* conceptually explicates Paul's declaration of the Son's "equality with God" (Phil. 2:6–11). It was a theological judgement, he argues, communicated with a different terminology in order to preserve a pattern of teaching regarding the ontological unity of Jesus and God. David S. Yeago, "The New Testament and the Nicene Dogma: A Contribution to the Recovery of Theological Exegesis," *ProEccl* no. 3 (1994): 152–64. In the present polemical discussion, it is not clear whether the doctrinal concept of an eternal functional subordination of the Son (EFS) preserves Nicaea's theological judgement of the Son's sharing the same substance (*homoousios*) with God the Father.

8. For recent discussions on the Trinity and its relations to other doctrines, see X. Pikaza, *Este es el hombre: Manual de cristología* (Salamanca: Secretariado Trinitario, 1997), 20; Kevin J. Vanhoozer, *The Drama of Doctrine: A Canonical-Linguistic Approach to Christian Theology* (Louisville. Westminster John Knox, 2005), 22; Gilles Emery and Matthew Levering, eds., *The Oxford Handbook of the Trinity* (New York: Oxford University Press, 2011). For challenges to social models of the trinity see Michael Welker and Miroslav Volf, eds., *God's Life in Trinity* (Philadelphia: Fortress, 2006); Giulio Maspero and Robert J. Wozniak, eds., *Rethinking Trinitarian Theology: Disputed Questions and Contemporary Issues in Trinitarian Theology* (New York: T & T Clark, 2012).

This shared optimism in the analogical use of Trinitarian categories for anthropology usually presupposes a "social model" of the Trinity. In this model, God's identity is conceived as an eternal *koinonia*, whereby the divine persons are rendered to be three perfect and co-eternal centers of consciousness who share the same nature, power, and glory, from which human analogies of personhood can be directly or indirectly extrapolated. Whereas their intuition to begin with Jesus's relationality is warranted, the limits of analogical applications become glaringly problematic. In this way, the theological consensual territory is abruptly fractured. If this demonstrates anything, it is that the analogical use of the Trinitarian economy for human relationships is extremely difficult, if not outright subjective in many cases. And in the worst cases, it is completely ideological instead of theological.

The concern of this essay is to bring to the forefront of the conversation an inspection of the methodological decisions employed in making christological judgements to inform Trinitarian theology among proponents of EFS, in order to understand their proposal, contributions, limits or problems.

Methodological Decisions among Advocates of EFS

It is quite evident that in this discussion we are seeking to articulate the nature of divine filiation, that is, the relationship between the Father and Son. The study of the paternity of God in the life of Jesus has garnered much attention in Christology and biblical research in the last fifty years. All sides agree that the language employed about God in the Gospels (and in Jesus's discourse specifically) is uniquely expressed with relational language: God is the Father of a Son, and the Father of a people. Furthermore, God is the Father of Jesus and God is the Father of his followers. This is significant because it reveals the purpose of theodramatic action. More specifically, the Son became human so that humans could become sons. This establishes for us an ordered life for disciples based on divine filiation, of which Jesus is our paradigmatic example. For this reason, it could be said that at the center of divine communicative action is the Father extending familial covenantal relations to his people. Edith Humphrey rightly notes, "The person and work of the Son . . . are cognitive and effective: the Son reveals the Father to the faithful; the work of the Son makes us faithful children of God."[9] Jesus's sense of filiation, generation (in eternity), and commission (in earthly ministry) by his Father is meant to shape our sense of filiation and adoption by God, the Father.[10] These analogical maneuvers are the general marks of this methodology, and are not widely contested.

---

9.   Edith M. Humphrey, "The Gift of the Father," in *Trinitarian Theology for the Church: Scripture, Community, Worship*, eds. Daniel J. Treier and David Lauber (Downers Grove: IVP Academic, 2009), 82.

10. One epistemic observation germane to this discussion is that in the New Testament, people know and worship the Father by knowing and worshipping the Son. This kind of sharing of divine prerogative undergirds Jesus's actions of judging, giving life, revealing the will of God, and receiving the same honor as God. Jesus is not "born of God"; he "comes from God." Coming from God not only signals

The agreement in methodology breaks when the proponents of EFS handle particular motifs embodied in the Son's earthly ministry. These narratives of the Son, which are charged with themes of submission and authority, are deployed as controlling principles for both divine and human relationality. So our task, then, becomes discerning the continuity and discontinuity of the Son's filial relationship with the Father. EFS is not neutral. The implication with EFS methodology is that *Jesus Christ's relationship of authority and submission to the Father in the economy of salvation is epistemically basic for conceptualizing the Son's ontological divine filiation from eternity past, present, and future.* If this is the case, it is problematic for a host of reasons and requires more investigation.

For example, Wayne Grudem has charged that it is only on the basis of the Son's obedience and submission that Christian faith can distinguish between the divine *personae* and avoid modalism, an ancient heresy. For him, an unwillingness to assume this hermeneutical proposition amounts to a denial of the testimony of the Bible where "the Son consistently, throughout eternity, submits to the authority of the Father."[11]

In light of Grudem's commitment to this hermeneutical method, his skepticism toward the traditional interpretation of the Trinitarian rule of the "inseparable operations" of God *ad extra*. For if the Son has a distinct and non-transferable role in the incarnation, a distinct submissive will (which includes suffering on the cross), then his work of condescendence is only his and not the Father's or the Spirit's work. Within this rationale, the undivided will of the Trinity might simply be the eternal agreement with which each hypostasis in the Godhead acts toward the other and toward the creation under the rule of authority and submission. Therefore, the distinctions of the divine persons must be found in their active "roles" as rendered in the economy of salvation, in the motifs of the Son as the one sent from the Father, which necessarily implies, for Grudem, submission. Hence, if

> the Son chooses people for salvation, he is simply following the directives of the Father. He is not acting independently of the Father's authority. Yes, both Father and Son participate in choosing, yet their actions are not identical but distinct.

---

a relationship of sending, a divine mission, but also a relationship of origin. M. M. Thompson avers: "Since he is the Son, Jesus's very life and being are to be found within the Father. He has life because 'the living Father' (John 6:57) gives it to him; in fact, he has 'life in himself' just as the 'Father has life in himself' (5:26), a remarkable statement that simultaneously affirms that the Son derives his life from the Father and yet has life in a distinct way, as the Father has it." Marianne Meye Thompson, *The God of the Gospel of John* (Grand Rapids: Eerdmans, 2001), 70, 72. Jesus delights in the reciprocal and profound knowledge (*epiginoskein*) of revelation he has from the Father, as well as the inherent authority to communicate that knowledge and life to whom he chooses.

11. Wayne Grudem, "Doctrinal Deviations in Evangelical-Feminist Arguments about the Trinity," in Ware and Starke, eds., *One God in Three Persons*, 20.

> The Father chooses; the Father shows the Son who has been chosen, and the Son chooses those who have been given to him by the Father (John 6:37).[12]

The theological analogy and payout for human relationships seem clear. Grudem explains:

> The Father and the Son relate to one another as a father and a son relate to one another in a human family; the father directs and has authority over the son, and the son obeys and is responsive to the directions of the father. The Holy Spirit is obedient to the directives of both the Father and the Son.[13]

While commenting on 1 Corinthians 11:3 he links divine filiation and human relations:

> Just as God the Father has authority over the Son, though the two are equal in deity, so in marriage, the husband has authority over his wife, though they are equal in personhood. In this case, the man's role is like that of God the Father, and the woman's role is parallel to that of God to the Son.[14]

Bruce Ware also supports the criteria that the only way to differentiate the divine persons is through their "roles," by their communicative actions in the economy towards one another. "Therefore, what distinguishes the Father is his particular role as Father in relation to the Son and Spirit and the relationships that he has with each of them."[15] In agreement with the creedal tradition, Ware confesses that God's Trinitarian self-differentiation is eternal, and therefore precedes the creative act of the cosmos. God's being in act is eternally and necessarily Trinitarian.

However, there seems to be discontinuity with the creedal tradition. Within the metaphysical grounds of self-differentiation of the persons in the Godhead lies a specific property, or a "role." This role, proponents of EFS infer, also precedes the economy of salvation. Notably, it precedes the created order. The Father's identity is distinguished by specific properties (i.e., propensity to send, choose, have authority, etc.). Whereas the greater tradition has used the theological grammar of "divine processions" and "relations of origins" (i.e. unbegotten, begotten, eternal generation),[16] Ware and others (wittingly or

---

12. Grudem, "Doctrinal Deviations in Evangelical-Feminist Arguments about the Trinity," 21.
13. Wayne A. Grudem, *Systematic Theology: An Introduction to Biblical Doctrine* (Downers Grove, IL: InterVarsity, 1994), 249.
14. Grudem, *Systematic Theology*, 459–60.
15. Bruce A. Ware, *Father, Son, and Holy Spirit: Relationships, Roles, and Relevance* (Wheaton, IL: Crossway, 2005), 43.
16. See Augustine, *The Trinity*, trans. Edmund Hill (New York: New City Press, 1991), Book I; Kenan B. Osborne, "The Trinity in Bonaventure," in *The Cambridge Companion to the Trinity*, ed. Peter C. Phan (Cambridge: Cambridge University Press, 2011), 108–27; Thomas Aquinas, *Summa*

unwittingly) introduce more narrative content to God's life, his "ontological self." The Father's distinction stems from his "supreme" monarchy;[17] while the identities of the Son and Spirit differentiate as the one submitted and the one proceeding respectively. Ware continues,

> Every essential attribute of God's nature is possessed by the Father, Son, and Spirit equally and fully. We cannot look at aspects of the *nature of God* as that which distinguishes the Father from the Son or Spirit; rather we have to look at the *roles and relationships* that characterize the Father uniquely in relation to the Son and the Spirit.[18]

Messianic psalms like Psalm 2:2–4 and eschatological texts like Revelation 19 are interpreted in support of the supremacy of the Father in the triune life, for it is the Father enthroning his Son as king over creation. And in devotional texts like the Lord's prayer (Matt. 6:9–10) Jesus is understood to be teaching that the Father is supreme over him for it is his will and kingdom that will be established. Ware argues: "It is (specifically) the Father's will that is to be done, and the Father's kingdom that is to come. The Father, then, has supremacy over all, as Jesus here acknowledges."[19] It seems that the kingdom is Jesus's kingdom only by virtue of receiving it. Seemingly, the kingdom is first and foremost the Father's, and derivatively, the Son's. This must mean, Ware believes, that the Father's authority over the Son is not simply that it is realized in history but it precedes history. For example, in Philippians 2:9–11, a key kenotic text where not only Jesus's deity is stated ("form of God") but also his divesting of divine prerogatives to become a slave, Ware extrapolates the following from God's immanent life: "It is the Father, then, who is supreme in the Godhead—in the triune relationships of Father, Son, and Holy Spirit—and supreme over all of the very creation over which the Son reigns as its Lord."[20]

Christopher Cowan also believes that God's sending Christ "into the world" in John's Gospel "appears" to assume a communicative hierarchical reality that precedes the incarnation (cf. John 3:16–17). Since the Gospel of John does not explicitly state that the Son's subordinate condition is temporary, then, Cowan infers than John must believe it. Cowan explains:

> While John clearly emphasizes Jesus's equality of divine essence with the Father— his activity in creation, his sovereignty over his death, and his glorious preexistence—he presents no testimony to counter the subordination theme and lead

Theologica, Volume 1, trans. Fathers of the English Dominican Province (New York: Cosimo, 2013), Questions 27–34.

17. Ware, *Father, Son, and Holy Spirit,* 46.
18. Ware, *Father, Son, and Holy Spirit,* 45.
19. Ware, *Father, Son, and Holy Spirit,* 47.
20. Ware, *Father, Son, and Holy Spirit,* 51.

one to believe that there was a time when it did not apply. One would think that if Jesus's submission to his Father's authority held only during his earthly ministry, the apostle would want to make sure his readers clearly understood this.[21]

The logic is as follows: Since Jesus is said to come "from heaven," the sending "implies a subordinate role for Jesus not only during his incarnation but prior to it as well. The Father's sending of the Son occurred prior to his being made flesh."[22] Notably, this last inference, an argument from silence, is a projection on John's understanding of the Son. This is a dubious conjecture. Maybe John, as the Nicene tradition affirms, assumed that divine relationality in the economy takes its form in the Son via the incarnation. The Nicene Creed, echoing Johannine language, states "Eternally begotten of the Father, God from God, Light from Light, true God from true God, begotten not made, of one being with the Father. Through whom all things were made. For our salvation, he came down from heaven."

It is not controversial in Christian thought to render God the Son as obedient and dependent within the economy of salvation to God the Father, for the Son is acting in *forma servi*. But how do we make these hermeneutical judgements regarding God's immanent life? Though wanting to maintain Nicaean orthodoxy, proponents of EFS claim that the submission of the Son incarnate in the economy of salvation *is* a revelation of the Son's eternal submission to the Father in eternity past. This is arguably a historical innovation. This method of theological conjecture makes one wonder as to the content of this eternal submission *ad intra*. If the submission were eternal and authority were only received in light of a specific communicative agency of the Son, "a role," then questions regarding the status of the shared essential divine attributes and the undivided divine will not cease. The Nicene tradition, as Lewis Ayres maintains, confesses authority, power, majesty, and glory in the mystery of Godhead as equally shared.[23] It is precisely this point that seems to be insufficient among EFS Trinitarian reflection.

To be sure, the obedience of the Son is an important motif and shares a broad Christian consensus. But this has not always been the case. Jesus's obedi-

---

21. Christopher W. Cowan, "'I Always Do What Pleases Him': The Father and Son in the Gospel of John," in Ware and Starke, eds., *One God in Three Persons*, 61. Amongst the many texts in dispute is 1 Corinthians 13. In a polemic about the proper practice of communal worship, Paul's admonition to the Corinthians is interpreted as establishing a programmatic hierarchical order: "authority and submission in human relations as a reflection of the authority and submission that exist in the eternal Godhead." For ultimately, God the Father is stated to be the head of Christ. Hence, the problem of the proper order in worship in Corinth is settled, in Cowan's hermeneutic, by a hierarchical portrayal of women and men relations that purportedly mirrors an eternal hierarchical relation of God the Father over God the Son.

22. Cowan, "I Always Do What Pleases Him," 62.

23. See Lewis Ayres, *Nicaea and Its Legacy: An Approach to Fourth-Century Trinitarian Theology* (New York: Oxford University Press, 2004), 279.

ence was controversial in the Arian debates of the fourth century because for them it logically implied ontological subordination of the Son, for which they wanted to deny *homoousious*. In the current debate, no one is seeking to deny this. What is controversial now is a new interest in positing the thesis that the Son's submission in salvation history corresponds to an eternal relational property that distinguishes him from the Father. This might appear benign until we interrogate the issue. One might ask: The Son is submitted to do what? Submission is a notion that has meaning when it is referencing a command. What is the content of the Son's submission when conceptualized before the creation of the world? Is there a salvific obedient role without an economy of salvation? Would not this thesis make the cosmos logically necessary for the Son? Is the Son, in his very nature, dependent upon the created order to be who he is? If so, this would be a tectonic-level departure from the Nicene Tradition. The aseity and freedom of the Trinity is at stake.

Christology and the Divine Will

At this point in our discussion we turn to examine the nature of the divine will. It seems that some proponents of EFS *construe the divine will as one in terms of unified in purpose, but based on an eternal order of willing, receiving, and completing that corresponds to the modes of subsistence of Father, Son and Spirit.*

Does the tri-personal God have three wills, three different but complementary centers of consciousness? What does Christology have to say on this matter? Chalcedonian Christology, which brought further conceptual clarification of the Nicene declaration of the Son's divine nature, posited that Jesus has two natures, human and divine, without confusion nor separation. Later, Maximus the Confessor (ca. 580–662), contended that consistency and loyalty to the Chalcedonian formula required the faith to affirm that Christ has two wills, a human will and a divine one. Evangelical Protestants mostly adhere to a dyothelite Christology, following the grammar rule that the human will of the Son is subordinate to the divine will.

As evangelical Protestants, we also affirm that personal distinctions in the Trinity do not stem from the undivided, perfect, and equally possessed divine nature. The Nicene tradition holds that the distinction of the divine *personae* is based on the relations of origin (i.e., eternal generation of the Son by the Father, the procession of the Spirit, etc.) in the Trinity. Proponents of EFS argue for another criterion, that is, the particular "expression" or "role" each subsistence reveals in the divine economy. It is accepted that the Son has a human will. And with the greater tradition, it is also acknowledged that the Son's divine will is one and the same as the triune God. But in practice this can be an ambiguous proposition. For example, Ware, Grudem, and Denny Burke argue that the eternal Son has a distinct will that characterizes his agency in relation to the Father. Ware says, "The submission of the Son in the incarnation is but a reflection of the eternal relationship that has always been true with his Father. The Son always seeks to do the will of the Father, and this is true eternally."[24] Moreover, he concludes, "In eternity, the Father commissioned the Son who then willingly laid aside the glory he had with the Father to come and purchase our pardon and renewal."[25] The Son's dependence and deference to the Father, according to this account, is communicated, but it is also a revelation of a hierarchical life *ad intra* within the Godhead. Apart from using authority and submission motifs to understand the interrelationality of the Godhead, they contend there would be no meaningful manner to tell them apart. A majority of proponents of EFS believe that the divine hypostasis of the Son would not be differentiable from the Father or the Spirit.

Consider Denny Burke, for example, who evaluates the will of the Son *simpliciter* without making an explicit logical distinction between the Son's human will. Arguing for a minority report translation of Philippians 2:6, which would render "form of God" and "grasping for equality" as referring to different realities (the former to an ontological condition, and the latter to a functional characteristic of Christ), Burke infers that Jesus's desire for equality with God the Father "would have precluded Jesus from his taking the form of a servant and from his becoming in the likeness of men. In his preexistent state, Jesus decided not to pursue 'equality,' but to pursue *incarnation*."[26] Here Burke envisages the divine will of the Son (which the tradition has rendered a singular divine will), as functioning as a distinct center of consciousness that is capable from eternity past to come to an agreement with another center of consciousness, the Father.

Now, then, we are reminded by J. N. D. Kelly how the Nicene tradition and Augustine parsed this issue: "where there is no difference of natures, there is none of wills either."[27] Kyle Claunch, while a proponent of EFS, rightly argues against the notion of distinct eternal wills, departing from Ware and Grudem's conception of the Son's will:

> In order for the Son to submit willingly to the will of the Father, the two must possess distinct wills. *This way of understanding the immanent Trinity does run counter to the pro-Nicene tradition, as well as the medieval, Reformation, and post-Reformation Reformed traditions that grew from it.* According to traditional

---

24. Ware, *Father, Son, and Holy Spirit*, 79. Ware explains: "It seems clear that if in Jesus coming, he did not do his own will but the will of his Father who sent him, then he acted in obedience to accord but came as the Father sent him, then he acted in obedience to fulfill the will of the Father in his coming to earth. It was not his own will per se that led him to come, but the will of the Father who sent him." Bruce Ware, *The Man Christ Jesus: Theological Reflections on the Humanity of Christ* (Wheaton, IL: Crossway, 2013), 62.

25. Ware, *Father, Son, and Holy Spirit*, 82.

26. Denny Burk, "Christ's Functional Subordination in Philippians 2:6. A Grammatical Note with Trinitarian Implications," in *The New Evangelical Subordinationism? Perspectives on the Equality of God the Father and God the Son*, eds. Dennis W. Jowers and H. Wayne House (Eugene, OR: Wipf & Stock, 2012), 103–4.

27. J. N. D. Kelly, *Early Christian Doctrines*, 5th ed. (New York: Continuum, 2000), 273.

> Trinitarian theology, the will is predicated of the one undivided divine essence
> so that there is only one divine will in the immanent Trinity.[28]

A key biblical text in conciliar discussions is John 6:38: "For I have come down from heaven not to do my will but to do the will of him who sent me." Olegario Gonzalez reports that exegetical theology has a long-attested history of identifying the speaker as the incarnate Logos who speaks in his human nature. The Son's human will is an absolute "yes" to the will of the Father. The will of Jesus "adheres to the one who is its foundation, as the Son adheres to the Father, without whom he would not be Son" and the Father would not be a Father.[29] And it is from the reality of the Son's human will that he assumes a destiny of solidarity with humanity. Here we find an ontological presupposition that at first is difficult to detect, but is of utmost importance. What is assumed is that the Son's temporal mission is based in the undivided eternal will of the Trinity. What is important here is the order. Everyone agrees to the submission and authority motif in salvation history. But some want to take the submission and authority motif and work it backwards into the Godhead. But what is evident here is a unified vision of the divine will, which is expressed in the economy of salvation as the obedience of the Son. Hence, the temporal mission of the Son Jesus, the redeemer, is the historical communication of his eternal procession.

An EFS conception of three coeternal divine wills in agreement is *de facto* a departure from creedal Trinitarian metaphysics. Phillip Cary is rightly concerned with the conception of multiple eternal wills. He contends:

> Father, Son and Holy Spirit are always necessarily of one will, because there is
> only one God *and therefore only one divine will.* And where there is but one will
> there cannot be the authority of command and obedience, for that requires one
> person's will to be subordinate to a will other than his own. . . . If there were rela-
> tions of command and obedience between the Father and the Son, there would
> be no Trinity at all but rather three Gods.[30]

The theological difficulty here is not only the contentious notion of an eternal subordination of the Son, but also the lack of clarity regarding a dyothelite Christology in relationship to God's immanent life. For this reason, Glen Butner contends that "to posit such terms as 'obedience' and 'submission' that imply a distinction of wills between the Father and the Son while

28. Kyle Claunch, "God Is the Head of Christ: Does 1 Corinthians 11: 3 Ground Gender Complementarity in the Immanent Trinity?," in Ware and Starke, eds., *One God in Three Persons*, 88 (emphasis mine).

29. Olegario González de Cardedal, *Cristología*, Sapientia Fidei (Madrid: Biblioteca Autores Cristianos, 2005), 284.

30. Phillip Cary, "The New Evangelical Subordinationism? Reading Inequality Into the Trinity," in Jowers and House, eds., *The New Evangelical Subordinationism?*, 6.

affirming dyothelite Christology entails a distinction of natures between the Father and Son (and Spirit) resulting in tritheism."[31]

Letham does not believe the language "obedience" and "submission" necessarily entails a distinction of natures, particularly because he makes recourse to the grammar of eternal generation. He, though, warns that the language of subordination among some EFS proponents is misguided, even if John V. Dahms and Wayne Grudem do not feel troubled by it. He writes, "The subject of active forms of the verb 'to subordinate' subordinates another. This could hardly be the case in the Trinity. It was typical of the Arian heresy." Nevertheless, he adds: "Instead, the idea of submission is compatible with an order among the Trinitarian persons and with their equality of status and identity of being."[32]

One way of avoiding this charge of tritheistic implications is suggested by Steven Boyer. He avers, "because the Father eternally generates the Son, one could reconcile the singularity of the divine will with the notion that the Father commands and the Son obeys by distinguishing between the divine will *qua* generative, which pertains to the Father, and the divine will *qua* receptive, which pertains to the Son."[33]

Allen and Swain propose another theological clarification that attempts to affirm obedience as a property of the eternal Son, while avoiding a revision of classical Trinitarian metaphysics. Hence their thesis: "the obedience of the eternal Son in the economy of salvation is the proper mode whereby he enacts the undivided work of the Trinity 'for us and for our salvation.'"[34] Furthermore, Allen and Swain contend: "The Son's personal property—that which is 'proper' to him and to him alone within the Godhead—is finally nothing other than the subsisting filial relation in which he eternally stands to the Father as a receptive communicant in the undivided divine essence."[35]

So proponents of EFS might want to consider Allen and Swain's articulation of the Son's property, as it appears to be consistent with Nicene metaphysics. However, we must see the distinction here. Obedience so conceptualized is an *ad extra* expression of the *taxis* within the triune God. It is a historical expression of the Son's eternal generation. It seems that Allen and Swain are proposing that obedience is a contingent or accidental property. In terms of modal characterization, it is a property that is not necessary for the holder to possess in every possible world. For if the property is essential, or necessary for the object to have it in all possible realities, then the holder must have it

31. Glen Butner, "Eternal Functional Subordination and the Problem of Divine Will," *JETS* 58, no. 1 (2015): 132.
32. Letham, "Eternal Generation in the Church Fathers," 122.
33. Steven D. Boyer, "Articulating Order: Trinitarian Discourse in an Egalitarian Age," *Pro Ecclesia* 18, no. 3 (2009): 265–66.
34. Scott R. Swain and Michael Allen, "The Obedience of the Eternal Son," in *Christology Ancient and Modern: Explorations in Constructive Dogmatics*, eds. Oliver Crisp and Fred Sanders (Grand Rapids: Zondervan, 2013), 75.
35. Swain, "The Obedience of the Eternal Son," 83.

in order to be what it is.[36] If the obedience of the eternal Son is a temporal expression of the eternal ordering of the Trinity (of the undivided divine will), then as the creation is a contingent reality, so is the property "being obedient" or "submissive" a contingent or accidental property. Therefore, it is fitting that the Son, Jesus, acts in history as the one who lives in obedience to the Father, as one who receives from the Father his eternal being and has "life in himself." But to present the *theologoumenon* of the EFS as an essential property, it seems that it would also require making creation a necessary reality for God and the life of the Son.

Christology and Eternal Generation

Should we choose between the eternal generation of the Son and EFS in order to distinguish the divine persons? Is eternal "submission" the new "eternal generation"? Proponents of EFS seem to argue that *eternal relations of origin/procession and relations of opposition do not possess sufficient explanatory power and should be better conceived as hierarchical relations of subordination in the Godhead anchoring the metaphysical distinctions of the divine hypostasis.*

Whereas a majority of Christian theology has maintained that God the Father generates the Son in the mystery of God's immanent life, and hence the incarnation of Jesus finds its metaphysical antecedent in the Father's begetting of the Son;[37] Supporters of EFS infer that filial texts about Jesus should be understood as referring not merely to the Son's kenotic condition, but to the Son's eternal life. In this case, submission, not eternal generation, is preferred to establish the identity of the Son. As I have shown, this is problematic. While many of the implications are overlapping, allow me to attend to the issue of procession more specifically.

A theological concern for those advocating the EFS thesis is that without allowing for the submission and authority motif to reach into the eternal relationality of the Godhead, it would be impossible to say why it was the "'Son and not the 'Father' or 'Spirit' who was sent to become incarnate."[38] Why is one sent, and not the other, if indeed there are no such categories of obedience prior to the divine mission? This apprehension seems somewhat strange in light of one principal consideration: Trinitarian orthodoxy has affirmed the eternal generation of the Son under a theology of divine processions that effectively grounds the Son being the Son of the Father. Letham, who has supported the EFS, nevertheless distances himself from a

---

36. Cf. Stephen Yablo, "Essentialism," in *The Routledge Encyclopedia of Philosophy*, ed. Edward Craig (London: Routledge, 1998), 417 22.

37. See the doctrinal account by Thomas G. Weinandy, "Trinitarian Christology: The Eternal Son," in *The Oxford Handbook of the Trinity*, eds. Gilles Emery and Matthew Levering (New York: Oxford University Press, 2011), 387–98.

38. Bruce Ware, "How Shall We Think About the Trinity?," in *God under Fire: Modern Scholarship Reinvents God*, eds. Douglas S. Huffman and Eric L. Johnson (Grand Rapids: Zondervan, 2002), 275.

revisionist metaphysics of God that downplays the capacity of the concepts of relations of origin and relations of opposition, and makes clear that eternal generation of the Son is of indispensable significance for Trinitarianism. This is hardly something that only late modern egalitarians believe. Letham affirms that the dogma of eternal generation, according to patristic theology, does indeed establish personal distinctions between the Father, Son, and Spirit. He explains:

> The Son is not the Father, the Father is not the Son, and the Holy Spirit is neither the Father nor the Son. Yet the three are one. Generation Highlights an Irreversible Hypostatic Order. . . . The relations of sending and being sent reflect the order of begetting and being begotten. Both the Western and Eastern churches have understood these as missions and processions. According to the processions, the Son and the Spirit are begotten and proceed eternally from the Father. The missions concern the sendings of both in history. There is a distinction but an inseparable connection.[39]

Letham also parts ways with Grudem and Ware. He warns about the use of the referents "father" and "son" *in directo* and simply applying it analogically to human relationships.[40] He explains the Nicene polemic regarding the naming of God and using human analogy:

> The Arian argument that human sons are subordinate to their fathers led to their contention that the son is subordinate to the Father. The church rejected this conclusion as heretical and opposed the premise as mistaken. Rather, the Son is equal with the Father in status, power, and glory. He is identical in being from

---

39. Letham, "Eternal Generation in the Church Fathers," 120–21. He continues: "The generation is eternal since the Father and the Son are eternal. As Bavinck puts it, 'Rejection of the eternal generation of the Son involves not only a failure to do justice to the deity of the Son, but also to that of the Father,' for 'it is not something that was completed and finished at some point in eternity, but an eternal unchanging act of God, at once always complete and eternally ongoing. . . . The Father is not and never was ungenerative; he begets everlastingly.' Since God is eternal and transcends time—which he created—the Trinitarian relations are eternal. There is not a punctiliar moment when the Father begat the Son, for that would place generation within the parameters of space-time and be contrary to its place within the eternal life of the indivisible Trinity."

40. There is an implicit theological rule working here: God's immanent life (apart from history) is revealed or displayed by God's life in the economy (in history). This order of knowledge and revelational experience is paradigmatically stated by Karl Rahner's axiom, "The 'economic' Trinity is the 'immanent' and the 'immanent' Trinity is the 'economic' Trinity." One way of understanding this axiom is that the working of the divine persons revealed in history—especially in the incarnation of the Son Jesus—truly reveals the same God who is constituted in eternity in these relationships. However, the communicative actions of the divine hypostases in the economy of salvation do not exhaust all that God is; there is an "excess" of divine reality. For a recent discussion of the reception of Rahner's Rule in evangelical theology, see Scott D. Harrower, *Trinitarian Self and Salvation: An Evangelical Engagement with Rahner's Rule* (Eugene, OR: Pickwick, 2012), Chapter 1.

eternity. In short, to take the creaturely reality as definitive of the life of God is a serious error, leading to dire results.[41]

So, there seems to be a lack of analogical awareness and equivocal language regarding the limits of the filial language amongst some proponents of EFS. This in turn posits a problem regarding the semantics of the language of submission and subordination that Christian faith needs to avoid.

On Imitating Divine Things

The thesis of EFS is not only provocative in terms of how it conceptualizes the Son's agency in the economy and in the immanent Trinity; how it tends to render the nature of the Son and the Father's will as centers of consciousness; and how it uses the obedience and submission as analytical to the eternal Son's identity; but especially, how it seeks to provide the ultimate theological justification for hierarchical relationships between men and women. It does so by arguing that gender complementarity is grounded in the immanent Trinity. Ware summarizes the case:

> For all eternity, the order establishes that God is the head of Christ; within the created sphere, there is an ordering such that Christ is the head of man; and within human relationships, the order establishes that man is the head of woman. Intrinsic to God's own nature is a fundamental *taxis,* and *he* has so designed creation to reflect his own being, his own internal and eternal relationships, in part, through created and designed relationships of *taxis.*[42]

K. Scott Oliphint, an advocate of EFS, is aware of the problems of unqualified extrapolations from properly trinitarian categories, attributes, or properties to anthropological ones. He admits that there are indeed theological discontinuities between how God is in himself and the analogical implications that might be inferred for human relations. He clarifies:

> when Scripture enjoins us in any way to be like God, or to reflect his character, or to take on his characteristics, it is enjoining us to be like, to reflect, to take on those characteristics that are his by virtue of creation—that is, covenantally— and not those that are his essentially. . . . So, for example, the order (*taxis*) of persons in the Godhead is an *ad intra* order.[43]

---

41. Letham, "Eternal Generation in the Church Fathers," 120–21; Dennis W. Jowers, "The Inconceivability of Subordination within a Simple God," in *The New Evangelical Subordinationism? Perspectives on the Equality of God the Father and God the Son,* eds. Dennis W. Jowers and H. Wayne House (Eugene, OR: Wipf & Stock, 2012), 397.

42. Ware, *Father, Son, and Holy Spirit: Relationships, Roles, and Relevance,* 72.

43. K. Scott Oliphint, "Simplicity, Triunity, and the Incomprehensibility of God," in Ware and Starke, eds., *One God in Three Persons,* 215.

And yet, despite a recognition of more or less ethical and ontological discontinuities, holders of EFS believe that one can assert EFS as an ontological and ethical analogue for the ordering of gender relations and the functional submission or subordination of women via *indirect inference*. Again, the immanent trinity is used as the grounds for gender complementarianism or male-led hierarchy.

On his part, although Letham thinks "that identity of nature and equality of status are compatible with an order" and "cannot be illegitimate in humanity," he admits that in extending implications to humanity "there are grave dangers lurking on both sides."[44] The dangers he has in mind are related to moral ethics and relationship breakdowns between men and women. He does not seem to worry about the problem of transposing properly theological conceptuality regarding the immanent life of God (for which we don't have equivalents in the created order), to anthropology where the order of being is ontologically other. Usually when the Scripture says that we should be like God or Jesus or Paul or the saints of the past, the indicative is based on communicative actions in history, not on the ontology of the divine being.

Conclusion

Complementarians who use Trinitarian dogma to advance their own socio-ethical construals have joined the legion of theologians in modern theology, particularly in the liberal tradition, who have developed ways to conceive God's life-in-act as an archetype for social organization. The now proverbial "the trinity is our social program," echoed by Leonardo Boff, Jürgen Moltmann, Miroslav Wolf, and Catherine LaCugna, has been adopted in evangelical discussions in the north-Atlantic latitudes.[45] Instead of using scriptural patterns of ordering ecclesiastical gendered relationships, or appealing to christological patterns of life, *imitatio Christi*, the Trinity is brought in to "close the deal."

Using the Trinity as inspiration for social practices is a highly subjective maneuver. As theologians we are susceptible to symbiotically project human things onto the divine things. The temptation is the ideological use God-talk. The function of trinitarian dogma is not to provide a model of utopic relationality or a legitimization of hierarchical relations. The dogma is fundamentally the confession of the God that has committed himself to human history

---

44. Letham, "Eternal Generation in the Church Fathers," 121. Letham compares the lack of distinctions between heterosexual gender roles to a danger "akin to a modalist error." This surely sounds rhetorically ingenious. But the basic problem is that this is a category mistake.

45. See for example Mark Husbands, "The Trinity Is Not Our Social Program: Volf, Gregory of Nyssa and Barth," in *Trinitarian Theology for the Church: Scripture, Community, Worship*, eds. Daniel J. Treier and David Lauber (Downers Grove, IL: IVP Academic, 2009), 120–41; Antonio González, *Trinidad y Liberación: La teología trinitaria considerada desde la perspectiva de la teología de la liberación*, 1st ed., Colección Teología latinomericana (San Salvador, El Salvador: UCA, 1994); Catherine M. LaCugna, *God for Us: The Trinity and Christian Life* (San Francisco: Harper, 1991).

through his Son and the Spirit. Various problems arise when we use the trinity as our "social program." First, the freedom of God can be compromised when the creator-creature distinction is not preserved. Proponents of EFS offer a maximal account of similarity between creature and creator, proposing analogical correlations between God's being in se and human relations. Secondly, there is a danger of falling into a simplistic analogy of being (*analogia entis*) without the dialectic of God's holy otherness and God's communicative irruption of human order. It is not pioneering, nor necessarily more faithful to Scripture, to find ontological legitimatizing of the *status quo* in what is already in the great majority of human societies: patriarchal hierarchy. This is the burden of those of us who serve in complementarian ecclesial traditions. In fact, we are called to speak and act as mutual servants, according to patterns of *imitatio Christi* in the wisdom of an ecclesial order of complementarity. We might call the notion of "Trinitarian complementarism" an exercise in "illegitimate Trinitarian transfer,"[46] that is, an illegitimate application of categories of the doctrine of the Trinity to anthropology.

The creed speaks of "the only Son of God, eternally begotten of the Father, God from God, Light from Light, true God from true God, begotten, not made, of one Being with the Father." The confession is the communication of a narrative-historical testimony in the language of ontology. The result is both a mirroring and a conceptual elaboration of the biblical testimony. To the reciprocal knowledge, love, authority, and being between Jesus and the Father, the church confessed *homognosis, homoagape, homoesksousía, homodoxa, homoousía.*[47]

In the filial and reciprocal relationships of Jesus, Son of the Father and bearer of the Holy Spirit, we stand before the life of the tri-personal God. The tri-personal God who revealed himself in history is the God whose inexhaustible life is from eternity. This is the life that is communicated in the history of Jesus's life act. Therefore, the economic Trinity is a manifestation of the immanent Trinity. This is the logical foundation for the history of the triune God's salvific temporal communication in Jesus: God's antecedent and inexhaustible triune life. As Kevin Vanhoozer states: "The economic Trinity is, or rather communicates the immanent Trinity."[48] The communication of divine life in and through Jesus is in itself the gateway to our communion with the Father and our experience of becoming his sons. Jesus's complete history finds intelligibility as God's history.

---

46. Kevin J. Vanhoozer coined the phrase "illegitimate Trinitarian transfer" in the context of polemics regarding what he terms "kenotic perichoretic relational theism" and the application of christological and Trinitarian categories to the God-world relation. I am using the phrase to refer to the unnecessary use of Trinitarian terminology to ground ecclesial complementarianism.

47. Olegario González de Cardedal, *La entraña del cristianismo* (Salamanca: Secretario Trinitario, 2001), 684.

48. Kevin J. Vanhoozer, *Remythologizing Theology: Divine Action, Passion, and Authorship*, Cambridge Studies in Christian Doctrine (Cambridge: Cambridge University Press, 2010).

From the reception of divine revelation in and through Jesus the Son, it is problematic to deduce that God's historical communication exhausts all that God is, or that God's life is inevitably dependent on or constituted in the history of the world. God's existence is fully in the eternal relationality of himself, independent from divine action in history. The missions of the Son and the Spirit—the creativity, servanthood, and sacrifice of Jesus and the sanctifying, regenerating work of the Spirit—are testified as a fruit of divine love and freedom.

Bibliography

Ayres, Lewis. *Nicaea and Its Legacy: An Approach to Fourth-Century Trinitarian Theology*. New York: Oxford University Press, 2004.

Boff, Leonardo. *Jesus Christ Liberator: A Critical Christology for Our Time*. Maryknoll, NY: Orbis, 1978.

Boyer, Steven D. "Articulating Order: Trinitarian Discourse in an Egalitarian Age." *Pro Ecclesia* 18, no. 3 (2009): 255–72.

Burk, Denny. "Christ's Functional Subordination in Philippians 2:6: A Grammatical Note with Trinitarian Implications." In *The New Evangelical Subordinationism? Perspectives on the Equality of God the Father and God the Son*, edited by Dennis W. Jowers and H. Wayne House, 82–107. Eugene, OR: Wipf & Stock, 2012.

Butner, Glen. "Eternal Functional Subordination and the Problem of Divine Will." *JETS* 58, no. 1 (2015): 131–49.

Cardedal, Olegario González de. *La entraña del cristianismo*. Salamanca: Secretario Trinitario, 2001.

———. *Cristología* Sapientia Fidei. Madrid: Biblioteca Autores Cristianos, 2005.

Cary, Phillip. "The New Evangelical Subordinationism? Reading Inequality Into the Trinity." In *The New Evangelical Subordinationism? Perspectives on the Equality of God the Father and God the Son*, edited by Dennis W. Jowers and H. Wayne House, 1–12. Eugene, OR: Wipf & Stock, 2012.

Claunch, Kyle. "God Is the Head of Christ: Does 1 Corinthians 11:3 Ground Gender Complementarity in the Immanent Trinity?" In *One God in Three Persons: Unity of Essence, Distinction of Persons, Implications for Life*, edited by Bruce A. Ware and John Starke, 78–87. Wheaton, IL: Crossway, 2015.

Cowan, Christopher W. "'I Always Do What Pleases Him': The Father and Son in the Gospel of John." In *One God in Three Persons: Unity of Essence, Distinction of Persons, Implications for Life*, edited by Bruce A. Ware and John Starke, 47–64. Wheaton, IL: Crossway, 2015.

Emery, Gilles, and Matthew Levering, eds. *The Oxford Handbook of the Trinity*. New York: Oxford University Press, 2011.

Erickson, Millard. *Who's Tampering with the Trinity? An Assessment of the Subordination Debate*. Grand Rapids: Kregel, 2009.

González, Antonio. *Trinidad y Liberación: La teología trinitaria considerada desde la perspectiva de la teología de la liberación*. 1 ed. Colección Teología latinomericana. San Salvador, El Salvador: UCA, 1994.

Grudem, Wayne. "Doctrinal Deviations in Evangelical-Feminist Arguments about the Trinity." In *One God in Three Persons: Unity of Essence, Distinction of Persons, Implications for Life*, edited by Bruce A. Ware and John Starke, 17–46. Wheaton, IL: Crossway, 2015.

_____. *Systematic Theology: An Introduction to Biblical Doctrine*. Downers Grove, IL: InterVarsity, 1994.

Harrower, Scot D. *Trinitarian Self and Salvation: An Evangelical Engagement with Rahner's Rule*. Eugene, OR: Pickwick, 2012.

Humphrey, Edith M. "The Gift of the Father." In *Trinitarian Theology for the Church: Scripture, Community, Worship*, edited by Daniel J. Treier and David Lauber, 79–102. Downers Grove: IVP Academic, 2009.

Hurtado, Larry W. *God in New Testament Theology*. Nashville: Abingdon, 2010.

Husbands, Mark. "The Trinity Is Not Our Social Program: Volf, Gregory of Nyssa and Barth." In *Trinitarian Theology for the Church: Scripture, Community, Worship*, edited by Daniel J. Treier and David Lauber, 120–41. Downers Grove, IL: IVP Academic, 2009.

Jowers, Dennis W. "The Inconceivability of Subordination within a Simple God." In *The New Evangelical Subordinationism? Perspectives on the Equality of God the Father and God the Son*, edited by Dennis W. Jowers and H. Wayne House, 375–410. Eugene, OR: Wipf & Stock, 2012.

Kelly, J. N. D. *Early Christian Doctrines*. 5th ed. New York: Continuum, 2000.

LaCugna, Catherine M. *God for Us: The Trinity and Christian Life*. San Francisco: Harper, 1991.

Letham, Robert. "Eternal Generation in the Church Fathers." In *One God in Three Persons: Unity of Essence, Distinction of Persons, Implications for Life*, edited by Bruce A. Ware and John Starke, 109–26. Wheaton, IL: Crossway, 2015.

Martínez-Olivieri, Jules A. *A Visible Witness: Christology, Liberation and Participation*. Emerging Scholars. Minneapolis: Fortress, 2016.

Maspero, Giulio, and Robert J. Wozniak, eds. *Rethinking Trinitarian Theology: Disputed Questions and Contemporary Issues in Trinitarian Theology*. New York: T & T Clark, 2012.

Oliphint, K. Scott. "Simplicity, Triunity, and the Incomprehensibility of God." In *One God in Three Persons: Unity of Essence, Distinction of Persons, Implications for Life*, edited by Bruce A. Ware and John Starke, 215–36. Wheaton, IL: Crossway, 2015.

Pannenberg, Wolfhart. *Jesus—God and Man*. 2nd ed. Philadelphia: Westminster, 1977.

Pikaza, X. *Este es el hombre: Manual de cristología*. Salamanca: Secretariado Trinitario, 1997.

Swain, Scott R., and Michael Allen. "The Obedience of the Eternal Son." In *Christology Ancient and Modern: Explorations in Constructive Dogmatics*, edited by Oliver Crisp and Fred Sanders, 74–95. Grand Rapids: Zondervan, 2013.

Thompson, Marianne Meye. *The Promise of the Father: Jesus and God in the New Testament*. Louisville: Westminster John Knox, 2000.

_____. *The God of the Gospel of John*. Grand Rapids: Eerdmans, 2001.

Vanhoozer, Kevin J. *The Drama of Doctrine: A Canonical-Linguistic Approach to Christian Theology*. Louisville: Westminster John Knox, 2005.

_____. *Remythologizing Theology: Divine Action, Passion, and Authorship*. Cambridge Studies in Christian Doctrine. Cambridge: Cambridge University Press, 2010.

Volf, Miroslav, and Michael Welker, eds. *God's Life in Trinity*. Philadelphia: Fortress, 2006.

Yablo, Stephen "Essentialism." In *The Routledge Encyclopedia of Philosophy*, edited by Edward Craig, 241–42. London: Routledge, 1998.

Yeago, David S. "The New Testament and the Nicene Dogma: A Contribution to the Recovery of Theological Exegesis." *ProEccl* no. 3 (1994): 152–164.

Ware, Bruce. *Father, Son, and Holy Spirit: Relationships, Roles, and Relevance*. Wheaton, IL: Crossway, 2005.

_____. "How Shall We Think About the Trinity?." In *God Under Fire: Modern Scholarship Reinvents God*, edited by Douglas S. Huffman and Eric L. Johnson, 6947–50. Kindle. Grand Rapids: Zondervan, 2002.

_____. *The Man Christ Jesus. Theological Reflections on the Humanity of Christ*. Wheaton, IL: Crossway, 2013.

Weinandy, Thomas G. "Trinitarian Christology: The Eternal Son." In *The Oxford Handbook of the Trinity*, edited by Gilles Emery and Matthew Levering, 387–99. New York: Oxford University Press, 2011.

CHAPTER 11

Pannenberg

The Submission of the Son
and the Heartbeat of Divine Love

JOHN MCCLEAN

Wolfhart Pannenberg, one of the great theologians of the late twentieth century, was an innovative and profound thinker.[1] Christology
and doctrine of God were central to his interests, so it is certainly
worth investigating his view of the relation of the Father and the Son. Indeed,
to consider this topic is to go to the heart of Pannenberg's thought and to
encounter some of the most distinctive features of his thought.

The final paragraph of Pannenberg's *Systematic Theology* offers a compact
summary of his theological vision, relating God's eternal existence and historical actions to redemption.

---

1. For an introduction to Pannenberg's life and thought see J. McClean, *From the Future: Getting to
   Grips with Pannenberg's Thought* (Milton Keynes: Paternoster, 2012), 1–43. See also T. Bradshaw,
   Pannenberg: A Guide for the Perplexed (London; New York: T & T Clark, 2009); S. J. Grenz, *Reason
   for Hope: The Systematic Theology of Wolfhart Pannenberg*, 2nd ed. (Grand Rapids: Eerdmans,
   2005); C. E. Gutenson, *Reconsidering the Doctrine of God* (New York; London: T & T Clark,
   2005); C. Mostert, *God and the Future* (Edinburgh/London/New York: T & T Clark/Continuum,
   2002); I. Taylor, *Pannenberg on the Triune God* (London/New York: T & T Clark, 2007); and G.
   Wenz, *Introduction to Wolfhart Pannenberg's Systematic Theology*, trans. P. Stewart (Göttingen:
   Vandenhoeck & Ruprecht, 2013).

> Here is the eternal basis of God's coming forth from the immanence of the
> divine life as the economic Trinity and of the incorporation of creatures, medi-
> ated thereby, into the unity of the trinitarian life. The distinction and unity of
> the immanent and economic Trinity constitutes the heartbeat of the divine
> love, and with a single such heartbeat this love encompasses the whole world
> of creatures.[2]

"Here" refers to previous discussion of the eschatological consummation of God's loving fellowship with the creation. God's works—his "coming
forth"—include the sending of the Son and his life of obedience as well as the
coming of the Spirit and, for Pannenberg, the final state is the *basis* for these
(more of that later). Pannenberg distinguishes the "immanence of divine life"
from the work of God in the economy, yet there is a deep unity. Together, the
two are the "heartbeat of divine love" which holds the whole of creation. The
imagery of a "heartbeat" tells us that the immanent-economic distinction will
be dynamic, the pulse of the life of God and creation.

Pannenberg's account of the subordination of the Son to the Father relates
closely to this wider theological vision. The Son's submission cannot be merely
located in the economy, though it is most certainly economic. Pannenberg
will insist that to bring creation into God's love, the work of God must be
related to his eternal unity. To trace how he does this is to grasp something of
the import of the breathtaking ultimate paragraph of his *magnus opus*.

While this study focusses on the Father-Son relationship, that should not
be taken to mean that Pannenberg's account is similarly limited. His doctrine
of God is equally pneumatological.[3] At points I will allude to this, though
due to space constraints only allusion will be possible.

Problems in the Doctrine of God

Pannenberg's theology is both genuinely conservative and remarkably
revisionist. He holds that the triune God of Christian theology is the one
true God. He returns constantly to affirm the basic insights of the traditional
account of God and his way. He also finds that the doctrine of God faces
several challenges which it has never fully overcome.

One problem Pannenberg identifies is the relation of unity and triunity in
the doctrine of God. He claims that theology has often moved toward subordinationism, tritheism, and modalism, each of which challenges the claim
that the one God is triune.[4] In the first instance he observes that pre-Nicaean
thought distinguished the three persons of the Trinity by appealing to different functions or realms of activity. That is, the Trinity was understood

---

2.   Wolfhart Pannenberg, *Systematic Theology*, trans. Geoffrey W. Bromiley (Edinburgh: T & T Clark,
      1991–1997), 3:646.
3.   See *ST* 1:371–83.
4.   *ST* 1:270–71.

primarily from the economy. Yet the early theologians lacked a clear basis for drawing valid conclusions about the immanent Trinity on the basis of the economy. Pannenberg's assessment is that this approach inevitably led to a form of subordinationism, since on the basis of the economy it seems clear that the Son is subordinate to the Father, and the Spirit subordinate to the Son.[5] In contrast Athanasius and the Cappadocians emphasized the unity of the persons in the work of God and found distinctions in the inner relations. This approach, Pannenberg claims, risked tritheism.[6] Finally, Augustine and Aquinas, as well as Hegel and Barth, assumed the unity of God and derived the doctrine of the Trinity from divine unity—risking modalism.[7] As Pannenberg surveys these problems, he highlights Athanasius's idea of distinct persons, whose relations constitute their identities as a key insight which was never fully developed.[8]

Pannenberg identifies a similar problem in the relation of the immanent and economic Trinity.[9] There has been a very strong tendency to isolate "God in himself" and "God revealed." Pannenberg argues that, after the Nicene-Constantinopolitan Creed, "the thought of the eternal and essential Trinity broke loose from its historical moorings and tended to be seen . . . as untouched by the course of history . . . and therefore also inaccessible to all creaturely knowledge."[10] The opposite problem has emerged in the twentieth century, following Rahner's axiom of the identity of the economic and immanent Trinity.[11] This approach encouraged the identification of the economic and immanent Trinity and the "absorption of the immanent Trinity in the economic"—most radically in process theology.[12]

Pannenberg also has a positive concern to ground the doctrine of God in the historical revelation of the Jesus Christ.[13] He dismisses speculative derivations of God's triunity: "[T]o find a basis for the doctrine of the Trinity we must begin with the way in which Father, Son and Spirit come on the scene and relate to one another in the event of revelation."[14]

---

5. *ST* 1:274.

6. *ST* 1:271–79.

7. *ST* 1:282–89, 295–98.

8. *ST* 1:278.

9. *ST* 1:307–8, 367

10. *ST* 1:332. Not all commentators see Nicaea-Constantipole as falling into this error; see T. F. Torrance *The Trinitarian Faith* (Edinburgh: T & T Clark; 1993), 146.

11. See K. Rahner, *Theological Investigations* IV, trans. K. Smyth (London: Darton, Longman & Todd, 1966), 94.

12. *ST* 1:331.

13. This was an emphasis in his thought from his earliest publication of the "Dogmatic Theses." See "Dogmatic Theses on the Doctrine of Revelation," *Revelation and History*, ed. W. Pannenberg, trans. D. Granskou (London: Macmillan; 1968), 139 and the discussion in McClean, *From the Future*, 52–58.

14. *ST* 1:299.

Pannenberg affirms Barth's concern to relate the doctrine of the Trinity to revelation and prior to the discussion of God's attributes and nature. Barth's approach depends on the fact of revelation—that "God reveals himself as Lord."[15] Pannenberg, in contrast, holds that "we must begin with the relation of Jesus to the Father as it came to expression in his message of divine rule."[16]

The Historical Jesus and God

Pannenberg is committed to a "Christology from below," which begins with the historical reality of Jesus and his message and ministry and then moves to a fuller doctrine of God. In the first place, he emphasizes that Jesus distinguished himself from God: "the differentiation of God as Father from his own person is . . . constitutive for Jesus's message and attitude." Jesus proclaimed God the Father and his kingdom, not himself; he witnessed to the Father, sought to glorify the Father and honoured the claims of the first commandment to have no other God. Pannenberg notes how often in the gospels Jesus turn attention away from himself to God (e.g. Matt. 7:21; 11:27; Mark 10:17–18; John 10:29; 14:28). When he does speak about himself, he is the one who has been sent as a messenger (Matt. 10:40; Mark 12:6; Luke 14:17). He depends on the Father for his work (John 5:19–22, 30) and is authenticated by the Father's testimony (John 5:31–38). He depends on God, so Pannenberg observes that "this self-distinction from God finds it clearest expression in the prayer of Jesus to the Father." For Pannenberg, Jesus's self-differentiation from the Father is inherent to his message of the kingdom; he announced the reign of God and was, himself, a subject of that kingdom.[17] Pannenberg summarizes that "the aim of the whole message of Jesus is that the name of God should be hallowed by honouring his lordship."[18]

Pannenberg notes another complementary movement in Jesus's life. Jesus brought people into an experience of the kingdom offering eschatological salvation in his public ministry and declaring that "the coming rule of God was present already to the salvation of those who received his message." He was "the mediator of the inbreaking of the rule and the forgiving love of God."[19] To encounter Jesus was not only to be directed to acknowledge God as the coming ruler, but to meet God as the Lord in the present.[20] Thus, his ministry and message implied an intimate connection between his own identity and God's (Matt. 11:27). His announcement of the kingdom tied God's

15. Pannenberg recognizes that Barth viewed the statement as a summary of content of revelation and not merely a formal statement of the fact of revelation; yet he insists that "derivation from this formula, or its analysis . . . was still normative for Barth's development of the doctrine"; ST 2:303f n. 149.
16. ST 2:304.
17. ST 1:263.
18. ST 1:309.
19. ST 2:328–34; quote from p. 334.
20. Pannenberg accepts "the dominant view of New Testament exegetes" of the mid-twentieth century that Jesus did not directly identify himself as the Messiah or Son of God, see ST 2:364, 391.

identity as Father to his own identity as Son. "Jesus is the Son inasmuch as it is in his message of the nearness of the royal rule of the Father, his subjection to the Father's will, and especially the function of his sending as a revelation of the love of God, that this God may be known as Father."[21]

Pannenberg sets Jesus's self-distinction from the Father alongside his "close link" to the Father, so it should not be taken to imply that Jesus is distant from the Father. In fact, just the opposite is the case. Pannenberg sees the movements of distinction and unity as complementary rather than competing, because of the resurrection.

Before the resurrection, it was not clear that Jesus could be the submitting servant and the presence of kingdom; these seem to be claims in unresolved tension. Jesus's death seemed to make his claim about the kingdom an "illusion," and the "ambivalence was set aside only by the resurrection of the Crucified."[22] The resurrection confirmed Jesus's claims and their implications since his life was taken into unity with God. The significance of the resurrection depends on it being understood as an eschatological event and as an anticipation of the unity of all things with God.[23]

> Only by his resurrection . . . did Christ attain to the dignity of the Kyrios. . . . Only thus was he appointed the Son of God in power. . . . Only in the light of the resurrection is he the preexistent Son. Only as the risen Lord is he always the living Lord of his community.[24]

Pannenberg's Eschatological Metaphysic

We have traced Pannenberg's argument that in Jesus's life there is a double movement of distinction from and unity with God and that this apparent tension is retained and taken up into a fuller eternal reality in the resurrection. Such a view depends on Pannenberg's distinctive metaphysic.

In classic Aristotelian metaphysics, essences determine ends. A thing exists for a certain purpose or goal because it has an essence and this essence brings the thing into existence. Taking the example of a sphere, Aristotle concludes that "there *is* no other cause of the potential sphere's being an actual sphere; this was the essence of each."[25] That is, the sphere existed as a sphere because it contained "spherical essence." Through time, things develop into a full expression of what they are in essence. A seed is potentially a great tree; under correct conditions it will germinate and grow into just that kind of

---

21. *ST* 1:264.
22. *ST* 2:335–43, quotes from p. 343.
23. *ST* 2:344. The facticity of the resurrection also has to be established, and Pannenberg argues carefully for this; see *ST* 2:347–63.
24. *ST* 2:283ff. Mostert, *God*, 43, shows that "the resurrection of Jesus is of foundational importance in Pannenberg's theology."
25. Aristotle, *Aristotle in Twenty-three Volumes*. Vol. 17. *The Metaphysics. Books 1–9*, trans. H. Tredennick (London: Heinemann, 1975), VIII.vi.5, 425.

tree, and not any other. The outcome of the historical process is grounded in the essence which existed at the beginning of the process.

Pannenberg inverts Aristotle's claims and argues that end determines essence. He holds that what comes about at the end constitutes identity, and because it comes about in the end it is present, in anticipation, all along. What exists in the present depends on what it will be in the future.

Pannenberg's point is not simply that what comes about in the future determines the meaning of the past, but that things have their essence or reality because of *God's future*. God's future brings an end which completes and stabilizes the history which precedes it. If history offered only constant variation, then the future would always simply change the past. What is true now, would turn out to be not so in time. Death is the most dramatic example of this. A flourishing human life develops its full meaning through time, but is suddenly extinguished and nullified at death.[26] Apart from consummation in God's eternity, nothing and no one would have a stable identity or existence. The Christian conviction that all things find their completion in unity with God gives a promise of a stable future. Security of identity now is based on the final state of all things in God's future. Pannenberg expresses this by stating that things are what they are now in anticipation of what they will be in God's eternal future.

By placing essence in God's future, Pannenberg holds that the whole flow of history is taken up into final identity. Eschatological completion does not cancel or diminish what has come before, but sums it up and brings it into perfect unity. That which has been distended through time is unified in the future of eternity. Pannenberg uses the image of a musical chord in which the notes played as a melody are unified as a harmony.

Pannenberg's metaphysic means that historical existence "anticipates" eschatological reality. The concept of anticipation is both epistemological and ontological.[27] The epistemological notion is straightforward: a thing is revealed as it is and known and understood in its essence at the end of its existence and fully at the end of the historical process. It is only when all events have played out that we can finally say what each thing is. The ontological notion is counterintuitive: What is revealed as the essence is *determined* from the end of the process, so that a thing has its essence during the temporal process in anticipation of the final reality. The correlate to this claim is that because the essence has been present, in anticipation, throughout the process, it can be known provisionally before the end.

Pannenberg claims that his metaphysic allows for the historicity of knowledge without conceding the case to a thoroughgoing epistemological relativism. This is particularly important in theology, for discussion of God

---

26. This is a line of thought developed by the existentialist philosopher Heidegger, who was a significant foil for Pannenberg; see the discussion in McClean, *From the Future*, 77–79.

27. See also Mostert, *God,* 116.

is impossible if the case of epistemological relativism is granted, since true knowledge of the Absolute cannot be ultimately relative.[28]

The Doctrine of God

Once Pannenberg's metaphysic is clear, his move from the human history of Jesus to the structure of the triune life of God becomes obvious. Jesus's human life consists of movements of distinction from and unity with God as Father, which are integrated in his resurrection when his obedience to the Father is rewarded by his being taken up into heavenly life. What comes about in the resurrection is what has been true about Jesus from the beginning: "[W]hat has become evident in the resurrection . . . has been on the stage from the very beginning" and "it had been on stage from the very beginning because Jesus has been raised from the dead."[29] Pannenberg's appeal to his eschatological metaphysic allows him to move from the historical Jesus—the submissive human servant—and identify him as the eternal Son of God. On that basis, Pannenberg justifies the New Testament texts which include elements that are not strictly historical but are reflections of what was proleptically true and, thus, genuinely true of Jesus during his preresurrection ministry.

Trinitarian and anti-Trinitarian thinkers have viewed the submission of Jesus and his unity with the Father as opposing aspects of New Testament revelation, which demand some resolution by appeal to two-nature Christology or the distinction between the economic and essential Trinity. That is, they have argued that the Son submits to the Father in his humanity, or in the work of the Trinity *ad extra*. Anti-Trinitarians have found evidence of the irrationality of the doctrine of the Trinity in this tension, arguing that since the Son submits to the Father he cannot be regarded as equal with the Father.

Pannenberg says orthodox theology missed "the point" of texts which spoke of the Son's submission.[30] In his approach, Jesus's self-distinction from and unity with the Father together constitute the identity and divinity of the Son. Jesus, in fully accepting the lordship of God whom he called Father, so thoroughly embodied the kingdom of God that he was the kingdom, and that since in the kingdom God is all in all, then "as Jesus glorifies the deity of the Father . . . he himself . . . is so at one with the Father that God in eternity is Father only in relation to him." That is, Jesus's distinction from the Father is at the same time his unity with the Father. Pannenberg declares that this is "decisive" and "constitutive" for the Son's divinity.

---

28.   For a fuller discussion of the reasons which promoted Pannenberg to develop his metaphysic, see McClean, *From the Future*, 70–86.

29.   W. Panneberg, *Jesus—God and Man*, trans. L. L. Wilkins and D. A. Priebe (Philadelphia: Westminster, 1977), 137.

30.   *ST* 1:310; cf. *ST* 2:385–89.

> As the one who corresponds to the fatherhood of God, Jesus is the Son, and
> because the eternal God is revealed herein as Father, and is Father everywhere
> only as he is so in relation to the Son, the Son shares in his deity as the eternal
> counterpart of the Father.

While Pannenberg's doctrine of God is grounded in the historical human
life of Jesus, he expands the discussion to include other relations of Father,
Son, and Spirit in the history of redemption, expounding the whole of revelation in terms of the "mutual self-distinction" of Father, Son, and Spirit. He
argues that all "active relations" have a place in the "richly structured nexus of
relationship" of Trinitarian life.[31] He treats all economic relations as constitutive for the distinctions between the persons and for their deity. For example,
the following are all treated as constitutive for God: The Father hands over
kingdom to Son and receives it back; the Son obeys the Father and honors
him as God; the Spirit confirms, raises, and extols the Son; the Father gives
the Spirit to the Son and to all creation; the Spirit sheds abroad the Father's
love.[32] Pannenberg's distinctive claim is that economic relations not only
reveal God's triune life but in fact constitute this life.[33] Olson has called the
claim that God's deity is established in his economic lordship, that is that
God's being is his rule, "Pannenberg's Principle."[34]

Developing a doctrine of God from concrete relations revealed in salvation history runs counter to a long-held theological rule, based on a commitment to divine unity: that the work of God *ad extra* is undivided.[35] Pannenberg questions this rule though he does not return to the theological method
of the second and third centuries, which distinguished the persons on the basis
of "spheres of operation."[36] Rather, he appeals to "inner relations," revealed in
and established by salvation history. His metaphysic implies that relations of
history must be included in God's being. He aims to show that "the events of
history in some way bear on the identity of [God's] eternal essence."[37]

Theological tradition has treated references to the "generation" of the Son
(John 1:14; 3:16; Luke 3:22) and the "procession" of the Spirit (John 15:26;
20:22) as insights into the immanent Trinity.[38] Pannenberg argues that

---

31. *ST* 1:320.
32. *ST* 1:308–16, 320–23.
33. "Pannenberg argues that the very being of God, not just our knowledge of God, is determined by the cross and the resurrection of Jesus"; Mostert, "Eschatology," 81.
34. R. Olson, "Wolfhart Pannenberg's Doctrine of the Trinity," *SJT* 43 (1990): 199.
35. T. C. Oden, *The Living God* (San Francisco: Harper & Row, 1992), 57–58.
36. *ST* 1:271. Pannenberg asks: "Might it not be that this rule itself stands in need of revision? We need not surrender the basic truth that the Father, Son and Spirit work together . . . because we accept the possibility of distinguishing the persons in these works."
37. *ST* 1:334.
38. Pannenberg (*ST* 1:305) notes T. Aquinas, *Summa Theologiæ: Latin Text and English Translation, Introductions, Notes, Appendices and Glossaries*, ed. T. Gilby, 61 vols. (London: Eyre & Spottiswoode, 1967), 1.43.2.

modern exegesis shows that all such passages in fact deal with Jesus's historical, human life and the ministry of the Spirit. Yet recognizing that these texts
deal with the economy of salvation does not make them irrelevant to understanding the immanent life of God. In fact, the situation is just the opposite,
since the only path to knowledge of God-in-himself is through this historical
revelation: "One can know the inter-trinitarian distinctions and relations, the
inner life of God, only through the revelation of the Son, not through the
different spheres of the operation of the one God in the world."[39]

Diagram A. shows some of the key features of Pannenberg's doctrine of
God. For simplicity it deals with the relation of the Father and the Son. In the
diagram, created time runs on the x-axis from left to right and the dark arrow
represents the "retroactive power" of the future. Temporal experience is
reflected in the lighter "anticipation" arrow. Within this temporal framework
lie a series of events (creation, the sending of the Son, Jesus's obedience, the
cross, and the resurrection) in which the Father and the Son are related, in
mutual self-distinction, which is at the same time their unity. This is shown
with the zigzag series of arrows. Through this process, the creation is brought
more and more into unity with God, and this is shown by the cone which
expands within the wider cylinder, until their cross-section is identical at the
eschaton. It is important to note that this "until" is only apparent on the grey
line; from the point of view of retroactive ontology the cone and cylinder
converge *because* they are identical at the eschaton. In the consummation,
God's life and his fellowship with the creation consist of both the self-distinction and the unity of the Father and the Son.

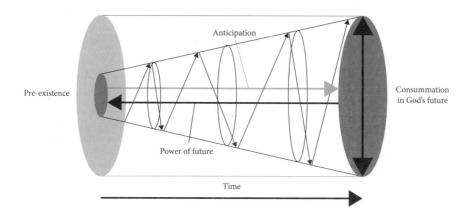

Diagram A: The self-distinction and unity of the Son and the Father through history

---

39.   *ST* 1:273.

Pannenberg's principle has further implications. He treats the relations as truly mutual, so that the Father-Son relation is constitutive for the Father as well as the Son. He extends Athanasius's argument that the Father could not be Father without the Son, asserting that not only is the Father's fatherhood found in relation to the Son, but his deity.[40] On Pannenberg's definition the lordship of the Father, mediated by the Son (Phil. 2:9ff.; 1 Cor. 15:24–25), "goes hand in hand with" deity. So, deity itself "has its place already in the intratrinitarian life of God, in the reciprocity of the relation between the Son, who freely subjects himself to the Lordship of the Father, and the Father, who hands over his lordship to the Son," and "the monarchy of the Father is itself mediated by the trinitarian relations."[41]

The assertion that the relationship of the Father with the Son constitutes the deity of the Father contrasts with a general view that the monarchy of the Father is foundational for the relations of the Trinity. Jenson identifies this as one of the three innovations in Pannenberg's doctrine of God.[42] Mostert confirms that this "is a departure from the classical doctrine of the priority of the Father over the Son and the Spirit."[43]

Pannenberg's conception of mutual relations must not be confused with "equivalent" relations, for "self-distinction" does not mean exactly the same thing for each of the three persons.[44] The mutual relations constitute the distinctions of the persons, and there is an order in the relations. Monarchy must be ascribed to the Father, while the Son is the "locus of the monarchy of the Father."[45] The Spirit is the condition and medium of fellowship between Father and Son.[46] Thus Pannenberg presents a doctrine of the Trinity in which the deity, distinctive identity, and unity of each of the persons is constituted in and through the others.[47]

Pannenberg uses the term "subordination," stating that "this uniqueness of Jesus rested on the unconditional subordination of his person to the lordship of God . . . only in this subordination to the rule of the one God is he

---

40.   *ST* 1:322.

41.   *ST* 1:325.

42.   R. Jenson, "Jesus in the Trinity: Wolfhart Pannenberg's Christology and Doctrine of the Trinity," in *The Theology of Wolfhart Pannenberg*, eds. C. Braaten and P. Clayton (Minneapolis: Augsburg, 1988), 199.

43.   C. Mostert, "From Eschatology to Trinity: Pannenberg's Doctrine of God," *Pacifica* 10 (February 1997): 82.

44.   *ST* 1:321.

45.   *ST* 1:322–25; "The relation of the Son to the Father is characterised in eternity by the subordination to the Father, by the self-distinction from the majesty of the Father, which took historical form in the human relation of Jesus to God"; *ST* 2:372–79.

46.   *ST* 1:316.

47.   "That means that each of the three persons must be understood as related to each other as *others* and as distinct from themselves. It does not mean . . . that they should be conceived individualistically. . . . Rather, they are constituted as distinct persons by their inner trinitarian relations, although these cannot be reduced to mere relations or origin"; Olson, "Pannenberg's," 191.

the Son."[48] He explains that by distinguishing the Father from himself as the one God, the Son moved out of the unity of the deity and became man, but in doing so he actively expressed his divine essence as the Son. The self-emptying of the Pre-existent One is thus not a surrender or negation of his deity as the Son, it is its activation.[49] While he uses the terms "subordination," it is not right to describe his view of the Son as subordinationist, because the Father is dependent on the Son. Pannenberg refers to the Father "handing over his lordship to the Son" and thus "his kingship [is] dependent on whether the Son glorifies him and fulfils his Lordship." This means that the reality of God's lordship "has its place in the intratrinitarian life of God, in the reciprocity of the relation between the Son . . . and the Father."[50]

Augustine rejected the view that the deity and attributes of the persons of the Trinity are conditioned and constituted in their mutual relations because it would mean that the persons would have neither their attributes nor their deity each for himself (*ad se*).[51] Pannenberg comments that "Augustine was not simply rejecting an inappropriate formulation of Nicene doctrine but missing one of its points . . . that the relations between the persons are constitutive not merely for their distinction but also for their deity."[52] Thus, Pannenberg reclaims what he takes to be the intent of traditional formulations, working through them more fully and setting them on better foundations.

Toward the end of his presentation of the doctrine of the Trinity, Pannenberg presents a fairly complete conceptualization of the triune God. He claims to have shown that theology should "understand the trinitarian persons, *without derivation* from a divine essence that differs from them, as centres of action of the one movement which embraces and permeates them all—the movement of the divine Spirit who has his existence only in them."[53]

Although he builds his doctrine of the God on the idea of mutual self-distinction of the persons of the Trinity, Pannenberg does not identify the economic and immanent Trinity in such a way that there is no eternal essence. He rejects a view of "a divine becoming in history"—that is, he does not hold to what is often termed "process" theology.[54] Although Pannenberg can, at points, seem to be a process theologian, this is to misunderstand him. Certainly, he holds that God's identity is determined by the events of history, but this is true only because the God dwells fully in his own future which is

---

48. *ST* 2:372–73.
49. *ST* 2:377.
50. *ST* 2:313.
51. *ST* 1:323, ref. to Augustine, *De trinitate* 6.1.2., 6.2.3., 7.1.2.
52. *ST* 1:323.
53. *ST* 1:385, original emphasis. Grenz, *Reason*, 49 summaries, "Pannenberg offers a radical reinterpretation of self-differentiation . . . namely, that the essence of person lies in the act of giving oneself to one's counterpart and thereby gaining one's identity from the other."
54. *ST* 1:331 and see Bradshaw, *Pannenberg*, 42.

anticipated in history. Pannenberg's eschatological metaphysic means he is not a process theologian.[55]

In Pannenberg's exposition of the Trinity "mutual self-distinction" and "salvation history" are inseparable. If inner Trinitarian relations are not constituted by salvation history, then the dynamic of mutual self-distinction cannot be maintained. Pannenberg argues that if the relations are already determined in terms of origin, and simply revealed in salvation history, then the doctrine of the Trinity will have to appeal to static and non-mutual relations as the basis for God's unity and deity. On his terms, if salvation history is removed from the presentation, then the description of God's triune life will collapse. On the other hand, if salvation history is not the story of God who is fully involved, then it will no longer be salvation history. For only as an expression of real involvement of God with his creation can it be the story of the "revelation of divine love," which "will finally lead . . . to participation in his glory."[56] Remove economic mutual self-distinction of the persons of the Trinity and salvation history is only history, and not really even that, for without its final horizon it will no longer be a "history" but only unrelated events.

Assessment

Pannenberg's innovative approach offers a dynamic description of the Trinity which presents God's eternity as simultaneity, rather than timelessness.[57] Divine eternity consists of Father, Son, and Spirit in mutual relation, moving together in distinction from one another and constituted in their own identities through their unity, realized in God's life with his creation; thus can eternity hold all time.[58] Pannenberg can affirm that the Son is subordinate to the Father and insist that the Father is dependent on the Son. He can include the "relations of origin" in his doctrine of the Trinity, but also insist that relations of origin are not the entirety of divine life.

Pannenberg's view of God's triune life is not one of submission and authority but intimate dynamic love. History is "the way in which the divine love declares itself."[59] Consequently, the mediation of time and eternity through

55. Olson, "Pannenberg's," 175–206 suspects that Pannenberg is Hegelian by tying God's self-actualization to history (and so a process theologian). Grenz shows that Pannenberg makes it very clear that he is not a process theologian, Grenz, Reasons, 186; and see Mostert, God, 227–30.

56. ST 3:642–44.

57. ST 1:405.

58. If the presence of the future were not a Trinitarian reality, then the thought of an eternal essence would become "a timeless abstraction" with no "temporal distinction" nor "the quality of life itself"; W. Pannenberg, "Eternity, Time and the Trinitarian God," in Trinity, Time and Church: A Response to the Theology of Robert W. Jenson, ed. Colin E. Gunton (Grand Rapids/Cambridge: Eerdmans, 2000), 70.

59. ST 3:644. Pannenberg writes: "If eternity and time coincide only in the eschatological consummation of history, then from the standpoint of the history of God that moves toward this consummation there is room for becoming in God himself, namely in the relation on the immanent and economic Trinity, and in this frame it is possible to say of God that he himself became something that he previously was not when he became man in his Son"; ST 1:438 and see 422–48.

the relation of the immanent and economic Trinity allows for the existence of plurality in the life of God. The God who is realized in the real relations of history cannot be solitary or static. This provides the basis for the plurality of creatures, and their sharing in the eternal glory of God; for if history is in fact the self-realization of God, then from the start creation already shares in the life of God.[60] Historical events participate in God's eternity not "vertically," in imitation of eternity; but "horizontally," along the timeline of history, in anticipation of their full participation in the eschaton. Since this involves all of history, it relates to the doctrine of creation and to the life duration of each creature, as well as to events which are particularly identified as salvific.[61]

Pannenberg relates the multiplicity of temporal reality to divine eternity. Multiplicity is found at every point of temporal experience: in the events of history, in the variety of divine attributes, in the uncertainty of truth claims and the relativity of knowledge, in the complex discussion of historical theology, in the many forms of revelation, in the diversity of human religious and cultural expression, in the proliferation of creatures, in the range of Christian denominations and their inability to reach unity, in the humanity of Christ and in the various works ascribed to the Spirit. He asks how the one God can truly be the source and goal of such a diverse reality? His answer is to understand all history as the work of a mutually self-differentiating triune God so diversity is the work of the one God who exists always in unity and distinction.

In the face of obvious diversity and little apparent unity, Pannenberg's claim would be bizarre and nonsensical, except that he appeals to the eschaton as the point at which true "unity in distinction" will emerge. At the same time, he claims that we must see that essence, which emerges in the eschaton, has been present all along. Reality in all its diversity is already, in anticipation, bound in "unity in distinction" in the love of God. This is Pannenberg's Christian ontology: proclaiming the love of God for all creation, revealed in Christ, completed in the Spirit, consummated in the eschatological and eternal life of Father, Son, and Spirit.[62]

Tonstad argues that Pannenberg's approach fails to deliver what he claims, and is, in fact, hierarchical and lacks "true reciprocity and mutuality" between the persons.[63] He argues that by insisting that the events of the life of Jesus constitute eternal relations, then Pannenberg cannot avoid the implication that obedience, and hence subordination, characterize the eternal relations. He notes that Pannenberg asserts that the Son's obedience "is not the alien obedience of the slave," but the "expression of his free agreement

---

60.   *ST* 1:407.

61.   *ST* 1:410.

62.   *ST* 1:432–41.

63.   Linn Tonstad, "'The Ultimate Consequence of his Self-distinction from the Father . . .': Difference and Hierarchy in Pannenberg's Trinity," *NZSTh* 51, no. 4 (2009): 390.

with the Father."[64] He argues that there is no basis to claim that economic obedience and submission are transformed into free agreement, rather that Pannenberg's logic implies "the missions are read back into the processions and mutually constitutive divine relations such that the eternal Trinitarian relations correspond fully to the submission seen in the life of Jesus." Presumably, Pannenberg's reply would be that the other elements of the relation, both economically and eternally, are the perfect unity of the Father and the Son, and the Father's own divinity being constituted in the work of the Son. Nevertheless, Tonstad's question about the success of Pannenberg's move from the economic to the eternal remains.

Tonstad is even more concerned that Pannenberg makes the self-emptying of the Son, most fully expressed in his death, the basis of the Son's self-distinction. He argues that "since the cross is remembered in eternity, the relation between self-distinction and death is part of the concrete self-distinction of Trinitarian persons that constitutes them as who they are."[65] For Pannenberg, the Son's self-distinction constitutes divine identity, it is not only to deal with human sin, thus it is difficult to see how Pannenberg can assert that the Father and Son have a mutually dependent relationship, when the self-distinction of the Son requires his abnegation.

Tonstad seeks a fully egalitarian doctrine of the Trinity, a "non-hierarchical, non-competitive account of the Trinity," and laments that Pannenberg's account is not able to provide this.[66] I am not persuaded by his alternative. Still, he is right to draw attention to the difficulties which flow from transposing Jesus's death into the eternal relations.

There is another feature of Pannenberg's account that raises questions about his approach. As I have noted, for Pannenberg, history is transformed into the eternal reality in which God's love "encompasses the whole world of creatures." For this to be so, God's love for the world must be the content of the history of Jesus, so history is an expression of God's love.[67] Love as the content of both history and eternity then constitutes essence of the triune life.

This intimate correlation of divine love in history and eternity with God's essence creates an ambiguity, at least, as to the status of God's wrath. On the one hand, the final state cannot include God's wrath, since this would compromise the consistent love of God in himself. In turn, Pannenberg must be able to show that the elements of history that seem not be an expression of God's love can be included into an eternity of love, so that together the movement between the two "constitutes the heartbeat of the divine love." Is it possible for Pannenberg to do so, on the basis of his own thought?

---

64. *ST* 2:316.
65. Tonstad, "Ultimate Consequence," 393.
66. Tonstad, "Ultimate Consequence," 398.
67. *ST* 1:422.

Pannenberg does not deny the reality of divine wrath but he will not allow that it is a divine attribute.[68] He states that when eternity enters time it does so as judgement, revealing the inner contradictions in all human lives. Apart from God's reconciling work "lives necessarily perish of the inner contradictions of their existence." If the outcome of judgement is destruction then the account of the economy as the expression of God's love and power in reconciliation is compromised.[69] It is only because God is the faithful Creator and Redeemer that eternity becomes *purifying* judgement.[70] Pannenberg holds out the strong hope that there is a "universal perspective" to salvation in Christ, and elements of life that have been lived in alienation from and enmity to God will be removed, leaving lives which can be fully incorporated into the love of God. So, "the judgement which is put in Christ's hand is no longer destruction, but a fire of purging and cleansing."[71]

There, is however, a "wrinkle" in Pannenberg's presentation. Because of the clear statements about eternal judgement and destruction in the New Testament, Pannenberg allows that some "who persist irreconcilably in turning aside from God" may be destroyed since "nothing may remain when the fire of divine glory has purged away all that is incompatible with God's presence." He insists that this is "a borderline case."[72] The predominant emphasis of the New Testament is the work of the Son and the Spirit to purify and unite creation.

Thus, Pannenberg seeks to isolate economic wrath and destructive judgement of destruction from the eternal state, so that wrath is not an attribute of God. Wrath is the historical manifestation of the God of love who purifies creation to bring all things into unity.

The "wrinkle" created by this approach can be seen in two ways. On the one hand, Pannenberg cannot express fully the biblical witness to divine wrath. It is not sufficient to suggest that there may be some "borderline cases" in which judgement leads to destruction.[73] On the other hand, his account that all of creation is included in the single heartbeat of divine love is compromised. Even a few creatures lost in judgement introduces a significant rupture in the divine heartbeat.

Mattes highlights this issue when he comments that Pannenberg "unwind[s] the tensions of certain Lutheran paradoxes." He refers to the dialectics in Luther's thought between grace and wrath ("gospel" and "law") in God's relation to the world and asks, "Can we not agree with Luther . . .

68. *ST* 1:439.
69. *ST* 1:420.
70. *ST* 1:610–11.
71. *ST* 1:619.
72. *ST* 1:620.
73. G. C. Berkouwer, *The Providence of God* (Grand Rapids: Eerdmans, 1974), 256 argues that any attempt to "get rid of the idea of Divine wrath . . . thrusts inimically at the entire revelation of God," and gives a summary of the importance of the theme of wrath in biblical revelation (258–61).

that the outworking of God's rule in the cosmos entails perhaps an economy of death?" He suggests that "if . . . wrath as an alien work can be seen as a legitimate aspect of God's quest to establish the divine rule in the cosmos," then Luther's dialectic "could be a helpful corrective to Pannenberg's metaphysics."[74] Luther recognized that God acts in judgement and adopted the language of Isaiah to call God's judgement an "alien work" (Isa. 28:21).[75] For Pannenberg, however, the presence of an alien work in history compromises the identity of God as the triune Infinite of holy love.

Placing God's wrath in a treatment of the attributes of the God of love is a challenge for all theology. Boersma, dealing with similar issues, recognizes this and the risk that the primacy of love may be compromised. However, he calls for an approach which allows even this element of Scripture to have a place in a theology: "fears of such a dualist understanding of God should not tempt us into ignoring the biblical expressions of God's wrath."[76] Pannenberg's theology is drawn into just this temptation.

Is it possible to adjust Pannenberg's thought to include wrath as a divine attribute, albeit a secondary one, while holding to his view of a rich mutual Trinitarian relations? Not on Pannenberg's term. For him, Jesus's life determines divine identity as the basis on which the totality of history is embraced in God's love. It is impossible for Pannenberg to separate the outcome of history as a whole from the reconciling work of God in Christ and the realization of the divinity of God. If Pannenberg conceived of the economy and God's identity as less tightly correlated, then his thought would be able to accommodate the tension. Such a reconception would, however, require a revision of his metaphysical proposal, since it would no longer hold the same relation of the eternal God with history.

Thus, for all the attraction of Pannenberg's doctrine of God, it does not seem to be sustainable; or at least there are significant questions, which mean that it is not preferable to classical formulations. Tonstad argues that his position cannot establish genuinely reciprocal relations in the Trinity. I have argued that his approach cannot successfully include God's wrath. Rather than seeking to transpose all the economic relations of the Father and the Son into an account of eternal mutually dependent relations, it seems better to continue with the classic tradition. This approach will affirm that the economic submission of the Son has to be understood in a twofold way—it is the proper human submission of the incarnate Son to his God and is it the fitting analogical expression of the *ad intra* Father-Son relation which we signify by the phrase "eternal generation."

---

74.   Mark Mattes, "Pannenberg's Achievement: An analysis and Assessment of His 'Systematic Theology,'" *CTM* 26 (February 1999): 60.

75.   M. Luther, "Lectures on Isaiah," *Luther's Works*, ed. J. Pelikan (St. Louis: Concordia, 1968), 16:233–34.

76.   H. Boersma, *Violence, Hospitality, and the Cross* (Grand Rapids: Baker, 2004), 48.

Bibliography

Aristotle, *Aristotle in Twenty-three Volumes.* Volume 17. *The Metaphysics. Books 1–9*, translated by H. Tredennick. London: Heinemann, 1975.

Berkouwer, G. C. *The Providence of God.* Grand Rapids: Eerdmans, 1974.

Boersma, H. *Violence, Hospitality, and the Cross*, Grand Rapids: Baker, 2004.

Bradshaw, Timothy, *Pannenberg: A Guide for the Perplexed.* London/New York: T & T Clark, 2009.

Grenz, S. J. *Reason for Hope: The Systematic Theology of Wolfhart Pannenberg.* 2nd ed. Grand Rapids: Eerdmans, 2005.

Gutenson, C. E. *Reconsidering the Doctrine of God.* New York; London: T & T Clark, 2005.

Jenson, Robert W. "Jesus in the Trinity: Wolfhart Pannenberg's Christology and Doctrine of the Trinity." In *The Theology of Wolfhart Pannenberg: Twelve American Critiques with an Autobiographical Essay and Response*, edited by Carl Braaten and Philip Clayton, 188–206. Minneapolis: Augsburg, 1988.

Luther, M. "Lectures on Isaiah." *Luther's Works*, vol. 16. Edited by J. Pelikan. St. Louis: Concordia, 1968.

Mattes, Mark. "Pannenberg's Achievement: An Analysis and Assessment of His 'Systematic Theology.'" *Currents in Theology and Mission* 26 (February 1999): 51–60.

McClean, John. *From the Future: Getting to Grips with Pannenberg's Thought.* Milton Keynes: Paternoster, 2012.

Mostert, C. *God and the Future.* Edinburgh/London/New York: T & T Clark/ Continuum, 2002.

Olson, Roger. "Trinity and Eschatology: The Historical Being of God in Jürgen Moltmann and Wolfhart Pannenberg." *Scottish Journal of Theology* 36 (1983): 213–27.

Pannenberg, Wolfhart. "Dogmatic Theses on the Doctrine of Revelation." In *Revelation and History*, edited by W. Pannenberg, translated by D. Granskou, 123–58. London: Macmillan, 1968.

_____. "Eternity, Time and the Trinitarian God." *Dialog* 39, no. 1 (2000): 9–14.

_____. *Jesus—God and Man.* Edited by L. L. Wilkins. Translated by D. A. Priebe. 2nd English ed. Philadelphia: Westminster, 1977.

_____. *Metaphysics and the Idea of God.* Translated by Philip Clayton. Grand Rapids: Eerdmans, 1990.

_____. *Systematic Theology.* Translated by Geoffrey Bromiley. 3 vols. Grand Rapids: Eerdmans; Edinburgh: T & T Clark, 1991, 1994, 1997.

_____. *Theology and the Philosophy of Science.* Translated by F. McDonagh. London: Darton, Longman & Todd, 1976.

Taylor, I. *Pannenberg on the Triune God.* London/New York: T & T Clark, 2007.

Tonstad, Linn. "'The Ultimate Consequence of his Self-distinction from the Father . . .': Difference and Hierarchy in Pannenberg's Trinity." *NZSTh* 51, no. 4 (2009): 383–99.

Torrance, T. F. *The Trinitarian Faith*. Edinburgh: T & T Clark, 1993.

Wenz, Gunther. *Introduction to Wolfhart Pannenberg's Systematic Theology*. Translated by P. Stewart. Göttingen: Vandenhoeck & Ruprecht, 2013.

CHAPTER 12

Classical Trinitarianism and Eternal Functional Subordination

Some Historical and Dogmatic Reflections

STEPHEN R. HOLMES

Introduction

There has been considerable energy in Anglophone evangelical theology in recent years devoted to the ideas of "eternal functional subordination" (EFS) or "eternal relationships of authority and submission" (ERAS).[1] Alongside a number of book-length engagements,[2] there have been many confer-

1. This paper was originally written for the 2016 ETS Conference, at the invitation of the Theology and Gender group. I am grateful for the invitation, and for helpful discussion at the conference.
2. To sample, merely: Kevin Giles, *The Trinity and Subordinationism: The Doctrine of God and the Contemporary Gender Debate* (Downers Grove: IVP, 2002); Giles, *Jesus and the Father: Modern Evangelicals Reinvent the Doctrine of the Trinity* (Grand Rapids: Zondervan, 2006); Millard J. Erickson, *Who's Tampering with the Trinity? An Assessment of the Subordination Debate* (Grand Rapids: Kregel, 2009); Denis Jowers and H. Wayne House, eds., *The New Evangelical Subordinationism? God the Father and God the Son* (Eugene, OR: Pickwick, 2012); Bruce A. Ware and John Starke, eds., *One God in Three Persons: Unity of Essence, Distinction of Persons, Implications for Life* (Wheaton, IL: Crossway, 2016).

ence papers and, in the summer of 2016, a whirlwind of blog posts. The debate
has been highly charged, with accusations of heresy being freely thrown on every
side; it has its origins in an attempt to link a particular account of gender roles
with the doctrine of the Trinity, through a leveraging of 1 Corinthians 11:3.

Whatever the merits of the appeal to that particular Pauline text, and so
of the argument about gender roles,[3] the claims about Trinitarian doctrine are
interesting. Both sides of the (regularly acrimonious) debate are apparently
convinced that there is a relatively monolithic tradition of Trinitarian orthodoxy that supports their position. I have argued before that, historically, the
church's teaching on the Trinity has been remarkably unified;[4] assuming that
argument was right, which side (if either) of this contemporary evangelical
debate can claim fidelity to that heritage? I argue in what follows that there is
no possible space for EFS/ERAS in classical Trinitarianism; any such doctrine
will necessarily be a departure from that tradition.

Defining "Trinitarian"

The confessional basis of the American Evangelical Theological Society,
like many other symbolic documents, includes a clause about the doctrine of
the Trinity: "God is a Trinity, Father, Son, and Holy Spirit, each an uncreated
person, one in essence, equal in power and glory." I reflect that this is not particularly well drafted; in particular, the natural grammatical reading of "one in
essence" is that it refers to the immediately prior subject, and so insists that each
person is one in essence, which is rather unfortunate. Grammar aside, though,
we can ask about theology: How adequate a definition of the doctrine of the
Trinity is this? There are two parts to this (my qualms about drafting aside):
there is clearly nothing here that is repugnant to Trinitarian orthodoxy; but is
believing this clause sufficient to Trinitarian orthodoxy? Or does one need to
believe not only this but something more to be adequately Trinitarian?

Asking such questions highlights that the word "Trinitarian" demands
definition, and the first point I want to make is that the only possible definition it may gain is historical. Scripture teaches us much about the nature of
deity, and about the relationships of the Son to the Father, and so on, and of
course we should believe all these things. But Scripture does not define for us
the word "Trinitarian"—the word is not a biblical one.

Now, of course, we could define the word by asserting that "Trinitarian"
means "believing that which the Bible teaches about Father, Son, and Spirit,"
but such a procedure would be unhelpful. Consider the ETS's confession: It
is a matter of record that the requirement to be Trinitarian was inserted to
prevent those who claimed to believe the Bible, but who denied the Trinity,
from seeking membership. This highlights the fact that the word "Trinitar-

---

3. I hold fairly strongly to the view that there are no good arguments from the doctrine of the Trinity to any
    human sociality, including gender roles in marriage or church, but that is not the theme of this essay.
4. See Stephen R. Holmes, *The Holy Trinity: Understanding God's Life* (Milton Keynes: Paternoster, 2012).

ian" has typically been used to judge the adequacy of various proposed readings of Scripture. Arians, Socinians, Unitarians, Jehovah's Witnesses, Oneness
Pentecostals, and various others all read Scripture wrongly because they fail
to read it in a Trinitarian way. That sentence only makes sense if we accept
that "Trinitarian" means something more definite than merely "whatever I
think the Bible teaches—that is, that the claim "Scripture teaches a Trinitarian
doctrine of God" is substantive, and not merely a tautology.

Perhaps a parallel example will help here: Consider the word "Calvinist";
it is similarly undefined biblically, and similarly proposes a body of teaching
that claims to be biblical, but that others regard as a poor reading of Scripture
(in this case, of course, the dividing lines are between evangelical believers).
Calvinists hold a particular set of ideas about fallenness, grace, faith, and election; they hold to these ideas because they believe that they are in fact taught
in Scripture, but the word "Calvinist" refers to that definite and limited set
of ideas, not to whatever doctrine someone claims to find in Scripture. The
Arminian may argue "The biblical doctrine of grace is not Calvinist" and have
something meaningful to say.

In both cases, then, there is no possible biblical challenge over the definition of the term, only over the correctness of the doctrine so denoted. Of
course, I might challenge the definition—the claim that it is not authentically
Calvinist to hold to a limited atonement is an example that has been essayed
more than once. The only meaningful court of appeal here will be to history:
"Calvinist" describes a historical tradition that has its origins in the Genevan
reformer, and is generally considered to find a key point of development in
the Synod of Dort; the idea of limited atonement develops during that history
(the first explicit articulation, I believe, was in Beza's responses to Andreae at
the Montbéliard Colloquy in 1586[5]); any argument that the idea is, or is not,
authentically "Calvinist" will turn on a telling of this history.

Mention of Dort takes me to a second point, slightly more controversial:
Not only must we define "Trinitarian" historically, we cannot do it by simple
appeal to this or that historical document. This is the thesis of Barnes's decisive essay, "The Fourth Century as Trinitarian Canon."[6] It is at least argu-
able that the Canons of Dort provide a definitive account of what it is to be
"Calvinist"—that argument must be historical in form, of course, but once
made and accepted permits a certain abstraction from history. I do not need
to know the details of the arguments surrounding Jacobus Arminius and
Johannes Wtenbogaert (the author of the *Five Articles of Remonstrance*) to be

---

5. On the various arguments adduced concerning predestination there see Jill Raitt, *The Colloquy of
    Montbéliard: Religion and Politics in the Sixteenth Century* (Oxford: Oxford University Press, 1993),
    147–55 and Gottfried Adam, *Der Streit um die Prädestination im ausgehenden 16. Jahrhundert: Eine
    Untersuchung zu den Entwurfen von Samuel Huber und Aegidius Hunnius* (Neukirchen: Neukirchener
    Verlag, 1970), 29–49.
6. Michel Rene Barnes, "The Fourth Century as Trinitarian Canon," in *Christian Origins: Theology,
    Rhetoric, and Community*, eds. Lewis Ayres and Gareth Jones (London: Routledge, 1998), 47–67.

able to determine whether a position is authentically Calvinist or not; I have a canon, or rather a set of canons, to measure it by. My claim here is that there is no similar canon, no similar defining symbolic document, for Trinitarianism.

This is not an obvious position, in that there are at least three apparent candidates, the decrees of the Councils of Nicaea and Constantinople, and the document we know as the Nicene Creed. It is not hard, however, to show that these are inadequate. The simplest summary of orthodox Trinitarianism, the one routinely taught to first year undergraduates, goes *"mia ousia, treis hypostases."* But none of our three documents teach this formula. Famously, Nicaea actually anathematises all who teach more than one hypostasis in the Godhead;[7] Constantinople, or at least that summary of it that has reached us, makes no mention of *ousia* or *hypostasis* at all;[8] the Creed will insist the Son is *homoousios ton Patri*, but says nothing similar of the Holy Spirit, and, again, does not use the word *hypostasis* at all. These documents, vital though they are, simply do not codify what we now call Trinitarianism.

So how do we define "trinitarian"? Barnes's argument in the paper cited above is that this core Christian doctrine is determined by the debate that, roughly put, occurs between Nicaea and Constantinople—I would want to add Augustine's interpretation of the Nicene heritage also (which I do not think Barnes would deny, but it was not the focus of his argument then). If we are to understand what the demand to be trinitarian means, we need to be attentive to the fourth-century debates, and to understand the doctrine that underlay the affirmations—and particularly the condemnations—made at Constantinople.

The first canon that has come down to us from that Council (one of the undisputed ones) affirms the faith of Nicaea and then condemns a series of positions by name alone. We are told that Eunomians, Arians, semi-Arians, Sabellians, Marcellians, Photinians, and Apollinarians are all wrong. The orthodox doctrine of the Trinity is that teaching which falls into none of these errors, but it is not spelled out. This is not a surprise; patristic theology tended to make progress by denying the possibility of various positions. We might on this basis assert that orthodox Trinitarianism is more of a space than a doctrine, and suggest that any account that does not fall foul of these various strictures can stand. There are two problems with this, however. The first is that it does not overcome the basic point that I am arguing here: even if we accept that claim completely, to determine the limits of orthodoxy we will need to discover what Eunomius, Sabellius, Marcellus, Photinus, and the rest taught. This will, inevitably, be historical work.

Second, the history is not generally read as leaving a blank space between these various heresies. What is left when they are all excluded is something

---

7. Τοὺς δὲ λέγοντας . . . Ἐξ ἑτέρας ὑποστάσεως ἢ οὐσίας φάσκοντας εἶναι . . . τούτους ἀναθεματίζει ἡ ἁγία καθολικὴ καὶ ἀποστολικὴ ἐκκλησία (from the Creed of Nicaea).

8. The closest to a Trinitarian formula comes in the fifth canon, which merely affirms the single deity of Father, Son, and Spirit.

quite specific and defined, which we might term Cappadocian Trinitarianism (locating Augustine as the most capable interpreter of that tradition). Now, Barnes certainly suggests in the paper I have cited that there were two strands of presentation here: one, represented by Rome, Alexandria, and later Augustine, locating Arius as the heresiarch of the century and interpreting later errors as different modes of repeating his core errors; and the other represented supremely by the Cappadocians seeing Arius as a fairly minor aberration, and seeing the great elenctic task as opposing Eunomius. There is not here, however, a difference of doctrine, so much as a difference over who the doctrine was to be defined against. Further, it is fair to say that in the two decades since Barnes wrote that paper there has been a massive and compelling body of patristic scholarship on the fourth century that has at least softened the edges of this picture, and that has found the presentation of later non-Nicene theologies as dependent on Arius to be a move more political than theological.[9]

The presenting problem for fourth-century theology was two equally biblical, but apparently contradictory, modes of discourse concerning the divine life. On the one hand, Christians, like the people of Israel, are called to an uncompromising loyalty to one God alone; on the other, Christians speak of Father, Son, and Spirit as each being divine. The Constantinopolitan list of heresies bears witness to this: Arians, semi-Arians, and Eunomians err in so stressing the diversity of Father and Son (or, in the case of the semi-Arians, Father and Spirit) that they deny the divine unity; Sabellians, Marcellians, and Photinians err in so stressing the divine unity that they deny any real distinct existence of the three divine persons.

I have written at some length elsewhere[10] on how these debates played out, and tried to delineate the careful theological moves that enable the Cappadocian statement of a convincing doctrine that falls into neither error. I do not intend to repeat that material here; but I reiterate that this history, famously complex as it is, is the only available definition we have of what it is to be Trinitarian. This does not mean, of course, that every one who wishes to claim to be Trinitarian must become an expert in fourth-century doctrinal history; it does mean that when a question arises about what is acceptably Trinitarian, then the only proper court of appeal is to a careful statement and consideration of this history. And so I turn to the novel—they are novel, as will become clear—ideas clustered around the slogans "eternal functional subordination" (hereafter EFS) and "eternal relations of authority and submission" (hereafter ERAS). How do these sorts of ideas relate to this complex and historically defined term, "Trinitarian"?

The first thing we must insist is that biblical exegesis has no purchase on this question. This is not a surrender of biblical authority, but a consequence of what I have so far argued about the term "Trinitarian" being only definable historically.

---

9.   Lewis Ayres, *Nicaea and Its Legacy: An Approach to Fourth-Century Trinitarian Theology* (Oxford: Oxford University Press, 2004) remains the key text here.

10. Holmes, *The Holy Trinity*, 82–120.

Suppose I came to be convinced both that the Scriptures teach EFS (or ERAS), and that the position was nonetheless incompatible with those positions developed in the fourth century: The proper claim then is not that EFS was compatible with Trinitarian orthodoxy, but that (so-called) trinitarian orthodoxy was unbiblical. I would have arrived in the position of the Jehovah's Witnesses, or the Oneness Pentecostals, of rejecting Trinitarianism out of faithfulness to (what I perceived to be) the biblical revelation. To return to my former analogy, I might attempt to prove that the doctrine of unconditional election is false from the Scriptures, but I cannot prove that it is not a proper tenet of Calvinism by exegesis. In exactly the same way, I can try to prove that a position, be it EFS, or confession of the *filioque*, or inseparable operations, or divine simplicity, is right by appeal to Scripture, but I cannot, necessarily, prove that a position is Trinitarian by the same procedure. That judgment can only ever be arrived at historically.[11]

The Distinction between God's Eternal Life and God's Actions in the World

Proposals such as EFS or ERAS, as their names suggest, are claims about the eternal life of God—about who God is *in se*. Just as the saying of the incarnate Son that "the Father is greater than I" does not lead to Arianism because it reflects the state of humiliation occasioned by the incarnation, not the eternal equality of Father and Son, so demonstrations of an obedience or submission of the Son to the Father that refer to the Son's state of humiliation are not adequate to prove an eternal subordination or submission. At one level, of course, this is uncontentious, but there is a point where we need to be careful. The proper distinction here is one that concerns the divine life, and is between theology and economy, not one that concerns the Son's state, and so is between pre-incarnate and incarnate, or humiliation and glorification.

This plays into the question at two points, corresponding to the beginning and the end of God's redemptive purposes. In seeking to order the divine works in the world using the concept of covenant, seventeenth-century Reformed authors proposed a "covenant of redemption," a pretemporal agreement between Father and Son (and, presumably, Spirit, although the point was generally left implicit) that the Son would assume a human nature, suffer crucifixion, and so bring salvation to the elect. Some have suggested that this covenant of redemption offers an example of an eternal, because pretemporal, ordering in the divine life that shows authority and submission.[12]

---

11. For this reason I have not even attempted to engage with the many exegetical defences of EFS/ERAS; if adequate, they establish it as *true*, but not as *Trinitarian*, and so they are not relevant to my modest argument here.

12. John Starke makes this error in arguing that John Owen taught an eternal authority of the Father over the Son; Owen is clear that this inequality stems from the *pactum salutis*, and so is not a reality of the divine life. Starke, "Augustine and his Interpreters," in Ware and Starke, eds., *One God*, 155–72, especially 159–65. Tyler Wittman's review of this volume in *Themelios* 40 (2015): 350–52, demonstrates the point about Owen and the *pactum* effectively.

The point appears powerful if we accept the reality of the *pactum salutis*: here is an event in eternity in which the Son submits to the Father's purposes. We might of course offer a rebuttal, which might take a strong form, that the *pactum* has in fact no basis in authority and submission, but instead results in the Father-Son relationship assuming that shape in the work of redemption.[13] A weaker form of the same point might instead insist that we know nothing of the character of the covenant, and so can claim nothing about the divine life from it. This seems to me to be properly modest, but I think we should go further.

The *pactum salutis* is eternal in that it is pretemporal, but it is not eternal in the sense that it belongs to the perfect life of God. It is very clearly the beginning of the works of God—the beginning of the great work of redemption. If God had chosen to remain alone in perfect eternal bliss and not to create, there would never have been a *pactum salutis*.[14] So the *pactum* tells us nothing about the eternal life of God (or at least nothing direct—I will come back to this). Similarly, the teaching of Paul in Corinthians that the last act of God's saving work will be the Son's handing over the kingdom to the Father might appear to speak of an act of submission or subordination in eternity, but again it is, if the language may be allowed, the wrong eternity. It is the consummation of the divine work, not an aspect of the divine life.

A defender of EFS/ERAS could respond to this in two obvious ways. One would be to embrace a broadly Barthian account of the divine life, in which God's eternal decision to be *pro nobis* is a determination of the divine life. (Famously, Barth includes the doctrine of election as the last word of the doctrine of God, not the first word of the works of God.[15]) Is such a move compatible with fourth-century Trinitarianism? There are obvious problems: an apparent suggestion of change in the perfect divine life being chief among them, but there is also a modification, at least, of divine aseity. That said, some of the most interesting theological work being done in the USA today is pushing in this sort of direction—I am thinking of projects like Jenson's and, particularly, McCormack's.[16] Suppose one of these projects worked, and it

---

13. This is in fact precisely what Owen teaches according to Wittman.
14. In the various blog posts that flowed on this issue in the summer of 2016, Jonathan Edwards was quoted more than once as an apparent defender of EFS/ERAS, but the defence relies on a failure to understand this point. The relevant text is *Miscellanies* 1062, which begins with an assertion that there is an economic order in the divine acts, "a subordination of the persons of the Trinity, in their actings with respect to the creature." Edwards immediately insists, however, that there can be no eternal subordination with respect to the divine will (i.e., no "authority" or "submission") and so faces a conundrum, which he solves by appealing to the *pactum salutis*: the economic subordination "must be conceived of as in some respect established by mutual free agreement." Edwards has more to say about the fittingness of this order, which I will consider below. (Quotations from the online Yale *Works of Jonathan Edwards*, vol. 20 (ed. Amy Plantinga Pauw).
15. Barth, *CD* II/2, 76–93.
16. Robert W. Jenson, *Systematic Theology. Vol. 1: The Triune God* (Oxford: Oxford University Press, 1997) and Bruce L. McCormack, "Election and the Trinity: Theses in Response to George Hunsinger," *SJT* 63 (2010): 203–24.

was in fact possible to show that there was a way of holding on to a recogniz-
ably orthodox account of immutability and aseity whilst accepting the act of
election, or the *pactum salutis*, as a determination of God's life, not just ours;
would the resulting doctrine be adequately Trinitarian?

The answer, unfortunately, must be "no," for all the reasons explored
above. Satisfying abstract doctrinal conditions is not enough to make a position "Trinitarian"; rather, we must be confessing the same sort of perfect divine
life as the fourth-century fathers confessed. A Barthian account, although it
might be attractive and even correct, is not this. If Barth is right about this
particular aspect of the divine life, then Basil, Gregory, and Augustine were
wrong—and an account that suggests that Basil, Gregory, and Augustine were
wrong about the divine life is, for that reason alone, already not adequately
Trinitarian on the only meaningful definition of "Trinitarian" we have.

The second obvious response would be to accept the argument above, that
the *pactum salutis* belongs to the works of God—not to the perfect life of God,
but to insist that the ordering of the works of God reflects the ordering of the
divine life. This is much stronger. Basil of Caesarea insisted on this point, that
because of the eternal order—*taxis*—of the divine life, all divine works are initiated by the Father, carried forward by the Son, and perfected by the Spirit. This
suggests that orthodox Trinitarianism recognized, indeed insisted upon, an
order in the life of God that is reflected in a created analogue of the Father
sovereignly proposing, and the Son apparently obediently acting in response.[17]
To answer this point, we need to reflect on the teaching encompassed in the
slogan *opera externa trinitatis indivisa sunt*. I will take up this reflection later.

The Son, Eternal and Incarnate

Much of the worthwhile work in the fourth-century debates depended on
clarifying the different ways in which Scripture refers to the Father-Son relation. The basic clarification, achieved most clearly by Hilary of Poitiers,[18] is
the one I have already made, between the eternal relation and the relation of
the Father to the incarnate Son. "I and the Father are one" refers to the eternal relation; "the Father is greater than I" to the incarnated relation. (Some
statements—"I have come from the Father"—are ambiguous, and Augustine
introduced a third category of distinction: statements of relationship that
apply equally to the eternal life and the incarnate life of the Son.)

This distinction is basic to the development of fourth-century Trinitarianism, and stands as a way of continuing to affirm the coequal glory of the

---

17.   This is Edwards's continuation in *Miscellanies*, 1062: There is, he suggests, "a natural decency and
      fitness" to the economic ordering. This is emphatically not any account of "eternal functional
      subordination"; he is clear that the only order in the eternal life of God is the relations of origin, but
      because the Son is from the Father in all eternity, there is a fittingness in the Son freely choosing to
      accept the authority of the Father in the economy.

18.   *De Trin.* IX.14.

Father and the Son without ignoring or explaining away biblical texts that speak of an unequal relationship. It becomes effectively an exegetical rule: Whenever a text speaks of any sort of subordination of the Son to the Father, the text is to be read as speaking of the economy, of the relation of the Father to the incarnate Son. Thus the basic doctrinal requirement of absolute equality and simplicity is maintained.

This raises a significant problem for the defender of EFS/ERAS: There is a programmatic basis to orthodox Trinitarianism which insists that any scriptural statement of authority, submission, or subordination in the Father-Son relationship is understood as referring to the economy of salvation, not to the eternal divine life. It is hard to see on this basis how any exegetical argument for EFS/ERAS can proceed without first rejecting a basic claim of the fourth-century Trinitarian consensus. Nonetheless, let us press on: What can we say about the eternal Father-Son relationship under the strictures of classical Trinitarianism?

The answer is fairly precise. All that is said of the eternal life of God is said of the single *ousia* save only that which refers to the relations of origin.[19] Thomas Aquinas, who understood this well, suggests that there are therefore five things only we can know about the persons of the Trinity: that the Father is unbegotten, that the Father begets the Son, that the Son is begotten of the Father, that the Father and the Son together spirate the Spirit, and that the Spirit proceeds from the Father and the Son.[20] This point is crucial to fourth-century Trinitarian theology because it defends the core doctrine of divine simplicity.[21] To surrender this point, on orthodox Trinitarian logic, is to deny the unity of Father, Son, and Spirit; it is to embrace polytheism.[22]

What are we going to do with EFS/ERAS under this stricture? Only one line is possible for the defender of these positions: to insist that in the relationship of begetting and being begotten there is either a functional subordination, or a relationship of authority and submission. This point has been recognized and accepted by defenders of these positions.[23] Let me specify the issue here more carefully:

Origen offered the standard defence of eternal generation,[24] a doctrine that of course is enshrined in the Creed. God does not change, and so the Son is coeternal with the Father, and yet the Son has his origin in being begotten

---

19. This is the way I summarized the point in *The Holy Trinity;* see 146.
20. *ST* Ia q.32 art.3.
21. On this, see (e.g.) Ayres, *Nicaea*, 280–81, 286–88.
22. Gregory of Nyssa argues this point explicitly in his classic work *Ad Ablab.*, often entitled in English "That we should not think of saying there are three gods."
23. See, e.g., Wayne Grudem, "Doctrinal Deviations in Evangelical-Feminist Arguments about the Trinity," in Ware and Starke, eds., *One God*, 17–46, especially 18–32.
24. He addresses it at various points in the extant works, but see for example *De Prin.* 1.2.2. The best interpretation is probably still Peter Widdicombe, *The Fatherhood of God from Origen to Athanasius* (Oxford: Clarendon, 1994).

from the Father—how do we square these three necessary biblical truths? By, Origen suggests, asserting that the generation of the Son is not the beginning of a new relationship, but the eternal way of being of the Father and the Son. The Father is eternally begetting the Son; the Son is eternally being begotten of the Father (and, to complete the list, the Father and the Son are eternally spirating the Spirit, and the Spirit is eternally proceeding from the Father and the Son). To press forward a bit from Origen, this is the best description—the only description—of the pure act that the life of God is, a single, simple event of ecstatic, perfect, and loving self-donation.

I am aware that some involved in defending EFS have also denied eternal generation;[25] I do not have much to say about that except that to deny eternal generation is certainly to deny the doctrine of the Trinity, and, given that "eternally begotten of the Father" is a confession of the Nicene Creed, is in grave danger of departing from what can meaningfully be called Christianity—it is, once again, to side with Unitarians and Jehovah's Witnesses in claiming that the Christian doctrine of God is unbiblical. Assuming then that the doctrine of eternal generation is accepted, if we are going to find an account of EFS/ERAS that is adequately Trinitarian, we are going to have to find it within our confession of eternal generation, as there is nothing else we can say about the Father-Son relationship.

This "nothing else" imposes a strict condition on our derivation: It is not just that our putative account of EFS or ERAS has to be coherent with eternal generation; it has to be shown to derive from that doctrine, because there is nothing other than eternal generation that we can say of the Father-Son relation. Now, this is not immediately hopeless: two lines suggest themselves. The first is to note that this relationship is asymmetric. There is, as we have noted, a proper *taxis*, an order, to the triune life. Durst's recent book is valuable both in reminding us that the biblical writers feel free to order the persons in every possible way, and that these different orderings invite us to reflect on different aspects of God's work in the world,[26] but *in se*, in the eternal divine life, it is clearly, on the biblical witness, proper to speak of the Father first, the Son second, and the Spirit third.

This asymmetry and order does not yet give us an account of authority or submission; it does give us an account of subordination, if that word is etymologically understood: the Son is second to the Father in order, and so is subordered. This point has been routinely made by Trinitarian theologians down the ages using language of order and suborder, a fact that a number of

---

25. I should note that there have been several verbal reports that two leading figures who have advanced this position in print, Bruce Ware and Wayne Grudem, indicated in public at the 2016 ETS conference that they have now accepted the doctrine of eternal generation. I cannot yet find any published statement to this effect, although I sincerely hope it is true, as all heaven rejoices when a sinner repents.
26. Rodrick K. Durst, *Reordering the Trinity: Six movements of God in the New Testament* (Grand Rapids: Kregel, 2015).

recent defenders of EFS have attempted to leverage. They are, unfortunately, mistaking the use of an unexceptional term for the embracing of a novel idea. Nothing may be derived from such usage save that the Son is most properly named after the Father and before the Spirit when we name God.[27] Nonetheless, reflection on this asymmetry might yet lead us to an account of authority and submission, unless there is some other reason to exclude such an account.

The second line we might push from the doctrine of eternal generation is to note that the relation between a human father and son, particularly in biblical context, certainly includes authority, submission, and subordination.[28] This has some *prima facie* plausibility: God chose to reveal the first and second modes of the divine being as "Father" and "Son," and so we are certainly invited to reflect on what we know of human paternal-filial relationships and to enquire whether we may predicate this of the eternal divine relationship also.

At the end of our investigation of what classical Trinitarianism has to say about the Father-Son relationship, then, we are left with two possible lines for the defender of some form of EFS/ERAS, one based around the ordering of the indivisible divine acts, which might be held to reflect an order in the eternal divine life, and the other inviting a reflection on Father-Son language, which might be held to suggest that eternal generation is a relationship of authority and submission. To test these further, we turn to what we must say of the *ousia*, the single, simple, divine life, in order to be faithful to fourth-century Trinitarianism.

The Simplicity of the Divine Life

Let me return first to the doctrine of the indivisibility of divine acts, which I discussed a little above. I have argued elsewhere[29] that this is in fact a crucial doctrine for the development of Cappadocian Trinitarianism, particularly in Gregory of Nyssa's much-anthologized *ad Ablabium*. Why should we not say Father, Son, and Spirit are three gods, asks Gregory? His answer turns on the inseparability of divine operations: Father, Son, and Spirit do one thing, and so are one being. Now, this argument is complex in its construction, and relies on a whole set of assumptions which Gregory does not stop to spell out. In the essay just referenced, I try to do some of this work, and suggest that the inseparability of divine saving acts is a corollary, and so a revelation, of the simplicity of the eternal divine life.

---

27. To take another text that was cited more than once in blog discussions in 2016, Charles Hodge speaks of "a subordination" in the Trinity (e.g. *ST* I.445) several times, but clearly means no more than this. It is "a subordination of the persons as to modes of subsistence and operation" that is summed up merely in the assertion that "the Father is first, the Son second, and the Spirit third" (again, 445).

28. A point Wayne Grudem has pressed several times in this discussion.

29. Stephen R. Holmes, "Trinitarian Action and Inseparable Operations," in *Advancing Trinitarian Theology: Proceedings of the Los Angeles Theology Conference*, eds. F. Sanders and O. Crisp (Grand Rapids: Zondervan, 2015), 60–74.

The arguments we have already seen point to a proper ordering in that simplicity, and here we get into the places where our language strains to speak well of God's life. God is pure act, the single, simple eternal act of the begetting of the Son by the Father and the proceeding of the Spirit from the Father and the Son. That is certainly to say that the relational distinctions that define the divine simplicity have a proper order to them—we most properly name God as the dominical baptismal formula does, Father, Son, and Holy Spirit. The Father is unbegotten, the Son is eternally begotten of the Father, the Spirit proceeds from the Father and the Son, and so there is a *taxis*, an order, in the eternal divine life. This, I take it, is the eternal analogue to the order we found in the inseparable divine acts, but there is no hint here yet of subordination, authority, or submission. This is the point made by Edwards:[30] that the shape of triune acts in the economy reflects the order of being in all eternity, but does not imply anything more than an order, that the Father is most properly named first, the Son second, and the Spirit third.

Further, this order is never division. The pure act that God is is single and simple. As we have seen, the confession of divine simplicity is crucial to fourth-century Trinitarianism, and so is a confession that is necessary for a theology to be adequately Trinitarian.[31] Now, divine simplicity demands the singularity of divine will, divine energy, divine action, and every other aspect of the divine life save only the eternal relations of origin.[32] There is one volitional inclination in the divine life, one intention, one activity, and so on. So, any proposal suggesting some form of EFS or ERAS must be consistent with there being a single divine act and a single divine will.

However, diversity of function requires diversity of act; this seems clear enough. Therefore, to hold to any form of functional differentiation, whether subordinationist or some other kind, within a single divine act is surely impossible; it would require an account of how two (or, in fact, three) different functions can exist within the same single and simple act.[33] There is an

---

30. See nn. 13 and 16 above.
31. See again Ayres, *Nicaea*, 286–88.
32. I take it that this is obvious, but it is spelt out by John of Damascus, *De fid. orth.* 8, and see now the exposition in Charles C. Twombly, *Perichoresis and Personhood: God, Christ, and Salvation in John of Damascus* (Eugene, OR: Pickwick, 2015), 29–32.
33. Grudem appears to realize and accept this impossibility, and so devotes space to insisting the doctrine of inseparable operations is unbiblical; unfortunately, this defence falls foul of my basic argument in this paper: Rejecting the ecumenical doctrine of the Trinity on the basis of a proposed private interpretation of Scripture is, once again, to side with Jehovah's Witnesses and others who have left the church on the grounds that the received doctrine of the Trinity is unbiblical. See Grudem, "Doctrinal Deviations," 18–27; Grudem focuses upon problems he perceives in the constructions of Erickson, Sumner, and Belleville, which in some cases do appear to be genuine problems, but the logic of his argument seems to require him to reject the doctrine of inseparable operations entirely, not merely to reject certain forms of it. There is an attempted retrieval on page 24, where Grudem accepts that "in some sense we only understand very faintly" that the whole Godhead is involved in every divine act; he denies, however, that this means "any action done by one person is also done by the other two persons," a line I find very

eternal analogue of the order of divine acts in the world, but it is in the order of relations of origin, and not otherwise. There is no space here for an account of EFS/ERAS, or for anything similar.

To assert relations of authority and submission within a single divine will is similarly impossible: authority and submission require a diversity of volitional faculties. Where there is one simple single will, there can necessarily be no authority or submission. This would appear to close off the second option outlined above for defending EFS/ERAS, that of an appeal to the language of "Father" and "Son." When we consider what we know of the divine life we are required to insist that the authority and submission we find in human paternal-filial relationships is not an analogue of anything real in the divine life; the language of Father and Son points to an asymmetrical relationship of origin and nothing more; it cannot be grounds for asserting EFS/ERAS, because to do so would be to offend against other necessary Trinitarian claims, particularly divine simplicity.

Conclusion

I have argued that the central Trinitarian doctrine of divine simplicity necessarily excludes any meaningful account of subordination, or of authority and submission, and so there is no space for an account of EFS, ERAS, or anything similar, within any recognisably orthodox Trinitarianism. I have accepted repeatedly that the defender of EFS/ERAS might choose, perhaps out of a desire to be faithful to his/her particular interpretation of Scripture, to hold to these doctrines by rejecting orthodox Trinitarianism, but such a rejection entails locating oneself outside of what is commonly understood to be the Christian church—hence my running comparison with Unitarianism and the Jehovah's Witnesses. It may be that EFS/ERAS is biblical and correct, but if it is, the classical Christian tradition of "orthodox Trinitarianism" must inevitably be unbiblical and wrong.

---

difficult to make any sense of. The most natural reading would be that Grudem thinks the "whole being of God" is something other than the three persons, but this would be merely bizarre.

Bibliography

Ayres, Lewis. *Nicaea and Its Legacy: An Approach to Fourth-Century Trinitarian Theology*. Oxford: Oxford University Press, 2004.

Barnes, Michel Rene. "The Fourth Century as Trinitarian Canon." In *Christian Origins: Theology, Rhetoric, and Community*, edited by Lewis Ayres and Gareth Jones, 47–67. London: Routledge, 1998.

Durst, Rodrick K. *Reordering the Trinity: Six Movements of God in the New Testament*. Grand Rapids: Kregel, 2015.

Erickson, Millard J. *Who's Tampering with the Trinity? An Assessment of the Subordination Debate*. Grand Rapids: Kregel, 2009.

Giles, Kevin. *Jesus and the Father: Modern Evangelicals Reinvent the Doctrine of the Trinity*. Grand Rapids: Zondervan, 2006.

———. *The Trinity and Subordinationism: The Doctrine of God and the Contemporary Gender Debate*. Downers Grove, IL: IVP, 2002.

Gottfried, Adam. *Der Streit um die Prädestination im ausgehenden 16. Jahrhundert: Eine Untersuchung zu den Entwurfen von Samuel Huber und Aegidius Hunnius*. Neukirchen: Neukirchener Verlag, 1970.

Grudem, Wayne. "Doctrinal Deviations in Evangelical-Feminist Arguments about the Trinity." In *One God in Three Persons: Unity of Essence, Distinction of Persons, Implications for Life*, edited by Bruce A. Ware and John Starke, 17–46. Wheaton, IL: Crossway, 2016.

Holmes, Stephen R. *The Holy Trinity: Understanding God's Life*. Milton Keynes: Paternoster, 2012.

———. "Trinitarian Action and Inseparable Operations." In *Advancing Trinitarian Theology: Proceedings of the Los Angeles Theology Conference*, eds. F. Sanders and O. Crisp, 60–74. Grand Rapids: Zondervan, 2015.

Jenson, Robert W. *Systematic Theology. Vol. 1: The Triune God*. Oxford: Oxford University Press, 1997.

Jowers, Denis, and H. Wayne House, eds. *The New Evangelical Subordinationism? God the Father and God the Son*. Eugene, OR: Pickwick, 2012.

McCormack, Bruce L. "Election and the Trinity: Theses in Response to George Hunsinger." *SJT* 63 (2010): 203–24.

Raitt, Jill. *The Colloquy of Montbéliard: Religion and Politics in the Sixteenth Century*. Oxford: Oxford University Press, 1993.

Starke, John. "Augustine and his Interpreters." In *One God in Three Persons: Unity of Essence, Distinction of Persons, Implications for Life*, edited by Bruce A. Ware and John Starke, 155–72. Wheaton, IL: Crossway, 2016.

Twombly, Charles C. *Perichoresis and Personhood: God, Christ, and Salvation in John of Damascus*. Eugene, OR: Pickwick, 2015.

Ware, Bruce A., and John Starke, eds. *One God in Three Persons: Unity of Essence, Distinction of Persons, Implications for Life*. Wheaton, IL: Crossway, 2016.

Widdicombe, Peter. *The Fatherhood of God from Origen to Athanasius.* Oxford: Clarendon, 1994.

Wittman, Tyler. Review of Bruce A. Ware and John Starke, eds., *One God in Three Persons: Unity of Essence, Distinction of Persons, Implications for Life.* *Themelios* 40 (2015): 350–52.

CHAPTER 13

The Trinity without Tiers

A Response to the Eternal Subordination/Submissiveness of the Son Debate

GRAHAM COLE

Introduction

W hy this topic?[1] It is an important topic because appealing to the inner life of God the Trinity has become quite popular in recent times. Some argue that the inner life of the Trinity is democratic, egalitarian, socialist, and nonhierarchical (e.g., Jürgen Moltmann and Leonardo Boff).[2] Others say it is hierarchical (e.g., Bruce Ware).[3] The inner life

---

1. A shorter version of this material was published in *Zadok Papers* S192 (2012): 2–5 with the title "Imitating the Trinity: A Response to the Eternal Subordination Debate." The intramural evangelical debate on the subject took on special prominence in 2016. See Caleb Lindgren, "Gender and the Trinity: From Proxy War to Civil War," http://www.christianitytoday.com/ct/2016/june-web-only/gender-trinity-proxy-war-civil-war-eternal-subordination.html (accessed January 27, 2017).
2. See Jürgen Moltmann, *The Trinity and the Kingdom of God*, trans. Margaret Kohl (London: SCM, 1981), 199, and Leonardo Boff, *Holy Trinity: Perfect Community*, trans. Phillip Berryman (Maryknoll, NY: Orbis, 2000), 8. For Boff's socialism, see his "Socialism Is Not in Limbo," https://leonardoboff.wordpress.com/2014/08/31/socialism-is-not-in-limbo/ (accessed January 21, 2017): "My evaluation is: we are headed for a socio-ecological crisis of such magnitude that, either we adopt socialism with a humanistic mode, or we will not have the means to survive."
3. Bruce Ware, *Father, Son, & Holy Spirit: Relationships, Roles, & Relevance* (Wheaton, IL: Crossway, 2005). Ware describes the inner life of the essential Trinity as "hierarchy without hubris," 157.

of the Trinity—so the argument runs for both points of view—is the model for gender relations in a marriage, in a family, in the church, and even, according to some, for society. Interestingly, the three theologians referred to above appear to represent variations of social Trinitarianism.

For the purposes of this essay, I especially will consider the hierarchical idea.[4] For many who hold the hierarchical view argue that the hierarchy within the eternal Trinity needs to be observed in ministry in the church and that leads to restricting the scope of women's ministry in the church. To put the matter less abstractly, the doctrine of the Trinity so conceived should exclude women from leadership of a congregation and thus constitutes a barrier to unrestricted women's ministry in the church. It is important to note that this doctrine of the Trinity is not a barrier to women's ministering per se, but is a barrier to unrestricted women's ministry. Anyone who believes the Bible supports women's ministry. The issue is scope.

1. A Classic Position on the Trinity

My concern is with any suggestion of hierarchy or "tiers" that involves some notion of a difference in rank or class especially in the light of the Athanasian Creed (fifth century), which for Anglicans is part of our confession and which says:

> So there is one Father, not three Fathers; one Son, not three Sons; one Holy Spirit, not three Holy Spirits.
>
> And in this Trinity none is afore, nor after another; none is greater, or less than another.
>
> But the whole three persons are co-eternal, and co-equal.[5]

The Athanasian Creed presents a Trinity without an eternal internal hierarchy. However, there were other points of view in the early church period.

2. An "Arian" Alternative

In the century before the Athanasian Creed, some in the early church wrestled with a very different way of conceiving of the Trinity and so to provide a way of contrast wrote "The Blasphemy of Sirmium" of A.D. 357:

> There is no question that the Father is the greater. For it can be doubtful to none that the father is greater than the Son in *honour, dignity, splendor, majesty,* and in the very name of Father, the Son Himself testifying, "He Who sent Me is

---

4. However, it is important to note that the general thrust of this paper is also critical of any "egalitarian" appeal to the inner life of the Trinity to norm human relations.
5. Article 8. Cf. *A Prayer Book for Australia: Shorter Edition* (Sydney: Broughton, 1999), 625 and 629.

greater than I." And no one is ignorant that it is the Catholic doctrine that there are not two Persons of the Father and the Son, and that the Father is greater and the Son subordinated to the father, together with all those things which the Father has subjected to Himself, and that the Father has no beginning and is invisible, immortal and impassible, but that the Son has been begotten from the Father, God from God, light from light, and that the generation of this Son, as has already been said, no one knows except his Father.[6]

Sirmium presents a "trinity" of sorts but one with tiers or rankings. Clearly, the Son does not stand at the same ontological level as the Father when Sirmium states: "For it can be doubtful to none that the father is greater than the Son in *honour, dignity, splendor, majesty,* and in the very name of Father, the Son Himself testifying, 'He Who sent Me is greater than I.'" Thankfully this view did not prevail in early Christianity.[7] It does show, importantly, why the concept of subordination became so problematical in the history of theological discussion unless carefully nuanced. And so with that background behind us let us turn to the present day.

3. The Present Controversy

The present controversy arises because some appeal to the doctrine of the eternal inner life of the Trinity as a pattern of headship over and subordination under that ought to norm gender relations. Many of these describe their position on the essential Trinity as eternal subordination with reference to the Father and Son relation. However, others, myself included, think that such an appeal is theologically mistaken. The latter argue, again myself included, that gender relations in the church need be informed by texts of Scripture that speak more clearly of male-female relations, rather than appealing to a speculative reconstruction of the eternal inner life of the Trinity and then drawing implications from it.

---

6. Quoted in J. N. D. Kelly, *Early Christian Creeds*, 3rd ed. (London/New York: Continuum, 2006), 286. My emphasis. The term "Arian" covers a variety of fourth-century subordinationist Trinitarian theologies that denied the full divinity of Christ. See the useful discussion of the term in Tarmo Toom, *Classical Trinitarian Theology: A Textbook* (New York: T & T Clark, 2007), 83–85. Since the term "Arian" covers a variety of positions and not just that of Arius himself, I have used "scare quotes." The definitive work on fourth-century Arianism is that of Lewis Ayres, *Nicaea and Its Legacy: An Approach to Fourth-Century Trinitarian Theology* (Oxford: Oxford University Press, 2006).
7. According to one eminent dictionary of church history the "Blasphemy of Sirmium" expressed the extreme Arian position and in so doing "marked the turning-point in the history of the Arian controversy." See F. L. Cross and E. A. Livingstone, eds., *The Oxford Dictionary of the Christian Church*, 2nd ed. (Oxford: Oxford University Press, 1978), 1280. It was Hilary of Poitiers who described the synod as "the blasphemy"; Kelly, *Early Christian Creeds*, 286.

4. The Anxiety

A further complication is that the idea of subordination has had a long and troubled history in Christian theology. One thinks, for example, of the "Arian" troubles of the fourth century and the Arminian "Arians" of the seventeenth and eighteenth centuries in England.[8] In particular, subordination language *prima facie* suggests that Jesus is a lesser being than God the Father. That's how the ancient "Arians" and the English "Arians" would have understood it. However I must emphasize that the present-day eternal subordinationists I know don't believe for a moment that the Father and Son are not equally God. For them, there is no ontological inferiority but a role or functional subordination of the Son to the Father in all possible worlds. Given the historical baggage associated with the idea of subordination, Robert Letham is wiser then to speak of "the eternal submissiveness of the Son" and Michael Bird, following Wolfhart Pannenberg, wisely speaks of "the Son's obedient self-distinction from the Father."[9]

5. What's at Stake?

What's at stake is how we are to live together before God in a God-pleasing way. We cannot do that unless we have revelation from God that tells us about his character, will, and ways. The idea of revelation brings us to the Scriptures as special revelation from God, and that raises the question of how those Scriptures are to be read. This is the hermeneutical or interpretative question, especially since there are some challenging texts in Scripture when it comes to the relation between the Father and the Son. To some of the key texts we next turn.

6. The Hermeneutical Issue: Some Challenging Texts

The ancient "Arians" believed their Bibles and used biblical texts as evidence for their beliefs. Here are some of the texts appealed to by them that are relevant to our subject.[10] Let me rehearse them without comment at this stage:

> . . . the Father is greater than I. (John 14:28)

> All things are yours, whether Paul or Apollos or Cephas or the world or life or death or the present or the future—all are yours, and you are of Christ, and Christ is of God. (1 Cor. 3:21–23)

---

8.   For the English story see Stephen Hampton, *Anti-Arminians: The Anglican Reformed Tradition from Charles II to George I* (Oxford: Oxford University Press, 2008), 162–91.

9.   Michael. F. Bird, *Evangelical Theology: A Biblical and Systematic Introduction* (Grand Rapids: Zondervan, 2013), 120.

10. See Athanasius, *Four Discourses Against The Arians*, Gregory of Nyssa, *Against Eunomius, Answer to Eunomius's Second Book*, Hilary of Poitiers, *On the Trinity*, and John Chrysostom, *Homilies on 1 Corinthians* in "The Fathers of the Church," in *New Advent: Featuring The Catholic Encyclopedia*, 2nd ed. (Pennsauken, NJ: Disc Makers, 2007, CD-ROM version).

I want you to realize that the head of every man is Christ, and the head of the woman is man, and the head of Christ is God. (1 Cor. 11:3)

But Christ has indeed been raised from the dead, the firstfruits of those who have fallen asleep. For since death came through a man, the resurrection of the dead comes also through a man. For as in Adam all die, so in Christ all will be made alive. But each in his own turn: Christ, the firstfruits; then, when he comes, those who belong to him. Then the end will come, when he hands over the kingdom to God the Father after he has destroyed all dominion, authority and power. For he must reign until he has put all his enemies under his feet. The last enemy to be destroyed is death. For he "has put everything under his feet." Now when it says that "everything" has been put under him, it is clear that this does not include God himself, who put everything under Christ. When he has done this, then the Son himself will be made subject to him who put everything under him, so that God may be all in all. (1 Cor. 15:20–28)

These texts were appealed to by the "Arians" to assert that Jesus was a lesser being than God the Father.

7. The "Arian" Approach

According to the "Arians," these texts must be taken at face value. For example, take John 14:28. Only a lesser being could say that the Father is greater than he is. Or take 1 Corinthians 15:20–28. Only a lesser being could be so described as subject to the Father. To speak anachronistically, this is no mere role or functional subordination; this is ontological inferiority. The Son stands on the creature side of the ledger only.

The early church rightly judged that this is a view that falls outside the bounds of Christian faithfulness.

8. The Eternal Functional Subordination Approach

The eternal functional subordination approach rests on an assumption. The scriptural presentation of Father, Son, and Holy Spirit needs to be seen as a window enabling us to "see" into the eternal inner life of the Trinity, or put another way, into the essential Trinity. In brief this becomes a hermeneutical principle for reading Scripture, i.e., what you see in the economy is true of eternity.[11] Now of course that is true concerning the divine character. There

---

11.   Karl Rahner was the most famous proponent of this idea and it has come to be known as Rahner's Rule. For Rahner's Rule, see Alister E. McGrath, ed., *Theology: The Basic Readings* (Malden, MA: Blackwell, 2008), 51: "the Trinity of the economy is the immanent Trinity and vice versa." For a discussion of loose versus tight readings of Rahner's Rule see Fred Sanders, "Entangled in the Trinity: Economic and Immanent Trinity in Recent Theology," *Dialog* 4, no. 3 (2001): 175–82. Randal Rauser suggests three possible readings of the rule: strict realist, loose realist, and anti-realist in "Rahner's Rule: An Emperor without Clothes?" *International Journal of Systematic Theology* 7, no. 1 (2005): 81– 94. For a fine critical discussion of Rahner's Rule see Scott Harrower, *Trinitarian Self and Salvation*

is no hidden God behind God. But it does not follow that that is true of inner Trinitarian relations given the incarnation.

On this view our challenging texts are expressions of the eternal functional subordination of the Son in function and role, but not of course in Godness.[12] Ontologically speaking, the Son is as much God as the Father and the Spirit are God. In earlier work, Bruce Ware was comfortable in speaking of the Father having greater dignity, honor, and majesty than the Son, and both the Father and the Son having greater dignity, honor, and majesty than the Holy Spirit.[13] Regarding the Spirit, Ware maintained that "the Spirit takes the position subordinate to both the Son and the Father."[14] He argued that this was true in "eternity past" and will be true "in eternity future," and was true of the Christ event.[15] However, theological debate brings changes in articulation and clarification of intent. Ware now argues that "the three persons having equal glory, dignity, honor, and majesty, while each reflects that glory in hypostatically distinctive ways, i.e., the Father's paternal glory distinctive yet equal to the Son's filial glory."[16] He maintains that this can be said of the Spirit too.[17]

Wayne Grudem draws an analogy from family life to illuminate his theological stance on the question of intra-Trinitarian relationships. As the husband exercises authority over his wife so too the Father over the Son, and both over the Holy Spirit who relates to them as a child to parents. In his words: "although it is not explicitly mentioned in Scripture, the gift of children within marriage, coming from both the father and the mother, and subject to the authority of both father and mother, is analogous to the relationship of the Holy Spirit to the Father and Son in the Trinity."[18]

Applications of eternal functional subordination to gender relations differ widely. For example, with regard to ministry in the church the mild application has no objection to a woman doing every ministry in a denomina-

---

(Eugene, OR: Pickwick, 2012). Harrower shows the difficulty that Luke-Acts constitutes for a strict reading of Rahner's Rule. In Luke, the Son is under the direction of the Spirit, whilst in Acts, the Spirit is under the direction of the Son (cf. Luke 4:1 and Acts 1:1–2). If the economy and eternity are isomorphic then has the essential Trinitarian *taxis* been changed?

12. As already argued, Bruce Ware is very clear that subordination has to do with function not with divine essence, *The Man Christ Jesus: Theological Reflections on the Humanity of Christ* (Wheaton, IL: Crossway, 2012), cf. 25 and 57. The philosophical question is whether this is a distinction without a difference if eternal functional subordination is true of all possible worlds.

13. Ware, *Father, Son, & Holy Spirit*, 1, 55, 65, 71, 72, 125, 131.

14. Ware, *Father, Son, & Holy Spirit*, 125.

15. Ware, *Father, Son, & Holy Spirit*, 125.

16. Email correspondence (2/14/2017) with permission to quote. Significantly, Ware says that this new more recent articulation of his position is truer to his intent of the last thirty years. Ware's new form of words reminds me of Jonathan Edwards's argument that there is a "peculiar honor" that is the Father's, and that this is also the case with the Son, and with the Spirit, "An Unpublished Essay on the Trinity," https://www.ccel.org/ccel/edwards/trinity/files/trinity.html (accessed January 30, 2017).

17. Ware, *Father, Son, & Holy Spirit*, 125.

18. Wayne Grudem, *Systematic Theology: An Introduction to Biblical Doctrine* (Leicester: Inter-Varsity; Grand Rapids: Zondervan, 1994), 257.

tion except lead it.[19] A moderate application would allow a woman do every ministry in a local church except lead it as pastor or senior pastor. The strong application maintains that a woman can only minister if males over a certain age are not present. With regard to society, the debate over Sarah Palin's vice-presidential candidacy shows some of the differences. On the one hand, according to John Piper's view, voting for Sarah Palin would have been a sin but a lesser one than voting for a pro-choice candidate.[20] On the other hand, Wayne Grudem would see no in principle theological problem with voting for her.[21] A friend of mine holds a similar position to that of Piper's, namely that subordination applies in the family, the church, and society. He argues that women should not have been given the vote. I admire the consistency of John Piper and my friend. If gender roles are based on the Godhead and creation then all of life should reflect the difference.

Although this is not my view and I find it highly problematical, it falls within the bounds of Christian faithfulness.[22]

9. The Economic Subordination Approach

Economic subordinationists[23] argue that the Son became subordinate to the Father for the economy or administration of salvation. In other words, the pattern of relationships between Father, Son, and Holy Spirit to be seen in the economy is not isomorphic with that within the essential Trinity. God now relates as Trinity in a new way through the humanity of the incarnate Son.[24] The economic subordinationist (for example, Millard J. Erickson)

---

19. For example, Craig L. Blomberg, "Neither Hierarchialist nor Egalitarian: Gender Roles in Paul," in *Two Views, On Women in Ministry*, eds. James R. Beck and Craig L. Blomberg (Grand Rapids: Zondervan, 2001), 369–70.

20. John Piper, "Why a Woman Shouldn't Run for Vice President, but Wise People May Still Vote for Her," Desiring God, http://www.desiringgod.org/blog/posts/why-a-woman-shouldnt-run-for-vice-president-but-wise-people-may-still-vote-for-her, 11/2/2008 (accessed October 10, 2010).

21. Wayne Grudem, *Evangelical Feminism and Biblical Truth* [Colorado Springs: Multnomah, 2004], 140. Women should not be discouraged from holding civil offices.

22. On 11/15/2016, at a public panel discussion at an Evangelical Theological Society Annual Conference meeting, both Wayne Grudem and Bruce Ware stated that they could now affirm the Nicene Creed's claim about the eternal generation of the Son. I was present on that occasion. Both Grudem and Ware were exemplary in showing how scholars can change their minds when faced with further evidence and convincing argumentation (*semper reformanda*). Ware now prefers the expression Eternal Relationship Authority Submission (ERAS) to capture the posture of the Son toward the Father in the taxis of the essential Trinity. Both he and Wayne Grudem make the same Trinitarian applications to human gender roles as they did before their change of mind on the eternal generation of the Son question. In email correspondence (17/1/2017), Wayne Grudem relates how he is comfortable with both the phrases "eternal subordination"—understood in relational and not ontological terms—and "eternal submission."

23. If the term "subordination" is to be retained, given competing understandings, it clearly needs some qualifier to distinguish the nature of the subordination on view. For some, "eternal functional" supplies that need. For others, "economic" is the key qualifier.

24. See the helpful discussion in Bruce Milne, *Know the Truth: A Handbook of Christian Belief*, 3rd ed. (Downers Grove, IL: IVP Academic, 2009), 200.

works on a different hermeneutical principle to the eternal subordination-ist, and whether knowingly or not on an ancient one at that.[25] Augustine distinguished between passages that spoke of Christ in the form of God and passages that speak of Christ in the form of a servant.[26] John 1:1–2 speak of Christ in the form of God (the Word) but John 4:6 speaks of Christ in the form of a servant (he was tired). Without some such distinction, the "Arians" played havoc with the biblical testimony. Even Charles Hodge, the patron saint of eternal subordinationism, recognized the distinction when it came to his commentary on 1 Corinthians.[27] He understood 1 Corinthians 3:21–23; 11:3, and 15:20–28 to be about economic not eternal sonship. In this he followed Calvin's own exegesis of these texts. I might add that it seems to me that the eternal subordination view cannot do justice—in contradistinction to the economic subordination view—to the great stooping represented by the incarnation as seen in texts such as John 17:5; 2 Corinthians 8:9; Philippians 2:5–11, and to the fact that although he was a son, Jesus learned obedience (Heb. 5:8).

The economic subordination view persuades me and I will say more about it anon. At this juncture though let me simply say that economic subordinationism too falls within the walls of Christian faithfulness, but I'd argue it is correct at key points in ways that the eternal subordination view is not.

10. Addressing the Challenging Texts

I believe that Augustine's hermeneutical rule that distinguishes between the form of God and the form of the servant is sound. The incarnation does not diminish the Trinity but it does mean that God the Trinity can relate in a new way through the humanity of the Son. In writing on the subject of economic subordination, John Murray states this idea well: "By the incarnation and by taking the form of a servant, the Son came to sustain new relations to the Father and the Holy Spirit. He became subject to the Father and dependent upon the operations of the Holy Spirit."[28] As the Athanasian Creed states

---

25.   Millard J. Erickson, *Who's Tampering with the Trinity? An Assessment of the Eternal Subordination Debate* (Grand Rapids: Kregel, 2009), 259. Also see Thomas McCall and Keith Yandell, "On Trinitarian Subordinationism," *Philosophia Christi* 11, no. 2 (2009): 339–58.

26.   See the helpful discussion of Augustine and of this principle in Toom, *Classical Trinitarian Theology*, 148–56.

27.   In fact Hodge posits three subordinations. The eternal concerns the Son's subordination to the Father as the second person of the Trinity to the first. The voluntary subordination is "the humbling" of the incarnation. The "economical" subordination is the Son's "official subjection" to the Father as the *theanthropos* (lit. "Godhuman") in his roles as redeemer and head of the church. See Charles Hodge's comments on 1 Corinthians 11:3 in his *An Exposition of the First Epistle to the Corinthians* (Grand Rapids: Eerdmans, 1959), 207.

28.   John Murray. "The Person of Christ," in *Collected Writings of John Murray 2: Systematic Theology* (Edinburgh: The Banner of Truth Trust, 1977), 139.

regarding the incarnation: "not of the conversion Godhead into flesh; but by taking of the Manhood into God."[29]

All our challenging texts assume the incarnation: John 14:28; 1 Corinthians 3:21–23; 11:3, and 15:20–28. With regard to John 14:28 the one who speaks is the Word become flesh (John 1:14). This is also true of the Corinthians passages. For example, the text does not say that the head of Son is the Father but that the head of the Christ—the definite article matters—is God (1 Cor. 11:3). Calvin and Hodge are right to argue that economic not ontological sonship is in view. As for 1 Corinthians 15:20–28 on the eternal subordination view this passage would teach two kinds of subordinations: an eternal one and an economic one, because at a future time we read that the eternally subordinate Son will be subject to the Father when the kingdom is handed over. The *regnum Christi* gives way to the *regnum dei*. In other words, the principle of an economic subordination is granted. If here, why not with the incarnation itself?

Indeed, in a review of a book on the Trinity, John Murray argues that not to carefully distinguish what may be said of the Trinity on the inside (*ad intra*) in eternity on the one hand and the Trinity in relation to us given the incarnation (*ad extra*) on the other hand, is "devastating for theology." He writes: "And this is why we must sharply contest such statements as these: 'we must make the doctrine of the immanent Trinity conform exactly in content to the economic Trinity'; God's whole essence is revealed to us in his operation."[30] Murray points out that to do so makes temporality/time an attribute of God. Murray's warning needs heeding.

11. Is It Time for a Moratorium?

Importantly, not all who argue for some kind of eternal submissiveness in the essential Trinity think that the eternal inner life of the Godhead provides a paradigm for social relations. Michael Bird and Robert Shillaker argued that it is time for a moratorium on appealing to the inner life of the Trinity to support any particular view of marital relationships.[31] This is sage advice especially given the New Testament's consistent appeal to the imita-

---

29. Someone may ask if there are any biblical texts that reveal something of the essential Trinity. Indeed there are. To look no further than the Johannine testimony, we learn that the Father and Son shared in love and glory before the foundation of the world (John 17:5 and 24); that God is spirit (John 4:24); that God is light (1 John 1:5) and love (1 John 4:8, 16).

30. John Murray's review of Claude Welch's *In This Name. The Doctrine of the Trinity in Contemporary Theology*, in *Collected Writings of John Murray 4: Studies in Theology* (Edinburgh: The Banner of Truth Trust, 1982), 281.

31. Michael F. Bird and Robert Shillaker, "Subordination in the Trinity and Gender Roles: A Response to Recent Discussion," *Trinity Journal* 29 NS (2008): 282. A very thoughtful piece. More recently, Bird has argued that "we have to propose that the Son's submission demonstrates something of the eternal relationships within the Godhead," *Evangelical Theology*, 120. Even so he does not apply this idea to gender relations given the uniqueness of the Trinity. Bird and Shillaker, "Subordination in the Trinity," 282.

tion of Christ as paradigmatic for our social relations and not the imitation of the eternal inner life of the Trinity. Some argue that John 17 is the counter example to this claim. However, there is no imperative predicated on the eternal internal life of the Trinity in the text. In fact John 17 is a prayer addressed to the Father, not ethical instruction. It is descriptive not prescriptive unless one wants to commit the naturalistic fallacy of moving from "is" to "ought."

In fact the genius of the New Testament is its accent on the imitation of Christ in relation to us. He washed his disciples' feet and left an example of service to follow that goes well beyond simple foot washing (John 13:1–13, 34–35). When Paul wants the Philippians to be other-person-centered he does not write of the eternal internal relation of Father and Son; instead, he works through the gospel story of how Christ took on the servant's role to serve wayward humanity even at the cost of his own death (Phil. 2:1–11). New Testament ethics are overwhelmingly evangelical because our behavior is to be informed by the evangel or gospel. There is a way of working from the eternal inner life of the Trinity that runs the risk of leaving the gospel behind.[32] Thomas à Kempis had a point in his classic work *The Imitation of Christ*.

12. Some Terminological Clarifications

In my view, the debate needs fresh vocabulary. As we have seen, Robert Letham writes of "the eternal submissiveness of the Son" and Michael Bird of "the obedient self-distinction of the Son." Millard J. Erickson suggests that the debate be conducted in terms of the gradationist view, in contradistinction to the equivalentist views of the eternal Trinity.[33] This is more helpful than casting the debate in terms of a complementarian view versus an egalitarian one. In fact there are those who argue for some kind of eternal obedience or "special submission" of the Son to the Father in the Godhead who are egalitarian on gender issues (e.g., Craig S. Keener).[34] Personally speaking, although these terms are well entrenched, I find the terms "complementarian" and "egalitarian" somewhat unsatisfactory when left unnuanced. In fact, increasingly there are so-called egalitarians whose preference is to be described as "complementarians without hierarchy" (e.g., Gilbert Bilezikian). It seems to me that Bible-believing Christians need to affirm some form of complementarianism because of the head-body analogy used by Paul of husbands and wives in Ephesians 5, and of Christ and the church in Ephesians 4–5. At the

---

32.   For a more developed discussion of the problem I see in trying to imitate the inner life of the essential Trinity see my "The Trinity, Imitation, and the Christian Moral Life," in *Building on the Foundations of Evangelical Theology: Essays in Honor of John S. Feinberg*, eds. Gregg R. Allison and Stephen J. Wellum (Wheaton, IL: Crossway, 2015), 312–28.

33.   Erickson, *Who's Tampering with The Trinity?* 17–18. "Gradationist" and "equivalentist" are Erickson's terms.

34.   Cf. Craig S. Keener, "Is Subordination within the Trinity Really Heresy? A Study of John 5:18 in Context," *Trinity Journal* 20 NS (1999): 47 and Craig S. Keener, "Women in Ministry," in Beck and Blomberg, eds., *Two Views*, 27–70.

same time, Bible-believing Christians need to affirm some form of egalitarianism (if not the term itself). Unlike the old covenant where only men were circumcised, in the new covenant both men and women are baptized. My preferred term is "Christo-complementarianism." This term I hope affirms the headship of Christ in relation to the church and Christologically informs the head-body analogy used of husbands and wives. It is instructive that Paul nowhere describes anyone but Christ as head of the church. I am uncomfortable then with loose talk about male headship in the church as it may obscure "the crown rights of the redeemer," to use an older phrase. As for hierarchy—of course there is hierarchy in Christianity. The Christian lives in a Christocracy. He or she lives under the reign of Christ as their Head, Lord and King.

13. In Sum

If what I have argued is sound then one of the putative barriers to unrestricted women's ministry in the church falls. Speculative reconstructions of the eternal inner life of the Trinity provide no model for concrete Christian behavior. The issue of the scope of women's ministry needs to be decided on other grounds theologically and exegetically (especially but not exclusively the exegesis and theological interpretation of Genesis 2–3 and 1 Timothy 2). In other words, there are more obvious biblical texts to explore.[35] There is much wisdom in Barth's advice to students on the occasion of his farewell before his expulsion from Germany in 1935: "And now the end has come. So listen to my piece of advice: exegesis, exegesis, and yet more exegesis! Keep to the Word, to the Scripture that has been given to us."[36]

---

35. Wayne Grudem, in an email to me dated 2/25/2017, clarifies his position as follows: "I see analogies between Trinitarian relationships and human relationships as a helpful supporting argument, and a valid one, but the primary arguments that I would make (and that I have done for many years) regarding relationships in marriage and in the church have to do with texts of Scripture that speak more explicitly of these matters." I myself am not convinced that such supporting arguments are sound.

36. Quoted in Gordon Fee, *New Testament Exegesis: A Handbook for Students and Pastors*, 3rd ed. (Louisville: Westminster, 2002), v.

Bibliography

Ayres, Lewis. *Nicaea and Its Legacy: An Approach to Fourth-Century Trinitarian Theology.* Oxford: Oxford University Press, 2006.

Cross, L., and E. A. Livingstone, eds. *The Oxford Dictionary of the Christian Church.* 2nd ed. Oxford: Oxford University Press, 1978.

Bird, Michael F. *Evangelical Theology: A Biblical and Systematic Introduction.* Grand Rapids: Zondervan, 2013.

Bird, Michael F., and Robert Shillaker. "Subordination in the Trinity and Gender Roles: A Response to Recent Discussion." *Trinity Journal* 29 NS (2008): 267–83.

Blomberg, Craig L. "Neither Hierarchialist nor Egalitarian: Gender Roles in Paul." In *Two Views, On Women in Ministry*, edited by James R. Beck and Craig L. Blomberg, 369–70. Grand Rapids: Zondervan, 2001.

Boff, Leonardo. *Holy Trinity: Perfect Community.* Translated by Phillip Berryman. Maryknoll, NY: Orbis, 2000.

Cole, Graham. "Imitating the Trinity: A Response to the Eternal Subordination Debate." *Zadok Papers* S192 (2012): 2–5.

_____. "The Trinity, Imitation, and the Christian Moral Life." In *Building on the Foundations of Evangelical Theology: Essays in Honor of John S. Feinberg*, edited by Gregg R. Allison and Stephen J. Wellum, 312–28. Wheaton, IL: Crossway, 2015.

Erickson, Millard J. *Who's Tampering with the Trinity? An Assessment of the Eternal Subordination Debate.* Grand Rapids: Kregel, 2009.

Fee, Gordon. *New Testament Exegesis: A Handbook for Students and Pastors.* 3rd ed. Louisville: Westminster, 2002.

Grudem, Wayne. *Evangelical Feminism and Biblical Truth.* Colorado Springs: Multnomah, 2004.

_____. *Systematic Theology: An Introduction to Biblical Doctrine.* Leicester: Inter-Varsity; Grand Rapids: Zondervan, 1994.

Hampton, Stephen. *Anti-Arminians: The Anglican Reformed Tradition from Charles II to George I.* Oxford: Oxford University Press, 2008.

Harrower, Scott. *Trinitarian Self and Salvation.* Eugene, OR: Pickwick, 2012.

Hodge, Charles. *An Exposition of the First Epistle to the Corinthians.* Grand Rapids: Eerdmans 1959.

Keener, Craig S. "Is Subordination within the Trinity Really Heresy? A Study of John 5:18 in Context." *Trinity Journal* 20 NS (1999): 39–51.

_____. "Women in Ministry." In *Two Views, On Women in Ministry*, edited by James R. Beck and Craig L Blomberg, 27–70. Grand Rapids: Zondervan, 2001.

Kelly, J. N. D. *Early Christian Creeds.* 3rd ed. London/New York: Continuum, 2006.

Lindengren, Caleb. "Gender and the Trinity: From Proxy War to Civil War." http://www.christianitytoday.com/ct/2016/june-web-only/gender-trinity-proxy-war-civil-war-eternal-subordination.html (accessed January 27, 2017).

McCall, Thomas, and Keith Yandell. "On Trinitarian Subordinationism." *Philosophia Christi* 11, no. 2 (2009): 339–58.

McGrath, Alister E., ed., *Theology the Basic Readings.* Malden, MA: Blackwell, 2008.

Milne, Bruce. *Know the Truth: A Handbook of Christian Belief.* 3rd ed. Downers Grove, IL: IVP Academic, 2009.

Moltmann, Jürgen. *The Trinity and the Kingdom of God,* trans. Margaret Kohl. London: SCM, 1981.

Murray, John. "The Person of Christ." In *Collected Writings of John Murray 2: Systematic Theology.* Edinburgh: The Banner of Truth Trust, 1977.

————. Review of Claude Welch's *In This Name: The Doctrine of the Trinity in Contemporary Theology.* In *Collected Writings of John Murray 4: Studies in Theology.* Edinburgh: The Banner of Truth Trust, 1982.

New Advent: Featuring The Catholic Encyclopedia. 2nd ed. Pennsauken, NJ: Disc Makers, 2007, CD-ROM version.

A Prayer Book for Australia: Shorter Edition. Sydney: Broughton, 1999.

Rauser, Randal. "Rahner's Rule: An Emperor without Clothes?" *International Journal of Systematic Theology* 7, no. 1 (2005): 81–94.

Sanders, Fred. "Entangled in the Trinity: Economic and Immanent Trinity in Recent Theology." *Dialog* 4, no. 3 (2001): 175–82.

Toom, Tarmo. *Classical Trinitarian Theology: A Textbook.* New York: T & T Clark, 2007.

Ware, Bruce. *Father, Son, & Holy Spirit: Relationships, Roles, & Relevance.* Wheaton, IL: Crossway, 2005.

————. *The Man Christ Jesus: Theological Reflections on the Humanity of Christ.* Wheaton, IL: Crossway, 2012.

CHAPTER 14

The Presence of the Triune God

Persons, Essence, and Equality

JAMES R. GORDON

I. Introduction: Subordination and the Trinity

Recent evangelical discussion of the doctrine of the Trinity has been disproportionately focused on the relationship between the persons of the Father and the Son. Proponents of so-called "eternal functional subordinationism" (EFS) insist that a necessary and eternal relationship of authority and submission obtains between the Father and Son (respectively) in a way that maintains fidelity both to the Nicene tradition of *homoousios* and the witness of Christian Scripture. While some might wish to downplay the concerns of EFS as a fringe movement of little importance to contemporary evangelical thought—often and unfortunately tied to other concerns, such as the roles of women in ecclesial ministry and familial life—the claims of EFS cut to the heart of orthodox Trinitarianism and as such deserve careful attention.[1]

---

1. By "orthodox" here I mean the views outlined in the seven ecumenical councils of the church. For example, there is no "orthodox" view of husband/wife relations, but there is an "orthodox" view on Christ's relationship to the Father, Mary's perpetual virginity, Christ's two (divine and human) wills, etc.

Many have already attempted to demonstrate the shortcomings of EFS from theological and philosophical perspectives,[2] but several proponents of EFS have offered what might initially appear to be a nuanced philosophical response to the objections to EFS.[3] In their essay, "An Examination of Three Recent Philosophical Arguments against Hierarchy in the Immanent Trinity," Philip R. Gons and Andrew David Naselli argue that the philosophical arguments of eternal function equality (EFE)—the view "that the Father and Son are completely equal in all noncontingent ways"[4]—fail to rule out hierarchy in the immanent Trinity.[5] In this essay, I will outline Gons and Naselli's responses to EFE, demonstrate that they are both independently problematic and inadequately aligned with traditional Trinitarian reflection, and use the divine attribute of omnipresence to show that more traditional accounts of the Trinitarian persons are able better to account for the scriptural witness to God's saving presence in general and in the work of redemption in particular.

II. On Personal Properties and Trinitarian Persons

One of the most serious objections to EFS concerns its creedal status. Christians confess that the one Lord Jesus Christ is "of one being with the Father" (i.e., *homoousios*), but some have claimed that EFS entails that Christ and the Father do not share the same essence—that is, that they are of a different being than one another.

Consider one recent argument to this effect from Thomas McCall and Keith Yandell.[6] McCall and Yandell argue that, if the Son is necessarily subordinate to the Father, such that there is no possible world in which the Son could *not* be subordinate to the Father, then the Son is *essentially* subordinate to the Father. But, if the Son is essentially subordinate to the Father, then the Son has an essential property that the Father lacks. And, if two persons do not share all of the same essential properties, then they are not identical.[7] The key here is that McCall and Yandell's argument against EFS is directed against the *essential* subordination of the Son—that is, that the Son's subordination

---

2. Most notably, Thomas McCall and Keith E. Yandell, "On Trinitarian Subordinationism," *Philosophia Christi* 11 (2009): 339–58; Thomas McCall, *Which Trinity? Whose Monotheism? Philosophical and Systematic Theologians on the Metaphysics of Trinitarian Theology* (Grand Rapids: Eerdmans, 2010), 175–88; and Millard J. Erickson, *Who's Tampering with the Trinity? An Assessment of the Subordination Debate* (Grand Rapids: Kregel, 2009).

3. I phrase it this way because the authors are clear that they are not attempting to offer a *defense* of EFS but merely to show that several common critiques of EFS are not as persuasive as they might initially seem.

4. Philip R. Gons and Andrew David Naselli, "An Examination of Three Recent Philosophical Arguments against Hierarchy in the Immanent Trinity," in *One God in Three Persons: Unity of Essence, Distinction of Persons, Implications for Life*, eds. Bruce A. Ware and John Starke (Wheaton, IL: Crossway, 2015), 197.

5. Gons and Naselli, "An Examination"

6. McCall and Yandell, "On Trinitarian Subordinationism," 339–58.

7. That is, assuming the principle of the Identity of Indiscernibles is true. As noted below, Gons and Naselli seem to reject what is known as "absolute identity" in favor of something like relative identity, but they offer no argument for doing so.

is a property of the immanent rather than the economic Trinity. Presumably, McCall and Yandell could be fine insisting that, for us and for our salvation, the Son submits to the Father during certain periods of his incarnate life, but that he does so *contingently* by an act of divine will—it could have been otherwise, in other words.[8]

III. *"Notions"* in God

In response to this argument, Gons and Naselli try to demonstrate that if McCall and Yandell's argument is sound, then orthodox Trinitarian doctrine would be doomed alongside of EFS. The reason for this is that, according to traditional treatments of the doctrine of the Trinity, there are five "notions" (*notiones*) in God: the unbegottenness and paternity of the Father, the filiation of the Son, the procession of the Spirit, and the spiration of the Spirit by the Father and the Son.[9] These notions pose a problem for McCall and Yandell—so say Gons and Naselli—because they entail that each of the individual triune persons have essential (not contingent) properties not shared by the other two triune persons. And, since the tradition of orthodox Trinitarianism was keen to avoid any sort of subordinationism, the Conciliar rulings were clear that eternal generation was an eternal and necessary act. This means, in other words, that there is no possible world in which the Son does not proceed from the Father and in which the Spirit does not proceed from the Father and the Son, since the acts are essential rather than contingent; they constitute the divine life. But, if the Son's procession is unique to the Son (and not the Father or the Spirit), then the Son has an essential property that neither the Father nor the Spirit share—the property "being begotten." And, as stated in the conclusion of McCall and Yandell's original argument, if two persons differ in their essential properties, they are essentially distinct (i.e., nonidentical). If McCall and Yandell's argument is sound, according to Gons and Naselli, "the historic doctrines of the eternal generation of the Son and the eternal procession of the Spirit, which the majority of the church has embraced in the East and West since at least the Council of Nicaea in 325 and arguably much earlier, would entail the denial of *homoousion*."[10]

Here Gons and Naselli could go in one of two directions: They could either show that *both* EFS and the traditional view of the eternal generation of the Son entail a denial of *homoousios*, or they could show that *neither* view entails a denial of *homoousios*. They at least entertain the former option, noting that "A growing number of theologians reject the historic doctrines

---

8. The idea of "submission" becomes more problematic between triune persons, however, when one begins to reflect on what it means for the triune God to have numerically one will.

9. Here I am using the historical language of the *notiones* in God, though it is absent from Gons and Naselli's essay. See Peter Lombard, *The* Sentences, *Book 1: The Mystery of the Trinity*, Mediaeval Sources in Translation 42, trans. Giulio Silano (Ontario: Pontifical Institute of Mediaeval Studies, 2007), distinctions XXVI–XXVIII.

10. Gons and Naselli, "An Examination," 199.

of eternal generation and procession,"[11] but they end up defending the latter position—that EFS's assertion of the Son's subordination is equivalent to the assertions present in the traditional view with respect to its affirmation of *homoousios.*

Gons and Naselli make the claim that "If this argument is valid,[12] not only does it refute EFS's proposal that the distinction between the Father and the Son is best understood in terms of authority and submission, but it also refutes the view held by the vast majority of the church for at least the last seventeen hundred years, namely, that the Father, Son, and Spirit possess unique personal properties that distinguish them from one another."[13] We will demonstrate this in greater detail below, but Gons and Naselli have not entitled themselves to the claim that "the vast majority of the church for at least the last seventeen hundred years" agreed "that the Father, Son, and Spirit possess unique personal properties that distinguish them from one another"—at least in the way that they mean it.[14] In fact, Gons and Naselli explicitly claim that they do not think this view needs defense for their argument to stand: "It is beyond the scope of this chapter to prove that the church has historically affirmed that the Father, Son, and Spirit each possesses one or more personal properties that make them distinct from one another."[15] As will become clear below, however, this point is precisely what is at issue in the discussion. Put differently, the question hinges on whether and to what extent the Son and Father can be differentiated in the immanent life of the triune God without being three distinct essences.

Naselli and Gons attempt to show that the Son's property "being generated" is equivalent to the property "being subordinate," such that if one of these properties entails a denial of Son's *homoousios* with the Father, then the other one does as well. But, since orthodox Trinitarians would claim that eternal generation does not entail a denial of—but rather secures!—*homoousios,* it follows that insisting on the eternal subordination of the Son, as does EFS, does not entail a denial of *homoousios* either.[16] In short, Gons and Naselli want to point out that those who claim the "traditional" or "orthodox" Trinitarian moniker cannot have things both ways: they cannot both maintain that

---

11. Gons and Naselli, "An Examination," 200, n. 18. But if the property that arises from the eternal generation of the Son is the same type of property that EFS posits of the Son, then rejecting eternal generation on the grounds of unorthodoxy would require abandoning EFS for the same reasons.
12. Presumably, however, they mean "sound" here rather than "valid," since a valid argument with one or more false premises will not guarantee a true conclusion.
13. Gons and Naselli, "An Examination," 200.
14. The claim is true in that the tradition has always said that five notions exist in God. But Gons and Naselli want to add other essential personal properties to the list of five, which is decidedly *not* traditional, as we will demonstrate.
15. Gons and Naselli, "An Examination," 200, n. 19. The key words here are "one *or more,*" as mentioned above. Further, it is somewhat ironic that, in a discussion that appeals to "historic Trinitarianism" quite frequently, there are no citations of historic discussions of the Trinity—save a cursory mention of Calvin.
16. Gons and Naselli, "An Examination," 200.

the eternal generation of the Son is not problematic and that the Son's having a distinct essential property (i.e., being subordinate) is problematic.

In order to show how the Son's essential submission to the Father does not entail a denial of *homoousios*, Gons and Naselli attempt to exchange the ontological language of "essentially" and "essence" for the terms *"fundamentally"* and *"substance,"* respectively. They state,

> An eternal function is a necessary function, and a necessary function does indeed find its grounding in one or more essential or fundamental properties. So the Son's eternal subordination to the Father in terms of his role or function in the Godhead derives from a fundamental difference between him and the Father.[17]

Further, since the triune God consists of one essence in three distinct persons, Gons and Naselli think that "Properties of the essence are just as essential or fundamental to the essence as properties of the persons are to the persons."[18] It follows from this, Gons and Naselli suggest, that "each person . . . has two sets of essential or fundamental properties," namely, the properties of the divine essence and the properties of the person, i.e., substantial and personal properties. This leads to four sets of essential properties in the Trinity: the properties of the substance, the personal properties of the Father, the personal properties of the Son, and the personal properties of the Spirit. This distinction allows Gons and Naselli to say that the triune persons—Father, Son, and Holy Spirit—share in common all the properties of the divine essence (or substance) even while having distinct sets of personal properties. They hold this view in contrast to the alternative view, which they attribute to McCall and Yandell, that "there is only one set of properties" in the Trinity.[19] And further, they claim the view that there is only one set of properties in the Trinity "clearly departs from historic Trinitarianism."[20] With this modification, Gons and Naselli think that McCall and Yandell's argument does not prove anything novel; it only shows that the Trinitarian persons are distinct, which is just what the tradition of orthodox Trinitarianism has asserted all along.

Gons and Naselli take their argument further (citing John Feinberg), accepting what appears to be a Relative Identity strategy to show that the properties *"being in authority over the Son"* and *"being in submission under*

---

17. Gons and Naselli, "An Examination," 201.
18. Gons and Naselli, "An Examination," This claim is somewhat confusing if, as traditional Trinitarian reflection maintains, the triune persons are identical to the divine essence given divine simplicity. Consider Emery's explication of Aquinas: "In the Triune God, the essence is not 'multiplied' by the three persons, but the three persons are one and the same identical essence" (Giles Emery, *The Trinitarian Theology of St. Thomas Aquinas* [Oxford: Oxford University Press, 2007], 144, *passim.*
19. Gons and Naselli, "An Examination," 203.
20. Gons and Naselli, "An Examination," Here they point the reader back to their claim that they do not think they need to demonstrate that the tradition thought that the persons possessed "one or more personal properties that make them distinct from one another" (Gons and Naselli, "An Examination," 200, n. 19).

the Father" both "inhere" not in what it means for the Father and the Son
(respectively) to be God, but in what it means for the Father to be the Father
and for the Son to be the Son. Or, put differently, "these are not properties of
the one essence, but unique incommunicable properties of the persons that
define their intratrinitarian relationships."[21] They therefore conclude, "Properties that inhere in the persons and not in the essence do not entail a denial
of *homoousion*."[22]

Finally, Gons and Naselli suggest that the original EFE argument could
succeed if it could show either that "The historic position of properties of the
persons as distinct from properties of the one essence is flawed; all properties
are properties of the one essence," or "The authority-submission properties
must be properties of the essence rather than the persons."[23]

In what follows, before turning to the divine attribute of omnipresence, I
will point out some serious problems with Gons and Naselli's argument and
show that a majority opinion within historic, orthodox Trinitarian *does not*
think that the persons of the Trinity have specific properties that are not also
properties of the divine essence (thus satisfying Gons and Naselli's condition
for the EFE argument against EFS to succeed).

IV. The Counting Problem

Consider first what I will call "the counting problem." On Gons and
Naselli's view, there are four sets of properties in God: the personal properties of Father, Son, and Holy Spirit and the properties of the divine essence or
substance. However, properties do not (and indeed cannot) exist abstracted
from a property bearer, which entails that there must be (on Gons and Naselli's view) four property bearers in God: God, Father, Son, and Holy Spirit. On
the face of things, Gons and Naselli's argument can be easily refuted:

1. If there are four sets of properties in God, then there are four property bearers in God.
2. There are not four property bearers in God.
3. Therefore, there are not four sets of properties in God (*modus
   tollens*).[24]

---

21. Gons and Naselli, "An Examination," 204–5. Gons and Naselli cite John Feinberg, *No One Like Him: The Doctrine of God*, Foundations of Evangelical Theology (Wheaton, IL: Crossway, 2001), 494–95.
22. Gons and Naselli, "An Examination," 205.
23. Gons and Naselli, "An Examination," 205.
24. This is a valid argument, but its soundness rests on whether the major premise is true (I doubt Gons and Naselli would deny the truth of the minor premise). Gons and Naselli might be tempted to accept a primary/secondary substance view, according to which, as Nathan Jacobs puts it, "the substance (*ousia*) in the Godhead is akin to secondary substance, which constitutes the common nature of the three particulars (*hypostases*), Father, Son, and Holy Spirit" (Nathan Jacobs, "On 'Not Three Gods'—Again: Can a Primary-Secondary Substance Reading of *Ousia* and *Hypostasis* Avoid Tritheism?," *Modern Theology* 24 [2008]: 335). However, it is not clear whether they would be comfortable with this solution.

If properties only exist in connection to some sort of property bearer, then Gons and Naselli's rendering of the tradition is inherently problematic, since it would entail that there are four things to count in God and that God is something in addition to Father, Son, and Holy Spirit.

The larger problem, however, concerns the relationship between the divine persons and the divine essence. Here I will briefly outline an alternative (and arguably, majority) view from the tradition: that of Thomas Aquinas. It will become clear that on Thomas's view of the Trinity, all of the properties of the Trinitarian persons are just properties of the one divine essence—this was one of the sufficient conditions Gons and Naselli stipulated for the EFE position to succeed. It will also become clear that Thomas's view solves other problems in the realm of divine presence that Gons and Naselli's view has difficulty with.

Consider first Thomas's claim regarding the relationship between the divine persons and the divine essence: "Just as relations in created things inhere in an accidental way, so relations in God are the divine essence itself. It follows from this that in God the essence is not really distinct from the person even though the persons are really distinguished from one another."[25] In other words, it is impossible to conceive of the divine essence as consisting in anything other than the subsistent divine persons. This seems to rule out Gons and Naselli's view that there are certain properties of the divine essence that are not properties of the divine persons or that there are certain properties of the divine persons that are not also properties of the divine essence. Or, as Thomas puts it elsewhere, "the divine essence is not something other than the three persons; so there is no quaternity in God."[26] The Trinitarian persons are merely subsistent relations within the divine essence.

Giles Emery provides a helpful summary of the motivation for Thomas's view. He writes, "The essence of the three persons should be 'one in number' (*una numero*). This phrase means that the three divine persons are not just of one specific nature, like the human persons in whom one recognizes 'the same nature' because they have the same humanity. In the triune God, the essence is not multiplied by the three persons, but the three persons are one and the same identical essence."[27] Or, in Thomas's words:

> if, among human beings, three persons are called three men and not one single man, that is because the human nature common to the three is theirs in a different way, divided up materially amongst them, which could not take place in God. This is because, since three men have three numerically different humanities, only the essence of humanity is common to them. But it must be the case

25. Aquinas, *ST* I, q. 39, a. 1, cited in Emery, *The Trinitarian Theology of St. Thomas Aquinas*, 144.
26. Aquinas, *Super II Decret.* (Leon edn., vol. 40, p. E 43), cited in Emery, *The Trinitarian Theology of St. Thomas Aquinas*, 146.
27. Emery, *The Trinitarian Theology of St. Thomas Aquinas*, 144.

that in the three divine persons, there are not three numerically different divinities but one single simple deity, since the essence of the Word [i.e., of the Son] and of Love [i.e., of the Spirit] in God is nothing but the essence of God.[28]

In short, the Trinitarian persons are identical to the divine essence, given the doctrine of divine simplicity, and as such, there is no fourth set of properties common to the three.[29]

IV. Trinitarian Personal Properties

McCall and Yandell's problem, according to Gons and Naselli, is that they ignore the distinction between properties that belong to the divine essence and properties that belong to the divine persons. Indeed, for Gons and Naselli, "It seems that in their view there is only one set of properties, which clearly departs from historic Trinitarianism."[30] Recall that Gons and Naselli maintain that the traditional view is that each of the Trinitarian persons—Father, Son, and Holy Spirit—has a particular and unique set of properties that distinguishes each person from the other two persons. For Gons and Naselli, in addition to the "notions" mentioned above, the Father has the essential property of "having authority over the Son" and the Son has the essential property of "being in submission under the Father." However, this is decidedly *not* the traditional view. The traditional view maintains that the *only* properties that distinguish the persons are the relational properties described in the notions (not the Son's "being subordinate" or the Father's "being authoritative"). Persons, in fact, *just are* relations within the divine essence—subsistent relations, to be sure, but relations nonetheless. Thus Emery: "The persons are not just *characterized* by means of a relative property, they *are* a relation which subsists, a 'subsistent relation.'"[31]

Perhaps Gons and Naselli would object and insist that eternal generation itself gives rise to an ordered relationship—the Father as the one who generates the Son and the Son and Spirit as those which are generated and spirated. This is another way of saying that the immanent act of eternal generation gives rise to the "notions" in God and further, that the ordering of the immanent relations gives rise to an appropriate manner of attributing specific terms of economic action to individual Trinitarian persons, even though the external works are indivisible. What is clear, however, is that "The accurate meaning of the expressions, 'first, second, third person' excludes any kind of priority of one person over the another. . . . Such expressions . . . designate the order of origin or 'order of nature' in God."[32]

---

28. Aquinas, *De rationibus fidei*, ch. 4, cited in Emery, *The Trinitarian Theology of St. Thomas Aquinas*, 144.
29. There is likely a deeper issue looming here: that of social Trinitarianism.
30. Gons and Naselli, "An Examination," 203. Here again they cite their footnote, which cites Calvin.
31. Emery, *The Trinitarian Theology of St. Thomas Aquinas*, 304.
32. Emery, *The Trinitarian Theology of St. Thomas Aquinas*, 136.

What then of the distinctions between the persons? Does McCall and Yandell's position eliminate all distinctions between the Trinitarian persons such that there is only one set of properties in the Trinity? To help answer this question, consider Russell L. Friedman's distinction between the two prominent Medieval accounts of the Trinity (i.e., the "relation" and "emanation" accounts). Despite the significant differences between the two accounts of the doctrine, Friedman notes that "these two explanatory approaches to trinitarian identity and distinction agreed . . . that each divine person was *constituted*; that is to say, each person took on his own distinct personal being, on account of a single characteristic that is unique to that one person and distinguishes that person from the other two persons. This single characteristic was called a 'personal property.'"[33] So far Gons and Naselli could agree. But, Friedman continues:

> The three divine persons, then, according to both the relation and the emana-
> tion account, are essentially identical (i.e., the share completely the same divine
> essence) apart from one difference, which is the unique personal property that
> makes each of the persons distinct from the other two persons. The personal
> properties thus bring about "merely" personal distinction, that is, a *real* but not
> an *essential* distinction.[34]

What then of the personal relations? As Friedman puts it, "compared to the divine essence, the relation's subject or foundation, the relation itself 'vanishes,' it disappears, since it is really the same as the essence. This is merely to say that the divine relations do not inhere in the divine essence, they are not different from the essence, and there is no composition in God."[35] The traditional view (which both Medieval views shared in common), in other words, is that the only "personal properties" that one can apply to the immanent life of the divine persons are the five "notions"—*not* things like "subordination" and "authority."

This is not to say, however, that one cannot distinguish the Father's action from the Son's action in the economy of redemption. Given the doctrine of appropriations, one can indeed add other things to the list of personal properties—but only to the list of personal properties that are contingent to God. That is to say, one has moved out of the realm of the eternal and essential being of God and into the realm of the temporal and contingent missions of the triune persons.

Gons and Naselli could respond in one of two ways. First, they could claim that while the tradition *did not* consider things like "subordination" and "authority" among the essential personal properties of the triune persons,

---

33. Russell L. Friedman, *Medieval Trinitarian Thought from Aquinas to Ockham* (Cambridge: Cambridge University Press, 2010), 6.
34. Friedman, *Medieval Trinitarian Thought*, 6–7.
35. Friedman, *Medieval Trinitarian Thought*, 11.

they *should* have (since there is no conceptual difference between the five notions and things like "subordination" and "authority"). This strategy would entail, however, that Gons and Naselli's view is *not* traditional, which, while not necessarily problematic in itself, would at least be problematic given the claims to tradition in their essay. Alternatively, Gons and Naselli could claim that the tradition *did in fact* consider things like "subordination" and "authority" as essential personal properties. But this strategy would require an argument, and there are significant reasons to think that the tradition thought there were five and only five notions in God. Ultimately, as we will see further below, "The communal presence of the persons thus rests on their *consubstantiality*. For what is implicated in this is that the three divine persons do not just have a similar nature, but the very same nature, identically one, that is to say, *numerically one*."[36] The distinctions pertinent to this discussion concern the precise way the triune God is present in the act of redemption.

V. Possible Incarnation?

We can move more quickly through Gons and Naselli's second reply to the EFE position,[37] which considers the triune persons' fitness for incarnation. McCall and Yandell's argument, as Gons and Naselli rehearse it, is that if the Father could not have become incarnate and the Son could have, then we have another instance in which the Son and Father have differing essential properties and therefore are not *homoousios*.

Gons and Naselli attempt to make a distinction between "a theoretical incarnation" and "*the* incarnation with all that it entails,"[38] and they claim that the nuanced position of Aquinas actually agrees with their claim that "The unique personal properties of the Son make him best suited to be united to human nature and fulfill the role of Mediator."[39] They conclude, "in all possible worlds that include biblical incarnation, the Son rather than the Father or the Spirit would have become incarnate because God's nature is such that he always does what is most fitting."[40]

Here it is important to ask what "unique personal *properties*" Gons and Naselli are intending to appeal to. Recall that here we are referring to essen-

---

36. Emery, *The Trinitarian Theology of St. Thomas Aquinas*, 303 (emphasis original).

37. This essay will not address Gons and Naselli's third reply, since it would take us out of the realm of Trinitarian doctrine and into the realm of Christology, given their appeals to the distinction between Christ's divine and human natures.

38. It is difficult to understand what this distinction means, since presumably, given the logic of possible worlds, the world that contains "*the* incarnation with all that it entails" *just is* one among many other possible worlds containing a "theoretical" incarnation. If Gons and Naselli mean to claim that God, as the Greatest Conceivable Being, could only possibly create the best of all possible worlds, they would need to show a) that this is the best possible world and b) that God could not create any other world than this one. This creates other difficulties, to be sure, but the argument is too underdetermined to figure out exactly what Gons and Naselli mean.

39. Gons and Naselli, "An Examination," 208.

40. Gons and Naselli, "An Examination," 208–9.

tial properties in the immanent life of God, apart from God's relating to creation (i.e., transitive actions). If the argument we have established above is right—i.e., that the only essential personal properties of the triune persons are the five *notiones*—then Gons and Naselli are misguided to suggest that certain personal properties of the Son and Father make one or the other fit or unfit for the incarnation.

While it is right to appeal to the idea of "fittingness" to talk about *why* the Son (and not the Father) became incarnate, it is wrong to speak of fittingness as grounded in anything other than the "notions" in God—that is, the personal properties that distinguish the Son and the Spirit and not anything like authority and submission. Gons and Naselli appeal to Thomas Aquinas, claiming he thinks "the Son is uniquely fit for the work of the incarnation," and they offer their reading as a "more sophisticated" reading than McCall and Yandell's.[41] It turns out, however, that an appeal to Thomas here hardly helps Gons and Naselli. As Frederick Christian Bauerschmidt has shown, "Thomas readily admits that the economy of salvation could have been ordered differently—e.g. it could have not included the incarnation or Christ's death on the cross."[42] Or, as Thomas puts it, "it was not necessary that God should become incarnate for the restoration of human nature. For God with His omnipotent power could have restored human nature in many other ways."[43] While it is the case that Thomas thinks incarnation is most fitting for the person of the Son, this does not entail that Gons and Naselli are right, for what grounds the fittingness is the order of subsistence of the Father, Son, and Holy Spirit. Gons and Naselli think conceding the fittingness of the incarnation of the Son allows them to point out that the Son and Father have different personal properties, among which they would include the properties of authority and submission. But it is just the triune relations—that is, the subsistent persons—and the "notions" that generate the Son's fitness for incarnation, not any additional properties like Gons and Naselli suggest. Indeed, the tradition has never added additional essential properties to the triune persons, and for good reason.

We see something similar in St. Anselm of Canterbury's discussion of the incarnation of the Son. He says, first of all, "If the Holy Spirit became flesh, as the Son became flesh, surely the Holy Spirit would be the son of a human being. Therefore, there would be two sons in the divine Trinity, namely, the Son of God and the son of a human being."[44] Anselm here has

---

41. Gons and Naselli, "An Examination," 208.

42. Frederick Christian Bauerschmidt, *Thomas Aquinas: Faith, Reason, and Following Christian*, Christian Theology in Context (Oxford: Oxford University Press, 2013), 141. For more on this, see Scott Swain and Michael Allen, "The Obedience of the Eternal Son," *International Journal of Systematic Theology* 15 (2013): 114–34.

43. Aquinas, *ST* III, q. 1, a. 2.

44. St. Anselm, "On the Incarnation of the Word," in *Anselm of Canterbury: The Major Works*, Oxford World's Classics, eds. Brian Davies and G. R. Evans (Oxford: Oxford University Press, 1998), 250.

the Son's relation of origin as the begotten one in mind, and it would be odd for the second person of the Trinity to be the eternal Son while the third person of the Trinity would be the temporal Son. The result would be that "some mixture of doubt would be generated when we were speaking of God the 'son.'"[45] Anselm's reason, it seems, is not that it would be inappropriate for God if the Spirit became incarnate; rather, it would be confusing *for us*. Indeed, the only problem *for God* of the Spirit's becoming incarnate is that it would entail an inequality between the Son and Spirit, which Anselm says is "inappropriate."[46] Consider Anselm's reasoning:

> There would also be a kind of inequality, as it were, of the different persons, who ought to be completely equal, by reason of the fact that they were sons, since one son would be greater by reason of the dignity of a superior parent, the other lesser by reason of an inferior parent. . . . Therefore, if the Holy Spirit were to have been born of the Virgin, one person would be greater, and the other person lesser, by reason of the dignity of their origin, since the Son of God would have only the more excellent origin from God, and the Holy Spirit only the lesser origin from a human being.[47]

Anselm also notes that this same issue would have been a problem had the Father become incarnate. In addition, "if the Father were to be the son of the Virgin, two persons in the Trinity would take the name of grandson, since both the Father would be the grandson of the Virgin's parents, and the Father's Son would be the Virgin's grandson, although the Son himself would have no part of him from the Virgin."[48] Anselm does claim that, by virtue of assuming a human nature, the Son is "less" that the Father and the Spirit, "yet the latter two persons do not on that account surpass the Son, since the Son also has the same majesty whereby they are greater than the Son's humanity, the same majesty whereby he himself with them is also superior to his humanity"—and this "majesty" to which Anselm refers is the divine nature.[49]

In short, while it is the case that Anselm thinks there is something about who the Son is essentially, who the Father is essentially, and who the Spirit is essentially that makes certain economic actions most fitting or appropriate for God, the "something" is always and only the relation of origin or the "notions" in God. As we have seen, then, Gons and Naselli's claim that "At least some versions of EFE eliminate any real property distinctions among the persons of the Trinity,"[50] is impossible to maintain, since the "real property

45.   Anselm, "On the Incarnation of the Word," 250.

46.   Anselm, "On the Incarnation of the Word," 250.

47.   Anselm, "On the Incarnation of the Word," 250.

48.   Anselm, "On the Incarnation of the Word," 251.

49.   Anselm, "On the Incarnation of the Word," 251.

50.   Gons and Naselli, "An Examination," 212. They also add, "This clearly departs from what the church has believed since at least Nicaea," but they provide no evidence from the tradition to support this claim.

distinctions" in the triune God *just are* the triune persons. Gons and Naselli try to smuggle in additional *essential* properties to be added to the Triune persons aside from the traditional "notions" without providing any historical precedent for doing so.

VI. Trinitarian Omnipresence

At this point, one might merely point out that Thomas Aquinas is not the only representative of orthodox Trinitarianism within the Christian tradition. That point would be fair enough—though one ought at least to recognize Thomas's debt to the Patristic tradition. Some might object, further, that Aquinas's understanding of God as a Trinity in unity is a speculative bit of theology proper disconnected from the practical concerns of redemption. But this is not the case. In fact, Aquinas's views of God's Triunity—of the divine essence—are intimately connected with his views of God's saving presence in the divine missions. We will now turn our attention to how Aquinas's account of the Trinity secures both the omnipresence of the Triune God in general and the saving presence of the triune God in particular.

With respect to Aquinas's understanding of God's omnipresence, the fact that the triune persons are *identical* with the divine essence secures God's ability to be present in all places. Aquinas writes:

> First, as He is in all things giving them being, power and operation; so He is in every place as giving it existence and locative power. Again, things placed are in place, inasmuch as they fill place; and God fills every place; not, indeed, like a body, for a body is said to fill place inasmuch as it excludes the co-presence of another body; whereas by God being in a place, others are not thereby excluded from it; indeed, by the very fact that He gives being to the things that fill every place, He Himself fills every place.[51]

For Aquinas, the "He" here is the none other than the triune God—Father, Son, and Holy Spirit—such that while Aquinas has in mind omnipresence as a property of the divine essence, it is this essence subsisting in the triune persons that is the way in which God is present. God is present, in other words, by God's essence in all places in modes particular to the persons' relations of origin. And, given the doctrine of divine simplicity, wherever God is, God is there wholly (and not partly).

Aquinas's understanding of the Trinity's omnipresence also secures God's present activity in the economy of redemption. Indeed, in his useful summary of Aquinas's *Commentary on the Gospel of St. John*, Matthew Levering suggests that the relation between the Father in the Son with respect to the divine essence is central to Aquinas's account of the Son's saving presence. This is the case, first of all, because Aquinas thinks that part of the way

---

51. Aquinas, *ST*, *Ia*, q. 8, a. 2.

Christ saves believers is by incorporating them into beloved friendship with
the triune God. Aquinas says, "because the Father perfectly loves the Son, this
is a sign that the Father has shown him everything and has communicated
to him his very own power and nature."[52] In the Father's generation of the
Son, the self-gift of the Father's own essence, believers see the invisible love of
God made visible in a human person. "The Father's love," says Levering, "is
a sign of what he has done for the Son in giving him everything that he, the
Father, possesses. It is love that manifests a giver who has generated his perfect
likeness."[53] When Jesus says "Whoever has seen me has seen the Father"
(John 14:9) or "All things have been delivered to me by my Father; and no
one knows the Son except the Father, and no one knows the Father except the
Son and any one to whom the Son chooses to reveal him" (Matt. 11:27), he is
claiming that there is nothing it is to be the Son that has not been given to him
by the Father. Or, as Levering puts it, "Since Christ is the Wisdom of God, his
wisdom is the Trinity, and learning his wisdom, as his friend, means to share
in his Trinitarian life."[54] To claim that the Father somehow possesses properties that the Son does not have—beyond the traditional divine "notions"—is
to make the Son's presentation of the Wisdom of the Father impossible, for
what would it mean for the submissive Son perfectly (and identically) to present the authoritative Father. Any difference in personal properties aside from
the subsistent relations would compromise the saving presence of the triune
God in the economy of redemption. Thus, as Maximus the Confessor claims,
"the whole of the Father and the whole of the Holy Spirit were present essentially and perfectly in the whole of the incarnate Son."[55]

While some might be inclined to think that the Son's self-giving in the
passion is an indication of his submission to the Father's will and thus a
confirmation of the EFS position—that Christ was revealing in the economy
of salvation that which was proper to his person and true from all eternity—
Aquinas thinks the opposite is the case: Christ's self-giving in his passion is a
mirroring of the Father's self-giving in the generation of the Son. In short, for
Aquinas, "the Paschal mystery does indeed reveal the Trinity."[56] The obvious
objection at this point is that it is proper to say the Son suffers on the cross,
and it is improper to say the Father suffers on the cross (at risk of Patripas-

52. St. Thomas Aquinas, *Commentary on the Gospel of St. John*, part 1, ch. 3, *lect.*2, n. 449 (trans. James A. Weisheipl and Fabian R. Larcher [Albany, NY: Magi, 1980], 191), cited in Matthew Levering, *Scripture and Metaphysics: Aquinas and the Renewal of Trinitarian Theology*, Challenges in Contemporary Theology (Malden, MA: Blackwell, 2004), 137.
53. Levering, *Scripture and Metaphysics*, 138.
54. Levering, *Scripture and Metaphysics*, 139.
55. St. Maximus the Confessor, "On the Lord's Prayer," in *The Philokalia*, compiled by St. Nikodimos of the Holy Mountain and St. Makarios of Corinth, Vol. 2, eds. and trans. G. E. H. Palmer, Philip Sherrard, and Kallistos Ware (Boston: Faber & Faber, 1981), 287, cited in Levering, *Scripture and Metaphysics*, 140.
56. Levering, *Scripture and Metaphysics*, 142.

sianism). Therefore, to speak of the whole triune God as present in the actions of Christ is necessarily problematic (so the objection goes).

In response, we will examine in passing the doctrine of inseparable operations and the idea of appropriation. The doctrine of the inseparable operations claims that the external works of the Trinity are indivisible (*Opera Trinitatis ad extra aunt indivisa*). Recall, importantly, that discussing the *external* works of the Trinity is to consider God's transitive acts *ad extra* (the *opera exeuntia*).[57] We are not considering God's immanent acts *ad intra*, all of which are, as Webster puts it, "constitutive, not accidental, activities . . . these activities are what it is for God to be God."[58]

Further, according to the concept of appropriations, it is proper to attribute specific economic works distinctly to the Father, Son, and Holy Spirit by virtue of their order of subsistence.[59] Consider, for instance, the incarnation, in which the Son assumes a human nature but the Father and Spirit do not. For Aquinas, actions such as this are divided into their principle and term (*principium actus et terminus*).[60] The principle of action in the incarnation is the divine nature, while the term of the action is the person of the Son. As Tyler Wittman puts it, "This distinction between the beginning (*principium*) and end (*terminus*) of the act of assumption enables Aquinas to say both that the divine nature acts in the assumption and that the Son alone becomes incarnate."[61] Certain Trinitarian actions "terminate" on one or other of the three divine persons because of the theological concept of appropriation, according to which it is proper to attribute specific actions to one or the other of the triune persons. At the same time, however,

> By definition, the appropriated attributes are no substitute for the personal properties, and are not to be conflated with them. It does not belong to appropriations to give us a proper notion that could really distinguish each divine person; this is the task of the properties or Trinitarian "notions," knowledge of which is assumed within the process of appropriation. Appropriation can never in any way replace theological study of the persons' properties, for it presupposes it.[62]

It might be proper to say, by way of appropriation, that the Son is subordinate to the Father during specific parts of his earthly incarnate ministry. But to move beyond this weak claim to the stronger claim that the Son's subordination is due to any eternal or necessary distinction between the Father and the

---

57. On this distinction, see John Webster, "Trinity and Creation," in *God without Measure: Working Papers in Christian Theology: Volume I: God and the Works of God* (London: Bloomsbury, 2015), 89–90.
58. Webster, "Trinity and Creation," 90.
59. See Emery, *The Trinitarian Theology of St. Thomas Aquinas*, 212ff.
60. Cf. Tyler R. Wittman, "The End of the Incarnation: John Owen, Trinitarian Agency and Christology," *International Journal of Systematic Theology* 15 (2013): 294–300.
61. Wittman, "The End of the Incarnation," 294–95.
62. Emery, *The Trinitarian Theology of St. Thomas Aquinas*, 337.

Son is to move outside of traditional theological reflection and into problematic territory.

VII. Conclusion

We have seen that Gons and Naselli's response to EFE's objections to EFS fail to give proper attention to traditional Trinitarian thought. And, we have argued that *if* Gons and Naselli's argument is correct, *then* it becomes problematic to specify the way the triune God is present in the work of redemption. To be perfectly clear: a view of the Trinity in which the Father, Son, and Spirit share distinct essential personal properties in addition to the five "notions" compromises the triune God's ability to enact God's saving self-presence. This saving presence is grounded not only on the fact of the Trinitarian processions and the full equality of the triune persons, but also on God's economic, united presence in God's actions for us and for our salvation.

Bibliography

Bauerschmidt, Frederick Christian. *Thomas Aquinas: Faith, Reason, and Following Christian*. Christian Theology in Context. Oxford: Oxford University Press, 2013.

Emery, Giles. *The Trinitarian Theology of St. Thomas Aquinas*. Oxford: Oxford University Press, 2007.

Erickson, Millard J. *Who's Tampering with the Trinity? An Assessment of the Subordination Debate*. Grand Rapids: Kregel, 2009.

Feinberg, John. *No One Like Him: The Doctrine of God*. Foundations of Evangelical Theology. Wheaton, IL: Crossway, 2001.

Friedman, Russell L. *Medieval Trinitarian Thought from Aquinas to Ockham*. Cambridge: Cambridge University Press, 2010.

Gons, Philip R., and Andrew David Naselli. "An Examination of Three Recent Philosophical Arguments against Hierarchy in the Immanent Trinity." In *One God in Three Persons: Unity of Essence, Distinction of Persons, Implications for Life*. Edited by Bruce A. Ware and John Stark, 195–213. Wheaton, IL: Crossway, 2015.

Jacobs, Nathan. "On 'Not Three Gods'—Again: Can a Primary-Secondary Substance Reading of *Ousia* and *Hypostasis* Avoid Tritheism?" *Modern Theology* 24 (2008): 331–58.

Levering, Matthew. *Scripture and Metaphysics: Aquinas and the Renewal of Trinitarian Theology*. Challenges in Contemporary Theology. Malden, MA: Blackwell, 2004.

Lombard, Peter. *The* Sentences, *Book 1: The Mystery of the Trinity*. Mediaeval Sources in Translation 42. Translated by Giulio Silano. Ontario: Pontifical Inistute of Mediaeval Studies, 2007.

McCall, Thomas. *Which Trinity? Whose Monotheism? Philosophical and Systematic Theologians on the Metaphysics of Trinitarian Theology*. Grand Rapids: Eerdmans, 2010.

McCall, Thomas, and Keith E. Yandell. "On Trinitarian Subordinationism." *Philosophia Christi* 11 (2009): 339–58.

St. Anselm. "On the Incarnation of the Word." In *Anselm of Canterbury: The Major Works*. Oxford World's Classics. Edited by Brian Davies and G. R. Evans, 233–59. Oxford: Oxford University Press, 1998.

St. Maximus the Confessor. "On the Lord's Prayer." In *The Philokalia*. Compiled by St. Nikodimos of the Holy Mountain and St. Makarios of Corinth, Vol. 2. Edited and translated by G. E. H. Palmer, Philip Sherrard, and Kallistos Ware. Boston: Faber & Faber, 1981.

St. Thomas Aquinas. *Commentary on the Gospel of St. John*. Translated by James A. Weisheipl and Fabian R. Larcher. Albany, NY: Magi, 1980.

———. *Summa Theologiae*. 61 vols. London: Eyre & Spottiswoode, 1964–1981.

Swain, Scott, and Michael Allen. "The Obedience of the Eternal Son." *International Journal of Systematic Theology* 15 (2013): 114–34.

Webster, John. "Trinity and Creation." In *God without Measure: Working Papers in Christian Theology: Volume I: God and the Works of God*, 83–98. London: Bloomsbury, 2015.

Wittman, Tyler R. "The End of the Incarnation: John Owen, Trinitarian Agency and Christology." *International Journal of Systematic Theology* 15 (2013): 294–300.

CHAPTER 15

Bruce Ware's Trinitarian Methodology

SCOTT HARROWER

This article makes a contribution to the current debates within evangelical theology about the nature of God the Trinity, by outlining Bruce Ware's Trinitarian hermeneutics and theology.[1] A number of Ware's key Trinitarian works are examined at length, which include his landmark *Father, Son, and Holy Spirit: Relationships, Roles, and Relevance*. As my description of his content is carried out, I will focus upon Ware's particular reading and methodological use of something analogous to "Rahner's Rule": *"The 'economic' Trinity is the 'immanent' Trinity and the 'immanent' Trinity is the 'economic' Trinity."* By way of this work, I will conclude that a number of theological and hermeneutical pressures drive Ware toward an inconsistent use of Scripture. This is accompanied by an inconsistent interpretation of, and theological construction with respect to, the relationships between the Father, Son, and Spirit in both the economy of salvation and in eternity. This article

---

1. This article is a revised version of an unpublished portion of my PhD dissertation undertaken under the supervision of Graham Cole and Thomas McCall at Trinity Evangelical Divinity School, completed in 2011. A revised version of my thesis was subsequently published as Scott D. Harrower, *Trinitarian Self and Salvation: An Evangelical Engagement with Rahner's Rule* (Eugene, OR: Pickwick, 2012). I am grateful to Dr. Cole and Dr. McCall for their influence, and this work reflects both their influence and input. My thanks also go to those who have helped develop and outline this piece as a discrete contribution, including Jonathan King and Patrick Senn from Ridley College, Melbourne, Australia.

concludes that despite the surface attractiveness of his methodology, Bruce Ware's work requires methodological and conceptual modification.

The Warrant for This Essay

Stephen R. Holmes, Senior Lecturer in systematic theology at the University of St. Andrews, recently reflected on a new volume on the Trinity, edited by Bruce Ware and John Starke.[2] Holmes proposed a series of snapshots of complementarian theology as it relates to a number of issues, including Trinitarian doctrine.[3] He wrote:

> There is a good book to be written by someone who has more patience than I do with bad arguments, narrating the various arguments used by complementarians in recent decades. A "narrow hermeneutic" argument based around close exegesis of two or three NT texts failed—the exegesis was not plausible; it was replaced by a "broad hermeneutic" argument appealing to a Biblical theology of gender. This also failed, and was replaced by an appeal to "eternal functional subordination" and a direct argument from the doctrine of God to gender relations.[4]

He continued:

> The book I am here treating seems to me to demonstrate that (at least some) "complementarians" themselves have realized what serious scholars already knew: this argument too fails. It relied on an extreme version of social Trinitarianism which had no purchase in the Christian tradition, and was unsustainable exegetically. In their different ways, Starke, Claunch, and others here offer chastened versions of the argument—but it is lost.[5]

Holmes's proposal will receive a contribution by means of this article that outlines various aspects of Bruce Ware's theology. It is written for both historical and theological purposes; I hope to preserve and clarify his arguments, sources, and hermeneutics. In particular, I shall undertake a study of his essay "How Shall We Think of the Trinity?" where he laid out his methodological assumptions and some of their concomitant theological claims. Following this, Ware's book *Father, Son, and Holy Spirit*[6] will also be explored in an effort to demonstrate how he fleshed out the assumptions he disclosed in "How Shall We Think of the Trinity?" Before proceeding, I will provide a

---

2. Bruce A. Ware and John B. Starke, eds., *One God in Three Persons: Unity of Essence, Distinction of Persons, Implications for Life* (Wheaton, IL: Crossway, 2015).
3. Steven R. Holmes, "Reflections on a New Defence of 'Complementarianism,'" http://steverholmes. org.uk/blog/?p=7507 (accessed October 20, 2015). See also Thomas H. McCall, "Gender and the Trinity Once More: A Review Article," *Trinity Journal* 36 (2015): 263–80.
4. McCall, "Gender and the Trinity Once More," 263–80.
5. McCall, "Gender and the Trinity Once More," 263–80.
6. Bruce A. Ware, *Father, Son, and Holy Spirit: Relationships, Roles, and Relevance* (Wheaton, IL: Crossway, 2005).

short biographical sketch of Ware, and some categories related to "Rahner's Rule," that will help articulate a description and critique of Ware's work. In the course of this work, I will also attempt to explain the attractiveness of his methodology to some evangelical theologians.

Bruce Ware

Ware has been the Senior Associate Dean and Professor of Christian Theology, at Southern Baptist Theological Seminary (Kentucky).[7] Ware is also on the council of a socially conservative movement which calls itself the "Council for Biblical Manhood and Womanhood." He received his doctorate from Fuller Seminary, and taught at various conservative seminaries including Trinity Evangelical Divinity School (Illinois) where he was the chair of the Biblical and Systematic Theology Department. Notably, Ware returned to Trinity Evangelical Divinity School for a Henry Center-sponsored debate on the evening of October 9, 2008. Ware partnered with Grudem in arguing for the eternal subordination of God the Son to God the Father. They debated Thomas McCall and Keith Yandell, who countered that the Ware/Grudem position undermines the full divinity of God the Son. This debate attracted great attention and follow-up.[8]

Ware's printed works reveal a keen interest in the attributes of God, in the doctrine of the Trinity, and in Christology. His works on the attributes of God, written and edited over a twenty-year period between 1986 and 2005, include *An Evangelical Reformulation of the Doctrine of the Immutability of God,*[9] *The Grace of God,*[10] *God's Lesser Glory: The Diminished God of Open Theism,*[11] *Their God Is Too Small,*[12] *God's Greater Glory,*[13] and *Still Sovereign.*[14] These works are directed towards those Ware considers as nonconservative evangelicals.

---

7.   I have spoken with Ware personally at some length on various occasions, and have found him to be approachable and sharp-witted. In undertaking this article I wish to make it clear that I respect him as a person, and hope to have described his position with charity, despite the significant theological differences between us. I am also aware that Ware's and Grudem's views have evolved, as noted by Dr. Cole's contribution to this volume.

8.   The Henry Center has a record of the arguments of each side of the debate. http://www.henrycenter. org/2008/10/09/trinity-debate-ware-grudem-vs-mccall-yandell (accessed November 20, 2008). Publications relating to this debate include Thomas H. McCall, *Which Trinity? Whose Monotheism: Philosophical and Systematic Theologians on the Metaphysics of Trinitarian Theology* (Grand Rapids: Eerdmans, 2010). The debate has continued in a number of well-known published works.

9.   Bruce A. Ware, "An Evangelical Reformulation of the Doctrine of the Immutability of God," *Journal of the Evangelical Theological Society* 29 (1986): 431–46.

10. Thomas R. Schreiner and Bruce A. Ware, *The Grace of God, the Bondage of the Will,* 2 vols. (Grand Rapids: Baker, 1995).

11. Bruce A. Ware, *God's Lesser Glory: The Diminished God of Open Theism* (Wheaton, IL: Crossway, 2000).

12. *Their God Is Too Small: Open Theism and the Undermining of Confidence in God* (Wheaton, IL: Crossway, 2003).

13. *God's Greater Glory: The Exalted God of Scripture and the Christian Faith* (Wheaton, IL: Crossway, 2004).

14. Thomas R. Schreiner and Bruce A. Ware, *Still Sovereign: Contemporary Perspectives on Election, Foreknowledge, and Grace* (Grand Rapids: Baker, 2000).

Ware's works on the Trinity, including his 2005 book *Father, Son, and Spirit: Relationships, Roles and Relevance* are focused on developing the case that the gospel, and its efficacy, is dependent upon certain eternal immanent relationships amongst the persons of the Trinity. These are also said to set the patterns for Christian living and ministry.[15] Ware's perspective on this is so comprehensive that he has written a book for children to the effect that his Trinitarian views have strong implications for them.[16] The purpose of his work is both to shape the opinions of conservative evangelicals, and to argue against others who would also take the Scriptures as their norming *norma*.[17] The evangelicals whom Ware seeks to confront are, to his mind, "evangelical feminists" or proponents of Trinitarian "egalitarianism."[18]

Since writing *Father, Son, and Holy Spirit* in 2005 (which I will examine anon), Ware has continued to write on the Trinity and its significant links to Christology. For example, in *Cur Deus Trinus?* (2006) Ware argues that the atonement and its efficacy are undergirded by the structures of the immanent Trinity.[19] Ware continued to reflect on Christology in the article "The Man Christ Jesus" (2010)[20] and the book *The Man Christ Jesus* (2012).[21]

Ware is deeply wary about the impact society and culture can have upon theology and Christian doctrine, especially on the doctrine of God. This is manifested in the tone of Ware's early published Trinitarian theology.[22] At the outset of "How Shall We Think About the Trinity?" he cites "the sobering

---

15. Ware, *Father, Son, and Holy Spirit*.

16. *Big Truths for Young Hearts: Teaching and Learning the Greatness of God* (Wheaton, IL: Crossway, 2009).

17. It is notable that, for Ware, the basis for Christian life and ministry is not the gospel but the eternal, inner-Trinitarian relationships. More on this issue anon.

18. Ware argues against "'evangelical feminists,' otherwise known as 'egalitarians'"; Bruce A. Ware, "How Shall We Think About the Trinity?," in *God under Fire*, eds. Douglas S. Huffman and Eric L. Johnson (Grand Rapids: Zondervan, 2002), 269.

19. "*Cur Deus Trinus?* The Relations of the Trinity to Christ's Identity as Savior and to the Efficacy of His Atoning Death," *The Southern Baptist Journal of Theology* 10 (2006): 48–56. This work is significant because, like Rahner, Ware aligns his Trinitarian methodology with central pastoral and theological concerns. For Rahner, the Trinity does not explain the atonement, rather it clarifies the structures of human beings—those who are created in such a manner as to receive a direct self-communication from God in grace. For Ware, the Trinity explains the atonement and the structure of families. Therefore, we note that both theologians seek to align what is primary in their theological systems with the doctrine of the Trinity. For Ware, as a conservative evangelical, it is the atonement and gender relationships; for Rahner, it is the human subject. In a more recent work, "The Man Christ Jesus," Ware argues against what he perceives as an overemphasis on the divinity of Christ by evangelicals. He outlines the significance of the humanity of Jesus within his identity as the God-man, as "the means by which he fulfilled his calling" in life and ministry. "The Man Christ Jesus," *Journal of the Evangelical Theological Society* 53 (2010): 5.

20. Ware, "The Man Christ Jesus."

21. *The Man Christ Jesus: Theological Reflections on the Humanity of Christ* (Wheaton, IL: Crossway, 2012).

22. It is an essay published in Douglas S. Huffman and Eric L. Johnson, eds., *God under Fire: Modern Scholarship Reinvents God* (Grand Rapids: Zondervan, 2002).

words" of Dr. Wainwright, former professor of Systematic Theology at Duke University:

> The signs of our times are that, as in the fourth century, the doctrine of the trinity [*sic*] occupies a vital position. While usually still considering themselves within the church, and in any case wanting to be loyal to their perception of truth, various thinkers and activists are seeking such revisions of the inherited doctrine of the Trinity that their success might in fact mean its abandonment, or at least such an alteration of its content, status, and function that the whole face of Christianity would be drastically changed. Once more the understanding, and perhaps the attainment, of salvation is at stake, or certainly the message of the church and the church's visible composition.[23]

With this warning in place, Ware proceeds to outline his Trinitarian theology and the assumptions which undergird it. In order to describe Ware's procedure as he pursues his Trinitarian theology, it will be helpful to briefly recap "Rahner's Rule," one of the most important methodological norms for Trinitarian theology.

Rahner's Rule

Most aspects of Trinitarian theology and its implications revolve around how to interpret the relationships between the Father, Son, and Spirit as these are revealed in the Bible's account of salvation history.[24] One way of distinguishing these interpretations is to designate them with reference to how they (either explicitly or implicitly) relate to a Trinitarian norm known as "Rahner's Rule" (RR).[25] Karl Rahner stated it as: "*The 'economic' Trinity is the 'immanent' Trinity and the 'immanent' Trinity is the 'economic' Trinity.*"[26]

One approach to RR has been designated as the "strict realist reading" (SRR).[27] This argues that there is an unqualified identification between the

---

23. Ware, "How Shall We Think About the Trinity?," 255.

24. This section is dependent upon Scott Harrower, *Trinitarian Self and Salvation* (Eugene, OR: Pickwick, 2012).

25. See my account of the significance of the norm, its various interpreters, and an assessment of the interpretations in conversation with Luke-Acts and the book of Hebrews. Scott Harrower, *Trinitarian Self and Salvation*.

26. Karl Rahner, *The Trinity* (New York: Crossroad, 1970), 22 (Rahner's italics). The economic Trinity "[r]efers to the various roles of the members of the Trinity in the administration (economy) of the plan of salvation." The immanent (or essential) Trinity is the "Trinity's own eternal, internal, life as Father, Son and Holy Spirit." Graham A. Cole, *He Who Gives Life: The Doctrine of the Holy Spirit* (Wheaton, IL: Crossway, 2007), 286–87; Werner Brändle, "Immanente Trinität—ein Denkmal der Kirchengeschichte? Überlegungen zu Karl Rahners Trinitätslehre," *Kerygma und Dogma* 38 (1992): 185–98.

27. See Dennis W. Jowers, *The Trinitarian Axiom of Karl Rahner: The Economic Trinity Is the Immanent Trinity and Vice Versa* (Lewiston, NY: Edwin Mellen, 2006). Shillaker sums up Jowers's conclusions as follows: "1) trivially obvious identity, 2) absolute identity, 3) copy theory, 4) merely de facto identity, of which only one option carries the title, 5) 'Rahner's actual meaning." Robert Shillaker, "Rahner's

immanent Trinity and the economic Trinity. This view of RR interprets it in such a way that it allows us to speak about the exact relational structure of God's life as Father, Son, and Spirit. This is known as the ontological approach to the rule.[28] In other words, it asserts that God acts and relates as Father, Son, and Spirit in the economy of salvation in exactly the same way that he eternally relates within himself as Father, Son, and Spirit.[29] This exhaustive interpretation of RR entails a number of ontological claims beyond the fact that God is the Father, Son, and Spirit. The theological consequences of these, such as what this means for the coherence of the will of God, are addressed in other papers in this volume and in the scholarly literature.[30]

Alternatively, one can approach RR via the "loose realist reading" (LRR).[31] This reading of RR refrains from stating that there is a direct mirroring between the Trinitarian relations in the economy of salvation and the eternal inner-Trinitarian relations within the immanent Trinity. This historically dominant theological position takes an epistemological, or methodological, rather than an ontological view of the Trinitarian relationships that take place in the economy of salvation.[32] If taken methodologically or epistemologically, these relations in history reveal that there is a triune God but do not reveal the precise mechanics of how this God is triune. Lincicum writes: "If we intend it [RR] as a methodological principle about the order of knowing, then we may certainly agree with the first half of his statement that the economic Trinity truly reveals the immanent Trinity. In this sense, salvation history is not a modalistic play, but really reveals God as he is."[33] In other words, this position

---

Axiom and the Hermeneutic Foundation of Thomas Weinandy's Reconceiving the Trinity," *European Journal of Theology* 25 (2016): 35; Michael Hauber, "Unsagbar Nahe: Eine Studie zur Entstehung und Bedeutung der Trinitätslehre Karl Rahners" (PhD thesis, Freiburg, 2008); William V. Dych, *Karl Rahner* (Collegeville, MN: Liturgical Press, 1992).

28. Reading the rule as an epistemological principle is the non-controversial claim that "*The ontological Trinity is the ground of being for the economic Trinity and the economic Trinity is the ground of cognition for the ontological Trinity.*" Seung Goo Lee, "The Relationship between the Ontological Trinity and the Economic Trinity," *Journal of Reformed Theology* 3 (2009): 106–7 (Lee's italics).

29. Randall Rauser, "Rahner's Rule: An Emperor without Clothes?," *International Journal of Systematic Theology* 7 (2005): 82–85.

30. D. Glenn Butner Jr., "Eternal Functional Subordination and the Problem of the Divine Will," *Journal of the Evangelical Theological Society* 58 (2015): 131–49.

31. Butner Jr., "Eternal Functional Subordination," 85–87, 90–91.

32. Lee, "The Relationship between the Ontological Trinity and the Economic Trinity," 106–7. On Augustine's work on this issue see Ricardo Ferri, "Le Missioni Divine nel de Trinitate di Agostino d'ippona: Commento ai Libri ii–iv," *Lateranum* 82 (2016): 56–57.

33. Lincicum continues: "The reciprocal aspect of Rahner's maxim, however, implicates one in an ontological construal of the copula [the 'is' in RR] and so endangers the distinction between God and world. This move has serious and detrimental theological consequences, and so must be rejected." David Lincicum, "Economy and Immanence: Karl Rahner's Doctrine of the Trinity," *European Journal of Theology* 14 (2005): 116. See also Butner, "Eternal Functional Subordination." On the centrality and relevance of the immanent Trinity, even in the absence of its exhaustive desciption, see Jason M. Smith, "Must We Say Anything of an 'Immanent' Trinity? Schleiermacher

holds that the extent and degree to which God's eternal triune relationships are revealed is limited by both the nature of revelation and our possibilities for comprehending God; therefore, it is not exhaustive and leaves room for the mystery of God's being. In addition, those who hold this position claim that the SRR of RR faces well-documented, insurmountable problems.[34]

Bruce Ware and His Unique Interpretation of the SRR of RR

In Ware's explicitly Trinitarian works, the use of a norm with striking resemblance to the SRR of RR is apparent as far back as 2002 in "How Shall We Think About the Trinity?" (2002).[35] In this work, Ware immediately follows the quote from Wainwright (above) with a discussion of the relationship between the economic and immanent Trinity. This argument is prefaced by four concerns, two of which are particularly relevant here. The first is, "Whereas once the immanent Trinity took priority conceptually, the shift today is to give pride of place to the economic Trinity."[36] The second is, "many contemporary evangelical egalitarians are urging the church to retain masculine language for God while denying that this masculine language indicates any kind of inner-Trinitarian distinction of authority."[37] Ware clarifies what he understands to be the terminology and relationship between the immanent and economic Trinities before dealing with the issue of the reduction of the immanent Trinity into the economic Trinity. He states:

> . . . in orthodox theology, God is, in himself, eternal, self-existent and fully self-sufficient. Yet he has freely chosen to create a world with which he is intimately and fully involved. In accounting for both sides of this . . . reality, church theologians from the beginning have distinguished senses in which we talk about God. God *ad intra* (or God in himself) must be distinguished carefully from God *ad extra* (or God in relation to the world). . . . [I]t is a mistake to so identify God with the world such that somehow God's independence from the world is lost.[38]

Ware then proceeds to underscore his primary concern in Trinitarian thinking: the avoidance of agnosticism about God. As he defends this priority he outlines the SRR approach to selected texts that are relevant to Trinitarian discussion:

---

and Rowan Williams on an 'Abstruse' and 'Fruitless' Doctrine," *Anglican Theological Review* 98, no. 3 (2016), 509–512.

34. I document nine categories of problems the SRR of RR faces in Harrower, *Trinitarian Self and Salvation* 23–24.

35. Ware, "How Shall We Think About the Trinity?" This work was written in the same year Ware wrote "Male and Female Complementarity and the Image of God," in *Biblical Foundations for Manhood and Womanhood*, ed. Wayne Grudem (Wheaton, IL: Crossway, 2002), 71–92.

36. Ware, "How Shall We Think About the Trinity?," 255.

37. Ware, "How Shall We Think About the Trinity?," 255.

38. Ware, "How Shall We Think About the Trinity?," 255–56 (Ware's italics).

... having insisted that God *ad extra* is logically and conceptually dependent on God *ad intra*, the theologians of the church have also insisted that this does not leave us with two gods. That is, because God reveals *who he is* when he makes himself known to his finite creatures, we can have confidence that we come to know God *in himself* through his revelation to us. . . . God is not different in himself from what he is in his revelation to us. If this were the case, the God we *know* would be a different god from the God *who is*.[39]

This explicit concern becomes a foundational assumption for Ware's Trinitarian theology. He writes, "[A]s the divine persons act in freedom to create and to relate, they likewise manifest in their economic dealings with the world what is true of their logically prior and intrinsic immanent relations."[40] In the absence of any conditioning caveats, we therefore take the two statements above as evidence of Ware's approach to RR, and conclude that this view has great affinity with the strict realist reading of RR.

Ware begins his section entitled "Reducing the Immanent to the Economic Trinity" (which addresses the first of the concerns he noted) with a discussion of Rahner's *Grundaxiom*. On RR he states:

> One might take this claim to mean, with Barth, that we do not have two triune beings when we speak of the immanent and economic Trinities. If this were all that Rahner meant, there would be no real reformulation. But clearly Rahner wants more. Since we know God only in his self-revelation . . . and more particularly only as he is savingly revealed through the incarnation of the Son, we must use as our starting point on Trinitarian understanding the historic and redemptive revelation of the triune God who, as Father, Son and Spirit, brings us to salvation. . . . [T]his reductionism of the immanent Trinity to the economic Trinity has become commonplace in current Trinitarian writings. . . . The result is that we are limited to God's historical manifestation of his triune being for understanding the nature of that divine Trinity. But, if all we see and therefore know of God is God in historical manifestation, then at least two problems arise.[41]

For Ware, the two problems within Rahner's view are the loss of God's independence from creation as One whose being is necessarily a mystery, and the diminished value accorded to propositional revelation about the Trinity in Scripture. Regarding these two problems, Ware writes:

> First, if God's immanent being is identical to his economic manifestation, then God's independence from creation is called into question. Concerning Rahner's

39.   Ware, "How Shall We Think About the Trinity?," 256 (Ware's italics).
40.   Ware, "How Shall We Think About the Trinity?," 257.
41.   Ware, "How Shall We Think About the Trinity?," 257–58.

own reduction of immanent to economic Trinities, John Thompson observes that Rahner has "failed to distinguish between the mystery of grace in the economy and the *necessary* mystery of the Trinity per se." . . . Second if our knowledge of God is limited to his economic and historical self-disclosure, this denies an important category of divine revelation by which we know God, namely, propositional revelation. Surely as God utilizes the medium of divine discourse to tell us about aspects of his divine reality that transcend our own limitations and historical conditioning, we should not reject such knowledge of God simply because we have not somehow experienced those aspects historically. . . . The glory of divine revelation is precisely that God has *made himself known* such that without his free self-disclosure, we would be fully in the dark.[42]

The quotation above shows that to his credit, there are points at which Ware is critical of Rahner. Even so, as this article demonstrates, the substance of Ware's Trinitarian work shares Rahner's focus on Trinitarian relations in the economy of salvation and their significance for the immanent Trinity.[43]

The next issue prioritized by Ware in his article is the issue he labels as "Evangelical feminists." Ware begins by providing a definition of "Evangelical feminists" who seek to retain masculine language for God yet reject eternal functional subordination; these people are "known as egalitarians." For Ware, the positive aspect of their position is that these people "view Scripture as God's inspired Word and self-revelation, [and] the vast majority of egalitarians have sought to defend masculine God-language against the criticism of their feminist colleagues."[44] However, the problem he sees is that, in tandem with retaining masculine language for God, "they deny that such masculine God-language implies that what is masculine is superior over what is feminine or that the eternal relations of Father, Son and Holy Spirit indicate any kind of eternal functional hierarchy within the Trinity."[45]

Ware's challenge to the egalitarian position over their rejection of an eternally static hierarchy of authority in the immanent Trinity has to do with the nature of language for God, the nature of special revelation, and the nature of gender. Ware interrogates the "egalitarian" position via a string of questions. Firstly, on the nature of language for God, he asks: "What *does* it mean that the Father is the eternal *Father* of the Son and that the Son is the eternal *Son* of the Father? Is not the eternal and inner-Trinitarian Father-Son relationship indicative of some eternal relationship of authority *within* the Trinity itself?"[46] Secondly, with an eye to the nature of special revelation he asks: "Further-

42. Ware, "How Shall We Think About the Trinity?," 258–59 (Ware's italics).
43. Hauber, "Unsagbar Nahe: Eine Studie zur Entstehung und Bedeutung der Trinitätslehre Karl Rahners," 2008.
44. Ware, "How Shall We Think About the Trinity?," 269.
45. Ware, "How Shall We Think About the Trinity?," 269.
46. Ware, "How Shall We Think About the Trinity?," 270 (Ware's italics).

more, if . . . the masculine language about God in Scripture is not a conces-
sion to a patriarchal culture but rather represents God's own chosen means of
self-disclosure, what *is* conveyed by this masculine terminology?"[47] Thirdly,
with respect to the nature of gender he makes the following links: "[W]hile
egalitarians and complementarians agree that masculine God-language never
indicates the superiority of the male or the inferiority of the female, one must
ask: Does this masculine language not intentionally link God's *position and
authority as God* with the concept of *masculinity* over femininity?"[48]

In Ware's mind, the "orthodox view" (his twin views on "the eternal nature of the Father-Son relationship within the Godhead" and "the
predominant biblical masculine language for God") has an obvious and
significant outworking in human relationships. That is, a view akin to the
SRR of RR is applied directly to human relationships: "[I]f an eternal relationship of authority and obedience is grounded in the eternal immanent
inner-Trinitarian relations of Father, Son, and Holy Spirit, then it gives at
least *prima facie* justification to the notion of creational human relations in
which authority and submission inhere."[49]

In the last part of "How Shall We Think About the Trinity?" Ware seeks to
overcome arguments put forward by egalitarians against his own position. He
summarizes the egalitarian argument in three points. The first of the egalitarian arguments is that the creation of men and women in God's image is the
basic category for human beings and their interactions, not their gender. The
second egalitarian rejoinder is that any subordination within the Godhead
entails a form of Arianism. Thirdly, the position argues that the incarnational
mission of the second person of the Trinity provides the logic for, and fully
accounts for, the temporary submission of God the Son to God the Father in
the economy of salvation. Ware concludes his article with a response to each
of these three points.

His responses are as follows. To counter the first argument, Ware states
that the choice of the word "Father" as the address for God (the Father)
by Jesus was deliberate because it conveys the nature of their relationship.
Furthermore, because being in authority is central to being a Father, and given
that Jesus referred to his mission as the Father's will, Jesus must be under the
authority of the Father. To counter the second egalitarian argument, Ware
states that though subordinationism was rejected in the early church, "nonetheless the church has always affirmed the priority of the Father over the Son
and the Spirit." Ware cites Augustine's *De Trinitate* 4.27 as evidence that the
Father and Son are distinguished by the authority-submission structure of
this relationship. Ware responds to the third argument by stating that Jesus
could only be Savior and Lord if he were male, because the male gender, and

---

47. Ware, "How Shall We Think About the Trinity?," (Ware's italics).
48. Ware, "How Shall We Think About the Trinity?," (Ware's italics).
49. Ware, "How Shall We Think About the Trinity?," (Ware's italics).

male gender language alone, and not female gender language, can reflect the absolute authority of God.[50]

Ware adds two further points to his counterargument against egalitarian responses to his stand on the eternal subordination of God the Son, the significance of the male gender language, and the revelation of God. Firstly, he argues that if it is not necessary that only the Son could become incarnate, then we are in an agnostic position as to why it was fitting that this person of the Trinity became incarnate and not another, and also why the names Father, Son, and Holy Spirit are relevant. If this agnosticism were the case, Ware claims that there would be no connection between Trinity and Christology. His second argument is that Scripture warrants the claim that God the Son was eternally submissive to God the Father, and that Jesus was not merely fulfilling a submissive mission in time and space.[51]

Ware's "Conclusion" to "How Shall We Think About the Trinity?" revisits the problems he countered in contemporary Trinitarian theology and pleads for a scriptural approach to the doctrine of the Trinity: "Because we have God's inspired Word and because God has made known his own triune life in his Word, we must with renewed commitment seek to study, believe, and embrace the truth of God made known there."[52]

Analysis of the Putative Biblical Basis for the Use of the SRR

Having surveyed a key exemplar of Ware's motivations, methodology, and theology, some preliminary observations of the putative biblical basis for Ware's approach to RR work will be carried out.

In "How Shall We Think About the Trinity?" Ware lays out the "biblical evidence" for what he calls the "eternal functional subordination of the Son to the Father." His primary evidence is that "As Jesus declares in well over thirty occasions in John's Gospel, he was *sent to the earth* by the Father to do the Father's will . . . [we] should . . . think of this sending . . . as having taken place in eternity past, a commissioning then fulfilled in time."[53] The basis of Ware's understanding of RR as a Trinitarian norm therefore presumes the "eternal functional subordination" of God the Son. This is ultimately based upon the economy of salvation. Thus, Ware begins his treatment with the economy of salvation despite earlier appealing to God's aseity and freedom. His reading of the relationships amongst the divine persons in the economy of salvation (with the exception of the Spirit's temporary authority over the Son) are then read as isomorphic reflections of these relationships in the immanent Trinity. Ware further marshals scriptural warrants for his argument for the eternal subordination of the Son to the Father as follows. Ware begins with two passages

---

50. Ware, "How Shall We Think About the Trinity?," 272–75.
51. Ware, "How Shall We Think About the Trinity?," 275.
52. Ware, "How Shall We Think About the Trinity?," 277.
53. Ware, "How Shall We Think About the Trinity?," 275.

attributed to the apostle Peter. Firstly, Peter's words about a "set purpose" of God (Ware assumes this means God the Father alone) in Acts 2:23. Ware speculates that these words may draw upon Old Testament passages such as Psalm 22; Isaiah 9:6–7, 53; and Micah 5:2, which predict the Messiah and his work. Secondly, 1 Peter 1:20 ("He was chosen before the creation of the world, but was revealed in these last times for your sake") is taken to speak not merely of the foreknowledge of a Savior, but that the commissioning of the Son was by God the Father within the immanent Trinity.

Two other passages (Eph. 1:3–5; Rev. 13:8) are put forward as exegetical proof. Ware takes these passages to argue for the pretemporal election of Christ by God the Father as necessary in order for Christ to come into the world. In Ware's understanding, this demonstrates that God the Father's purpose for God the Son was set within the life of God, independent of creation. Ware consolidates his argument by stating that the submissive relationship of Jesus is established by looking back into eternity, as well as looking forward to the consummation when Jesus will again be submitted to the Father. Ware appeals to 1 Corinthians 15:27–28 to make this case.[54]

Ware's understanding of the relationship between the Father and Son in eternity and the economy of salvation is grounded in the will of God the Father alone: "Yet we have scriptural revelation that clearly says that the Son came down out of heaven to do the will of his Father. This sending is not ad hoc."[55] Further, if one does not follow his argument, then Ware claims that they compromise the glory of the Son who "willingly laid aside the glory he had with the Father to come and purchase our pardon and renewal. Such glory is diminished if there is no eternal Father-Son relation on the basis of which the Father sends, the Son willingly comes, and the Spirit willingly empowers."[56]

All of Ware's efforts combine to present a key assumption in Rahner's theology: only God the Son could become incarnate. In what constitutes a departure from classical theism, Ware identifies the Father's will as the basis for the fittingness of the Son's incarnation.[57]

Ware believes that there is an exegetical foundation for the authority-submission structure between the Father and the Son in the immanent and economic Trinities. This relies heavily upon the presupposition that father-

---

54. Ware, "How Shall We Think About the Trinity?," 275–76.
55. Ware, "How Shall We Think About the Trinity?," 275.
56. This argument may not work in view of Philippians 2:5–11. In this passage, what highlights the glory of the Son is the fact that he did give up his relational equality with God the Father in eternity to become subordinate to him in the economy of salvation. If the second person of the Trinity is always in an authority-submission relationship to God the Father, then what "glory" is there in reduplicating this relationship in the economy of salvation?
57. Peter Lombard, Giulio Silano, and Pontifical Institute of Mediaeval Studies., *The Sentences: Book 3, On the Incarnation of the Word* (Ontario: Pontifical Institute of Medieval Studies, 2008), Dist. 1, ch. 2, "Whether the Father or the Holy Spirit could have become incarnate or could do so now," 5. See Harrower, *Trinitarian Self and Salvation*, 74–75.

hood language designates God the Father's identity as the authority in the Godhead. This assumes a fatherly kind of maleness as the bearer of this authority in the created world. Ware bases this on John 1:14–18 into which he imports his view of fatherhood and sonship. The specifics of the passage, and the Johannine view of what fatherhood and sonship mean, are not dealt with. Instead Ware states:

> Clearly, at the pinnacle of this self-disclosure of God stands the revelation of Jesus the Christ, who became flesh [the second person of the Trinity became flesh] that we might know in visible form what the invisible, nonphysical God is like (John 1:14–18). . . . That Jesus is the Son sent by the Father is so deeply and widely reflective of God's self-revelation in and through the Incarnation that to alter this language would suggest, even if only implicitly, that one speak of a different deity. Divine self-revelation, then, requires the glad retention of God as Father, Son and Holy Spirit.[58]

The connection between fatherhood and authority is not worked out exegetically from within John's own writings, but is instead fleshed out by an appeal to Malachi 1:6 (NIV 1984): "A son honors his father, and a servant his master. If I am a father, where is the honor due me? If I am a master, where is the respect due me?' says the LORD Almighty." Ware's comment on this is that: "God as Father is rightfully deserving of his children's honor, respect, and obedience. To fail to see this is to miss one of the primary reasons God chose such masculine terminology to name himself."[59]

Ware offers Jesus's role as the second Adam as the basis for Jesus's male gender, and as necessary for him to be Savior and Lord. However, Ware extends this into an argument in which he contends that the authoritative nature of the male gender is revealed in the fact that Christ was male. Ware merely states that Christ's maleness communicates and reflects the authority and lordship of God; therefore, maleness is authoritative by its nature. He offers no biblical warrant for his position.[60] The problem Ware's argument faces at this point is that the male Jesus is himself under authority, therefore, maleness alone cannot be defined as authority, but must (at least in this case) be taken in tandem with obedience.

It is highly significant that Ware's use of the SRR of RR entails a literalistic linguistic argument. By means of this approach, Ware seeks to apply his interpretation of the relational character of the names "Father" and "Son" from the economy of salvation to the immanent Trinity. This is not surprising since the SRR of RR, and Ware's close affinity with it, employs a univocal approach to Trinitarian relations, and therefore the language of Father receives the same

58. Ware, "How Shall We Think About the Trinity?," 267–68.
59. Ware, "How Shall We Think About the Trinity?," 272–73.
60. Ware, "How Shall We Think About the Trinity?," 274–75.

univocal treatment.[61] Further, Ware introduces his own view of what the Father-Son relationship entails, plus the univocal application of this language from creation to the Creator. In this way he establishes a Father-Son relationship of authority and subordination in the immanent Trinity because he can claim to have found it in the economic roles of the Father and the Son.[62] Secondly, as noted above, Ware follows Rahner (in part) in his argument that only the second person of the Trinity could become incarnate. It is noteworthy that both theologians' views entail a subordinationism of some kind.

Father, Son, and Holy Spirit

I began this article by outlining Ware's basis for the use of a hermeneutic which can be described as approximating the SRR of RR.[63] I carried this study out on a work which is dedicated to the relationship between the economic and immanent Trinity, "How Shall We Think About the Trinity?" The underlying motivations, concerns, sources, hermeneutical criteria, content, christological implications, and practical outworking of a Trinitarian theology based upon the SRR of RR in *Father, Son, and Holy Spirit* are unchanged from those in "How Shall We Think About the Trinity?" For example, in *Father, Son, and Holy Spirit* the methodological nexus between gender roles leading to an authority-subordination structure, the economy of salvation being the basis of constructing eternally fixed roles within the Godhead, and confirmation of these roles by appeals to God the Father's will before creating, is followed without deviation.[64] Ware also employs what may fairly be called the SRR of RR (or the SRRT as per footnote 74) as his norm for positing Trinitarian relationships. He writes:

> Clearly, then, Scripture teaches that Jesus's submission to the Father extends from eternity past to eternity future, and what we see in the incarnational mission of Christ over and over again is simply the manifestation here and now, of what is eternally true in the relationship between the Father and the Son. . . . Authority and submission reside eternally in this Father-Son relationship, as taught clearly in Scripture and affirmed by the fathers of the church.[65]

61. On the history of the priority and uses of creaturely language in the Arian and post-Nicene neo-Arian debates see R. P. C. Hanson, *The Search for the Christian Doctrine of God: The Arian Controversy 318–381* (Grand Rapids: Baker Academic 1988), 557–97; Maurice Wiles, *Archetypal Heresy: Arianism through the Centuries* (Oxford: Clarendon, 1996), 27 ff.; Jan-Heiner Tück, "The Father without the Son Would Not Be the Father," *Communio* 42 (2015): 7–25.
62. Ware is very clear about this. In "How Shall We Think About the Trinity?," 270, Ware wrote that he believed that within God there exists an "eternal relationship of authority and obedience grounded in the eternal immanent inner-Trinity relations of Father, Son and Holy Spirit."
63. I noted it could be described as a SRRT, even though Ware deploys the SRRT selectively.
64. Ware, *Father, Son, and Holy Spirit: Relationships, Roles, and Relevance*, 71–86.
65. Ware, *Father, Son, and Holy Spirit*, 85.

The first of the main areas of difference between these works is the inclusion of work on the Holy Spirit in *Father, Son, and Holy Spirit*. This work discloses the extent to which the use of the SRR of RR significantly affects Ware's pneumatology. The Holy Spirit is clearly in a "third-string" position in the way in which Ware conceives of the eternal Trinitarian relationships. He "embraces eternally the backstage position in relation to the Father and the Son."[66]

In a revealing paragraph, Ware explains the Spirit's relational position in the context of his SRR view of RR:

> What has been true in eternity past, in the incarnation of the Son upon the earth, and throughout all of the work of the Father and the Son in lives now . . . is also true in eternity future, as the Spirit takes the position subordinate to both the Son and the Father.[67]

Ware explores the significance of his SRR of RR-based view for the inner-Trinitarian relationships and the missions of the persons of the Trinity. He writes:

> . . . notice the difference between the Son and the Spirit. . . . The Son said constantly that he came from heaven to do the will of his *Father*, and that the *Father* had sent him into the world. There is no mention of the Spirit . . . as involved in the sending of the Son, and yet when the Spirit comes into the world, it is so clear that even though the Spirit proceeds from the Father, he is also sent from the Son (John 15:26; Acts 2:33). Yet, although the Spirit is sent from both the Father *and the Son*, he shows no resentment. The Spirit accepts this role. He embraces it. He joyfully, willingly takes the position of being third—all the time third.[68]

In light of the quote above, how Ware describes the successive subordinations of God the Son and God the Holy Spirit to each other in the context of Jesus's earthly and ascended ministry is instructive. Ware makes the following observation about the relationship of Jesus to the Spirit in his ministry:

> As a man, Jesus submitted fully to the Spirit, even though in terms of rank within the Trinity, Jesus has authority over the Spirit. For the sake of his mission, he humbled himself. In taking on our human nature, he submitted to the very one over whom he has rightful authority.[69]

On the Spirit's role under the authority of Jesus after the resurrection, Ware writes that: "Jesus says that the Spirit who is coming will not speak on his own

---

66. Ware, *Father, Son, and Holy Spirit*, 104.
67. Ware, *Father, Son, and Holy Spirit*, 125.
68. Ware, *Father, Son, and Holy Spirit*, 129 (Ware's italics).
69. Ware, *Father, Son, and Holy Spirit*, 91.

authority but will speak what Jesus tells him to speak."[70] Ware draws together the successive subordinations of the Son and Spirit to one another in Jesus's earthly ministry and his post-ascension state in the following conclusion: "Jesus made it clear that although he has submitted to the Spirit in his life as the incarnate Son of the Father, the order of relationship between himself and the Spirit was fundamentally reversed."[71]

This succession of subordinations creates a prima facie internal problem of coherence and contradiction within Ware's argument for static relational patterns within God. It raises the question of how this economic pattern could accurately and directly reflect the relational patterns within the inner life of God. Ware must find a way to argue that *only one* of these relationships directly mirrors the strict authority-submission structure within God. In order to resolve this problem, Ware grounds his argument in John 16:12–14. For Ware, the fact that the Spirit "will speak what *Jesus* tells him to speak" is highly significant.[72] This is taken to mean that there is no doubt that the Spirit is under the authority of the Son from eternity. Ware consolidates his argument for a strictly ordered authority structure that exists in the manner of Father over Son and both over the Holy Spirit:

> Jesus does not say, "Just as I spoke only what the Father taught me, and just as I glorified the Father, so the Spirit, when he comes, likewise will only speak what the Father teaches him, for he will glorify the Father." No, the direct lines of authority and submission here run between the Spirit and the Son, not the Spirit and the Father. Although Jesus submitted fully to the Spirit in his incarnate life, still, the Spirit's eternal role is to uphold the will and the word of the Son; in his coming, the Spirit seeks in all he does to glorify Jesus.[73]

This revelatory aspect of the Son-Spirit relationship, and this aspect alone, is taken to be normative for the structure of the Son-Spirit relationship. However, Jesus's earthly ministry under the Spirit is not taken as normative. This is a marker for describing Ware's view as a selective use of the SRR of RR.[74] That is, the life of Jesus and his divine relationships are interpreted via theological conclusions drawn from his reading of John 16:12–14. Thus, we see that Ware's realism is conditioned by a selective use of texts.

A further point in Ware's argument relates to the ascension. By his return to the Father, Jesus is understood to demonstrate the true structure of inner-Trinitarian relationships: "Although the Son is in submission to the Spirit

---

70. Ware, *Father, Son, and Holy Spirit*, 94. Ware's exegetical conclusion from John 16:12–14, upon which he bases such an authoritarian view of the relationships between Jesus and Holy Spirit, is questionable.

71. Ware, *Father, Son, and Holy Spirit*.

72. Ware, *Father, Son, and Holy Spirit* (Ware's italics).

73. Ware, *Father, Son, and Holy Spirit*, 94–95.

74. Or, a selective SRRT, a SSRRT (selective strict realist reading of texts).

in the incarnation, in his exaltation the Son 'returns' to his place under the Father yet over the Spirit. So the Spirit is the 'Spirit of Jesus,' . . . and the Spirit comes to 'glorify' Jesus."[75]

Given the above, Ware's methodological use of the SRR cannot accurately be captured by labeling it as the SRR of RR alone. A qualification needs to be made. Ware has employed a selective strict realist reading of the text (SSRRT) in order to resolve a key problem for those who take the SRR of RR. By means of his selective reading of texts, Ware resolved the problem which the successive subordinations of the Spirit and the Son to each other poses for the SRR of RR. He achieves this by concluding that because the Spirit ultimately serves the Son, then even though the Son is submissive to the Spirit in the economy of salvation, the eternal Father-Son-Spirit order within the Trinity is preserved. That is, by Jesus teaching that the Spirit is under his authority, seen in that after the ascension the Spirit will remind the disciples of Jesus's words, then the fact that Jesus is under the authority of the Spirit in the economy of salvation is not a problem. The Trinitarian *taxis* is normatively expressed *in the teaching of Jesus* rather than in economic relations.[76]

In attempting to overcome a problem passage in terms of the SRR of RR, Ware appears to undermine his principle that the relationships seen in the economy of salvation are strict reflections of the relationships within the immanent Trinity. The fact that he has destabilized this principle is highly significant for his ecclesial and social project because the application of the intra-divine relationships to the realm of human relationships is not as clear-cut as Ware would suggest. In fact, in order to preserve his view of a set authority structure within the Trinity, Ware added a qualifying caveat to all patterns of relationships in the economy of salvation. We can restate his norm in our own words as "divine inner-relations in the economic Trinity strictly mirror the relationships in the immanent Trinity *unless one of the persons of the Trinity teaches something corresponding to the Father-Son-Spirit structure of authority that can be used to qualify problematical texts that* prima facie *point in a different direction*."[77]

This means that by these two relativizing caveats Ware demonstrates that he has indeed effectively moved beyond the SRR of RR into a Selective Strict Realist Reading of Texts (SSRRT) as an alternative Trinitarian norm. This sub-category of the SRR of RR may be stated as the following norm: "*despite any apparent evidence to the contrary, any relationship between persons of the*

75. Ware, *Father, Son, and Holy Spirit*, 97.
76. Ware, *Father, Son, and Holy Spirit*, 94–95.
77. Please note that these are my words, I am describing Ware's framework for dealing with biblical data that does not fit within his theory on pages 94–98. Ware is aware of texts that are defeaters for his interpretive scheme. However, they are not taken seriously, for example on Ware, *Father, Son, and Holy Spirit*, 95. Ware also adds another qualifying factor onto the changing nature of the relationship between the Son and the Spirit. This factor is the "broader Trinitarian context" in which the Father-Son-Spirit order of relations is established, see Ware, *Father, Son, and Holy Spirit*, 94–98.

Trinity in the economy of salvation must correspond to the authority-submission structure of Father over the Son, to both of whom the Spirit is subordinate."

The second area of difference between "How Shall We Think About the Trinity?" and *Father, Son, and Holy Spirit*, lies in the treatment of Jesus's faithfulness toward God in his human nature and his mission.[78] Ware argues that Jesus's human nature entailed some limitations; however, these negative limitations are restricted to Jesus's intellect:

> [Jesus] accepted the limitations of what it is to be a human, in order to grow in understanding, to grow in wisdom, as the Spirit would help him see things more clearly and understand God's Word with greater clarity and greater forcefulness as he grew older. In this sense then, he was like any child born. . . . In accepting these limitations . . . Jesus did not discard or give up any attributes of deity . . . . he accepted the limitation or restriction of the use . . . of certain of his divine attributes in order to live life fully as a man.[79]

The positive demand placed upon Jesus by his human nature is the demand to "live by faith."[80] This demand is an outworking of his intellectual constraint: "In his divine nature, he retained omniscience, but in the consciousness of Jesus, the God-man, he accepted a restricted knowledge so that he would have to trust his heavenly Father. He had to live by faith. . . . He had to . . . be 'made perfect' (Heb. 5:9)."[81] Ware's theology may need further development in terms of the fullness of Jesus's messianic vocation, as the fulfillment of the Old Testament's call for a new faithful human person, and a righteous people of God.

The Attractiveness of the SRR of RR or SRRT

One important driving force for Ware is to avoid agnosticism about God. In an article included in *God Under Fire*—in which Ware had his piece "How Shall We Think About the Trinity?"—Mark R. Talbot dealt with an issue central to evangelical Trinitarian theology. This issue was captured in the title of the work as: "Does God Reveal Who He Actually Is?"[82] In Ware's own article he underlines the weight he gives in his own thinking to special revelation:

> [I]f our knowledge of God is limited to his economic and historical self-disclosure, this denies an important category of divine revelation by which we know God, namely, propositional revelation. Surely as God utilizes the medium of

---

78. Ware, *Father, Son, and Holy Spirit*, 92–102.
79. Ware, *Father, Son, and Holy Spirit*, 92.
80. Ware, *Father, Son, and Holy Spirit*, 93.
81. Ware, *Father, Son, and Holy Spirit*, 93.
82. Mark R. Talbot, "Does God Reveal Who He Actually Is?," in Huffman and Johnson, eds., *God under Fire*, 43–70.

divine discourse to tell us about aspects of his divine reality that transcend our own limitations and historical conditioning, we should not reject such knowledge of God simply because we have not somehow experienced those aspects historically. . . . The glory of divine revelation is precisely that God has *made himself known* such that without his free self-disclosure, we would be fully in the dark.[83]

As noted above, for Ware, whenever there is a clash between the economic relations between members of the Trinity and Ware's view of the nature of these relations, Ware holds that our understanding of the Trinitarian *taxis* is ultimately normed by *the teaching of Jesus* rather than by economic relations.[84]

The attractiveness of the SRRT is that it enables people to state what they claim to know with great certainty. An extension of this is a simplistic way in which to posit a distinction between persons of the Trinity. On this issue, Ware's debating partner Grudem writes:

[T]he different functions that we see the Father, Son and Holy Spirit performing are simply outworkings of an eternal relationship between the three persons, one that has always existed for eternity. God has always existed as three distinct persons: Father, Son and Holy Spirit. These distinctions are essential to the very nature of God himself, and they could not be otherwise. . . . Each person is fully God and has all the attributes of God. *The only distinctions between the members of the Trinity are in the ways they relate to each other and to creation.* In those relationships they carry out roles that are appropriate to each person. This truth about the Trinity has sometimes been summarized in the phrase . . . "equal in being but subordinate in role." Both parts of the phrase are necessary to a true doctrine of the Trinity: If we do not have ontological equality, not all the persons are fully God. But if we do not have economic subordination, then there is no difference in the way the persons relate to one another, and consequently we do not have the three persons existing as Father, Son and Holy Spirit for all eternity. For example, if the Son is not eternally subordinate to the Father in role, then the Father is not eternally "Father" and the Son is not eternally "Son." This would mean that the Trinity has not eternally existed. This is why the idea of eternal equality in being but subordination in role has been essential to the church's doctrine of the Trinity since it was first affirmed in the Nicene Creed, which said that the Son was "begotten of the Father before all ages" and that the Holy Spirit "proceeds from the Father and the Son."[85]

---

83. Ware, "How Shall We Think About the Trinity?," 258–59 (Ware's italics).
84. Ware, *Father, Son, and Holy Spirit*, 94–95.
85. Wayne Grudem, *Systematic Theology: An Introduction to Biblical Doctrine* (Grand Rapids, MI: Zondervan, 1994), 251 (Grudem's italics). It is very important to note that at that point in Grudem's career, his historical conclusions were under-supported. The substance of his recent change of view

In articulating this rationale, Grudem and other evangelicals are essentially seeking the same assurance Rahner did. This desire for certainty drives the deployment of a number of theological points required to establish their argument. In Ware's and Grudem's case their Trinitarian theology is grounded upon issues of gender, language, and authority as these are used to establish distinctions in the Godhead. Rahner's motivation was different, but his procedure was similar in that he made systematic connections to ground his unique perspective. He was driven to make the arguments about the incarnation in order to bolster his strict realist Trinitarianism. O'Byrne notes this connection in Rahner's work:

> Rahner reasons that when God acts in the economy, we must hold that such action is the reliable self-revelation of God. Thus, we do indeed come to know the tripersonal God directly through the economy of salvation, without need for recourse to complicated strategies like that of appropriation. . . . When Rahner insists, against Thomas and others, that only the Logos could have become incarnate, his reasoning is related to the reliability of God's self communication.[86]

At this point I note that there is a danger that a desire for certainty by evangelicals may lead to nonbiblical and inappropriate assumptions and bases for theology.

The Challenge Ahead for an Evangelical Use of the SRR of RR or SRRT

Those who apply views with close affinity to the SRR of RR (including the SSRRT), together with those who employ the LRR of RR, need to demonstrate its exegetical basis and fruitfulness for the Trinitarian doctrine of God. Sanders puts this challenge for both those who take the SRR of RR (radicalizers) and the LRR of RR (restricters) as follows: "If the formally articulated doctrine of the Trinity ought to serve as an aid to further exegesis, then one way of estimating the two sides in the argument over Rahner's Rule is to ask which position enables its adherents to do better exegesis."[87] I pursued this question at length in *Trinitarian Self and Salvation*, and found that Trinitarian projects that stem from the SRR of RR are NOT exegetically warranted and as such do not provide a secure basis for the doctrine of God. In this article, I have argued that the selectivity demonstrated by Ware in his SSRRT stems from the need to select a canon within the canon for the sake of holding his

---

on begetting remains unclear. See Graham Cole's article in this volume as well as John Jefferson Davis, "Incarnation, Trinity, and the Ordination of Women to the Priesthood," *The Deception of Eve and the Ontology of Women* (2010): 14.

86. Declan O'Byrne, *Spirit Christology and Trinity in the Theology of David Coffey*, Studies in Theology, Society and Culture (Berlin: Peter Lang, 2010), 169.

87. Sanders, *Image*, 167.

own version of the SRR of RR.[88] I have also described the inner working of Ware's writings and found that his Trinitarian theology does not live up to his own claim that the correct interpretation of Scripture is normative for all evangelicals.[89] Furthermore, his use of a sub-category of the SRR of RR, the SSRRT, ultimately undermines his exegetical, hermeneutical, and Trinitarian efforts. This article has been mostly descriptive. Further work will yield a deeper biblical, historical, and theological *assessment* of Bruce Ware's theology. This will be a welcome effort to the discussion currently underway within significant evangelical Trinitarian communities.

---

88. The fact is that the SRR of RR cannot handle the diversity of Trinitarian relations seen in Scripture and thus the highly selective and exegetically questionable SSRRT is a corollary of the attempt to employ the SRR of RR. Harrower, *Trinitarian Self and Salvation*; Sanders, *Image*, 167–68. Significantly, Sanders believes this problem is insurmountable: "this 'problem of economic diversity' poses an obstacle, perhaps an insuperable one, to using Rahner's Rule in developing a Trinitarian theology from Scriptural sources." Sanders, *Image*, 168 n.16.
89. Ware, "How Shall We Think About the Trinity?," 275.

Bibliography

Brändle, Werner. "Immanente Trinität—Ein Denkmal Der 'Kirchenge-schichte'? Überlegungen Zu Karl Rahner's Trinitätslehre." *Kerygma und Dogma* 38 (1992): 185–98.

Butner Jr., D. Glenn. "Eternal Functional Subordination and the Problem of the Divine Will." *Journal of the Evangelical Theological Society* 58 (2015): 131–49.

Cole, Graham A. *He Who Gives Life: The Doctrine of the Holy Spirit.* Wheaton, IL: Crossway, 2007.

Davis, John Jefferson. "Incarnation, Trinity, and the Ordination of Women to the Priesthood." *The Deception of Eve and the Ontology of Women* (2010): 10–20.

Drecoll, Volker Henning, ed. *Trinität.* Tübingen: Mohr Siebeck, 2011.

Dunard, Emmanuel. "L'identité Rahnérienne Entre la Trinité Économique et la Trinité Immanente à L'epreuve de ses Applications." *Revue Thomiste* 103 (2003): 75–92.

_____. "'Trinité Immanente' et 'Trinité Économique' selon Karl Barth. Les Declinaisons et la Distinction et son Dépassement (Aufhebung)." *Revue des Sciences Philosophiques et Théologiques* 90 (2006): 453–78.

Dych, William V. *Karl Rahner.* Outstanding Christian Thinkers. Collegeville, MN: Liturgical Press, 1992.

Erickson, Millard J. *Who Is Tampering with the Trinity? An Assessment of the Subordination Debate.* Grand Rapids: Kregel, 2009.

Ferri, Ricardo. "Le Missioni Divine nel de Trinitate di Agostino d'ippona: Commento ai Libri ii–iv." *Lateranum* 82, no. 1 (2016): 55–75.

Grudem, Wayne, ed. *Biblical Foundations for Manhood and Womanhood.* Wheaton, IL: Crossway, 2002.

_____. *Systematic Theology: An Introduction to Biblical Doctrine.* Grand Rapids: Zondervan, 1994.

Hanson, R. P. C. *The Search for the Christian Doctrine of God: The Arian Controversy 318–381.* Grand Rapids: Baker Academic, 1988.

Harrower, Scott D. *Trinitarian Self and Salvation: An Evangelical Engagement with Rahner's Rule.* Eugene, OR: Pickwick, 2012.

Hauber, Michael. "Unsagbar Nahe: Eine Studie zur Entstehung und Bedeu-tung der Trinitätslehre Karl Rahners." PhD thesis, Freiburg, 2008.

Huffman, Douglas S., and Eric L. Johnson. *God under Fire: Modern Scholar-ship Reinvents God.* Grand Rapids: Zondervan, 2002.

Jowers, Dennis W. *The Trinitarian Axiom of Karl Rahner: The Economic Trin-ity Is the Immanent Trinity and Vice Versa.* Lewiston, NY: Edwin Mellen, 2006.

Lee, Seung Goo. "The Relationship between the Ontological Trinity and the Economic Trinity." *Journal of Reformed Theology* 3 (2009): 90–107.

Lincicum, David. "Economy and Immanence: Karl Rahner's Doctrine of the Trinity." *European Journal of Theology* 14 (2005): 111–18.

McCall, Thomas H. "Gender and the Trinity Once More: A Review Article." *Trinity Journal* 36 (2015): 263–80.

_____. *Which Trinity? Whose Monotheism: Philosophical and Systematic Theologians on the Metaphysics of Trinitarian Theology.* Grand Rapids: Eerdmans, 2010.

_____. "Deus Trinitas: David Coffey on the Trinity." *Irish Theological Quarterly* 67 (2002): 33–54.

Molnar, Paul D. *Divine Freedom and the Doctrine of the Immanent Trinity: In Dialogue with Karl Barth and Contemporary Theology.* New York: T & T Clark, 2005.

O'Byrne, Declan. *Spirit Christology and Trinity in the Theology of David Coffey.* Studies in Theology, Society and Culture. Berlin: Peter Lang, 2010.

Peter, Lombard, Giulio Silano, and Pontifical Institute of Mediaeval Studies. *The Sentences: Book 3, On the Incarnation of the Word.* Ontario: Pontifical Institute of Medieval Studies, 2008.

Rahner, Karl. *The Trinity.* New York: Crossroad, 1970.

Rauser, Randall. "Rahner's Rule: An Emperor without Clothes?" *International Journal of Systematic Theology* 7 (2005): 81–94.

Sanders, Fred. *The Image of the Immanent Trinity: Rahner's Rule and the Theological Interpretation of Scripture.* Issues in Systematic Theology 12. New York: Peter Lang, 2005.

Schreiner, Thomas R., and Bruce A. Ware. *The Grace of God, the Bondage of the Will.* 2 vols. Grand Rapids: Baker, 1995.

_____. *Still Sovereign: Contemporary Perspectives on Election, Foreknowledge, and Grace.* Grand Rapids: Baker, 2000.

Shillaker, Robert. "Rahner's Axiom and the Hermeneutic Foundation of Thomas Weinandy's Reconceiving the Trinity." *European Journal of Theology* 25 (2016): 33–43.

Smith, Jason M. "Must We Say Anything of an 'Immanent' Trinity? Schleiermacher and Rowan Williams on an 'Abstruse' and 'Fruitless' Doctrine." *Anglican Theological Review* 98, no. 3 (2016).

Stolina, Ralf. "'Ökonomische' und 'Immanente' Trinität? Zur Problematic einer Trinitätstheologischen Denkfigur." *Zeitschrift für Theologie und Kirche* 105 (2008): 170–216.

Talbot, Mark R. "Does God Reveal Who He Actually Is?" In *God under Fire*, edited by Douglas S. Huffman and Eric L. Johnson, 44–70. Grand Rapids: Zondervan, 2002.

"Trinity Debate: Ware-Grudem vs. McCall-Yandell." Carl F. H. Henry Center, October 9, 2008. http://www.henrycenter.org/2008/10/09/trinity-debate-ware-grudem-vs-mccall-yandell.

Tück, Jan-Heiner. "The Father without the Son Would Not Be the Father." *Communio* 42 (2015): 9–23.

Vanhoozer, Kevin. "Forward." In *Communion with the Triune God: John Owen*, edited by Kelly M. Kapic and Justin Taylor, 11–13. Wheaton, IL: Crossway, 2007.

Ware, Bruce A. *Big Truths for Young Hearts: Teaching and Learning the Greatness of God*. Wheaton, IL: Crossway, 2009.

_____. "*Cur Deus Trinus*? The Relations of the Trinity to Christ's Identity as Saviour and to the Efficacy of His Atoning Death." *The Southern Baptist Journal of Theology* 10 (2006): 48–56.

_____. "An Evangelical Reformulation of the Doctrine of the Immutability of God." *Journal of the Evangelical Theological Society* 29 (1986): 431–46.

_____. *Father, Son and Holy Spirit: Relationships, Roles, and Relevance.* Wheaton, IL: Crossway, 2005.

_____. *God's Greater Glory: The Exalted God of Scripture and the Christian Faith*. Wheaton, IL: Crossway, 2004.

_____. *God's Lesser Glory: The Diminished God of Open Theism*. Wheaton, IL: Crossway, 2000.

_____. "How Shall We Think About the Trinity?" In *God Under Fire*, edited by Douglas S. Huffman and Eric L. Johnson, 254–77. Grand Rapids: Zondervan, 2002.

_____. "Male and Female Complementarity and the Image of God." In *Biblical Foundations for Manhood and Womanhood*, edited by Wayne Grudem, 71–92. Wheaton, IL: Crossway, 2002.

_____. "The Man Christ Jesus." *Journal of the Evangelical Theological Society* 53 (2010): 5–18.

_____. *The Man Christ Jesus: Theological Reflections on the Humanity of Christ*. Wheaton, IL: Crossway, 2012.

_____. *Their God Is Too Small: Open Theism and the Undermining of Confidence in God*. Wheaton, IL: Crossway, 2003.

Ware, Bruce A., and John B. Starke, eds. *One God in Three Persons: Unity of Essence, Distinction of Persons, Implications for Life*. Wheaton, IL: Crossway, 2015.

Wiles, Maurice. *Archetypal Heresy: Arianism through the Centuries*. Oxford: Clarendon, 1996.

CHAPTER 16

The Intergenerational Impact
of Theological Beliefs

SCOTT HARROWER

W
hy do debates about the doctrine of the Trinity matter today?[1] They matter because they generate and shape the theological cultures of future generations. A theological culture is a social matrix, that includes theological and interpretative attitudes about the nature of God, Jesus Christ, the Holy Spirit, and how these relate to Christian worship, works, scriptural exegesis, and personal piety. Such cultures are developed over time, and either stabilize or problematize Christian faith and experiences; they have enormous impacts upon Christian communities.[2]

---

1. My thanks go to Graham Cole for a number of conversations in which he pointed out Wiles's work and impressed on me the importance of the theologies that one generation passes down to another. An earlier video version of this article was published by Logos in their Mobile Ed course TH 361, "Perspectives on the Trinity: Eternal Generation and Subordination in Tension," 2016, used here with their permission.

2. Both Lewis Ayres and Khaled Anatolios note the importance of theological cultures in their important works on the reception and development of Nicene theology. For example, see Lewis Ayres, *Nicaea and Its Legacy: An Approach to Fourth-Century Trinitarian Theology* (Oxford; New York: Oxford University Press, 2004); *Augustine and the Trinity* (Cambridge: Cambridge University Press, 2010); "Irenaeus vs. The Valentinians: Toward a Rethinking of Patristic Exegetical Origins," *Journal of Early Christian Studies* 23, no. 2 (2015): 153–87; Khaled Anatolios, *Retrieving Nicaea: The Development and Meaning of Trinitarian Doctrine* (Grand Rapids: Baker Academic, 2011); *The Holy Trinity in the Life of the Church*, Holy Cross Studies in Patristic Theology and History (Grand Rapids: Baker Academic, 2014).

The clash between theological cultures forged early Christian beliefs, identity, worship, and mission. A number of our earliest sources for early Christianity, such as Irenaeus's and Tertullian's works record these clashes, their arguments, and how they justified their respective positions. In time, the seven ecumenical councils were called to resolve large-scale versions of these battles to do with the identity of Christ and God in particular. What is interesting is that though measures were taken time and time again to keep individual and community beliefs and practices aligned with apostolic preaching, some beliefs were stubbornly persistent. For example, semi-Arian or homoian theological cultures persisted for a number of centuries after the First Council of Nicaea (A.D. 325). Though they adapted and changed slightly, they were passed on from generation to generation.

The phenomenon of receiving theological cultures and passing them onwards cannot be ignored. It goes on today, though it is at times subtle. Consider the following example from the college where Mike Bird and I work, Ridley College in Melbourne, Australia. Our library is named the Leon Morris Library. Leon Morris's theological efforts in affirming the atoning death of Christ, as well as the usefulness of the Old Testament for theology, are ever-present reminders to those of us who work there. Leon's portrait looks down upon us kindly as we go about our activities. Our college has a theological culture that is influenced by Leon Morris and his heirs, those principals that followed him and shared his theological convictions.

Theological cultures of today matter for the sake of our churches and also for future generations. What we teach and commend to our students, churches, and friends will influence them and their children and grandchildren. In the same way that I am grateful to the evangelical Anglicans that came before me, I hope that future evangelical Anglicans will be thankful to my generation for passing on a particular theological culture.

As an Anglican I am reminded that when it comes to the doctrine of God I don't have to look back to the fourth century to appreciate the importance of one generation passing down a particular theological culture to do with the Trinity to another. The seventeenth and eighteenth century saw a number of nuanced homoiousian or "semi-Arian" subordinationist theologians in the Anglican church. Perhaps the most famous were Isaac Newton (d. 1727), William Whiston (d. 1752), and Samuel Clarke (d. 1729).[3] Isaac Newton's successor at Cambridge, William Whiston, wrote that Newton opened his eyes to the fact that "what has long been called Arianism is no other than old uncorrupt Christianity."[4] They self-identified with "Arianism" not because they held exactly the same theological positions as the Arianism of the fourth

---

3. Thomas C. Pfizenmaier, *The Trinitarian Theology of Dr. Samuel Clarke (1675–1729): Context, Sources, and Controversy* (Leiden: E.J. Brill, 1997).

4. This section is dependent on Maurice Wiles, *Archetypal Heresy: Arianism through the Centuries* (Oxford: Oxford University Press, 2001), 77.

century, but because their views were more closely aligned with that than with creedal orthodoxy. Arianism was an umbrella term that included what today we would call homoianism, or homoiousian, or crypto-Arianism, according to its particular inclinations.[5]

The sources of Newton's theology are noteworthy because they are biblical texts. However, they are interpreted through a particular theological grid. His christological views were driven by hermeneutical principles that stemmed from his close exegesis of texts such as 1 Corinthians 8:5–6; Philippians 2:5–11; John 5:26. These included the distinction between the kind of divinity the Father has as God, and the Son has as Lord; the primacy of God the Father over the Son; the different grounds for worshipping the Father and the Son; and a reading of the divinity of the Logos which is (in a relative sense) distinct from and lower than the divinity of God the Father.[6] Importantly, Wiles notes that "On the scriptural side, a small number of texts or short passages stand out as the controlling influences on his [Newton's] understanding of the person of Christ. By and large it is the same selection of scriptural evidence that had shaped Arian understanding in the fourth century."[7] Newton also appealed to historic theologians, such as Justin Martyr, as models of those who prefigured his christological and subtrinitarian position. He rejected the normative value of the *homoousion*. In sum, Newton was an example of "homoiousian" theology—the Son is like the Father with respect to his divinity.[8]

Samuel Clarke was Newton's theological successor. He was influenced by Newton and published the infamous neo-Arian *The Scripture-Doctrine of the Trinity* in 1712.[9] It had a devastating effect on the piety, worship, and theology of the clergy and also of the laity of both the Church of England and the Presbyterians. This in turn fueled the development of Unitarianism and Deism in future generations.[10] The point to note here is that sub-Nicene tendencies in one generation may well lead to committed subtrinitarian and nontrinitarian believers in the next. Indeed, many of these will be determined antitrinitarians. The cautionary intergenerational tale outlined above illustrates the fact that important theological beliefs and practices are relevant for both

---

5. Gilliam notes the range of terms that may be used to describe Whiston's noncreedal and crypto-Arianism. Paul R. Gilliam, "William Whiston: No Longer an Arian," *The Journal of Ecclesiastical History* 66, no. 4 (2015): 755–71.

6. Wiles, *Archetypal Heresy: Arianism through the Centuries*, 77.

7. Wiles, *Archetypal Heresy: Arianism through the Centuries*, 79.

8. For discussion on this issue, see Stephen D. Snobelen, "Isaac Newton, Heretic: The Strategies of a Nicodemite," *The British Journal for the History of Science* 32, no. 4 (1999): 381–419. He argues against Thomas C. Pfizenmaier, "Was Isaac Newton an Arian?," *Journal of the History of Ideas* 58, no. 1 (1997): 57–80. Snobelen's methodology anchors his more robust conclusions, see Snobelen, "Isaac Newton, Heretic: The Strategies of a Nicodemite," 382.

9. Pfizenmaier, *The Trinitarian Theology of Dr. Samuel Clarke (1675–1729): Context, Sources, and Controversy*.

10. James Byrne, *Religion and the Enlightenment: From Descartes to Kant* (Louisville: Westminster John Knox, 1997).

the present and for the future. Hence, our trinitarian theology matters for its churchly impact in both the present and the future. An expanded awareness of the intergenerational impact of our beliefs should lead us to reticence when it comes to trinitarian speculation.

So, ask yourself: "What kind of theological culture do I want to commend to future Christians with respect to the divinity of Christ?" I know I want to commend God the Son "true God from true God . . . of one being with the Father," and nothing short of that. Do you?

Bibliography

Anatolios, Khaled. *The Holy Trinity in the Life of the Church*. Holy Cross Studies in Patristic Theology and History.   Grand Rapids: Baker Academic, 2014.

_____. *Retrieving Nicaea: The Development and Meaning of Trinitarian Doctrine*.   Grand Rapids: Baker Academic, 2011.

Ayres, Lewis. *Augustine and the Trinity*. Cambridge; New York: Cambridge University Press, 2010.

_____. "Irenaeus vs. The Valentinians: Toward a Rethinking of Patristic Exegetical Origins." *Journal of Early Christian Studies* 23, no. 2 (2015): 153–87.

_____. *Nicaea and Its Legacy: An Approach to Fourth-Century Trinitarian Theology*. Oxford; New York: Oxford University Press, 2004.

Byrne, James. *Religion and the Enlightenment: From Descartes to Kant*. Louisville: Westminster John Knox, 1997.

Gilliam, Paul R. "William Whiston: No Longer an Arian." *The Journal of Ecclesiastical History* 66, no. 4 (2015): 755–71.

Pfizenmaier, Thomas C. *The Trinitarian Theology of Dr. Samuel Clarke (1675–1729): Context, Sources, and Controversy*. Studies in the History of Christian Thought. Leiden; New York: E.J. Brill, 1997.

_____."Was Isaac Newton an Arian?" *Journal of the History of Ideas* 58, no. 1 (1997): 57–80.

Snobelen, Stephen D. "Isaac Newton, Heretic: The Strategies of a Nicodemite." *The British Journal for the History of Science* 32, no. 4 (1999): 381–419.

Wiles, Maurice. *Archetypal Heresy: Arianism through the Centuries*. Oxford: Oxford University Press, 2001.

Scripture and Ancient Sources Index

Name Index